"NEW NEGROES
FROM AFRICA"

T0350068

"NEW

SLAVE TRADE ABOLITION

NEGROES

AND FREE AFRICAN SETTLEMENT

FROM AFRICA"

IN THE NINETEENTH-CENTURY CARIBBEAN

ROSANNE MARION ADDERLEY

Indiana University Press
Bloomington & Indianapolis

This book is a publication of

Indiana University Press
601 North Morton Street
Bloomington, Indiana 47404-3797 USA

http://iupress.indiana.edu

Telephone orders   800-842-6796
Fax orders   812-855-7931
Orders by email   iuporder@indiana.edu

The paper used in this publication meets the minimum
requirements of American National Standard for Information
Sciences—Permanence of Paper for Printed Library
Materials, ANSI Z39.48-1984.

Manufactured in the United States of America

Library of Congress Cataloging-in-Publication Data

Adderley, Rosanne Marion.
    New negroes from Africa : slave trade abolition and free African
settlement in the nineteenth-century Caribbean / Rosanne Marion
Adderley.
        p. cm. — (Blacks in the diaspora)
    Includes bibliographical references and index.
    ISBN 0-253-34703-3 (cloth : alk. paper) — ISBN 0-253-21827-6
(pbk. : alk. paper)
    1. Blacks—Bahamas—Social conditions—19th century—Case
studies. 2. Blacks—Trinidad and Tobago—Trinidad—Social conditions—19th century—Case studies. 3. Africans—Bahamas—Social
conditions—19th century—Case studies. 4. Africans—Trinidad
and Tobago —Trinidad—Social conditions—19th century—Case
studies. 5. Blacks —Cultural assimilation—Bahamas—Case studies.
6. Blacks—Cultural assimilation—Trinidad and Tobago—
Trinidad—Case studies. 7. African diaspora.   I. Title. II. Series.
    F1660.B55A63 2006
    305.89607296—dc22
                                                        2006001257

1 2 3 4 5   11 10 09 08 07 06

FOR MY PARENTS,

Paul Lawrence Adderley

AND

Lilith Rosena Thompson Adderley

CONTENTS

Acknowledgments *xi*

Introduction   1

1. Potential Laborers or "Troublesome Savages"?
   Settlement of Liberated Africans in the Bahamas   23

2. "Binding them to the trade of digging cane holes":
   Settlement of Liberated Africans in Trinidad   63

3. "A fine family of what we call creole Yarabas":
   African Ethnic Identities in Liberated African
   Community Formation   92

4. "Assisted by his wife, an African":
   Gender, Family, and Household Formation
   in the Experience of Liberated Africans   126

5. Orisha Worship and "Jesus Time":
   Religious Worlds of Liberated Africans   153

6. "Powers superior to those of other witches":
   New African Immigrants and Supernatural Practice
   beyond Religious Spheres   182

7. "Deeply attached to his native country":
   Visions of Africa and Mentalities of Exile
   in Liberated African Culture   203

Conclusion: African Creoles and Creole Africans   234

*Appendix 1. Reports of Liberated African Arrivals
   in the Bahamas from Governors' Correspondence*   241

*Appendix 2. Reports of Liberated African Arrivals
   in Trinidad from Governors' Correspondence*   245

Notes   249

Select Bibliography   303

Index   317

[S]ome hundreds of savages from Africa have been turned loose amongst them—unshackled from the restraints which the Laws imposed on the slaves.

—Alexander Murray, Former Collector of Customs,
Nassau, Bahamas, 1832

ACKNOWLEDGMENTS

The research and writing of this project was supported two Andrew W. Mellon Grants through the University of Pennsylvania, a Bernadotte Schmitt Award from the American Historical Association, and a Fulbright-IIE Fellowship. A year of writing was made possible by a Mendenhall Fellowship at Smith College, Northampton, Massachusetts.

Between 1997 and 2000 several grants from the Roger Thayer Stone Center for Latin American Studies at Tulane University facilitated research trips to archives in Havana, Cuba, and multiple trips to conferences to present work related to this project. Conference trips have also been supported by the Tulane University School of Liberal Arts and Sciences and the Department of History. In the summer of 1997, a grant from the Committee on Research of the School of Arts and Sciences at Tulane funded a proposed research trip to the Sierra Leone National Archives in Freetown to examine records of the Liberated African Department that existed there in the nineteenth century. Renewed war in that country and a U.S. State Department advisory against travel made that trip impossible. During the academic year 1999–2000, I enjoyed the always-incalculable benefit of an uninterrupted year of research and writing through a postdoctoral fellowship at the Carter G. Woodson Institute at the University of Virginia. In 2004 and 2006 grants from the Georges Lurcy Charitable and Educational Trust funded some final manuscript preparations, most significantly the production of maps and the preparation of the index. These grants were administered through the Department of History and the School of Liberal Arts and Sciences at Tulane. Map expenses were also supported by a grant from the Stone Center for Latin American Studies.

Archive staff at the following repositories made this project possible through their efficiency and exceptional diligence in the face of voluminous and often-last-minute requests: Public Record Office, Kew, England; Department of Archives, Commonwealth of the Bahamas, in Nassau; National Archives of Trinidad and Tobago, Port-of-Spain, Trinidad; Archivo Nacional, Havana, Cuba; Wesleyan Methodist Missionary Society Archives, School of Oriental and African Studies, London; Baptist Missionary Society Archives, Oxford University; Church Missionary Society Archives, University of Birmingham; Rhodes House Library, Oxford University. I owe similar gratitude to college and university library staff at the University of Pennsylvania, Smith College, the University of Virginia, the University of the West Indies, the College of the Bahamas, and Tulane University.

Although the oral history portion of this project is relatively modest, it is critical. After I completed those interviews, I often told friends that even if I never produced the written history, the time spent with my oral history participants in the Bahamas and Trinidad would always count as some of the richest experiences of my career. This sentiment and my profound gratitude have not changed a decade later. In addition to providing one of those interviews, the late Father William Thompson also mentored me through much of my graduate career as I moved back and forth between my home in the Bahamas and various other research and writing locations.

The content and writing of the book have benefitted over time from the careful critiques of my advisors, Richard Dunn and Lee Cassanelli, and during my postdoctoral year from feedback offered by various colleagues affiliated with the Woodson Institute at the University of Virginia, including Adrian Gaskins, Joseph Hellweg, Joe Miller, Rolland Murray, and Dylan Penningroth. Two anonymous readers for Indiana University Press provided generous readings of the book's promise and meticulous recommendations for its final revisions. My longtime friend Rhonda Frederick read the final version of Chapter 1 in November of 2003 and performed the truly heroic task of prodding and guiding me into producing a final version of everything else.

Since my arrival at Tulane University in 1996, I have benefited from the intellectual and professional communion that make university life so rewarding and any scholarly production possible. Among colleagues and friends in the History Department, Jim Boyden has offered uniquely timely advice and support, especially in the last two years of releasing this book from my desk. George Bernstein, Linda Pollock, Larry Powell, Randy Sparks, Lee Woodward, Justin Wolfe, and Trudy Yeager have also been critically supportive colleagues in numerous ways. To have had the mentorship, professional support, and friendship of a historian of Sylvia Frey's distinction and grace over the past eight years has been an incalculable privilege. I can only hope that this book in some small measure lives up to the faith that Sylvia has invested in it and in me. Cora Ann Presley was also a particularly important mentor during the years we shared at Tulane and has remained so since her 1998 move to Georgia State University.

Beyond the History Department, I have enjoyed extended communities of colleagues and friends at Tulane in the interdisciplinary programs in Latin American Studies and in African and African Diaspora Studies (ADST). A small writing group of ADST colleagues read the original version and played an important role as I began the process of excavating this book from that thesis. That writing group consisted of Gaurav Desai, Christopher J. Dunn, and Adeline Masquelier. In countless less-specific but no-less-important ways, I have benefited from the support and friendship of Pamela Franco, Marilyn Miller, Gayle Murchison, Supriya Nair, Olanike Orie, Ben Reiss, Frank Ukadike, and Richard Watts. It was especially fortuitous that I arrived at Tulane during the same academic year as Michael Cunningham. Michael has steadfastly supported me and my work in all ways—from abstract needs such as encouragement and professional guidance to more mundane but equally necessary tasks, such as twice driving versions of this manuscript to the post office minutes before closing time. Last, in my most optimistic imaginings of my career, I could not have envisioned a more faithful or more generous mentor, colleague, and friend than Felipe Smith. More so than any other person, I am not sure whether without his support this project would have ever been completed.

For the past three summers, the Super Scholar/EXCEL program at Xavier University of New Orleans has given me the most rewarding academic job I may ever have. To take on a new summer teaching job in the midst of trying to finish a major research project seems perhaps counterproductive. Yet, for nurturing my life as a historian, teacher, and human being, I owe a debt that is profound and almost indescribable to the students, staff, and faculty of that program, particularly to its director, Dereck J. Rovaris, Sr.

My students at Tulane University, Smith College, the University of Virginia, and in the EXCEL Program at Xavier have been a source of inspiration to me in more ways than they could ever imagine.

Tobie and Ming-Yuen Meyer Fong, two of my oldest friends, have provided constant moral support and a standing invitation for days of calm and rejuvenation in the warmth of their home. Although she may not remember this fact, Tobie Meyer-Fong is also the person who persuaded me over fifteen years ago to embark upon this journey of trying to make a life out of being a historian. (Saul Liwen Meyer-Fong sent a lovely picture to cheer up my study and kindly agreed to wait until the book was finished before insisting that I come to celebrate his birth in person.) Among other fellow scholars and friends who have supported this book and its author in innumerable ways over far too many years are Giselle Anatol, Edward Baptist, Fitzroy Baptiste, Bridget Brereton, Marsha Brooks, Michael Crutcher, Greg Dorr, Lisa Lindquist, Edda Fields, Michele Frank, Herman Graham, Virginia Gould, Frank Guridy, Marsha Houston, Judith Lee Hunt, Tera Hunter, Natalie J. Ring, Renee Romano, D. Gail Saunders, Ian G. Strachan, Martha Vail, Laura Watts, Rhonda Williams, Edith Wolfe, Betty Wood, Kirsten Wood, and Jacqueline Woodfork.

At various points of disillusionment or more casual discontent with this project, I have selfishly sought refuge among friends safely outside the peculiar and often insular world of professional historians and university life.

Sydney D. Lewis has always been a willing listener and a source of much happiness, inspiration, and peace. Doug Anderson, Ajamu Baraka, Angelica Benton-Molina, Damian Cassells-Jones, Suha Dabbouseh, Kelly Frisch, Robert Horton, Pamela Johnson, Nicole Kirby, Bridget Lehane, Laura Moye, and Sunita Patel are also due particular thanks. I met a significant number of these friends during periods of volunteer work with Amnesty International and the People's Institute for Survival and Beyond (an anti-racist community-organizing collective). I especially thank my activist colleagues from Amnesty International and the People's Institute for giving me an abundance of *truly* rewarding work to do.

Jonah Sollins-Devlin arrived in this world long after I was exhausted of this project, therefore just in time to be a perfect friend and playmate, giving endless hours of respite from this book and joy as only he could provide. Many thanks are due his parents, Rachel Devlin and Stephen Sollins for so willingly sharing with me their son and their home. In addition to parenting a remarkable child, Rachel Devlin is one of the most challenging historians I know, in every sense of that adjective. Her reading and comments specifically strengthened the arguments on gender and family in Chapter 4. If I have succeeded in executing that chapter (and other parts of this book) with anything resembling intellectual boldness or courage, it is much to Rachel's credit. She is further a friend beyond compare.

At Indiana University Press, my editor Robert Sloan and assistant editors Kendra Boileau Stokes and Jane Quinet have brought this project to fruition with faith and patience, regularly tested by my dogged postponement of more deadlines than I care to remember. The inevitable and innumerable weaknesses which remain in *"New Negroes from Africa"* are of course all my own.

This book and its author have been blessed for more than a decade by the prayers and support of communities of faith in five different countries, including mostly Christian churches but also a Hindu pundit who raised prayers for the successful completion of my Ph.D. during Diwali celebrations in Trinidad in the fall of 1993. This book has been completed only through the grace of God, whose mercies and blessings are without number.

My sisters Catherine and Paula Adderley are model siblings and my best friends who brighten and enrich my life daily, even across thousands of miles. They have done more to sustain me and this book than they will ever realize. Finally, this book is dedicated with love to my parents, Paul Lawrence Adderley and Lilith Rosena Thompson Adderley, who have made everything possible.

"NEW NEGROES FROM AFRICA"

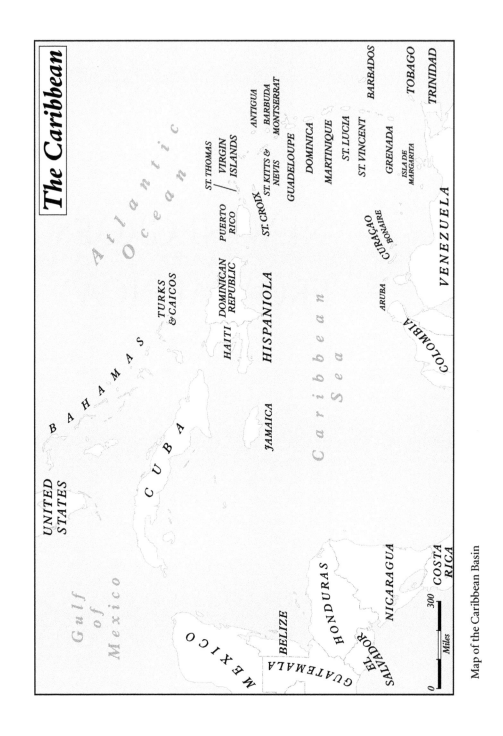

Map of the Caribbean Basin

Introduction

"Queer customs are those of these black africans who form a lively part of my charming population."[1] A French priest, the Abbé Armand Massé, penned this description in December 1879 from his mission field in southwestern Trinidad. In this instance, Massé refers specifically to his experience with a parishioner he describes as "a man from the Congo." This man had asked the missionary to say a special mass in honor of his father, who had died years ago. After enthusiastic participation in the Roman Catholic ritual, the Congo man then organized a celebration and feast, followed by dancing which lasted "all day and . . . all night again."[2] In his journal entry, Massé seems to marvel both at the enthusiasm the man expressed for the mass and the extravagance of the celebration which followed. That a European in the West Indies should express amazement at the behavior of "black Africans" hardly seems remarkable. Massé's comments merit attention as much because of their timing as because of their content. By the 1870s, when Massé wrote, the black populations of the British Caribbean consisted overwhelmingly of people who had not been born in Africa. Indeed, Caribbean-born people had formed such a majority since at least the early 1830s. Massé and other observers described this majority as negro or creole. They reserved the adjective African, in almost all cases, for those who had been born in Africa and sometimes for their first-generation descendants. And like the Abbé Armand Massé, observers throughout the West Indies marveled at the persistent and distinctive role played by the African segment of the larger black population during the nineteenth century.

For more than 200 years, between the seventeenth and nineteenth centuries, Britain had imported hundreds of thousands of African slaves into her Caribbean possessions. However, the end of the legal slave trade during the first decade of the nineteenth century accelerated the demographic creolization of the British West Indian slave population. After the Act for the Abolition of the Slave Trade of 1807, the percentage of African-born slaves would gradually decline. But that same abolition act also created a new special category of African immigrants to the British Caribbean who had been rescued from illegally operating slave ships by the British navy: they were officially designated as liberated Africans. Over a six-decade campaign of slave trade suppression the Royal Navy would detain more than 500 ships that were found in violation of anti–slave trade laws and of various bilateral treaties that Britain negotiated with other European and American governments. From such vessels over 40,000 rescued Africans ended up settled in British Caribbean territories, mostly under diverse arrangements of apprenticeship or indenture.[3] And by the second half of the nineteenth century, these liberated Africans made up the majority of the African-born population. Throughout the century, the distinctive behavior and experience of these free African settlers—what Massé called queer customs—repeatedly drew the attention of both colonial authorities and ordinary citizens as the "new negroes from Africa" crafted a unique place within the larger African-Caribbean community.[4]

Upon their arrival in British Caribbean colonies, liberated Africans encountered preexisting populations of African descent, themselves mostly enslaved up until British slave emancipation in 1834. The arrival of the slave trade refugees—"new Negroes from Africa"—received great attention not only from colonial authorities but also from both the black and white populations in general. All segments of the population seemed to agree that the arrival of such Africans constituted a significant development that would measurably affect economic, social, and cultural life in these Caribbean colonies. Since the nineteenth century, scholars and other observers have likewise pointed to liberated Africans as a body of immigrants who in various ways shaped the culture of the colonies where they settled. For example, in some instances liberated Africans have been credited with (or blamed for) adding new or renewed African influences to different aspects of African-Caribbean culture such as religion or folk beliefs. In other cases historians have pointed to ways liberated Africans established their own cultural practices or institutions, distinct if not necessarily separate, from the wider black community. Some such institutions and practices survived well into the twentieth century. And even where specific cultural influences did not survive, commentary about the arrival of these unusual African immigrants persisted in the oral histories of the various Caribbean territories where they settled. This study explores the experience and impact of liberated African immigrants in the nineteenth-century British Caribbean by examining two colonies—the Bahamas and Trinidad—that together received about 15,000 liberated African settlers, accounting for roughly one-third of the total number settled in British Caribbean territories.

In June 1806, the British Parliament passed a law ending legal British participation in the transport of enslaved Africans or persons of African descent for sale across the Atlantic Ocean or by any other route.[5] This law, which came into effect on May 1st, 1807, ended a period of almost three centuries during which Great Britain had played a leading role in the Atlantic slave trade and in the establishment of European colonies in the Caribbean and the Americas that depended in varying degrees on the labor of enslaved Africans and their descendants. Historians have long hailed this enormous legal accomplishment, which, according to many observers, marked the beginning of the end for British systems of slavery in the Caribbean and constituted one of the most significant milestones in the dawn of the nineteenth century as the age of emancipation. That age embraced hundreds of legal and human dramas as European colonial powers and independent states in the Caribbean and the Americas ended the legal enslavement of people of African descent and both white and black people set about the process of establishing new modes of social, economic, and cultural interaction. This study explores one particular human drama of the emancipation age that has so far received only moderate attention from historians: the experience of tens of thousands of Africans rescued from illegally operating slave ships by the British navy between 1807 and the mid-1860s as a direct result of the passage of the slave trade abolition act.

During the early nineteenth century, other European nations and the newly independent United States also passed legislation outlawing the transoceanic trade in African slaves. Great Britain, however, took the lead in international enforcement. For example, British authorities used diplomatic pressure to encourage other countries to pass anti–slave trade legislation. They also sought treaty agreements whereby other nations would allow the British navy to police illegal slave trading by both British and foreign subjects. Under the terms of the 1807 Abolition Act, Africans found aboard illegally operating slave ships were "forfeited to His Majesty . . . in such Manner and Form, as any Goods or Merchandize unlawfully imported." However, unlike other confiscated "goods," these enslaved persons were immediately emancipated from their condition as slaves. The British described such slave trade refugees as liberated Africans (or African recaptives),[6] and for more than half a century the fate of these people was a central concern of British abolitionist policy. Of the more than 100,000 liberated Africans rescued by the British navy, more than half ended up settled in the British West African colony of Sierra Leone, which had been formed in 1787 by British abolitionists as a settlement for free blacks from England and elsewhere in the British empire and had become a crown colony in 1808.[7] More than 40,000 ended up settled in various British Caribbean territories, most through a system of labor emigration that operated from Sierra Leone in the 1840s and 1850s.[8] Other liberated Africans were transferred to British Caribbean colonies from captured slave ships processed at an Anglo-Spanish Mixed Commission Court established in Havana, Cuba, in 1819 after Great Britain and Spain had entered into treaty agreements for the suppression of the slave trade.[9] A similar process of transfer moved some liberated Africans from a Mixed Commission Court in Rio de Janeiro, Brazil.[10] A small number of liberated Africans ended up in British Caribbean colonies more or less by accident after illegally operating slave ships wrecked or otherwise foundered at sea near British territories or British naval vessels.

This exploration seeks first to contribute in general to the broad field of the cultural history of the African diaspora that encompasses both the ever-growing body of community studies, especially from the era of slavery, and the many recent works in cultural studies of the African diaspora focused either on specific theoretical or conceptual concerns or specific themes or issues over time.[11] In particular, this project seeks to speak to two related trends in this scholarship. The first is the sense that there is always more that historians can know about how enslaved Africans and people of African descent conducted their day-to-day lives and made the choices that formed the black cultures of the seventeenth, eighteenth, and nineteenth centuries and the roots of the diverse cultures of the contemporary African Atlantic world.[12] Recent decades have seen a near-universal acceptance of the need to better understand how African inputs contributed to the processes of culture- and community-building among Africans and their descendants in the diaspora. It has been a widely accepted fact for more than half a century that, contrary to prior scholarship, Africans did not arrive in the New World as blank cultural slates. Nor were they reduced to such a condition by the traumas of slavery. Quite the contrary, these involuntary immigrants came from diverse, complex cultures and despite the restrictions of slavery and other forms of anti-African or anti-black oppression, African influences had an ongoing input in the formation of black cultures and black communities.

These kinds of in-depth and African-sensitive community studies were pioneered in the late 1960s and early 1970s with works such as Orlando Patterson's study of Jamaica, *The Sociology of Slavery* (1967), and John Blassingame's study of the southern United States, *The Slave Community* (1972). Also important from the mid-1970s was an essay jointly authored by anthropologists Sidney Mintz and Richard Price entitled *An Anthropological Approach to the Afro-American Past: A Caribbean Perspective.*[13] Although it no doubt arose in part from an impulse to compare and explain why African influences on black culture in the Caribbean appeared more prominent than those in the United States, the essay raised broad methodological challenges for historians and other scholars addressing the cultural history of Africans and people of African descent in the diaspora. In particular, Mintz and Price drew attention to the need to consider broad principles shared by diverse West and West-Central African cultures and the way such principles could have shaped cultures in the diaspora, not necessarily in the transmission of identifiable African forms but functioning more subtly as a kind of underlying cultural grammar. They also urged historians to quite specifically consider how displaced Africans in the Americas would have set about carrying out both routine and ritual matters as people separated from their home societies and facing the constraints of New World slavery. In other words, how did individual African actors and later their descendants literally set about the process of making African-American culture?

Since the mid-1970s, scholarship asking precisely these kinds of questions has flourished—a development reflected in the publication of an updated, revised, and moderately expanded version of the Mintz and Price essay under the new title *The Birth of African-American Culture: An Anthropological Perspective* in 1992.[14] In the past two decades, studies have become ever more ambitious, either in the depth with which they have examined individual slave communities or the extent to which they have incorporated the African backgrounds of their subjects. One of the most ambitious of all is Philip Morgan's monumental work *Slave Counterpoint* (1998) on slave life in the Chesapeake and Lowcountry Regions of the United States in the eighteenth century. Morgan not only achieves a detailed social and cultural history of unprecedented breadth but also deploys throughout his vast study sustained attention to the constant cultural and social dialectic at work between African inputs or influences and American adaptations or innovations. Morgan writes: "[A]t the fundamental level of epistemological beliefs, interpersonal relations and expressive behavior, slaves kept alive a measure of their African 'character.'"[15] My study seeks to maintain a constant attention to this critical cultural and social dynamic, not simply as one part of understanding the experience of liberated Africans but as one of the most critical lenses through which all history of the African diaspora should be scrutinized. Another major current in the cultural history of the African diaspora is the growing understanding that historians can often pin down with previously unimagined specificity the geographic and therefore ethnic origins of the enslaved Africans who arrived in particular areas of the Americas and the Caribbean. The case of liberated Africans fits well within this trend in two respects. First, because of their visibility as specially rescued Africans and the interest of British authorities in developing policies for liberated Africans as a part of British benevolence, significant (although by no means comprehensive or even) records exist about the origins and arrivals of large groups of liberated Africans. Second, at a more general level, using bodies of data collected during the process of slave trade suppression and existing scholarship on the African geographic and ethnic origins of the mid-nineteenth-century slave trade, this study attempts to attend to the ways particular African ethnic backgrounds played into the lives of liberated Africans once they settled in the Caribbean.

It is also important to note that in nineteenth-century records for the British Caribbean, historians can often trace liberated Africans as a distinct African-born group amidst black populations which had declining numbers of Africans who had arrived as slaves. After the abolition of the Atlantic slave trade in 1807, British colonies saw very little illegal slave trading, and the institution of slavery itself was abolished in 1834. Because there was no other major new source of African immigration, for most of the century, most people identified as African-born immigrants—especially people who were not elderly—can also be identified as liberated Africans.

Chapters 1 and 2 summarize the processes by which liberated African immigrants settled in the Bahamas and Trinidad over the period between 1808 and approximately 1860. These two chapters set the stage for examining liberated African populations in the two locales chosen as case studies for this project. However, as introductory chapters, they also offer an overview of changes in British policy toward slave trade suppression during this half-century period. Such policy changes affected the military and legal means of dealing with captured slave ships and shaped the strategies used to settle liberated Africans over the long term. To some extent, the question of long-term settlement always focused most heavily on what liberated Africans would do as a working population.

In many ways, the book's central project of exploring the specific social and cultural worlds experienced and created by these free African immigrants truly begins with chapter 3, which takes up the question of African ethnic identity. The chapter examines the representation of particular ethnic groups among the liberated African population and considers the ways that these more specific forms of ethnic identification shaped liberated African life. The persistence of specific African ethnic labeling has at times been cited as one of the things that made liberated Africans stand out in the post-emancipation British West Indies, as people in effect clinging to continuing Africanness even among subsequent generations.[16] The phenomenon of African ethnic labeling in fact occurred throughout the Americas, including among populations that remained enslaved. Examining such identities here brings liberated African perspectives from the Bahamas and Trinidad to a significant area of the cultural history of the African diaspora. Chapter 4 takes a different demographic focus, examining issues of gender distribution and family formation among the liberated African population. In the nineteenth-century Atlantic slave trade, gender ratios were often such that men and boys outnumbered women and girls by approximately two to one. Because British colonial officials viewed settlement of liberated Africans with a spirit of social engineering, this gender imbalance regularly received official attention, most often focused on difficulties that new arrivals might encounter in forming heterosexual families. Chapter 4 explores these issues of gender balance and family formation as a way of illuminating some of the striking ways that gender shaped the experience of liberated African women in particular but also the community as a whole. Turning to more particular cultural questions, chapter 5 draws these unique African immigrants into the long-standing exploration of religious and supernatural life among Africans and their descendants in the Caribbean and the Americas. The chapter looks at both the practice of African-derived religion and the experience of liberated Africans who converted to Christianity. Chapter 6 meanwhile explores the role of liberated Africans in the more informal (and often pernicious) supernatural practices commonly called obeah in the British West Indies. Finally, chapter 7 looks at the way that these immigrants remembered the homelands from which they had come over the long term, with some particular attention to the often considered but rarely achieved idea of repatriation.

Although liberated Africans receive regular (albeit passing) attention in much literature on the nineteenth-century slave trade, only two major monographic studies treat the question of liberated African settlement in the Caribbean at length: Johnson U. J. Asiegbu, *Slavery and the Politics of Liberation 1787–1861: A Study of Liberated African Emigration and British Anti-Slavery Policy* (1969); and Monica Schuler, *"Alas, Alas Kongo": A Social History of Indentured African Immigration into Jamaica, 1841–1865* (1980).[17] More than thirty years after its original publication, Asiegbu's work remains the single authoritative text that outlines the ways Great Britain at first established its policy of using liberated Africans as indentured labor, how the colonial government carried out the policy, and how and why that policy ultimately failed. Asiegbu's work in some respects bridges studies of abolitionist policies and politics and social history works concerning the lives of the Africans and their descendants most affected by those abolitionist activities. That is to say, although Asiegbu situates his work mostly within the historiography of British anti-slavery policy, the book also provides some important insights into the study of the life experiences of liberated Africans. Asiegbu focuses almost entirely on the organized emigration of liberated Africans from the British colony of Sierra Leone to labor-hungry sugar colonies such as British Guiana, Jamaica, and Trinidad, mostly between

1840 and 1860. Thus, in his work the experience of liberated Africans who ended up in the Caribbean by other routes receives rather marginal attention. Furthermore, while *Slavery and the Politics of Liberation* provides a much-needed portrait of the politics and economics involved in African rescue, resettlement, and indenture, it hardly begins to address the cultural complexities of the experience of liberated Africans. Most significant for this study is that fact that as a historian of Africa and of British colonial policy, Asiegbu devotes little attention to the fate of liberated Africans after their arrival in the Caribbean.

This issue is the subject of Monica Schuler's *"Alas, Alas Kongo."* In her study, Schuler argues that two factors shaped the character of the African immigrant experience. In the first place, the new arrivals sought to separate themselves not only from the world of their white plantation employers but also from the African-Caribbean world that had developed before their arrival. Secondly, she finds that within liberated African communities, individual ethnic differences played a significant role. According to Schuler, most of Jamaica's nineteenth-century immigrants fell into two cultural groupings, Yorubas and Central Africans (also called Congos), who not only lived separately but also responded differently to the cultural stimuli of the New World. Schuler paints a portrait of an immigrant community that on the one hand distinguished itself from the society around it but on the other hand also maintained significant cultural distinctions within a larger African immigrant unity.

This model of African cultural maintenance is in many ways convincing and fits well with recent efforts to explore the strength of African-American communities in European-dominated New World societies. However, the Jamaican community on which Schuler's portrait is based constituted only 10,000 people—about a quarter of the liberated Africans who entered the British Caribbean during the nineteenth century. British Guiana, which received 14,000, received the largest number. Trinidad received about 8,000, while smaller colonies combined probably received about 10,000. The Bahamas received roughly 6,000 of this group.[18] These other communities can serve to test and expand Schuler's model of African acculturation in the post-slavery Caribbean. My study will attempt to take a closer look at the complexities of social and cultural negotiation—exploring the important African inputs of these unusual immigrants but also seeking to more fully understand the genesis of African-Caribbean forms and the interaction of liberated Africans with the wider black population.

The Caribbean colonies that received African immigrants may be divided into two categories, large plantation colonies and smaller peripheral islands. In the former group, planters and administrators viewed the liberated Africans as a convenient source of labor that could replace the thousands of slaves who rejected plantation employment after emancipation. In the smaller islands, liberated Africans were seen more as unanticipated new additions to the existing laboring population. Both government officials and private citizens expected the new immigrants to accept apprenticeship or indenture in a variety of occupations as the economy demanded. Trinidad fits into the larger category and the Bahamas into the smaller. In all territories, liberated Africans made a variety of choices concerning the conduct of their lives. Many of these choices were shaped by various African antecedents. Other decisions were dictated by peculiar local circumstances. By comparing two very different colonies, this study will be able to explore the tension between pragmatic adaptation and the reshaping of African traditions. Trinidad and the Bahamas form ideal cases for such a comparative exploration.

During 1797, Great Britain acquired Trinidad from the Spain. Thus, in the early nineteenth century the island was just beginning to develop a thriving sugar economy modeled after other British possessions. Many would-be planters obtained land grants from the British government and created vast new plantations in addition to those that already existed from previous French and Spanish efforts. Before long, however, these new developments faced two major setbacks. First, in 1807, the abolition of the slave trade deprived the new plantations of the unlimited cheap labor of previous centuries. Second, and even more problematic, in 1838 Great Britain declared full emancipation and thousands of freed slaves abandoned the estates. In the wake of this "catastrophe," Trinidad planters asked the British to help them find new workers. The thousands of Africans being seized by the British navy seemed an obvious choice. Trinidad received fewer than 1,000 liberated Africans between 1808 and 1840, but once organized projects began to use these slave trade refugees as emigrant labor for British sugar colonies, the southern Caribbean island became a major destination for African recaptives. At first, labor agents acting on behalf of Trinidad planters attempted to recruit Africans who had been settled in Sierra Leone for several years and had already received lessons in language and religion from English missionaries. However, after only one group of settlers had been taken to Trinidad, the English-speaking Africans in Sierra Leone began to hear rumors about the harsh working conditions their peers had encountered on Caribbean estates, and established African settlers decided to reject the offers of West Indian recruiters. The recruiters turned instead to those Africans who had literally just been liberated from the slave ships. These people belonged to a variety of ethnic groups, did not speak English, and no doubt still suffered from the shock of their captivity. After landing at Sierra Leone, such people were "persuaded" to emigrate to Trinidad and other colonies with shortages of labor. When these immigrants arrived at Port-of-Spain, their appearance, language, and behavior set them distinctly apart from the New World society around them, unlike the initial cargo of English-speaking, Christian-educated Sierra Leonians. According to contemporary observers, this distinctiveness remained for at least half a century.[19] Planters, travelers, and British officials all described the unique culture developed by these new immigrants. This group clearly constitutes a compelling case for the study of African cultural response to the New World.

The Africans who settled in the Bahamas are an equally compelling example. The tiny British colony included several hundred small islands scattered in the Atlantic between Florida and Hispaniola. In 1621, Charles I granted property rights in the islands to his attorney general, Sir Robert Heath, but the islands were first settled some twenty years later by a group of Puritans seeking to establish a community of full religious freedom. The colony grew steadily over the course of the next century but never developed a large-scale agricultural economy like the more southerly islands. During the nineteenth century, these islands achieved distinction more for their location than for their economy. Located halfway between Cuba and the southern United States, Bahamian waters saw significant traffic both from illegal slavers and British naval patrols. With no significant plantation economy, Bahamian colonists did not clamor for liberated Africans as a source of labor. However, between 1811 and 1841, at least two dozen ships bringing over 6,000 Africans landed in the islands. In some ways, the Bahamas might be described as the Sierra Leone of the northern Caribbean. The local government made arrangements for the new immigrants to be indentured, apprenticed, or employed in diverse occupations, including agricultural labor. Travelers, administrators, and eventually missionaries all remarked on the unique character of the new immigrants in comparison with other Bahamian people of African descent. In some cases, "hostility" was even described between the two groups.[20] As late as the mid-twentieth century, local historians claimed to be able to trace the specific African origins of Bahamian families descended from these nineteenth-century communities. A study of the Bahamian liberated African communities thus provides another very fruitful avenue for attempting to understand this unique African-Caribbean experience in the nineteenth century.

No single body of documents addresses the liberated African populations of the British Caribbean. However, a combination of several different sources provides a quite detailed portrait. Records of the British Colonial Office include regular dispatches from Caribbean governors about local affairs throughout the nineteenth century. War Office records include not only papers from naval vessels involved in slave trade suppression but also slave lists and logbooks from the Spanish and Portuguese ships the navy intercepted. Foreign Office records include a diverse range of correspondence concerning Britain's often-contentious interactions with foreign governments over the critical international aspects of slave trade suppression. Some Treasury Department records even detail specific expenses incurred in the transport and settlement of the rescued Africans. The materials from the Foreign Office, War Office, and Treasury Department are used primarily to establish demographic, economic, and political frameworks for the experiences of liberated Africans. Meanwhile, the Colonial Office dispatches and some similarly descriptive materials from Colonial Land and Emigration Office sources provide more narrative and anecdotal data for cultural interpretation. Records of Christian missionary organizations that worked in the African immigrant communities serve a similar purpose, as does a small body of travel accounts written by tourists and other visitors to these colonies during this time period.

In libraries and archives in both the Bahamas and Trinidad, local records supplement these colonial and missionary sources. Of particular use are a variety of community history projects prepared mostly by students at the College of the Bahamas and the University of the West Indies but also on occasion by local archivists and other scholars. Oral interviews were conducted with people who either claim descent from liberated Africans or who have early-twentieth-century memories of the African presence in their various communities. Although the last Africans arrived over a century ago, many average citizens are still aware of the existence—if not the exact history—of these special communities.

The heavy reliance on British public documents seems perhaps incongruous in a study of African-Caribbean culture and community. However, British administrators in both the Colonial and Foreign Offices recognized the situation of liberated Africans as one that involved potential changes in the very nature of culture and society in British West Indies, and that these issues were not simply matters of diplomacy regarding the slave trade or labor supply for plantations. These administrators did not discuss the issues of culture development and community formation that form the subject of the present work. However, they did discuss—at great length—the questions of which colonies should receive African emigrants and under what circumstances. These questions in turn produced additional discourse on the possible impact of these Africans on their destinations. Junior (or even senior) civil servants of the nineteenth century seem unlikely arbiters for a study rooted in the concerns of late-twentieth-century scholarship on the African diaspora. Yet these men devoted pounds of paper and months of attention to considering the fate of these unique African immigrants to the Caribbean.

In particular, British authorities expended much anxiety wondering about the interactions between liberated Africans and the existing population of African descent. Their concern often reached levels of absurdity when considering the possible impact of the presumed new "Africanness" these immigrants would bring to West Indian colonies then three centuries old. One official went so far as to warn against the "contagion of savage life" that liberated Africans might carry into British territories.[21] This warning presents "African culture" as discrete, identifiable, pernicious, and in some way communicable. In the opinion of nineteenth-century British authorities, acculturation was not a nuanced process of both exchange and creativity between European and other peoples. Instead, they viewed the creation of culture in the West Indies as the process of moving other people toward British norms. Hence, despite all their criticisms of creole populations, they viewed these people as inevitably "improved" by dint of their longer experience with British governance. One authority even suggested that British officials scatter the African immigrants in groups as small as possible throughout the sixteen West Indian territories and thereby "weaken and dilute . . . the apprehended evil."[22] While these ideas sound preposterous given modern understandings of the nature of culture, they in fact highlight the rationale for this study: the settlement of liberated Africans was a unique and consequential development in the African diaspora in the Caribbean. In the New World, Africanness did become something discrete, however difficult to bound or identify. And the Africanness of newly arrived immigrants would have necessarily differed from the Africanness of people with older or different arrival experiences. While it does not accept this newly arrived Africanness as pernicious or communicable, my study posits that a collective identity did exist for liberated Africans and their descendants and that the evolution over time of this community identity and its effects on populations around it can be traced.

The integration of liberated Africans into the wider African-descended community occurred in large measure through their status as members of an immigrant working class who were destined to become a part of the local laboring populations. In an 1832 letter to his superiors at the Colonial Office, the governor of the Bahamas, Sir James Carmichael-Smyth, made the following prosaic observation concerning the behavior of liberated African immigrants in the colony under his governance: "The real truth is, as far as I have been enabled to see, that the African, like every other Man, will exert himself or not exert himself in the exact proportion as he finds his own interests affected."[23] In much of the British West Indies during the years after emancipation, this description would have applied equally well to the behavior of former slaves. After 1834, planters and other employers complained quickly and at great length that once freed, their black working population would no longer cooperate with the long-established labor demands of the Caribbean agricultural economies. Unlike the sympathetic Governor Carmichael-Smyth, these white West Indians usually did not address the interests of the emancipated slaves and the ways those interests affected the behavior of workers. As historians such as William Green in *British Slave Emancipation* (1976) and, more recently, Thomas Holt in *The Problem of Freedom* (1992) have demonstrated, these post-emancipation labor complaints focused on the vain hope of planters that freedpeople would perform the same amount of labor they had as slaves, under roughly the same working conditions, for whatever meager wages or other compensation employers deemed appropriate.[24] Nevertheless, even the most intransigent former slaveholder recognized the inevitability of some disarray of the post-emancipation world. In other words, while they expressed displeasure at the uncooperativeness of their former chattel, they did not claim surprise at the problems they encountered. Quite the contrary, most planters portrayed their labor difficulties as evidence of the folly of emancipation, a fulfillment of their predictions that economic and social collapse would follow the end of slavery. Even the most ardent abolitionists did not anticipate an uncomplicated transition to free labor. Many British antislavery activists hoped (unrealistically) that the majority of newly freed slaves would continue as plantation laborers and that, with encouragement and oversight from the British government, former slaveowners would pay their new employees fairly and treat them well. However, abolitionists also expressed concern about the ability of the newly emancipated to handle their novel status. Some leaders expressed this concern in terms of straightforward matters such as the need for education or the desirability of continued efforts to convert freedpeople to Christianity and provide religious instruction. Other voices worried more abstractly about the capacity of former slaves to function independently without the dependency and supervision of slavery. Some couched these worries in terms of perceived African or "Negro" inferiority, while others criticized the institution of slavery for hindering the development of Britain's black Caribbean subjects as potential free workers and citizens. Thus, people from both sides of the emancipation issue viewed the universal establishment of free labor in the West Indies as an experimental process fraught with practical and cultural difficulties.

In contrast, such justifiable concern and even pessimism usually did not characterize discussion of the various labor experiments embarked upon with liberated Africans both before emancipation in the Bahamas and after emancipation in both the Bahamas and Trinidad. Carmichael-Smyth, a committed although not strident opponent of slavery, made his comment about the "real truth" about African labor in the context of a statement comparing the "industry" of liberated Africans settled in the Bahamas with the alleged lack of industry on the part of Bahamian slaves. The governor argued that while slaves had no incentive to work diligently, free African men exerted themselves "as readily and cheerfully as labourers in any part of the world" because they had families to support.[25] This kind of argument followed standard antislavery rhetoric of the period. Carmichael-Smyth's positive review of liberated African behavior, whether it was exaggerated or not, reflected a widespread optimism about the role these people would play in British West Indian economies. Even in the Bahamas, where white inhabitants initially expressed hostility toward these unusual immigrants, both agricultural and other employers came to view the slave trade refugees as a promising supplement to their local laboring population. Governor William Colebrooke, who succeeded Carmichael-Smyth in the mid-1830s, described the liberated Africans as a "most useful and valuable people."[26] One finds no hint of caution in this accolade or fear about the capacity of the newly arrived Africans to function effectively as free laborers. Even more strikingly, in Trinidad the whole process of labor recruitment of liberated Africans rested on the belief that the immigrants would serve local labor needs where recently emancipated slaves had proven either insufficient in number or were unreceptive to the wages and working conditions desired by sugar planters.

Unwittingly, in his 1832 statement, Governor Carmichael-Smyth in fact foreshadowed the failure—or perhaps more accurately the underfulfillment—of labor schemes for liberated Africans both in his colony and elsewhere. On the whole, liberated Africans did indeed "exert themselves" according to "their own interests." And those interests often did not coincide with those of their employers. Much like freed slaves, after the conclusion of their indentures, liberated Africans balanced wage labor with more-independent economic activities. Furthermore, liberated Africans did little to change the patterns of labor usage in either colony even during their periods of indentured servitude. The mixed economy of the Bahamas involved a combination of subsistence agriculture, some plantation agriculture, and maritime pursuits such as fishing and wrecking, salt-raking in southern parts of the archipelago, and a variety of trades and shopkeeping activity within the town of the Nassau. During the roughly thirty years of liberated African immigration to the colony, new arrivals found themselves serving indentures in all of these activities. In contrast, in the sugar-dominated economy of Trinidad, most economic activity revolved around the production of this staple crop on plantations. The majority of liberated African immigrants began their Trinidadian lives serving terms of indenture on sugar plantations. The only notable exception to this rule involved the practice of assigning children under the age of twelve to indenture as household or personal servants, often with individuals living in the town of Port-of-Spain. That liberated Africans became integrated into the working population of each colony, and indeed served required periods of indenture ranging from three to fourteen years, seems to demonstrate a significant degree of success for those people who viewed the rescued Africans as a potential labor source. But these immigrants neither solved the complaints of Trinidadian planters about the shortage of labor nor provided Bahamian employers—particularly in agriculture and salt-raking—with a workforce that was any more productive, stable, or guaranteed than that of former slaves.

One reason for this lack of radical success for employers lay in the special protected status liberated Africans possessed. The labor-management mores of both the Bahamas and Trinidad were rooted in the institution of slavery. Therefore, when local whites and even the colonial governors looked hopefully at the labor potential of liberated Africans, they envisioned arrangements that would grant large measures of control to employers and minimal autonomy to workers. The Colonial Office, however, exercised especially vigilant oversight of the treatment of these unique refugees, regularly intervening to protect the Africans from treatment as quasi-slaves or captive free workers. For the most part, this policy did not reflect London's hostility to the exploitation of the Africans as menial laborers. Rather, it demonstrated a mixture of genuine concern and political sensitivity on the part of various civil servants. Many abolitionists within the civil service justifiably feared the possibility of African mistreatment at the hands of planters who had developed abusive habits under slavery. Most Colonial Office functionaries, whatever their political views, felt vulnerable to criticism that alleged that the practice of slave trade suppression in fact served as a scheme through which Great Britain seized slaves bound for Cuba or Brazil only to misuse them as laborers in its own colonies. Significant contrasts of course existed between the experience of Africans who worked as tradesmen or personal servants in Nassau or Port-of-Spain and those who worked on plantations in the Out Islands of the Bahamas or in rural Trinidad. However, there was not a simple distinction between greater exploitation of labor in the profit-hungry plantation economy of Trinidad and less harsh conditions in the Bahamas. In both places, employers made various attempts to restrict the scope of freedom of liberated Africans only to have colonial authorities intervene—never to remove the expectation that the Africans, like the rest of the black population, should function primarily as laborers but rather to attempt to protect them from violence and other treatment too closely akin to slavery. Such interventions had two effects. First, liberated African laborers never became the tightly controlled labor force for which many employers had hoped. Second, through their observation of the actions taken on their behalf, the Africans came to recognize their unique status and the ways official policy regarding liberated Africans often turned to their advantage. This recognition not only affected their behavior in some dealings with employers but also later influenced the development of their understanding of their social and cultural place within the British Caribbean world. All the same, in both colonies, in the disposition of their labor these African immigrants blended quickly with prevailing local patterns.

One important difference between the Bahamian and Trinidadian cases lay in the fact that over one-third of all liberated Africans who entered the Bahamas arrived before emancipation. Most evidence indicates that these people often worked and sometimes lived directly alongside slaves. Indeed, much of the early concern of Bahamian whites about the consequences of accepting liberated African immigrants revolved around fears that these free strangers would disrupt the discipline of the slave community. Ultimately, white Bahamians did receive liberated Africans into their slave society, and those early fears proved largely unfounded. However, the situation of free African immigrants working among slaves raises automatic questions about the treatment of the free group. During the 1820s, the British Parliament established a commission to investigate the condition of liberated Africans settled in the West Indies. Two commissioners involved with this effort visited the Bahamas in 1827 and 1828 and compiled lengthy reports that provide some sense of the work experience of the earliest liberated African arrivals.[27] These men traced the whereabouts and circumstances of hundreds of rescued Africans, even though by 1827 many of these immigrants had lived in the Bahamas for over a decade and had already completed any terms of indenture or apprenticeship established when they first arrived. In the commissioners' records some people are listed as domestics or washerwomen, occupations they may have begun during their indentureships. Other entries indicate clear changes from one occupation to another. Thus, for example, one man apprenticed as a "herdsman" ended up working as a "porter." No direct evidence exists about the nature of the initial apprenticeships for a significant number of people—especially those described as self-employed in subsistence cultivation. But given the fact that slavery dominated the laboring sector of the economy, liberated Africans and slaves inevitably shared the world of work.

Anecdotes illustrate not only the intermingling that occurred between these two groups but, more important, the way the African immigrants seemed to become an integral yet free component of the slave society. One group of ninety-three liberated Africans arrived in the Bahamas in May 1827 and had therefore spent less than a year in the colony at the time of the parliamentary investigations. These newcomers were still serving six-year indentures when the commissioners arrived. An "Ebo" woman from this group provided the following report concerning her employment: "That she is employed by her Holder in Agriculture. Has no fixed allowance but gets quite enough to eat. Receives also proper clothing and is very well treated. Cohabits with a slave of her Holder by whom she has one child."[28] The phrase "cohabits with a slave" in fact appeared frequently in the 1828 report. Yet most strikingly, most of this description suggests a work experience indistinguishable from slavery, except for the fact that this woman knew that she would serve only a limited term and perhaps also the claim of very good treatment. At the same time, however, the mere fact that emissaries from London actually interviewed hundreds of these immigrants about their condition sent a powerful message to both Bahamian society at large and to the Africans themselves about the special position they held. In fact, reports on the condition of liberated Africans continued during this pre-emancipation era. The 1828 effort had a unique quality both in its thoroughness and in the fact that it originated from a specific parliamentary mandate, but during the first two decades of slave trade suppression, the employers of liberated Africans also faced an annual check from the collector of customs.

This pattern of special attention continued in the post-emancipation years, although, the annual reports by the customs collector did not. What also continued was the pattern of African immigrants intermixing with the wider laboring population—all of whom were now free—rather than occupying any separate niche. Thus, for example, in 1838, when Lieutenant Governor Cockburn ordered the preparation of written agreements for the apprenticeship of over 1,000 Africans who had arrived in the colony that May taken from two Portuguese slave ships—the *Diligente* and *Camoens*—local officials drafted three formats: one for "Minors or domestics &c under 16 years," one "for Prodial [*sic*] laborers above the Age of Sixteen" and one for "Mariners & others above the age of 16 years."[29] This latter category in particular reflected the economic diversity of the Bahamian archipelago. In less than two weeks after the arrival of this extraordinary number of people, the lieutenant governor had executed over 800 apprenticeships, leaving no room for doubt about the demand for these laborers.

These particular indentures, however, did not last. As will be discussed in chapter 1, Africans rescued from Portuguese vessels in the Caribbean ended up in the Bahamas as a measure of expediency while the Royal Navy escorted the illegal slave ships to the British-Portuguese court at Freetown, Sierra Leone. The Colonial Office informed Lieutenant Governor Cockburn that he should not have executed such agreements until the conclusion of the legal matters at Freetown. Cockburn at first protested, saying that it would prove impractical to cancel the indentures, as so many employers had taken their new laborers to islands away from the capital. He also questioned whether or not he could legally nullify the agreements at all.[30] However, after several months of arguing via transatlantic communications, in November 1838 the lieutenant governor capitulated and published a notice canceling the adult apprenticeships and indicating that the apprenticeships of minors should end when they reached the age of 16.[31]

In addition, Cockburn advised stipendiary magistrates in the various islands that "should this arrangement be such as to throw any Africans out of employment, without affording them the means of elsewhere obtaining wherewithal to duly support themselves, you will take the necessary measures for sending them to the charge of the African Board in Nassau."[32] (The African Board consisted of a group of local authorities responsible for the management of immigration of liberated Africans.) Cockburn expressed concern that a large number of Africans would end up returned to government custody. He also worried that the employment of future African arrivals would prove difficult without the control of indentures. During this period, most liberated Africans who entered the Bahamas came from similar Portuguese ships for which legal work had to be completed in Sierra Leone.

In 1831, facing a parallel situation, Governor Carmichael-Smyth settled a group of roughly 150 people from the Portuguese slaver *Rosa* in their own independent village, called Adelaide, on the southwest coast of the island of New Providence.[33] Cockburn, however, seems never to have considered this kind of free village settlement as practical or even desirable for the large number of African immigrants he faced in 1838. Indeed, even as he stated his concern that liberated Africans would prove more difficult to hire out without the power of apprenticeships, he expressed confidence that the immigrants would find employment. In December, Cockburn reported that 300 Africans had returned to government supervision as a result of the canceled indentures, but he anticipated that "many of these would be disposed of very shortly."[34] The experience of the 1,000 Africans from the ships *Diligente* and *Camoens* presented a fair reflection of the broad experience of liberated African laborers in the Bahamas. The Africans were dispersed throughout the economy to perform the same range of occupations (although most were agricultural) performed by the rest of the black laboring population, both in and around Nassau and in the Out Islands. However, the laboring experience of liberated Africans in the Bahamas involved special monitoring and review by local officials and officials in London, motivated by the social-management imperatives inherent in British policies toward liberated Africans.

In Trinidad, liberated Africans likewise followed a pattern of labor similar to that long established for the island's working classes as a whole. That is to say, the majority of liberated African immigrants became menial agricultural laborers in the sugar plantation economy. Rev. Thomas Gilbert, an Anglican priest who supervised a parish in south-central Trinidad, characterized the life of the recently arrived Africans as follows: "[T]he Planters . . . are almost to the exclusion of others, the persons under whose superintendence and care the African are placed."[35] Gilbert wrote this comment during the summer of 1850 in the context of a lengthy letter enumerating his concerns about the treatment of these immigrants. In 1849, well over 1,000 liberated Africans arrive in the colony via programs of labor recruitment from Sierra Leone and the island of Saint Helena. Indeed, as will be discussed in chapter 2, the entire decade of the 1840s marked the height of such immigration. Addressing his remarks to Lord Harris, the governor of the island, and to the colonial government in London, Gilbert offered a detailed critique of what he perceived as the failure of the British at both local and imperial levels to properly attend to the physical and spiritual needs of the Africans. It is no surprise that the most serious concerns of the priest were the related issues of conversion, church attendance, and both religious and secular education. However, Rev. Gilbert's letter and the months of controversy it generated also provide a review of the overall integration of liberated Africans into the world of Trinidadian agricultural labor—a world which they shared in most, although not all, respects with the colony's former slaves.

In promoting the cause of Christian conversion and instruction, Rev. Gilbert more than once in his letter advocated the implementation of measures to either induce or require the employers of liberated Africans to set aside the Sunday Sabbath for their attendance at church and at religious classes. Gilbert lamented of "the habit, which is not uncommon[,] of occupying the Africans on Sundays."[36] On this subject, he implied a significant contrast between the experience of the newly arrived Africans and that of other segments of the laboring population: "I have seen [the Africans] when others from different directions have been assembling in the house of prayer, gathering Cane tops in the field, in the same dirty, ill-clad condition in which they appear through the week."[37] This statement suggests that some employers may have taken advantage of the immigrant laborers by setting them to work on Sundays at times when the emancipated slaves would not do work. This interpretation requires some caution; as people not yet converted to Christianity, the Africans may very well have viewed their Sunday labor as no more or less intolerable than their work on other days of the week. Also, in a letter written to support Gilbert's appeal, the bishop of Barbados pointed out that the roots of the problem with the Sabbath with respect to liberated Africans lay in part in patterns of Caribbean agricultural life carried over from slavery. Slaves and free laborers often made use of whatever time off they had on Saturdays or Sundays "engaged in marketting [sic], or in cultivating their own provision grounds, or even in sleep or amusement."[38] Bishop Parry recommended the most specific provisions possible to mandate Sunday religious activities for the African immigrants. Like many planters (and even some abolitionists) who hoped that liberated Africans might function as model free laborers, Bishop Parry seems to have believed that, given the opportunity, Rev. Gilbert and others could shape these people into idealized converts to Christianity, independent of the habits or mores of the wider laboring population with whom they worked.

Liberated Africans would eventually express some of their greatest distinctiveness in their religious lives, although not at all in ways the Anglican bishop would have approved of! Their incorporation into the society as laborers, however, proceeded in ways that followed the experience of emancipated slaves and the rest of the black agricultural workforce. Rev. Gilbert and Bishop Parry did not achieve any of the aggressive socioreligious programming attached to plantation employment for which they had hoped. Also, in the early 1850s, the Colonial Office had fallen into a pattern of allowing only limited one-year indentures for all free African immigrants sent to the Caribbean under labor recruitment schemes. Thus, approximately a year after their arrival, liberated Africans faced roughly the same set of choices about how to dispose of their time and labor in rural plantation Trinidad as emancipated slaves had. Rev. Gilbert gave indirect testimony that, like newly emancipated slaves in previous decades, liberated Africans immediately took advantage of the option of changing employers. In the context of his concern that the Africans receive good treatment and adequate education, Gilbert made a strong plea for longer periods of indenture. With language that seems incongruous in a letter written by a priest, he argued that with the short indentures, individual planters had no incentive to provide the best possible clothing or accommodation for their African immigrant workers. If such workers elected to leave after twelve months, the planter had no way to recoup his investment. Gilbert explained, for example: "If [a planter] erects consonant [*sic*] houses for [liberated African] reception, they may leave his Estate for any where or reason or for none at all . . . and his capital which might be otherwise usefully employed is thus locked up in an unoccupied dwelling."[39] In this statement, the reverend clearly seems to argue not from hypothesis but rather from his observation of such behavior by immigrant Africans. And indeed, complaints about precisely this problem appeared with regularity in the voices of planters and other prominent citizens who wrote editorials and letters contemplating the economic future of the colony in Trinidad's newspapers. By "leaving estates for anywhere, any reason or for no [reason] at all," liberated Africans did nothing more than follow in the emergent patterns established by former slaves and other segments of the black laboring population. In Trinidad's post-slavery sugar economy, the combination of labor-hungry planters and available land for squatting gave all of these workers a measure of mobility and bargaining power in the disposition of their labor, resources liberated Africans made use of just as other groups had done.

When Governor Harris responded to Gilbert's various criticisms and requests, he in fact argued that as laborers, these Africans constituted nothing more than one component of the black working population as a whole. And as such, he had neither the resources nor the inclination to make extra or legally binding provisions for their religious and secular education, beyond the efforts already in progress for the "Creole [or black Trinidadian] race." Lord Harris asked:

> Are these [liberated Africans] to be placed in a more advantageous position than the rest of the population? [I]f so, can it be effected? Doubtless it would be very desirable to achieve a superior degree of civilization for them and for the others also, but I have great doubts whether it be possible to do more for them than for the rest of the laborers.[40]

Ultimately therefore, in neither the Bahamas nor Trinidad did the immigration of liberated Africans result in a set-apart class of workers. The immigrants stood out because of their special status and the attention they received and because of their cultural difference, as African-born people, from the rest of the black population. They did not, however, carve out separate economic niches or alter the existing labor markets in any dramatic fashion. Trinidad eventually turned to East Indian indentured labor in order to create a set-apart class and created a new body of restrictive rules to bind these new workers more effectively to sugar plantations. The Bahamas did not have a heavy demand for labor after the immigration of liberated Africans had ceased. Most important, in neither colony did the integration of these immigrants into existing economic frameworks imply their disappearance into the wider population. Quite the contrary, while these "new Negroes from Africa" did not inhabit separate economic spaces, they did very much create distinctive cultural ones.

1

Potential Laborers or "Troublesome Savages"?

SETTLEMENT OF LIBERATED
AFRICANS IN THE BAHAMAS

"Africans . . . introduced into the Colony under Indentures from condemned Slave Ships constitute the most worthless and troublesome class of black people in the town of Nassau and its vicinity."[1] Thus proclaimed a group of prominent white Bahamian inhabitants in the summer of 1816, when liberated African immigrants numbered only several hundred, less than 15 percent of the roughly 6,000 who would arrive over the next half-century. Especially during these early years of settlement, little direct evidence exists about the everyday lives of these Africans, whether they were "troublesome" or not. But both whites and blacks noted their arrival as something special in the social and cultural history of the colony. The processes by which liberated Africans arrived in the Caribbean varied widely during the sixty years of their immigration. Most writing about this population has focused on those liberated Africans who entered Jamaica, Guyana, and Trinidad during the 1840s and 1850s under a government-organized indenture scheme. In his work *Slavery and the Politics of Liberation*, Johnson Asiegbu chronicles the rise and decline of this organized immigration project which transported rescued Africans from Sierra Leone or the island of Saint Helena to Caribbean colonies seeking plantation workers to replace the labor of recently emancipated slaves. In *"Alas, Alas Kongo": A Social History of Indentured African Immigration into Jamaica*, Monica Schuler traces the experience of indentured liberated Africans in Jamaica.[2] More than half of the liberated Africans who entered the British Caribbean arrived under indentures during the critical post-emancipation decades. However, the settlement of a significant number of free African immigrants had begun thirty years earlier, almost immediately after the initial passage of the abolition

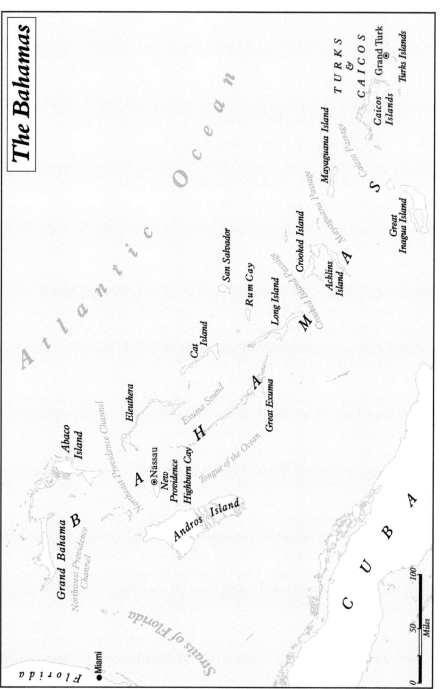

Map of the Bahamas

law. In the territory of the Bahamas, these early arrivals made up a significant portion of the total number of liberated Africans the colony received.

In examining the British abolition law, historians of the abolition and
suppression of the Atlantic slave trade have mostly addressed the many
clauses that dealt with the mechanics of seizing illegal slave ships and successfully prosecuting the resultant criminal actions. These clauses constituted the majority of the law and perhaps had greatest relevance in Britain's
diplomatic dealings with other countries on matters of enforcement.[3] In
fact, only one of the twenty-seven original clauses of the abolition act directly addressed the human consequences of the new law. That seventh
clause, however, placed an immediate and unequivocal burden on the British Crown to "receive, protect, and provide for such Natives of Africa" as
would be found on board confiscated slave ships.[4] The law required an interesting legal maneuver to effect this requirement. Under the terms of the
act, slave ships seized by the navy (or detained by private citizens) fell under
the jurisdiction of the nearest British vice admiralty court. If the court concluded that the vessel had violated the abolition law and had been properly
detained, the ship was to be "condemned as Prize of War" and forfeited to
the Crown. Under the seventh clause, the human cargo was also to be condemned as prize of war and likewise forfeited; in the words of the act, "for
the sole use of His Majesty, His Heirs or Successors." The clause immediately
continues, however, that this forfeiture of people as property would take
place solely for the purpose of superseding any other prior or even future
property claim. In other words, the British government took ownership of
the illegally transported slaves in order to prevent anyone else from ever
owning them.

For reasons that partially relate to the intricacies of antislavery politics
within the British Parliament, terms such as "emancipation" or "freedom"
do not appear anywhere in the 1807 act. Under future policies, some liberated Africans would receive emancipation certificates in the course of being
processed under this law. But in explicit terms, the act gave them a not-
slave-but-not-quite-free status under the protection and to a large extent
the control of British authorities. On the one hand, the act stipulated that
liberated Africans "should in no case be liable to be sold, disposed of, treated
or dealt with as Slaves" by the Crown or its subjects. On the other hand, the
law also stated that "Officers Civil or Military" designated by the Crown
would have the authority to enlist rescued Africans in the armed forces or
"to bind the same . . . as apprentices" to private citizens for up to fourteen
years. In March 1808, the king would issue an Order in Council designating
the collector or other chief officer of customs in each colony as the civil officer charged with the responsibility of disposal of liberated Africans. Among

other duties, he would be responsible to find work for them and supervise their relationships with their employers. The collector in effect would serve as a kind of ombudsman, addressing the concerns of liberated Africans on matters related to the housing, subsistence, payment, and general treatment their new employers provided. Thus, decades before any organized indenture scheme, all British colonies became potential sites of settlement for slave trade refugees.

In practice, most liberated Africans fell under British sovereignty through condemnation as prize of war at Freetown, Sierra Leone. Predictably, the navy's West African squadron carried the largest share of slave trade suppression duties, and most captured slave ships met their fate off the West African coast. Founded in 1787 as a settlement for free blacks from England and Nova Scotia, Sierra Leone proved a logical site for the adjudication of slave trade matters and the disposition of rescued Africans.[5] But while this African colony received the majority of such settlers, many others were rescued in the West Indian islands. Between 1807 and 1834, thousands of liberated Africans settled in the British Caribbean, in at least some cases forming the foundation of larger communities that would develop later in the nineteenth century.

This early era of slave trade suppression highlights a major difference between smaller and larger colonies in the settlement of these immigrants. In the later era of organized immigration, large labor-hungry plantation colonies would dominate the process. By contrast, in this earlier era, any British colony with a vice admiralty court was eligible to receive freed Africans. No single colony in this early period saw a greater impact from this process than the archipelago of the Bahamas in the northwestern Caribbean, stretching between the Florida Keys and the island of Cuba. Cuba's sugar economy took off in the early nineteenth century, creating a demand for a large number of African slaves from the turn of the century through the 1850s. According to Spanish colonial authorities, Cuba imported approximately 200,000 slaves between 1790 and 1817 and an additional 110,000 between 1817 and 1827.[6] Given the notoriously high mortality rate of sugar-plantation laborers, Cuban planters developed a virtually insatiable desire to acquire African slaves by either legal or contraband trade.

Spain did not pass any regulation against the slave trade until 1814, and at that time the law simply stated that Spanish traders should transport slaves only to Spanish possessions. The first Anglo-Spanish treaty against the slave trade did not develop until 1817, and there were numerous problems in its implementation and enforcement. The two countries did not sign a rigorous and comprehensive treaty until the summer of 1835.[7] This long delay did not prevent the British navy from seizing Cuban-bound vessels during the first two decades of slave trade suppression. Historian David Murray explains that the Royal Navy operated under the assumption that most of the Cuban trade relied on British and American vessels which falsely flew the Spanish flag. Supported by British legal opinions, the navy seized many Cuban-bound ships and took them for condemnation. Once at the vice admiralty court, "the onus would be on the captain and crew to prove [that] they were really Spanish and not . . . operating under false colours."[8] Slave ships bound for Havana and other ports on Cuba's northern coast regularly traversed the waters of the Bahamas. Thus, the vice admiralty court at Nassau quickly emerged as the court of choice for many early cases related to the Cuban trade. Indeed, in 1811, Bahamian chief justice William Vesey Munnings described his colony as "the Turnpike Road to the [slave] market of Cuba."[9] The proximity of the Bahamas to the southern United States also placed the colony in the path of illegal slavers bound for North America. This trade was only a fraction of that bound for Cuba, but ships with U.S. connections also sold slaves in the Cuban market, further augmenting the position of the Bahamas as a crossroads for the illicit traffic.[10] Most important, during this early period virtually every seizure by the navy resulted in the settlement of liberated Africans at the site of condemnation. According to David Murray, the vice admiralty courts almost never ruled in favor of accused slave traders who claimed to be Spanish subjects and therefore legal operators. (Even if a vessel had only a single British owner among multiple owners or had received any supply at a British port, the 1807 law deemed the entire voyage illegal and therefore subject to capture by the navy.)[11] The owners of slave vessels had a right of appeal, but under the abolition act, successful appellants would receive financial compensation, not the restoration of their human cargoes.

In 1808, three years before the complaint by Chief Justice Munnings, Charles Cameron, the British governor, transmitted a deceptively simple dispatch to the Colonial Secretary in London: "I have received the honor of your Lordship's circular letter of the 2nd of October last enclosing the Act for the abolition of the slave trade. I have made the necessary communication to the Judge of the Vice Admiralty and the other public officers here who it concerns."[12] The governor added that he would carry out the future "instructions on this subject," which the Colonial Secretary had promised. Cameron's perfunctory tone betrays his unpreparedness for, or at least lack of anticipation of, the population the colony under his control would soon receive, a population that would transform the colony.

For a brief time, the governor may have felt vindicated in his casual attitude. Existing records suggest that the court at Nassau saw almost no slave trade cases for over eighteen months after the law came into effect. What were probably the first three cases occurred in June, August, and September of 1809 and look almost insignificant given the small number of African slaves involved. In the September incident, a Spanish vessel called the *San Rafael* came into port at Nassau seeking to sell "six Negro slaves." Perhaps ignorant of the British law, or perhaps hoping for lenient treatment, the master of the vessel applied to the searcher of customs for permission to conduct the sale. When the searcher refused this request, the *San Rafael* quit the port and conducted the sale at sea with buyers who traveled out to the ship in a small boat. Despite this ruse, the searcher of customs learned of their transaction and seized the illegally imported slaves from their new Bahamian owners. The vice admiralty court declared the seizure proper and transferred the rescued slaves to the jurisdiction of the Crown.[13] Neither court records nor communications to the Colonial Office indicate the fate of these six people; they presumably became either soldiers or apprenticed laborers according to the terms of the abolition act. This case hardly seemed to portend any large influx of African refugees. Indeed, the fact that the court records referred to "Negro slaves" rather than "Africans" leaves open the possibility that this incident involved people transferred from elsewhere in the Caribbean rather than brought recently from Africa. (Although aimed primarily at the importation of new slaves via the Atlantic, the abolition act in fact outlawed all overseas trafficking in people of African descent for the purpose of enslavement.)

The August 1809 case likewise offered no hint of a looming influx of Africans. The British schooner *Little Dick,* which was seized by the searcher of customs in August, faced prosecution and forfeiture in the vice admiralty court in December for violation of the abolition act. Although the December litigation concerned the forfeiture of the ship, a notation from Attorney General William Wylly refers to "Africans" from the vessel who had been condemned as prize of war in a previous prosecution. Neither court records nor letters from the governor's office make any further reference to these forfeited slaves. Like the slaves from the *San Rafael,* the Africans from the *Little Dick* probably constituted a small group. Even less information is available concerning the June 1809 case which involved only six Africans liberated from a captured slave ship called *La Sentinelle.*[14] Following these three cases, over a year would pass without any new prosecutions related to suppression of the slave trade. This lull would end in 1811 with the arrival of no less than eight captured slave ships at the Nassau vice admiralty court. Although less than half of these seizures resulted in successful prosecutions, by the end of that year the colony had taken in more than 400 liberated African settlers—the first major wave of a sporadic but continuing migration that would last for the next half-century.

Of the 1811 cases, the five unsuccessful prosecutions reveal a certain legal conservatism, even tentativeness, on the part of the court in its application of the relatively new law. The least-controversial of these cases concerned a ship empty of any human cargo but suspected of slave trade involvement by the commander of a British naval vessel. Captain Henry Wylkes Byng of H.M.S. *Goree* detained a ship identified as the *San Carlos* and, after examining her papers, concluded that "the said Ship was an American Ship Engaged in the African Slave Trade under Spanish Colours."[15] Byng escorted the vessel to the port of Nassau, where Attorney General William Wylly conducted the vice admiralty prosecution. Unfortunately, the captain's suspicions that had convinced Wylly to proceed did not persuade Surrogate Judge Peter Edwards, who ruled in favor of the owners of the *San Carlos* and ordered the vessel released.[16] In this instance, it seemed that Wylly did indeed stand on shaky legal ground. Britain then had no treaty with either the United States or Spain concerning slave trade matters. And with no other evidence put forth, the case rested entirely on the interpretation of the ship's papers as falsified documents. Edwards's decision therefore seems understandable. The other failed cases, however, are far less straightforward.

In September 1811, H.M.S. *Indian* under Captain Henry Jane brought in a vessel called the *Bom Amigo,* which was sailing under Portuguese colors. Like the *San Carlos,* this ship did not have a full cargo of African slaves. But according to the evidence presented to the court, she had recently delivered 350 Africans to be sold as slaves at Havana. Eleven captive Africans remained on board. In addition, the *Bom Amigo* had left Havana equipped with an oversized crew, "immense quantities of Water Casks, Mess Tubs, large Boilers, Fetters . . . and all the other apparatus of an African Slave Ship."[17] With this evidence, the attorney general only had to prove that the British court had jurisdiction over the allegedly Portuguese vessel. Under the 1807 law, Britain claimed jurisdiction over any vessel in which any British subject held even a minor interest as either an owner or member of the crew. Wylly made two distinct arguments on this issue before the court. First, he pointed out that after the sale of the Africans at Havana, the officers of the *Bom Amigo* had sent a portion of their profits to England via the London packet, strongly suggesting British financial involvement. Second, Wylly noted that the *Bom Amigo* carried London-based insurance, which likewise suggested British monetary interest in the slaving venture.[18] Nonetheless, Surrogate Judge Edwards once again erred on the side of caution, ordering the Portuguese vessel to be released along with the eleven Africans. The Africans thus remained slaves.[19] The abolitionists who had written the anti–slave trade act clearly hoped to avoid this kind of outcome more than any other: Africans temporarily brought under British protection with the prospect of freedom, only to have that prospect revoked with their return to slave dealers. In these early days of enforcement, however, neither Surrogate Judge Edwards nor his superior colleague Henry Moreton Dyer prioritized any such antislavery concerns.

In Attorney General Wylly's three other unsuccessful prosecutions, these two judges returned more than 600 rescued Africans to the hands of slave traders. The captured vessel *Alerto* that was returned to its owners in December 1811 carried an unspecified number of "African Negroes" which the court returned along with the ship's other cargo.[20] The *Carlota Teresa*, which was returned in May 1811, carried 274 Africans. The vessel *El Volador*, returned in July, carried 323.[21]

The case of the *El Volador* offers a revealing perspective on the social drama that liberated Africans would initiate in the Bahamas and elsewhere. The British brig *Moselle* brought this slave ship to Nassau on July 17, 1811, but the final judgment did not occur until October 1, after months of legal wrangling. During the ten-week interim, a dispute developed between Attorney General Wylly and the masters of the slave ship. Two weeks after the initial claim against the ship had been filed, Wylly returned to court with a request that Judge Edwards allow some or all of the Africans held captive on the slaver to disembark. Armed with the opinion of a doctor who had inspected the group, Wylly argued that conditions of extreme overcrowding prevailed on board *El Volador*, where the Africans were housed "in the proportion of two to each ton or thereabouts."[22] Given the nature of the slaving business, a doctor might have made an argument based on concerns about health with respect to any slave vessel temporarily detained pending prosecution. Perhaps the conditions on board this vessel did prove more onerous than the usual unpleasant norm. However, it also seems possible that Wylly filed this petition in the hope that once the Africans had left the slave ship, the judge might feel a greater reluctance to order them returned. This strategy obviously did not work, but in the interim Judge Edwards agreed to temporarily house the Africans at Hog Island, a small cay situated roughly one mile north of the island of New Providence.[23] Under this arrangement the *El Volador* group became de facto liberated Africans, although court records remain unclear about which colonial official had direct supervision over their activity while they were on Hog Island.

Although himself a slaveholder, Attorney General Wylly progressively established a public persona as a suspected gradual abolitionist and certainly a man in favor of ending the slave trade and improving the treatment of slaves—the two issues that dominated the British abolitionist agenda before emancipation.[24] During this first decade of slave trade suppression, Wylly played a prominent role not simply in performing his professional

duty with respect to slave trade cases but also in promoting the policy of settlement of liberated Africans, sometimes in the face of local criticism. However, the attorney general had no such opportunity in the case of *El Volador,*
in which the cautious vice admiralty court again prevailed. Captain Ferrity's
ship and the 323 Africans on board were returned to him on October 1,
1811.[25]

In the long run, though, the successful prosecutions of 1811 proved
more predictive than the failures. Over the course of the century, Great
Britain strengthened her legal hand until virtually all ships seized by the
navy resulted in successful condemnations and the release of African captives. But in March 1811 this process still constituted a novelty. In that
month, the colonial government of the Bahamas oversaw its first significant
settlement of liberated Africans. On March 14, H.M.S. *Colibre* brought in a
ship identified as *El Atrevido* whose papers indicated a previous name of
South Carolina. The processing lasted some two months. According to the
court records submitted by Attorney General Wylly, over 100 pieces of evidence from the ship's papers were presented, but the surviving court records
do not explain precisely why this case proved successful where others
failed.[26] After passing its sentence, the court ordered a full inspection of the
Atrevido Africans. The brief court minutes begin to paint the first sketchy
portrait of the new migration. The group consisted of one hundred and six
men, fifty-two women, twenty-nine boys, and seventeen girls; the juveniles
were identified as those "apparently under the age of fourteen years."[27] This
early demographic profile turned out to be a rough model of the pattern
that would emerge among future arrivals of liberated Africans.

The administrative community in the Bahamas replayed this scenario
twice more in 1811. In June, H.M.S. *Rattler* brought in a vessel that had originated in Boston but was then sailing under Portuguese colors with a cargo
of 115 Africans. Surrogate Judge Edwards condemned the vessel, called the
Sancta Isabel, in July and ordered the Africans delivered to the collector of
customs according to the abolition act. This group consisted of forty men,
seventeen women, twenty-six boys, and thirty-two girls. The court-ordered
inspection of the *Sancta Isabel* Africans also found seven of the number "in
a state of bad health."[28] Health problems would grow in importance as the
number of liberated Africans arriving in the Bahamas increased. Indeed, the
reality of dealing with a large number of sick or convalescent refugees would
become a distinguishing feature between the happenstance community of
liberated Africans in the Bahamas and liberated Africans who were more deliberately recruited as laborers in Trinidad. In the Bahamas, a significant
number of liberated Africans always remained in and around the capital of
Nassau and sought public assistance for their various health problems. In

contrast, in Trinidad, where almost all liberated Africans were dispersed to plantations well away from Port-of-Spain, the inevitable health problems of these slave trade refugees did not become a major administrative concern for the local government.

The final successful case of 1811 took place in August with the seizure of a second slaver that was reputedly from the United States but was using Portuguese papers. The *Joanna* carried 129 Africans whom the collector of customs received for enlistment into the armed forces or for entrance into terms of indenture with private citizens.[29] These seventy men, sixteen women, and forty-three children ended the first wave of immigration of liberated Africans into the Bahamas.

After 1811, the next large number of liberated Africans did not arrive until 1816. Only with hindsight do the 448 Africans of 1811 appear as the beginning of a major migration for the colony. Indeed, one might suspect that these early immigrants, numbering only in the hundreds, exerted little effect on the society they entered. To even refer to them as a community seems questionable. It is an irony that with a mixture of foresight, paranoia, and bigotry, the prominent white inhabitants of the Bahamas provided the first suggestion of incipient community formation by such immigrants. In the midst of the flurry of slave trade prosecutions in August 1811, 148 citizens presented a petition to Chief Justice William Munnings expressing their concern over the possible negative effects of liberated African settlers on the local community. (Munnings was acting as the administrator of government in the absence of Governor Cameron.) For the most part, this petition reflected the typical anxieties of slaveholders with respect to free people of color within their slave society. The petitioners complained that the colony in general and the capital in particular already had a surplus population of free blacks and coloreds who lacked adequate means of employment. They alleged that such people placed a disproportionate drain on the public funds for poor relief and implied that in many cases the want of employment among this group led to criminal or immoral activity.

> The Introduction of these Africans in such considerable numbers in fact increases a species of Population of little use and already too numerous in this Colony, named [*sic*] that of Free People of Colour. Already indeed there are numbers of that class of People on these Islands, and particularly in this Town and its vicinity, who from a dearth of employment, or want of disposition to work, lead the most wretched lives, without Education or moral habits to counteract the incitements of Vice, and other dangerous resources of Indolence and Want, to which the immediate pressure of their necessities too often impel them.[30]

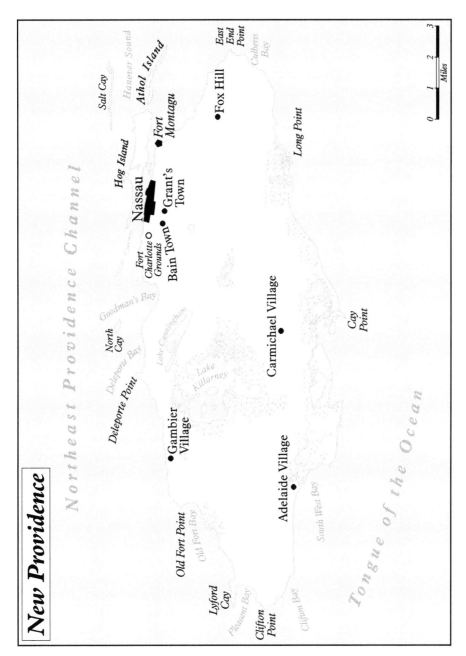

Map of New Providence

These accusations reveal far more about the fears of the petitioners than about the actual behavior either of free people of color or liberated African immigrants. Nevertheless, the complaint confirms that even a relatively small number of liberated Africans, scattered as individual indentured servants, formed an immediately perceptible presence in the local community.

Ultimately, nothing substantive came of this early protest. Munnings initially feared that the Bahamas House of Assembly would attempt to pass a law imposing a tax on individuals who accepted liberated Africans as indentured servants. In an apparent attempt to forestall that kind of legislative effort, Munnings responded to the petitioners with a letter offering to convene the assembly in order that they might devise "precautionary Measures" that would address their concerns about the African settlers without interfering with the obligation of the colony to carry out slave trade suppression as mandated by the 1807 act of Parliament. The assembly did not attempt to impose a tax to discourage the process of apprenticing such people. Nor indeed did it take up Munnings's proposal that it enact additional regulations for the settlement process. Rather, four months after the August petition of "Inhabitants," the members of the House of Assembly and Legislative Council filed a second petition in which they attempted to make a better case concerning the perceived social and economic threats posed by newly arriving Africans. The speaker of the House of Assembly, William Kerr, appeared as the principal signatory to both petitions and it seems probable that both documents represented the opinions of substantially the same group of prominent citizens.

In the second petition, filed in November and addressed directly to the British Crown rather than to the local chief executive, the authors seem to have become less adamant in their opposition to the concept of liberated African settlement. Instead they expressed for the first time the dual attitude that came to characterize much of white popular opinion in the Bahamas during the subsequent fifty years of liberated African immigration. They were still concerned that the immigrants would become a burden to the public treasury by ending up unemployed or underemployed and requiring poor relief, not to mention the additional suggestion of "more formidable evils" such as "beggary or crime" that might arise from an unsettled and unsupervised population, particularly within the town of Nassau.[31] However, in this November petition the legislators also conceded that liberated African immigrants could become a positive good for the colony, at least in economic terms, and only in those roles the prominent white inhabitants deemed appropriate:

> Your petitioners indeed willingly admit that could this increase to the Population be applied to agricultural purposes and a reasonable hope indulged that

such of these Africans as should be so employed would after the expiration of their Indentures, continue to cultivate the soil by hiring themselves as Field Laborers or otherwise, your Petitioners would have perhaps but little reason to regret their Introduction.[32]

Even with this concession, the remainder of the petition describes at length the authors' skepticism that free African immigrants would actually accept such terms. According to these complainants, in the Bahamas and elsewhere in the Caribbean, free people "of all descriptions," but especially those of African descent, sought to avoid agricultural labor in general.[33] The petitioners failed to point out the obvious reasons for this aversion. They spoke suggestively of "habits and prejudices springing as it were from the soil."[34] But they did not mention in so many words the unreasonable demands of agricultural employers in the region or the fact that much of the prejudice against field labor arose from the abuses of slavery!

This petition won greater sympathy from William Munnings. As the temporary administrator of the Bahamian government, Munnings had forwarded the previous petition to the Colonial Office with a letter that expressed his worries that local authorities might somehow obstruct settlement of liberated Africans. This second petition went beyond mere protest. In addition to suggesting that liberated Africans might in fact prove useful to the colony, the citizens had specifically requested that the central colonial government provide the Bahamas with some sort of relief to deal with the new population. Although this November appeal still contained a fair amount of complaining about possible social problems, the request for assistance clearly implied a degree of acquiescence on the part of local authorities to the unusual human consequences of slave trade suppression. In seeking unspecified assistance—"such relief therein as to your Majesty's royal wisdom shall seem most meet"—the legislators most likely hoped for some kind of financial help either to directly cover expenses related to liberated Africans or salaries to pay local functionaries who would oversee the immigration. Beyond monetary aid, they may have also hoped that in the future the Crown would grant them the authority to apprentice liberated Africans as field laborers for lengthier periods of time than the fourteen years indicated in the abolition act. Munnings willingly sent the November petition to London, no longer expressing apprehension at the attitudes of William Kerr and his colleagues but in fact asking the Colonial Office to respond positively to their request.[35] It makes sense that the local chief executive would have little objection to seeking extra financial or other assistance from London. During the ensuing decades, the Colonial Office and Bahamian officials would negotiate various agreements governing both the employment and treatment of liberated Africans and the cost of supervising them.

The secretary of state for the colonies did not promise the Bahamas anything specific in answer to this petition. The brief reply of the Earl of Liverpool merely indicated that the Colonial Office would confer with the military to make sure that the maximum number of rescued Africans entered the West India corps.[36] While this strategy would, at least in theory, reduce the number of liberated Africans who might come to Bahamian civil authorities as potential indentured immigrants, the Bahamians still had no guarantee of extra assistance in their new and unwanted social responsibilities. Direct monetary aid from the British treasury would eventually come in bits and pieces in response to requests pertaining to particular needs and sometimes immediately related to individual newly arrived groups of Africans. In the mid-1820s, detailed local legislation that prescribed the terms and conditions for liberated African apprenticeship began. However, for almost twenty years the process of liberated African settlement in the Bahamas, and elsewhere in the West Indies, remained a somewhat haphazard process that local authorities treated with a mixture of both wariness and confusion even as they began to consider both the labor potential and likely social and cultural inputs of the group.

Evidence of the continuation of this state of affairs through the 1810s emerges clearly from the 1816 case of a vessel called *La Rosa,* one of two successful slave trade prosecutions that occurred during that decade, both involving purportedly Spanish vessels. The ship *La Rosa* was wrecked at Green Turtle Key, Abaco, in 1816. (The second case involved a ship called the *Experiencia,* which was captured by an "insurgent" privateer near the island of Inagua in 1818.) In the *La Rosa* case, the tension between Attorney General Wylly and other white residents less sympathetic to the African refugees escalated to a level of open hostility. This ship ran aground on reefs near the island of Abaco in the northern Bahamas in June 1816. Learning of the wreck, Captain John Pakenham of the Royal Navy conducted his vessel, H.M.S. *Bermuda,* to Green Turtle Key, where he took custody of more than 300 African slaves and brought them to Nassau for legal proceedings in the vice admiralty court. The fate of the slave ship and its crew is not clear from the Colonial Office correspondence on the incident. It appears that the vessel did not survive the wreck and only its human cargo ended up in Nassau. Unlike previous cases where court records referred to the names of both slave ships and their captains, in this matter the court identified the case only as "Pakenham [and] Certain Natives of Africa"; it did not mention *La Rosa* by name.[37] Once in Nassau, Pakenham apparently left the Africans in the care of the collector of customs, presuming, with the support of Attorney General Wylly, that the vice admiralty court would deliver a favorable ruling according to the abolition act. Surrogate Judge Edwards, however, ruled the seizure improper and ordered that Pakenham, who had picked up the Africans, would have to pay not only court costs but also an amount of almost £26,000 as the "appraised value of the Africans."[38] (The ruling does not make clear to whom Pakenham would have paid such money, presumably to the owners of *La Rosa,* who apparently had fled the scene of the wreck.) Judge Edwards in effect ruled that there was not sufficient evidence to confirm that the ship *La Rosa* had been engaged in illegal slave trading; therefore Captain Pakenham should not have delivered the more than 300 slaves to Nassau, expecting them to be treated as liberated Africans.

William Wylly responded to this ruling with an angry letter to Governor Cameron in which he not only questioned Edwards's decision in this case but also alleged that the judge in fact had such severe deafness that he perhaps should not continue to serve on the bench at all. Wylly wrote with unsubtle sarcasm: "Mr. Edwards is so extremely deaf, that I do not suppose he will venture to assert that he has, for the last seven years, distinctly heard one word in ten that has been addressed to him."[39] This verbal attack represented less a personal animosity between Edwards and Wylly than a general frustration on the part of the attorney general concerning the disposition of this particular case and possibly also prior slave trade matters. Wylly pointed out in his letter that he had for many years supported Peter Edwards in various judicial and other public positions and that only "within the last few years" had found cause for criticism.

Even before this controversial ruling, a group of prominent white inhabitants had yet again petitioned the governor to protest the expected role of their colony as a refuge for liberated Africans. On this occasion the petitioners requested that the slaves wrecked at Abaco be sent for adjudication to a British West Indian port other than the Bahamas.[40] Like the 1811 petitions, this effort yielded no result. Within West Indian colonies, white elites such as these petitioners exercised enormous power in their control over slaves and other members of the nonwhite populations. However, as in most colonial populations, they had little hope of overturning British imperial policy on any matter, particularly not in the area of slave trade suppression during these years of antislavery ascendance both in Parliament and in the British civil service. West Indians and their allies had made their stand in Parliament against the abolition act through the end of the eighteenth century. After that act finally came into effect in 1807, the Colonial Office—polite responses notwithstanding—largely ignored protests such as this petition, which in effect sought to alter or interfere with the operation of the abolition law. In the matter of "Pakenham's seizure," an appeal by Attorney

General Wylly won a reversal of the initial vice admiralty court ruling and the Africans from *La Rosa* became the latest addition to the Bahamas's population of new African immigrants.[41]

While the legal explanations for these decisions by the vice admiralty court remain murky, the Pakenham incident provides significant evidence of nascent community formation among the earliest arriving segments of this unique body of immigrants. The petitioners who sought to divert the Africans from *La Rosa* to some other colony described the liberated Africans already in the Bahamas as "the most worthless and troublesome class of black people in the town of Nassau and its vicinity where unluckily their [*sic*] are nearly all centered."[42] While one must obviously question the accuracy of the petitioners in their description of the Africans as "troublesome," even this prejudicial characterization proves useful insofar as it points to the existence of some kind of distinctive behavior (or even culture) that singled out the newly arrived Africans within the wider population of people of African descent. Specifically, the petitioners contended that liberated Africans held themselves separate from both slaves and free people of color, "assimilat[ing] and associat[ing] principally with each other." The authors even implied that the new immigrants considered themselves "superior" because of the special circumstances of their arrival and their awareness of their eventual status as fully free persons after their terms of apprenticeship:

> Assured of the time at which the period of their servitude is to end they submit to it, some with a good and some with bad grace, according to accident, and the fluctuating suggestions of individual caprice; all of them however awaiting with impatience that hopeful change in their condition, with minds infinitely more intent on the indulgences and enjoyments fancifully connected in their anticipations, with a state of total exemption from restraint or coercion, than on the means of entitling themselves to those enjoyments by any certain, safe or honest exertion of their own. This thoughtlessness is naturally incident to the savage state from which they in fact can scarcely be said to have emerged.[43]

This obviously biased description suggests little more than the fact that liberated Africans preferred leisure over their enforced servitude. The white complainants offered no details about the "indulgences" or "enjoyments" allegedly desired by the Africans, and other evidence from later years, as the liberated African community grew, challenges this claim of aloofness on the part of the new immigrants. Even without such evidence, complete aloofness would seem both unlikely and impractical given the dispersion of the Africans either singly or in small groups to different employers, not to mention the presence of most of these new Africans in and around the city of

Nassau, where they undoubtedly faced regular interaction with the existing free black and colored population and with slaves.

In fact, Collector of Customs Alexander Murray would provide a revealing discussion of this question of aloofness in a letter he wrote in 1832, years after his retirement from his post as collector. Murray wrote to an under secretary of state at the Colonial Office seeking permission to transfer slaves from his New Providence plantation to another property he owned on Long Island in the central Bahamas, well away from Nassau. (Although the abolition act aimed to prevent the importation of slaves from Africa, after 1807 the Colonial Office sought to regulate all transport of slaves by sea, even within a single colony such as the Bahamian archipelago.) Murray complained that while they were in New Providence, his slaves failed to work with sufficient diligence on his behalf. He reported that, consistent with common practice near the capital, he had permitted some of the slaves to hire their time and pay him from their wages.[44] According to his account, these slaves did not earn amounts that he considered to be sufficient. Murray seemed to argue that the culture of slaves and other people of African descent in and around the colonial capital consisted of disorganization, poor discipline, and insubordination. Like the men who complained about the new Africans in 1816, he pointed to liberated African immigrants as one of the sources of these problems. While the 1816 petitioners had spoken of aloofness, Murray alleged that the new African immigrants "constantly up-braid[ed] and goad[ed]" their enslaved creole associates, pointing out the "advantage which [they] . . . possessed" as free and protected refugees from the illegal slave trade. Murray further claimed that the creole slaves viewed these "savages from Africa" as "certainly . . . inferior," and they resented the privileged status of the new group. Finally, Murray lamented that prior to the arrival of the liberated Africans, Bahamian slaves had proved "docile" and cooperative but had since become less tractable and more difficult to control.[45]

The former customs collector presented these arguments as justification for his desire to transfer his slaves from New Providence to his Long Island plantation. In other words, he sought to remove them from the negative influence of the free African immigrants who, although they were not absent from other Bahamian islands, largely ended up apprenticed in or near the capital. At first glance, Murray's criticisms might seem to lend some credence to the earlier portrait of liberated Africans as holding themselves apart from the remainder of the African-descended population. However, upon closer examination, the letter of the former civil servant not only proves self-serving and disingenuous but in fact suggests that, far from holding themselves aloof and superior, the liberated Africans more likely communicated at length with the resident population about their experience of slave trade suppression and the role of British authorities as advocates and protectors rather than enslavers. Contrary to the scenario painted by Murray, it seems far more plausible that liberated Africans served as a kind of inspiration to Bahamian slaves, motivating at least some of them to test the boundaries of their masters' authority—perhaps in the belief that British government officials who had rescued the liberated Africans from foreign slave ships might also come to the aid of local slaves.[46] This kind of testing of authority might explain, for example, Murray's complaint that slaves who hired their time had begun to deliver lower wages or that the slaves who remained on his plantation did not work as hard as they had before. Where Murray suggested that Bahamian-born slaves resented the liberated Africans who had received instant freedom, it seems more likely that the instant freedom granted to liberated Africans led some slaves to resent their enslavers (including Alexander Murray) all the more. When Murray described the new African immigrants as "arrogan[t]" as well as "a scuroless [sic] and vagabond set,"[47] he clearly highlighted characteristics that would have proved a far greater irritation to employers than to the slaves or resident free blacks who may have worked alongside the recently arrived immigrants.

Murray's true complaint lay in the fact that he could not command absolute authority over liberated African workers in the way that he, at least in theory, commanded authority over his slaves. To his mind, this lesser authority with the immigrants encouraged a lesser level of obedience from the enslaved. In an all-too-brief but nevertheless suggestive anecdote, Murray singled out a house servant named Julia (or Judy) who he wished to transfer to Long Island. Among her infractions, Julia allegedly had the habit of bringing her "paramour" into Murray's home after he and his family had gone to sleep. Although Murray nowhere identified this man as such, one cannot help but wonder whether Julia had selected her paramour from the liberated African population. According to other records, Murray employed some twenty-eight liberated Africans as apprentices.[48] From this small group, or even from others on the island of New Providence, Julia would have no doubt had the opportunity to meet such a person. And it certainly seems probable that a free African immigrant might have had less compunction about transgressing Murray's authority as both slave master and householder for the purposes of such nighttime visits. When Alexander Murray complained of formerly well-behaved slaves corrupted by liberated African influence, he may in fact have spoken with a particular indignation about specific transgressions in his own household. But perhaps most important, these attempts by Murray and other whites to characterize the impact of liberated Africans on their society point to the immediate and noticeable social and cultural presence these immigrants developed in the nineteenth-century Caribbean. That presence would only grow as the number of liberated African immigrants steadily increased over the half-century between 1810 and roughly 1860. Furthermore, even if one grants only a fraction of credibility to Murray's complaints, the liberated Africans from the start exhibited consciousness of themselves as a community, consciousness of their role in the politics of black freedom and unfreedom, and engagement with the wider population of people of African descent, including the enslaved.

With respect to the Pakenham (or *La Rosa*) Africans of 1816, Collector of Customs Murray, in his role as their superintendent, provided one of the first lengthy descriptions of the settlement process for such early refugees from the slave trade. He sent a series of communications to his superiors in London on this subject in August and September 1816. In the first of these letters, Murray boasted to the secretary of state for the colonies of his diligence in superintending the 500 Africans already under his charge in the Bahamas. He compared his performance with a report from Antigua that suggested that customs collectors in the Windward Islands viewed their responsibilities to liberated Africans solely as a matter of finding them positions of apprenticeship with no subsequent monitoring. Murray asserted that he, in contrast, had become a kind of ombudsman for the African immigrants, hearing their complaints about their employers or other matters and accepting renewed responsibility for those individuals whom employers rejected for reasons of ill health. Murray presented detailed testimony describing African immigrants "left in his yard or out offices covered with the most loathsome Diseases," which in one instance even resulted in the death of a child on his premises.[49] Murray probably exaggerated his good conduct in the hope of obtaining additional "remuneration . . . for the sacrifices made."[50] However, his description also betrays the somewhat passive attitude that existed among the white population concerning the potential of liberated Africans as laborers in this early period. In stark contrast to the later pleas of planters in sugar colonies such as Jamaica, British Guiana, and Trinidad, and even in contrast to the requests of some planters and salt producers in the Bahamas, at least some of the earliest New Providence employers who received liberated Africans viewed their apprentices as a useful but hardly necessary or overly valuable convenience. It should perhaps surprise no one that an employer would reject an apprentice suffering from a "loathsome Disease." The practice of outright abandonment, however, seems particularly heedless. From Murray's account, dissatisfied employers did not even complain about having received useless laborers. In future years, authorities who supervised the Africans and the employers who used their labor would become much more determined, organized, and serious about the process of distributing liberated African immigrants. During this first decade, however, the process revealed a sense of uncertainty among all parties involved.

All the same, the 1816 experience did not present a picture of either complete disinterest on the part of potential employers or complete disorganization on the part of the customs collector. Quite the contrary, other aspects of Murray's communications with London exhibit the early inklings of British attempts at both labor control and social management that would characterize the experience of the majority of liberated African immigrants later in the nineteenth century. In a list of itemized questions accompanying one of his letters, Murray sought official policy instructions on a variety of matters ranging from the cost of care for "incapacitated" and therefore unemployable Africans to the manner of dealing with immigrants after their apprenticeships ended. Several queries in particular point to the birth of deliberate attempts by Bahamians to take maximum advantage of liberated African labor instead of seeking to avoid accepting such immigrants into the colony at all. The authors of the various petitions protesting such immigration may not have changed their minds but rather may have simply resigned themselves to making the best use of an immigrant population they apparently could do nothing to prevent. One of Murray's queries spoke directly to the question of using liberated Africans for agricultural labor, an issue that had been raised in the November 1812 House of Assembly complaint. Murray asked his Colonial Office superiors whether or not he should allow liberated Africans to be apprenticed to persons living in Nassau who intended to use the labor of their apprentices on plantations located on other Bahamian islands.[51] These Out Islands contained the majority of Bahamian plantations and presented few opportunities for nonagricultural employment, apart from the equally arduous labor of salt-raking, which grew as an industry in the southern Bahamas throughout the nineteenth century. To transport these immigrants to plantations on other islands would presumably not only make better use of their labor than household or trade service in Nassau but would also have the advantage of reducing the possibility that they would fall into begging, crime, or unemployment, as local elites feared. Such planters quite possibly hoped to in effect trap the new immigrants on islands away from the capital, where there would be no alternative to undesirable field labor.

In his designated role as protector of the liberated Africans, Collector of Customs Murray wondered whether or not such Out Island apprenticeships would prove problematic because employers living in the capital would not be able to monitor the "individual treatment" of their apprentices. He also presented to the Colonial Office a question concerning what one might describe as the intended cultural management of the new immigrants. Referring again to the report from Antigua that had criticized lax supervision of liberated Africans in the Windward Islands, Murray expressed concern that Out Island apprenticeships would also prevent employers from "attend[ing] to the moral Instruction" of the Africans entrusted to them.[52] Taking into account Murray's attitudes expressed elsewhere, it seems likely that this concern reflected less his commitment to religious or other instruction for liberated Africans than his awareness of the fact that these issues were important components of official British policy toward these refugees. Throughout the years of slave trade suppression, Colonial Office functionaries not only engaged in much self-congratulation for their role in saving Africans from Cuban or Brazilian slavery, they also touted the added benefit of bringing the alleged advantages of British civilization to such Africans.

The subjects of civilization and morality arose in several other questions Murray asked. For example, he questioned whether or not all apprentices should become "free" at the end of their respective contracts regardless of any "good or depraved" character they might have manifested. The customs collector also requested instructions concerning the manner of dealing with female apprentices who "violate[d] all principals of good conduct and [chose to] pursue an abandoned course of life."[53] Given nineteenth-century British morality, one can reasonably speculate that such language referred to Murray's fears either of actual prostitution or of some other kind of extramarital sexual impropriety. In the context of his list of queries, Murray does not provide evidence that such behavior did in fact occur among the Africans already in the Bahamas, but merely by asking the question he certainly implies that it did. Concerns about female sexual misbehavior would not have particular prominence in the long-term attempts by British authorities to manage the social and cultural development of these immigrants. However, Murray's questions on such matters previewed what would become a core belief of the British government: that it both could and should attempt through various policy initiatives to socioculturally engineer the experiences of liberated Africans.

In the matter of the Pakenham Africans, Murray betrayed that his primary concern was their potential as laborers when in a second communication of September 1816 he openly advocated in favor of apprenticing them on Out Island plantations. Murray reported to the Colonial Office that he had sent 80 percent of these new arrivals to such distant agricultural employment. Apparently anticipating objections from his superiors, the customs collector went on to explain that he had advised their employers that female Africans should not perform most agricultural labor, just the supposedly lighter tasks of "weeding, picking Cotton, and Provisions, and of assisting in [the] planting of [provisions]."[54] He had also warned employers that should the Colonial Office object to these plantation apprenticeships, he would require them to return the laborers in question to his custody. However, seeking to forestall any objection from London, Murray concluded his letter with a transparently biased claim about the superior behavior and potential for future success of Africans sent to outlying islands in comparison with those who remained in the capital. He described the Out Island apprentices as "an orderly, quiet & industrious set of people" who had developed "habits of Industry" that would make them useful workers and good citizens even after their contracts expired. In contrast, he characterized the liberated Africans settled on the island of New Providence as "a more worthless race than . . . will seldom be met with anywhere."[55]

This characterization seems to be an early articulation of the complaints Murray made in 1832 concerning the role of liberated Africans in encouraging less-cooperative behavior among the nonwhite laboring population in and around Nassau. The customs collector thus gave an early idea of his reluctance to accept the idea of a body of nonagricultural and potentially independent free African laborers within the colony. As Murray implied, much of the colony's white elite shared this attitude and expressed it with regularity and increasing frequency as the number of liberated African immigrants received by the colony grew. Even without the heavy demands of the sugar islands for laborers, Bahamian planters, and increasingly salt producers, would come to view liberated Africans not simply as acceptable or inevitable refugee immigrants but as immigrants they could use to further their own economic interests. Their needs would never compete with those of larger colonies, and the Bahamas would certainly never become a labor-recruiting colony. But when the unusual circumstances of slave trade suppression continued to direct liberated Africans to the northern Caribbean colony, Murray and others of his class would at least attempt to take maximum economic advantage of these immigrants, with varying degrees of success.

As Murray's letter suggests, their success in such efforts often depended on how well local intentions coincided with the vision of the Colonial Office that oversaw much of the process of suppressing the slave trade. Where legal tentativeness and attempts to formulate settlement policies characterized this first decade after passage of the abolition act, during the remainder of the nineteenth century levels of planning and organization increased as immigration of liberated Africans not only increased in volume but became a far more deliberate and carefully managed process. The pre-1820 liberated African immigrants, numbering roughly 800 people, constituted less than 20 percent of the total number of approximately 6,000 who would settle in the Bahamas between 1807 and 1870. Furthermore, in the 1820s, only one additional group—93 slaves from a wrecked French vessel—were processed through the local vice admiralty court.[56]

The expansion of the legal apparatus related to slave trade suppression contributed significantly to the growth of liberated African settlement as a more calculated and organized phenomenon. Most important, after the first Anglo-Spanish and Anglo-Portuguese treaties in 1817, Britain succeeded in negotiating a series of increasingly powerful agreements with Spain, Portugal, and Brazil for the mutual policing of illegal slave traffic. With these major slave-trading nations (and with the Netherlands) Britain established a group of bilateral courts of mixed commission staffed by officials from each nation involved and charged with determining the legal fate of ships seized for allegedly participating in the illegal African slave trade. The commissions had no authority to either detain or prosecute suspected slave traders whose fate fell under the jurisdiction of their own respective nations. The commissioners would simply declare a seizure either proper or improper; in the case of vessels properly seized, they would condemn the ship as prize of war and liberate the Africans on board. By the end of 1820, a total of six mixed commissions existed: an Anglo-Portuguese commission at Rio de Janeiro, an Anglo-Spanish commission at Havana, an Anglo-Dutch commission in Suriname; and three commissions, Anglo-Spanish, Anglo-Portuguese, and Anglo-Dutch at Freetown, Sierra Leone. When Brazil declared its independence from Portugal in 1822, Britain pursued comparable anti–slave trade treaties with the new nation, and by 1828 two Anglo-Brazilian mixed commissions existed, one at Rio de Janeiro and one at Freetown.[57] Most of Britain's naval campaign against the slave trade continued to take place off the coast of West Africa, and the mixed commissions at Sierra Leone saw the greatest volume of activity. According to historian Leslie Bethell's calculations, between 1819 and 1845 the mixed commissions at Sierra Leone addressed a total of 528 cases, in comparison to fifty cases at Havana and only forty-four cases at Rio de Janeiro.[58] However, in the settlement of liberated Africans in the British West Indies, the mixed commission at Havana in particular would prove to have great importance.

Under the provisions of the treaties and related agreements that established the mixed commissions, the governments involved initially agreed that Africans liberated from slave ships at these sites should become free people in the territory—Cuba, Brazil, or Sierra Leone—where the adjudication took place. This provision was not a problem in the British colony of

Sierra Leone, but in the slave societies of Cuba and Brazil numerous observers reported that the *emancipados* were treated little better than slaves. In addition, Cuban and Brazilian authorities did not welcome the responsibility of monitoring the distribution and subsequent well-being of hundreds or even thousands of free Africans. Such authorities also worried that the introduction of these uniquely emancipated Africans might foment rebellion among local slaves. After years of diplomatic exchanges on this matter, in 1833 Britain and Spain finally came to an agreement under which British, not Spanish, authorities would take responsibility for Africans liberated at the Havana mixed commission for the suppression of the slave trade and Britain would transfer such Africans to its Caribbean possessions.[59]

The two nations formalized this agreement in the 1835 revision of the Anglo-Spanish Treaty for the Abolition of the Slave Trade. (The treaty stated that rescued Africans would fall "under the disposition of the Government whose cruiser had made the capture."[60] In practice, given the virtual non-participation of Spanish naval vessels in capturing slave ships, this clause placed most liberated Africans under British jurisdiction.) British officials engaged in similar discussions with their counterparts in Brazil, but they never arrived at a formal treaty agreement on such transfers.[61] Nevertheless, during the 1830s and early 1840s, Britain and Brazil transported liberated Africans from Rio de Janeiro to British West Indian colonies in a process similar to that applied at Havana. These transfers from Cuba and Brazil contributed several thousand Africans to the British Caribbean and constituted what one might describe as the second major phase of liberated African settlement.

The early 1830s also marked the dawn of British emancipation; the law ending British slavery was passed by Parliament in 1833. Historian David Murray rightfully points out the opportunistic concerns that shaped British behavior in developing this new policy of settlement of liberated Africans. With respect to the removal of liberated Africans from Havana, Murray writes: "As usual British motives were mixed. The abolition of slavery had led to labor shortages in the British West Indies and the liberated slaves, or *emancipados*... might help to fill the gap."[62] Murray points out that British West Indian governors even competed with one another for African immigrants under these new arrangements. The Colonial Office, however, did not give automatic priority to the most labor-hungry or plantation-dominated territories in this process. Quite the contrary, the body of civil servants charged with the everyday implementation of slave trade suppression policies debated at some length about what course of action they should follow in the distribution of rescued Africans from Cuba among different British colonies. These debates have particular pertinence for this study, because the Colonial Office authorities considered the benefits of sending liberated Africans to the nearest available colony regardless of its labor needs or demands—in this case the Bahamas—versus sending them to more-distant colonies with larger economies and very vocal requests for labor—particularly the island of Trinidad and the colonies of British Guiana and British Honduras, which also expressed interest. While nineteenth-century British bureaucrats seem unlikely guides for an evaluation of the social and cultural experiences of liberated Africans in the Caribbean, their comparative discussion in this case provides preliminary insights into the different material and conceptual concerns that would shape that experience in Trinidadian and Bahamian societies.

In October 1835, the Colonial Office prepared a detailed "Minute on the Condition and Disposal of Captured Africans at the Havana."[63] This document, apparently written by several under secretaries of state, sought to answer four specific questions. First, should the process of transferring liberated Africans from Havana continue? Second, if the policy should continue, should officials continue to try to organize emigration groups according to criteria of age, gender, and health? In the groups already sent to Trinidad between 1833 and 1835, the governor of that colony had asked for equal proportions of males and females, that none be over thirty years of age, and that everyone be in good health. As will be discussed in chapter 4, the question of gender balance would linger for many years as a key social concern in the speculations of British authorities about the possible impact of liberated African immigrants on West Indian societies. In their third question, the Colonial Office bureaucrats asked one another explicitly:

> If [the liberated Africans at Havana] are all to be removed how shall they be disposed of? Shall they be sent to Trinidad & those Islands only in which their labor may be profitable for commerce? Or shall some be sent to the Bahamas to be located there: providing their own subsistence & receiving the benefit of British Laws & Manners?[64]

Finally, as a concluding question, the "Minute" invited respondents to suggest alternative solutions to distributing the refugee Africans—although given the fact that transfers of liberated Africans to Britain's West Indian colonies had already begun, this last inquiry seems something of an afterthought.

The "Minute" in fact arose in part as a response to the competing claims of different West Indian governors. In addition to the arrangements with Governor George Hill of Trinidad, the British commissioners at Havana had received requests from Governor Carmichael-Smyth of British Guiana and Governor Cockburn of British Honduras.[65] Cockburn sought liberated

Africans not as plantation laborers but as woodcutters for the colony's intended development as a timber exporter. But perhaps even more than responding to these predictable requests, the Colonial Office "Minute" sought to respond to a "fourth application of a somewhat different nature" presented by Lieutenant Colonel William Colebrooke, governor of the Bahamas. Passing through Havana on his way to Nassau, Colebrooke had had the opportunity to observe stranded Africans from captured slave ships and learn of the plans then afoot to send them to British colonies that had requested them for use as laborers. Colebrooke did not directly criticize the proposals of other colonies; however, according to the Colonial Office, the Bahamian governor "made up his mind that a considerable number of [the Africans] *might be favorably (for themselves at least)* settled in the Bahamas" (emphasis added).[66] This suggestion prompted the Colonial Office to consider precisely the criticism posited by twentieth-century historians such as David Murray (as well as by some nineteenth-century antislavery activists) concerning the self-serving quality inherent in Britain's use of liberated Africans to fill its need for labor in the West Indies and in that self-interest a possible departure from the best interests of the Africans.

The early part of the 1835 "Minute" engaged this debate largely as a moral abstraction, considering whether or not Britain would compromise the "spirit of [her] national policy" on slave trade suppression if the Colonial Office chose a course of action that would benefit both the liberated Africans and British commercial interests "in preference to" a course of action that would benefit the Africans alone. The authors seemed particularly worried that the less economically attractive option—sending the Africans to the Bahamas—would in fact prove more beneficial to the Africans. If this were found to be the case, to send such emigrants to labor-hungry plantation colonies would seem almost certainly immoral. Consistent with much British public discourse in the wake of the 1833 Emancipation Act, these Colonial Office functionaries conceived of their government as the unquestionable benefactor of Africans whom other less-honorable nations continued to enslave. The several authors of the "Minute" therefore concluded, at least in principal, that the "moral & physical improve[ment] of the Africans liberated at Havana" should form the "single object" of any policy decision.[67] Their document, however, would go on elsewhere to explore in more detail the specifics of the different settlement options, and these officials would ultimately rationalize the viewpoint that both choices for settlement had sufficient positive qualities to justify their use.

Regardless of the eventually inconclusive policy position, these explorations of the hypothetical advantages and disadvantages of different settlement programs in fact highlighted several of the distinctions that would differentiate the experience of liberated Africans not only between the very different colonies of Trinidad and the Bahamas but also within each individual colony under different settlement circumstances. To begin with, the authors of the "Minute" presented a clear case favoring the idea of "forming [the Africans] into independent settlements" on "lands granted for the purpose" and having them cultivate that land for their own subsistence. These Colonial Office functionaries argued that while arrangements such as this would prove more costly, they had the advantage of placing the immigrants under the direct "care of the Government, and under the influence of moral civilization."[68] The language of "care" implies a skepticism that planters or even other employers would treat liberated Africans fairly or well. The officials further seem to have envisioned that government authorities could arrange a missionary presence for such settlements and perhaps other education as well. In the Bahamas, such missionary arrangements had already begun for previously established communities of liberated Africans and would continue at least through the 1840s. In reviewing the advantages of "independent liberated African settlements," the Colonial Office authorities even suggested that new African immigrants might simply be "unaccustomed" or "unfitted by their previous habits" to the kind of "regular labor" employers would require either on sugar plantations or in other contexts.[69] This suggestion seems strange indeed in the writings of British government bureaucrats. After all, during the nineteenth century, even the most ardent emancipationists and professed advocates of Africans generally viewed people of African descent as little more than potential labor for European-dominated economies. And in fact, the same authors who made the case for "independent [African] settlements" proved equally adept at arguing in favor of planters and other private citizens hiring liberated Africans.

In support of the proposals to use liberated Africans as plantation labor, the Colonial Office authors suggested that such "a system of dependence and subjection" and the inevitable interaction with other "more civilized" segments of the population could prove even more effective in guiding liberated Africans to become productive and socially adjusted members of West Indian societies. In presenting this argument, the officials expressed a concern that separate communities of liberated Africans would encourage these immigrants to maintain African-derived patterns of culture, custom, or behavior instead of adopting the norms of British colonial society. Attorney General Stephen Rothery had already expressed this concern in response to regulations prepared by the Board of Council in Trinidad for the distribution of liberated African laborers in that colony. Rothery had argued that allowing the immigrants to congregate in large numbers would encourage them to "form a society of themselves and . . . retain the savage habits of their nation."[70] He recommended instead that Trinidadian authorities distribute such Africans widely "amongst small proprietors . . . resident on their own property & superintending the work of their own laborers."[71] Although Rothery's preference for small proprietors did not become the practice in Trinidad, the principal of dividing the Africans from Havana into small groups for consignment to individual employers became a defining feature of this phase of liberated African immigration to that colony.

The Colonial Office "Minute" further pointed out that the idea of creating subsistence communities of liberated Africans might prove difficult given the gender imbalance of cargoes on slave ships, which had far more males than females: "A body of men without women . . . cannot form a community by themselves."[72] The Trinidadian government did seek to maintain a practice of accepting only gender-balanced lots of Africans brought from Cuba. However, gender imbalance was part of the broader pattern of immigration of liberated Africans to both the Bahamas and Trinidad. But, contrary to the compartmentalized musings of these Colonial Office authors, the pursuit of marital liaisons would become only one of many levels of social interaction between the new immigrants and existing nonwhite populations.

It is a paradox that in the effort to determine whether the Bahamas or the sugar colonies would be preferable as settlement locations for the Africans from Havana, the Colonial Office "Minute" moved away from attempts to measure comparative material and social environments and returned once more to the realm of moral abstraction. In a somewhat tortuous argument, the authors pointed out that the placement of liberated Africans as sugar workers in Trinidad or British Guiana might actually prove beneficial to the greater cause of slave emancipation internationally. They contended that if the use of liberated African laborers successfully improved the efficiency of sugar production in these territories and thereby lowered the price of nonslave sugar, Britain could strike an economic blow at the slave economies of Cuba and Brazil. The authors thus implied that even if liberated Africans might fare better if they settled in the Bahamas, they could in theory assist in improving the lives of thousands of other Africans by going to the sugar colonies because their labor would help reduce the economic incentives that continued to fuel slavery and the illegal slave trade.[73] British authorities would return to this argument in later years when they implemented the planned emigration of thousands of liberated Africans from Sierra Leone and the island of Saint Helena to work as indentured labor in Trinidad and other sugar colonies.

Before this premeditated immigration scheme begun, however, Trinidad received "over eleven hundred" liberated Africans from Cuba as the island's first major influx of this unique immigrant group.[74] Labor-hungry colonies, however, did not monopolize this transfer process. Although the Colonial Office "Minute" provided more than sufficient justification for prioritizing such colonies, the Bahamas nonetheless received over 900 Africans from the Havana mixed commission between 1836 and 1841.[75] One of these vessels, the *Jesus María,* which was condemned in 1841, included almost exclusively very young children, and one might speculate that this fact motivated British authorities to choose the Bahamas over colonies with greater demands for labor. This explanation, however, would not account for the other two groups of Africans sent from different vessels in 1836 and 1841. According to David Murray, the island of Grenada received one group of liberated Africans from Cuba during this era and the colony of British Honduras received two groups.[76] In the last pages of the 1835 Colonial Office "Minute," the authors suggested that the Bahamas might prove most appropriate as a settlement site for those liberated Africans who somehow did not fit with the more economically motivated shipments to other colonies. (For example, they proposed that the Bahamas might receive "surplus males" left over from the gender-equalized groups requested by Trinidad.)[77] However, consistent with the balanced or perhaps indecisive arguments of the "Minute's" earlier pages, a somewhat flexible discretion prevailed among British authorities at Havana as they distributed the African refugees liberated by the Anglo-Spanish Commission.

One key explanation for this state of affairs probably lay in the identity of the two men appointed to help the mixed commission supervise the African refugees. During the mid-1830s and early 1840s the post of superintendent of liberated Africans at Havana fell successively to two committed longtime emancipationists and advocates for African well-being: Dr. Richard Robert Madden and David Turnbull. Both men belonged to the British and Foreign Anti-Slavery Society and both sought to discharge their duties by holding the interests of the liberated Africans as their primary concern. Madden even came into open personal conflict with one of his British colleagues in Havana, Commissioner Edward Schenley, who owned slaves.[78] During his tenure as superintendent, David Turnbull several times faced threats of incarceration or worse at the hands of Spanish authorities who accused him of interfering with legal slave ownership in Cuba. On more than one occasion, such threats forced him to flee the island in fear for his freedom and safety. During the course of one such escape, Turnbull passed through the Bahamas on his way to London, and while in the town of Nassau he visited and worshiped with a group of liberated Africans then under the tutelage of a British Methodist missionary.[79] Yet in the end, even these two activists had only a short-lived effect on the shape of the settlement patterns of liberated Africans in the British Caribbean. Historian David Murray explains that the debate over where to send liberated Africans from Havana would prove to have limited consequence. Four groups of liberated Africans emigrated from Cuba to Trinidad before the formalization of the transfer policy in the 1835 Anglo-Spanish treaty. After that formalization, between 1835 and 1841, the Havana mixed commission condemned only six cargoes of Africans, which they distributed between the Bahamas, Grenada, and British Honduras.[80]

The experience of those Africans transferred from Havana to the Bahamas mostly repeated patterns established for the distribution of liberated Africans at the end of the first decade of slave trade suppression. By the time of the arrival of the Africans from the Spanish schooner *Empresa* in 1836, the colony had established an "African Board" composed of leading citizens (including a medical doctor) who supervised the logistics of such immigration, removing some of that responsibility from the sole province of the collector of customs. The local government also constructed a "convalescent establishment" west of the town of Nassau that received African immigrants who arrived too ill for employment or enlistment in the armed forces.[81] One cannot overemphasize how much these Africans, although emancipated, continued to suffer medically as victims of the Atlantic slave trade. The Africans from the *Empresa* traveled to Nassau in a hired vessel with a journey of two days at sea. In that time eleven people (almost 3 percent of the group) died either from scurvy or diarrhea; their misery was exacerbated by particularly rough weather at sea. Of the 393 survivors, eighteen people went to the "African hospital," or "convalescent station," upon arrival, half suffering from diarrhea and the remainder with a litany of complaints including dropsy, yaws, joint pain, and oral tumors.[82]

During the early 1830s, Bahamian governor James Carmichael-Smyth also established several settlements of the independent and subsistence character described in the 1835 Colonial Office "Minute." But from the *Empresa* group, 100 teenagers and adults went as apprenticed laborers to Long Island and twenty to Rum Cay.[83] This large consignment to islands away from the capital, presumably to labor on plantations or at salt ponds, demonstrated the full commitment of seemingly all Bahamian authorities to the use of liberated Africans in this fashion. Unlike the questioning of Customs Collector Murray in 1816, two decades later there appeared to be no sign of doubt about the acceptability of apprenticeships on the Out Islands. Nor did there seem to be any attempt to keep large groups of the African immigrants away from the colonial capital of Nassau, where in previous decades white inhabitants had bemoaned the possibility of "beggary, unemployment or crime" among such newcomers to the town. This concern had perhaps dissipated because of the creation of two outlying liberated African settlements ten and sixteen miles from the town. The former of these, called Carmichael in honor of the governor who had established it, received the remaining 147 adults and teenagers from the *Empresa.* There they would join other previously settled liberated Africans in both subsistence agriculture and the clearing of roads under government supervision. Finally, a local newspaper reported that the "boys and girls" from the slave ship—those under 14 years of age—would "be placed with families,"[84] presumably in some status as apprenticed servants. (It is interesting that in practice, local authorities placed such children with both white and free black families.) While many of these placements with families almost certainly occurred within the town, white inhabitants perhaps felt less potential disruptive threat from these younger immigrants than they might have felt from a similar number of adults so situated. White inhabitants may have simply become accustomed to or resigned to the presence of liberated Africans in their midst, having had such immigrants among them for two decades without the development of the various social problems anticipated in previous years. After slavery was abolished in 1834, white proprietors no longer complained about the free African newcomers as potential threats to slave control.

Several demographic features of the *Empresa* group illuminate the nature of liberated African settlement in the Bahamas. Unlike the gender-balanced groups the governor of Trinidad had requested from Havana, the three groups from the Anglo-Spanish mixed commission that went to the Bahamas included the whole population of Africans from each individual ship. Thus the colony received heavily male-dominated immigrant groups. The *Empresa* group included only forty-seven females in the body of almost 400 people. That kind of gender distribution (in addition to other factors) would inevitably lead to significant degrees of interaction between the new arrivals and the existing population. Another question of community formation arises from the decision of the Bahamian African Board to assign the large group of 100 people to work for employers at Long Island. The newspaper account that reported this decision did not give any indication of how (or even if) authorities had separated these people among different employers. But even assuming some such separation, it seems at least possible that some segments of this large group would have had the opportunity to maintain some sense of community based on their experience of arrival together. This expectation would apply even more to the group of 147 sent to the district of Carmichael. These people would have had a tailor-made opportunity to form community both among themselves and, virtually by government design, with other liberated Africans at the specially designated settlement.

Apart from the groups taken from Spanish slave ships, other liberated Africans also entered the Bahamas from Portuguese slave vessels captured by the British navy during the early 1830s, but not immediately processed by any mixed commission court. According to the bilateral treaties, the condemnation of these ships and the liberation of their slaves would have to take place at the Anglo-Portuguese court in Sierra Leone, despite the fact that British naval captains often doubted the legitimacy of the Portuguese papers the ships carried. Prior to the advent of the treaty-mandated mixed commissions, British authorities would have attempted to prosecute such ships in one of their own vice admiralty courts and would have apprenticed any liberated Africans according to their own abolition law. The system of mixed commissions, however, created a new legal process and a unique humanitarian problem: when the Royal Navy seized Portuguese slave ships near Cuba, what should British authorities do with the captive Africans if they had to escort those ships back across the Atlantic for prosecution at Sierra Leone?

The first such case occurred in June 1831 when Lieutenant Taplin of H.M.S. *Pickle* seized a Portuguese vessel under the name *Rosa* in Bahamian waters. Taplin at first took the vessel to Havana, where British authorities advised him that the Anglo-Spanish commission had no jurisdiction. Commissioner William Macleay suggested that Taplin take the Africans to the nearby colony of the Bahamas, where he might leave them while H.M.S. *Pickle* escorted the *Rosa* to Sierra Leone. James Carmichael-Smyth, then governor of the Bahamas, accepted this arrangement when Taplin arrived at Nassau. In the governor's words, "[I]t was not possible to send the one hundred and fifty-seven human beings back again across the Atlantic cooped up in the hold of the small vessel . . . without the moral certainty of a considerable mortality amongst them."[85]

Opposite: A document like this was apparently prepared for each African legally emancipated by the mixed commission court. This example refers to Africans from the Spanish merchant schooner *Empresa,* seized in 1836. Although these liberated Africans were assigned European names, the certificate also allows space for the individual emancipated person to be initially identified by the "name he or she was known by in Africa." The court gathered this and other information with assistance from people of the same nationality (i.e. ethnic or geographic background) and interpreters speaking the same language as each newly arrived African. The bottom left corner of the document sets aside space for what officials considered to be basic personal data: nationality, age, height, identifying marks. For many of these Africans the identifying marks included cultural scarifications. *Courtesy of the Public Records Office of the United Kingdom, CO 318/127.*

D. JOSÉ MARÍA HERRERA Y HERRERA,

CONDE DE FERNANDINA, PRÓCER DEL REINO, GRANDE DE ESPAÑA HONORARIO DE PRIMERA
CLASE, GRAN-CRUZ DE LA REAL ÓRDEN DE ISABEL LA CATÓLICA, Y CABALLERO DE LA DE
CÁRLOS TERCERO, GENTIL HOMBRE DE CÁMARA CON EJERCICIO, Y CORONEL AGREGADO AL
REGIMIENTO DE CABALLERÍA DE ESTA PLAZA; Y DON EDUARDO WINDHAM HARRINGTON SCHEN-
LEY, MIEMBROS DEL TRIBUNAL MIXTO DE JUSTICIA ESTABLECIDO EN ESTA CIUDAD DE LA HA-
BANA PARA EL CUMPLIMIENTO DEL TRATADO CELEBRADO ENTRE SUS MAGESTADES CATOLICA
Y BRITANICA EN VEINTE Y OCHO DE JUNIO DE MIL OCHOCIENTOS TREINTA Y CINCO SOBRE ABO-
LICION DEL TRAFICO DE ESCLAVOS; EL PRIMERO EN LA CLASE DE JUEZ ESPAÑOL; Y EL SEGUN-
DO EN LA DE JUEZ INGLES DURANTE LA AUSENCIA DEL SEÑOR DON WILIAM SHARP MACLEAY CON
PERMISO DE SU GOBIERNO.

N.°

Certificamos que en el espediente obrado en este Tribunal Mixto
de Justicia sobre la detencion que hizo la Corbeta de Guerra Inglesa
nombrada Vestal, su Comandante D. Guillermo Jones, del Bergan-
tin Goleta Mercante Español Empresa con cargamento de negros
bozales; se pronunció sentencia difinitiva, declarándose bien y le-
galmente hecha la mencionada detencion, y de consiguiente por li-
bres los negros que conducía el buque apresado. Y siendo uno de
éllos el que en Africa era conocido con el nombre de
segun su informe dado por medio de

individuos de su misma
nacion é intérpretes de su idioma, presentes en este acto para ser
en todo tiempo testigos de la identidad de su persona; cuya filia-
cion se anota al pié, al cual se le ha puesto ahora por nombre
le consignamos la presente, rubricada de
nuestra mano, y refrendada por el Sr. Secretario, quien toma razon
de este documento en el libro particular formado al efecto, para
que le sirva de carta de emancipacion, quedando sujeto al destino
que, en conformidad de dicho tratado, habrá de darle el Superior
Gobierno.—Habana y Noviembre 7 de 1836.

El Conde de Fernandina.   *Eduardo Windham Harrington Schenley.*

Nacion
Edad
Estatura
Señales

The career of Governor Carmichael-Smyth uniquely demonstrates the role that the economics of different colonies played in shaping the nature of the settlement of liberated Africans. In the case of the *Rosa,* Carmichael-Smyth developed a set of settlement and employment arrangements for the rescued Africans that were consistent both with their ambiguous legal status and the Bahamian economy. Four years later, in a new appointment as governor of British Guiana, Carmichael-Smyth became an aggressive advocate in favor of importing liberated Africans to his new colony as plantation laborers. For the *Rosa* Africans in 1831, Carmichael-Smyth created a settlement on the southwestern end of New Providence, sixteen miles from the town of Nassau. He named the village Adelaide in honor of the wife of King William IV and described the new community as follows:

> I have directed [the *Rosa* Africans] to be landed and hutted on an ungranted piece of ground in the neighbourhood of an unfrequented anchorage of this Island. . . . There is a small creek which abounds with fish; and after a certain length of time, partly by cultivating the ground & partly by fishing they will be able to take care of themselves. As at present these Negroes are quite naked & in a perfect savage state, I have been obliged to authorize the Collector of Customs to hire an overseer *& a few intelligent free black people* to remain with them for the present & to instruct them in cultivating the ground.[86] (emphasis added)

The governor considered the possibility of apprenticing these Africans but decided that he could not do so without a formal ruling on the case, something that would not occur until the slave ship *Rosa* reached the Anglo-Portuguese mixed commission in Sierra Leone.[87] Carmichael-Smyth's small description of the settlement of the *Rosa* Africans says much about the way liberated African life and community would evolve in the Bahamas. Colonial authorities regularly provided these immigrants opportunities to live in independent communities, even with the ever-present preference of elite whites that nonwhite laborers be employed under white supervision. Setting aside the ethnocentrism inherent in the word "savage," one also sees here the important dynamic of culturally and socially distinct newly arrived Africans beginning Caribbean lives with the opportunity to take some cues from the more long-standing black population.

In July 1832, Lieutenant Potbury of H.M.S. *Nimble* delivered to the Bahamas 401 Africans from another captured Portuguese slave ship, the *Hebe,* destined like the *Rosa* for prosecution in Sierra Leone. In January 1832, the Colonial Office had raised the possibility that rescued Africans from Portuguese slavers might use the Bahamas as a temporary refuge until they were transferred to the labor-hungry plantation colony of Trinidad. Thus, anticipating the transfer of the *Hebe* Africans, Carmichael-Smyth settled this group on the small island of Highburn Cay in order to "prevent them merging, more or less, in the existing [black] population."[88] In fact, the *Hebe* Africans never left the Bahamas. They remained in a supervised settlement on Highburn Cay until May 1833, when word arrived from London that after a successful prosecution at Sierra Leone, these Africans had full emancipated status. Governor Carmichael-Smyth then directed the collector of customs to supervise the enlistment of the group into either military service or some form of labor apprenticeship.[89] According to an 1835 report, the group ended up dispersed as follows: thirty enlisted in the 2nd West India Regiment, 149 apprenticed to employers in New Providence, and sixty-six apprenticed to employers on other islands. Most tragically, 134 had died during the year on Highburn Cay and an additional six died between 1833 and 1835.[90] When the *Hebe* case was wrapped up, Bahamian authorities also noted that they had yet to receive any official notice about the conclusion of the earlier case of the slave ship *Rosa.* By that time, the *Rosa* Africans had lived in the Bahamas for almost two years at their specially created settlement of Adelaide. Governor Carmichael-Smyth concluded that with no further instructions after such a long period, this special settlement would remain as originally organized. The problem of the long delay between the time that Portuguese ships arrived in the Bahamas and the conclusion of legal matters in Sierra Leone was one of several factors that prevented these "Portuguese" groups from being transferred to Trinidad.

Carmichael-Smyth left the Bahamas in June 1833 to begin a new position as governor of British Guiana. During the following year his interim successor, Lieutenant Governor Blaney T. Balfour, became an aggressive advocate in favor of sending liberated Africans taken from Portuguese slavers to plantation colonies. In the summer of 1834, two additional groups of Africans arrived in the Bahamas from such vessels. The schooner *Despique* arrived in June, in the custody of H.M.S. *Firefly,* bringing a group of 205 rescued slaves. Balfour reported to the Colonial Office that in settling this group, he had "followed precisely the steps" Governor Carmichael-Smyth had pursued in the case of the *Rosa.*[91] This statement implies that the *Despique* Africans joined the village of Adelaide, although Balfour does not explicitly say this. He may have settled the group at the village of Carmichael, which was also occupied by liberated Africans receiving various forms of subsidy and superintendence from the government. When H.M.S. *Nimble* brought another Portuguese ship to Nassau in August 1834 with 162 Africans, Balfour again reported that he had "followed precisely the same steps" as before. On this occasion, however, the lieutenant governor also took the opportunity to argue in favor of removing such people from the Bahamas altogether:

I have now to suggest to you Sir, the very good results which an immediate transference to Trinidad would produce—our Land in the Bahamas is not sufficiently fertile for the future support of these large Gangs, and moreover their presence is dreaded here, whereas it is sought in Trinidad.[92]

Balfour did not clarify his comment about the fertility of Bahamian land. Did he mean that local soils could not support subsistence farming sufficient to feed the liberated Africans? Or was he alluding to the fact that the Bahamas did not have lands conducive to plantation agriculture in which the Africans might be employed? As for the local population "dreading" further African arrivals, many years had passed since the last formal complaints about the introduction of these immigrants. Balfour conceded that local salt proprietors would have likely welcomed a supply of apprenticed laborers. He went on, however, to criticize the Bahamian system of apprenticeship of liberated Africans. The lieutenant governor contended that except in cases of domestic service, the Africans who worked under apprenticeship gained little benefit, "neither learn[ing] English, nor any useful occupation" and were "often subject to harsh and cruel treatment."[93] Transferring such Africans to Trinidadian plantation economy would have almost certainly exacerbated these kinds of problems.

This question became moot in 1835 when the Bahamas received its new governor. Lieutenant Colonel William Colebrooke, who assumed the Bahamian governorship, opposed the idea of removing newly settled Africans to plantation colonies. Unlike Lieutenant Governor Balfour, Colebrooke argued that liberated African immigrants in the Bahamas could reasonably support themselves from agriculture and, to a lesser degree, fishing. He also argued that the system of apprenticing these immigrants to various employers had proved successful and that sufficient demand for labor existed to continue the process. The new governor contended that through the placement of superintendents and missionaries at settlements such as Adelaide, the newly arrived Africans could receive cultural benefits including instruction in the English language and in Christianity. Perhaps most persuasively, Colebrooke suggested to his superiors in London that the Africans—"having been established [in the Bahamas] for some time and having formed connexions"—would find removal to Trinidad (or anywhere else) undesirable.[94] In the 1835 "Minute" that explored the process of settlement of liberated Africans in the West Indies, the Colonial Office officially endorsed Colebrooke's judgment on this matter. While the authors of that document argued back and forth about the fate of liberated Africans legally processed at Havana, they agreed that the refugees left in the Bahamas pending legal decisions from Sierra Leone should not be displaced.[95] Thus, in January

1836, the Earl of Aberdeen informed Governor George Hill of Trinidad that Africans from Portuguese vessels could not become a source of plantation labor for his southern Caribbean colony. The secretary of state for the colonies explained: "[T]heir long establishment [in the Bahamas] and the accounts I have received of their satisfactory condition have determined me to let them remain where they are."[96]

This decision would have greater consequences for the Bahamas than it would for Trinidad or other sugar colonies clamoring for laborers. Africans taken from Portuguese vessels became the single largest source of liberated African immigration to the former colony. By 1835, when the Colonial Office formally adopted this policy toward the Portuguese slave ships, the Bahamas had accepted approximately 900 Africans from four captured vessels. Between 1836 and 1838, the colony would receive roughly 2,400 more refugees from seven captured Portuguese vessels. Over 1,000 of these arrived in May 1838 on only two ships: the *Diligente* with 474 enslaved souls aboard and the *Camoens* with 569.[97] In addition, during 1837 and 1838, the Bahamian government took in approximately 400 Africans rescued from three Portuguese slavers that ran aground and sank in Bahamian waters. After some legal debate, British authorities agreed that refugees from such wrecks should enjoy the same status as liberated Africans emancipated under the laws and treaties governing slave trade suppression. As Governor Colebrooke had recommended in 1835, these arrivals from Portuguese ships joined Bahamian economy and society under a mixture of arrangements involving both subsistence-oriented settlement and diverse indentured labor. In total, during the 1830s almost 3,700 liberated Africans entered the Bahamas from Portuguese slave ships. Together with the groups transferred from the mixed commission court at Havana and those settled during the first two decades of slave trade suppression, the addition of these 3,700 people meant that by the end of 1841, the Bahamas had received over 5,000 of these African immigrants. Almost two decades would pass before any further Africans arrived, and these would number less than 500. Thus, at the beginning of the 1840s the process of migration of liberated Africans into the Bahamas had virtually run its course.

After a twenty-year hiatus, that migration reemerged at the beginning of the 1860s. Several times during the first year of that decade Governor Charles Bayley received reports from seamen that they had discovered evidence of slave ships traversing Bahamian waters, in some cases using small cays in more remote regions of the archipelago as depots where they waited with groups of slaves they intended to transport clandestinely into Cuba.[98] By this decade, Great Britain had for many years concentrated her military efforts against the slave trade on the West African coast, and although Cuban authorities had begun to make some attempts to police the traffic, observers repeatedly reported the continuation of slave importation to the Spanish island.[99] In the summer of 1860, the Bahamas received one last large group of African refugees from this illegal Cuban traffic. These Africans arrived from a vessel wrecked off the island of Abaco. In this case both Governor Bayley and his colleagues in London proceeded somewhat tentatively, looking first to laws and precedents set in previous years and then attempting to craft new regulations in case a renewed influx of liberated Africans should begin. After the slaver (in at least one account referred to by the name *Heroina*) ran aground at Lanyard's Cay near Abaco Island, a convoy of three salvage vessels brought 389 rescued slaves to Nassau along with three white crewmen. Bayley at first quarantined the group four miles offshore at Athol Island under the supervision of the quarantine and immigration officers. He also supplied the new arrivals with food and clothing "as well as cooks, nurses, and interpreters belonging to their own race, the Congo."[100]

The governor initially decided that he would engage the Africans as "servants or apprentices for periods of two and four years." However, after complaints from local residents, he extended the terms to five years for adults and six for children. The complainants had argued that if apprenticeships lasted four years or less, employers would expend time and money feeding, clothing, and instructing the Africans only to lose their services just at the point when they had learned sufficient English and work skills to become most useful. During these deliberations the quarantine officer approved the transfer of the Africans from Athol Island to new temporary quarters at the Fort Charlotte military barracks west of the town of Nassau. After the modification of his apprenticeship plan, Governor Bayley supervised a process by which potential employers filed written applications, and those who were successful received their new indentured workers during three mass distributions. In the end, forty-two adults and 188 children were assigned as apprentices to employers in and around the town of Nassau, fifty-nine adults and sixty-one children went to similar engagements in the Out Islands, and five adults and three children were "sent sick to hospital." In his report to the Colonial Office, Bayley elaborated that of the people sent to the Out Islands, thirty had gone to salt ponds while the remainder had gone either to fruit plantations or to household employment. A "reasonable proportion" of the Nassau apprentices had received assignments with tradespeople such as "joiners, carpenters, boat-builders and blacksmiths."[101] In addition, Bayley had permitted Lieutenant Colonel James Travers, who commanded the 1st West India Regiment, to enlist twenty-five of the adult men as soldiers. According to Travers, they enlisted only after he had ensured through interpreters that the men had a full understanding of the military service which they would enter.[102]

The arrival of the *Heroina* Africans initiated some illuminating dialogue among colonial authorities and others about the nature of settlement for liberated Africans. From the Colonial Office, Under Secretary of State T. F. Elliot expressed concern about the employment of some of the new arrivals in field labor and salt-raking rather than in "arts, crafts or trades." He also questioned the wisdom of sending apprentices to the Out Islands away from the closer monitoring by the government that was available near the capital.[103] In reply to Elliot, Governor Bayley launched a robust defense of the policies he had followed. Among a variety of justifications, he argued that the field work required for pineapple and orange farming in the Bahamas involved nothing like the hardships of sugar production elsewhere in the West Indies. Bayley also informed the Colonial Office that he had recently sent an acting magistrate to Inagua to investigate the condition of newly arrived Africans apprenticed in the salt ponds. He promised that he would cancel their apprenticeships if the magistrate returned a negative report.[104] These exchanges between Bayley and Elliot obviously revived debates from the 1830s and earlier over what constituted an acceptable, an appropriate, or even a "good" life for newly arrived Africans settling in the Caribbean outside the framework of slavery.

Colonial authorities such as the governor had disproportionate power in shaping that settlement experience. Yet in Bayley's letters about the *Heroina* one also has intriguing hints of ways the nonwhite population at large also intervened in such debates. Bayley reported that some Bahamian-born or "creole negroes" from the "lower ranks of life" had expressed interest in hiring some of the *Heroina* Africans under the apprenticeship scheme. The governor strongly opposed this idea, claiming that it would encourage idleness among what he called the "lower ranks" and would also deny the African immigrants what he viewed as the inevitably superior material, cultural, and social benefits of having white employers. Bayley portrayed the Bahamian-born blacks as looking down upon the African newcomers and being anxious to exploit them.[105] As will be seen, relationships between these special African immigrants and the so-called black Creoles in fact developed along much more complex lines.

Liberated African immigrants who had arrived in previous decades also expressed special interest in the *Heroina* Africans. The process of formally distributing this group as apprentices stretched over several days; delay was caused by multiple factors, including the decision of some employers to "return" the Africans originally assigned to them. Bayley complained about this slowness because of the alleged effects it had among the colony's other African residents:

> [O]ne consequence of this delay was that—before the distribution was completed—Congo men and women already settled in the island found means of communicating with their compatriots and succeeded in dissuading the greater portion of the female adults, and the elder girls from allowing themselves to be assigned to any one.[106]

One sees in this brief description evidence of solidarity among Kongo-identified people, most, if not all, of whom would have arrived in the Bahamas rescued from slave ships several decades before.[107] One also sees a sense of community among liberated Africans based on their shared experience as slave trade refugees. Unfortunately, Bayley gave no hint about what reasons lay behind the apparent campaign to keep the newly arrived women and girls free from terms of apprenticeship. Motives may have included the hope that members of the gender-imbalanced local Kongo group would marry and form families with these new females. (Chapter 4 will address issues of gender ratio and possible ethnic or cultural preferences in the creation of households by liberated Africans.) Perhaps the longer-term Kongo residents had found their apprenticeships abusive or simply too restrictive. Maybe they had their own ideas about the social roles of girls and women. Probing these kinds of issues will form a critical part of this book's effort to understand how liberated African immigrants integrated with one another and with the largely African-Caribbean communities of which they became a part.

Following the *Heroina* case, the Colonial Office recommended that authorities write a new Bahamian law to set updated, clear, and accessible guidelines for the settlement of any future slave-ship arrivals. After months of official study and debate, a new law passed in 1861.[108] However, a renewed influx of liberated African refugees did not materialize. The 389 Africans shipwrecked at Lanyard's Cay in July 1860 thus constituted the last recorded settlement of this class of immigrants in the Bahamas.[109]

2

"Binding them to the trade of digging cane holes":

SETTLEMENT OF LIBERATED AFRICANS IN TRINIDAD

While the Bahamas began receiving liberated African immigrants within only a few years of the passage of the abolition act, in the colony of Trinidad, located in the southern Caribbean far away from Cuban slave trade routes, the process of liberated African settlement had hardly begun during the decades prior to 1830. In an 1819 report, the Trinidad customs collector reported that since the abolition of the slave trade he had supervised the processing of only fourteen individuals who had been liberated as a consequence of the new law.[1] Moreover, most of these fourteen seem to have involved not slaves newly brought from Africa but rather people whose owners had improperly sought to transport them from one part of the Caribbean to another.[2] Colonial Office correspondence on the subject and the returns from other colonies indicate that most liberated Africans seized in the Caribbean during the first decade and a half of slave trade suppression arrived through vice admiralty courts in the Bahamas, Antigua, and Tortola, with other islands such as Trinidad playing only minor roles. Attempts by British officials to quantify this early immigration of liberated Africans to the British West Indies placed the total number of immigrants at about 3000 people during the first fifteen years after the abolition law.[3]

One notable exception to this prevailing pattern occurred in Trinidad. In 1808, Sir Alexander Cochrane, then commander of British naval forces in the Leeward Islands, used his military position to transfer a group of rescued Africans from the island of Tortola to work as laborers on his sugar estates in Trinidad. According to an 1813 letter written by a former magistrate from Tortola, early in 1808 the vice admiralty court at that island completed proceedings against two U.S. slave ships, condemning the vessels and their

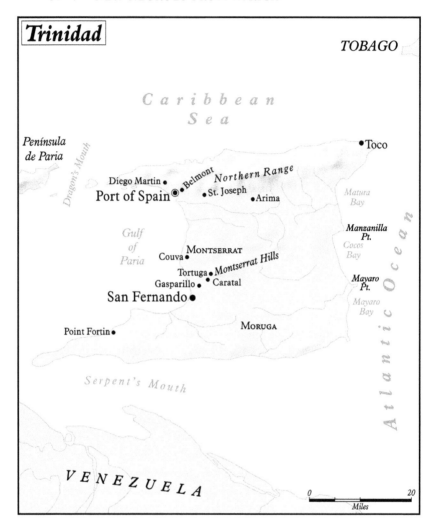

Map of Trinidad

cargoes as prize of war. The Africans from these vessels reportedly numbered between one and two hundred individuals. The former magistrate explained that instead of attempting to enlist any of these people in the armed forces or apprentice them at Tortola, Cochrane obtained two vessels in which he sent the whole group to his properties in Trinidad, where he apprenticed them for the maximum term allowed under the abolition law: fourteen years. The magistrate considered this self-interested arrangement a violation of the abolition act, and he directed his letter to the antislavery activist William Wilberforce, asking him to confront Sir Alexander to "call him to . . . account" and presumably persuade him to undo the apprenticeships.[4] The magistrate also sent a copy of his letter to a Colonial Office official to ask that he use his authority to "promote the attainment of the ends of Justice" on behalf of the Africans in question.[5] However, the magistrate's protest yielded no result, no doubt in part because the Cochrane arrangement had already existed for almost five years. Although Cochrane's liberated Africans constituted only a tiny fraction of the approximately 8,000 that Trinidad would finally receive, the experience of Cochrane's group previewed many attitudes and policies which would prevail in later years.

Trinidadian governors and other officials referred to "Cochrane's African Apprentices" repeatedly in discussions through the 1820s; they wondered about the adjustment of these new African arrivals to the local society and compared their behavior with that of slaves and other people of African descent. Such discussions gave particular consideration to the performance of these Africans as free peasants or workers after the end of their term of apprenticeship in 1822. Most significant, however, the success of Cochrane's scheme in effectively seizing these people for labor on his sugar plantations gave an advance indication of the dominant role the demands for plantation labor would play in the experience of Trinidad's liberated Africans. The Tortola magistrate protested bitterly in his 1813 letter that he did not believe that the abolition act ever "intended to bind . . . liberated Africans to the trade of digging cane holes and other operations of a sugar plantation."[6] In fact, according to his interpretation, when the law spoke of "binding [liberated Africans] . . . as apprentices," the legislators had intended that the African immigrants involved should work at a specific trade, not that they should perform routine manual labor and certainly not that they should "be . . . worked and flogged on a Sugar Estate."[7] The language of the law, however, does not justify that interpretation. Although it is very detailed on some matters, the abolition law left the question of the nature of the proposed apprenticeships quite vague. Colonial Office authorities still might have questioned whether it was proper for Admiral Cochrane to consign such a large group of African refugees for his own use, but they did not. And historians may reasonably interpret their acquiescence as the first step in what would become a forty-year commitment to viewing liberated Africans in the Caribbean less as a puzzling new class of immigrant refugees and more as potential plantation laborers.

Trinidad received its first major waves of liberated Africans through the transfer of rescued Africans from the Anglo-Spanish mixed commission court at Havana in the mid-1830s—although only after major debates in the Colonial Office about how best to disperse the immigrants. The logistical arrangements for the process of removal illustrates one of the most obvious differences in character between transferring liberated African immigrants from Cuba to Trinidad and transferring them to the Bahamas. Unlike the groups of Africans who entered the Bahamas from the Havana mixed commission, most of the Africans who went to Trinidad did not emigrate as complete cargoes from individual slave ships. Although the authorities at Havana had in fact hired a private vessel—"the *Cuba* of Hamburgh"—to transport liberated Africans to Nassau, groups from individual slave ships usually remained intact from the time of capture by the British navy.[8] By contrast, the majority of the roughly 1,000 liberated Africans who went to Trinidad via the Havana mixed commission traveled in carefully engineered groupings according to the requests of the Trinidad government, which expressly sought gender-balanced groups of healthy potential laborers from the Havana officials. The gender requirement in particular inevitably led to the disaggregation of groups taken from individual ships; in practice, this requirement also led to the combining of Africans taken from different condemned vessels. For example, in January 1834, the captain general of Havana wrote to Governor George Hill to inform him that a Spanish schooner, *Manuelita,* had departed for Trinidad with a party of liberated African immigrants. This group consisted of 212 people, "paired in sexes" derived from the cargoes of two Spanish slavers condemned by the mixed commission during the previous December.[9] Such mixing of separately rescued groups would have disrupted to some degree any patterns of ethnic distribution on board particular slave ships. This would not necessarily have had any predictable influence on the communities liberated Africans would form once they arrived in Trinidad. After all, the random combination of people from two slave ships might not have yielded ethnic patterns any more or less diverse than those that already existed on individual vessels.

Discussions on the subject of how to organize labor immigration from the mixed commission had begun as early as 1832, involving Spanish and British authorities at Havana, the governor of Trinidad, and officials from both the Colonial and Foreign Offices in London. Some of the conditions agreed upon in these early exchanges addressed technical and financial matters such as the British request that the Spanish government should cover the cost of such removals or the stipulation that the governor of Trinidad should receive advanced notice of at least one month before the scheduled arrival of any immigrant ship. Other regulations, however, stipulated matters of more human consequence such as the mandate that "children [should] not to be sent without one or both of their parents [and that there should be] . . . no forced separation of families."[10] To a great extent, these rules would have had only a limited effect because slave-ship cargoes rarely involved family units, at least not in any western definition of such terms. It is probable that siblings formed the most common category of persons eligible for such protections. Governor Hill claimed that when sending liberated Africans who arrived from Havana in the *Manuelita* out to employers, he sought to respect not only bonds of "relationship" but also bonds of "friendship."[11] In their now classic essay on *The Birth of African-American Culture,* anthropologists Sidney Mintz and Richard Price point out that connections between pairs of slave trade "shipmates" often lasted long after arrival in the Americas. These authors further contend that "the 'shipmate' relationship became a major principle of social organization and continued for decades or even centuries to shape ongoing social relations."[12] They support this contention with anecdotal and linguistic evidence from across the New World diaspora, and one may reasonably speculate that similar dynamics formed within the liberated African groups. Corroboration of these connections, however, proves elusive. For instance, in one intriguing example from the *Manuelita* case, the notation "Queen" appears next to the name of a woman included on a list of ten Africans hired by Trinidadian planter John Wilson.[13] This woman had arrived from Africa with the given name Taza and had received the Spanish name Dionisia in Havana. Unfortunately, nothing in the available documentation illuminates what relationship (if any) existed between the designated "Queen" and the nine Africans who joined her on Wilson's estate. Another glimpse of such relationships appeared in Governor Hill's description of his distribution of a group of Africans brought from Havana in the Spanish vessel *Siete Hermanas.* Governor Hill assigned eight people—three males and five females—to an estate in Arouca. He explained this uneven gender arrangement as follows:

> The reason of giving five females to this lot was that four of the five are sisters and the fifth a sort of governess over them. Their distress at the threat of separation was so loudly and so feelingly expressed [that] I placed them together.[14]

Governor Hill recounted this explanation mostly to show off his careful attention to the needs of the African immigrants. In this brief description one does not even know whether the four girls were in fact blood siblings. We do see that they made specific and even dramatic efforts to maintain relationships developed before their arrival in Trinidad. Predictably, the details of preexisting personal relationships among newly arrived Africans generally prove elusive.

Whatever the ongoing importance of prior bonds of friendship, the lives of liberated Africans arriving in Trinidad from Havana were most powerfully shaped by the distribution and employment practices Governor Hill set in motion once the African immigrants disembarked in the British colony under his control. The arrival of the *Manuelita* group in February 1834 provides a window into the experience of the transfers from Havana to Trinidad. Unlike the apprehension or at least hesitation that had greeted the arrival of the first significant groups of liberated Africans in the Bahamas twenty years before, these groups arriving in Trinidad from Havana met with aggressive enthusiasm from planters facing the economic uncertainty engendered by the ending of the slavery. These men desperately sought ways to perpetuate the profitability sugar monoculture had brought to so much of the British West Indies for centuries. Governor Hill reported to the Colonial Office that upon the arrival of the *Manuelita* Africans, "immediate applications were made to the amount of 938 . . . for their services."[15] In other words, planters collectively requested over 900 laborers—way more than were available in this single group. The Trinidad governor had a motive for exaggerating the enthusiasm of local planters. Hill made no secret of his desire to demonstrate Trinidad's willingness and suitability to receive a large groups of such immigrants. The governor reported that when local employers learned of the prospect of receiving "a large number of freed Africans" from Cuba, a group of them had sent him a memorial indicating their collective desire and preparedness to employ no less than 5,000 refugees. They also proposed that if the government could arrange to apprentice such Africans for a period of six years, they would accept as many as 10,000.[16] Both the governor and his petitioners probably overstated the demand in the local economy for liberated African laborers. Nevertheless, these claims served clear notice of the aggressive recruitment and focus on plantation employment that would characterize the entrance of this class of immigrants into Trinidadian society.

Nowhere did these characteristics appear more evident than in the meticulous scheme through which twenty planters in the colony received their first liberated African workers from the *Manuelita*. Of the 207 people who arrived aboard the vessel, only seven did not go to plantations. Governor Hill described "seven little girls under ten years of age" as "too young to go to the Estates," and he explained that he had therefore "placed them with respectable families," probably as household servants.[17] The governor divided the remaining 200 Africans from the *Manuelita* into twenty groups of ten—five males and five females in each—for distribution to twenty agricultural employers under six-month terms of apprenticeship.[18] Hill's arrangements in this early case provide insight into some of the factors that would shape patterns of community formation among liberated African immigrants in Trinidad. At first glance, the division into relatively small groups would seem to have created an obstacle to significant interaction between any broad collectivity of newly arrived Africans. And the size of the island of Trinidad—which is reasonably large in Caribbean terms—might have made matters worse if the small cadres of immigrants ended up widely dispersed on separate estates. Indeed, in planning the transfer of liberated Africans from Cuba to Trinidad, the crown law officer had expressed the hope that separating such immigrants into small groups would discourage them from "form[ing] a society of themselves and . . . retain[ing] savage habits."[19] However, the dispersal of the Africans among so many different properties did not necessarily preclude wider community formation.

In the first place, as in most plantation societies in the Caribbean, sugar estates in Trinidad usually did not exist in isolation but rather in clusters in particular areas that were sometimes determined by the agricultural advantages of individual locations. During the nineteenth century, this situation was prevalent in parts of southern Trinidad, which became the dominant area for sugar cultivation in this era. Thus, although they were sent to employers in lots of ten (or even fewer), liberated African immigrants almost certainly had the opportunity to form some networks of interaction among their fellow immigrants who were assigned to closely neighboring estates. Numerous historians have documented the existence of this kind of interaction between slaves from different plantations. As free laborers, the liberated African immigrants would have had even more opportunities to form such connections. Second, in some instances, the total number of liberated Africans on particular estates would increase when the estate owner received additional African workers from newly arriving immigrant groups. When a second vessel with Africans from Havana, the *Reyna Cristina,* arrived in March 1834, only one month after the *Manuelita,* Governor Hill selected thirty-one new agricultural employers, who each received lots of five or six people.[20] However, when the ship *Las Siete Hermanas* delivered its group of Havana Africans in September 1835, six of the *Manuelita* employers seem to have received new allotments, as apparently did two individuals who had received immigrants from the *Reyna Cristina.*[21] If repeat allocations occurred only eighteen months apart, they almost certainly also occurred in later years when much larger groups of liberated African immigrants entered the colony. Furthermore, and perhaps most important, the Africans from Havana and those who came later from Sierra Leone and Saint Helena all went to their various plantations as workers hired for fixed periods of apprenticeship or indenture. Once they completed such terms, these immigrants acquired even greater liberty to form whatever associations they wished—cultural, familial, or residential—with other liberated African immigrants.

In his report on the African immigrants brought from Havana by *Las Siete Hermanas* in 1835, Governor Hill offered early evidence of the prospective meaningfulness of such associations. The *Siete Hermanas* group included fifty-four girls under the age of twelve whom Hill arranged to place mostly as household servants with various women, almost all in Port-of-Spain. Before these children took up their positions, the governor's wife arranged a meeting between the fifty-four new arrivals and twenty-two girls who had come from Havana on previous occasions and had received comparable situations of employment and guardianship. Governor Hill described the encounter as follows:

> The decent dress, manners & appearance of the 22 made an evident and favorable Impression on the 54 newcomers; *some were of the same Nation,* and their joy and reception were interesting to observe.[22] (emphasis added)

The first part of this description makes an obvious attempt to demonstrate to the Colonial Office that the program of domestic apprenticeship had successfully moved African children toward British social norms. Indeed, by citing the so-called "favorable Impression" in the eyes of the newcomers, Hill implied that even the children viewed the westernizing process as desirable! However, the governor must have found the communion between those of "the same Nation" particularly striking, because his mention of this phenomenon did nothing at all to enhance his presentation of Trinidad as the ideal settlement colony for liberated African immigrants. If anything, the Colonial Office might have viewed this kind of national or ethnic bonding as a hindrance to the so-called civilizing process. We cannot take the experience of these girls as necessarily representative of that of liberated African immigrants in general. However, both their intra-ethnic interaction and their perceived sense of connection as fellow newly arrived Africans give some intimation of the patterns of community creation that probably prevailed more widely.

The majority of Trinidad's community of liberated Africans, however, would not arrive for over a decade. And they would not come via the Havana mixed commission. In fact, the *Siete Hermanas* group was the last body of liberated Africans to enter Trinidad from Cuba. Throughout 1835 and into 1836, Governor Hill continuously appealed to the Colonial Office for more immigrants from the Havana mixed commission. Authorities in both Trinidad and British Guiana attempted to impress London with their commitment to the good care of liberated African immigrants by preparing competing legislative packages to govern the reception of such immigrants in their respective colonies. For example, in March 1835 Trinidad enacted an "Ordinance for the Protection of, and the Promoting [of] the Industry and Good Conduct of Africans Transferred to [That] Island," copies of which went to both the Colonial Office in London and the British commissioners in Cuba. This ordinance codified routine matters such as the proper way to exchange documentation on each group of Africans transferred to British colonies. Other provisions laid out the language for the indentures of such Africans and fixed the maximum period of service at three years. Some provisions of the law established mechanisms to monitor the well-being of the immigrants. For example, the lengthiest clause of the Trinidad ordinance detailed "Provisions for the maintaining of the Africans" and listed the precise quantities and types of food employers would have to provide for each indentured African. Additional clauses set out specific requirements for wages, clothing, and medical care.[23] It does not require excessive cynicism to recognize these fastidious provisions—and the almost equally detailed "Penalties for neglect or omission"—as part of a strategy designed to impress the Colonial Office with Trinidad's superior preparedness to receive liberated African laborers. Governor Hill and his counterpart Governor James Carmichael-Smyth of British Guiana (who was formerly governor of the Bahamas) also wrote directly to the British commissioners in Cuba, likewise hoping to impress them. In 1836, Governor Hill even sent an angry letter to the Colonial Office complaining that one of the Havana commissioners had declared a preference for the terms of British Guiana's ordinance regarding liberated Africans without giving the Trinidadian government the opportunity to improve their own law and thus compete for the potential laborers.[24] As historian David Murray points out, all such competition became irrelevant when the number of Spanish vessels condemned at the Havana mixed commission "dropped off sharply" during the late 1830s; such vessels yielded only the six cargoes noted in chapter 1 between 1836 and 1841.[25]

Even before the final collapse of the supply of liberated Africans from the Havana mixed commission, Hill had begun to consider the possibility of obtaining liberated African workers from other sources, most notably Sierra Leone. As the home of three mixed commission courts for slave trade cases, this colony had become the principal site of settlement for rescued Africans. In March 1835, even before the completion of the ordinance regulating the experience of liberated Africans from Havana, Governor Hill made inquiries with the Colonial Office about the possibility of receiving immigrant African laborers from this source. In response to this initial inquiry, Hill met with an unequivocal denial. The secretary of state expressed "grave doubts" that the move to the Caribbean would provide a better way of life for liberated Africans, and he doubted that British officials could successfully persuade them to go.[26] An internal Colonial Office memo discussing Hill's request also surmised that should Britain attempt such an emigration scheme, "Foreign Nations would suspect the motives of the transference & call it a Slave Trade."[27] Yet in less than a decade the Colonial Office would abandon these reservations and supervise a series of emigration schemes that would bring approximately 14,000 liberated Africans from both Sierra Leone and the island of Saint Helena as laborers to Trinidad and other West Indian colonies.

Colonial Office support for the emigration of liberated African laborers from Sierra Leone finally came in 1840. In his study of *Liberated African Emigration and British Anti-Slavery Policy,* Johnson Asiegbu suggests three reasons that worked together to produce this policy reversal. First, the termination of the apprenticeship system involving ex-slaves in 1838 produced more urgent demands from West Indian planters for a new solution to their labor needs.[28] In Asiegbu's opinion, the Colonial Office believed that a real possibility existed that West Indian colonies would secede over this issue. Second, the rising price of West Indian sugar had provoked complaints of "economic hardship" from merchants and consumers in Great Britain. And finally, Asiegbu points to the failure of the Niger Expedition, which lasted from 1840 to 1841, as a key event that provided a "humanitarian argument" in favor of emigration of laborers from Sierra Leone. Sponsored by abolitionist Sir Thomas Buxton and others, the Niger Expedition attempted to establish a model settlement in West Africa using the labor of liberated Africans and others to develop a community based on European-led agricultural production and missionary Christianity. When the experiment disintegrated, even many abolitionists began to suggest that Africans "could only be civilised or evangelised" by removing them from Africa under schemes such as the proposed emigration to the West Indies.[29] With these motivations and justifications in place, the Colonial Office finally gave West Indian planters and administrators what they desired: official acquiescence and assistance in the transfer of liberated Africans from the West African coast to the Caribbean as laborers.

Legal changes in the prosecution of slave trade cases in this era smoothed the transformation in British policy. During the early 1840s, the mixed commission system fell into decline, partly because of the expiration or alteration of some of the treaty arrangements involved and partly because of a disinclination among the contracting parties to maintain the complexities of joint law enforcement. After 1839, most slave trade cases ended up once again in Britain's vice admiralty courts, mostly at Sierra Leone and Saint Helena. Foreign governments had become less willing to invest serious effort in slave trade suppression, and even some slave traders preferred this arrangement. Although British courts could usually muster legal justification to condemn almost any slave ship and emancipate its slaves in the 1840s and 1850s, these vice admiralty courts did not have jurisdiction to prosecute foreign slave traders.[30] Processing slave ships at the vice admiralty courts meant that British officials had sole and uncomplicated authority in determining the disposition of liberated Africans from these vessels. Between 1840 and 1860, sending such Africans to the British West Indies became the principal course of action.

During those two decades, emigration procedures went through several variations. At first, emigrants left Sierra Leone in private vessels separately hired by the three major immigrant-receiving colonies: British Guiana, Jamaica, and Trinidad. Each of these colonies also employed an agent who worked at Freetown to recruit their immigrants in competition with one another. During the initial years of recruitment, the agents focused not on recently arrived liberated Africans but rather on those who had already spent at least several months settled at Sierra Leone. Many of these people had learned some English and in some cases had converted to Christianity. Beginning in 1843, however, the British government decided to take more direct control over the emigration scheme, partly to ensure proper treatment of emigrants on the journey across the Atlantic. Almost as soon as the emigration program began in 1841, criticism emerged from foreign governments and from some British abolitionists that the program amounted to a variation on the slave trade that Britain claimed to oppose. In 1843, the Colonial Office took control of the recruitment process away from the individual agents and vested that authority in the Colonial Land and Emigration commissioners. Emigration commissioners employed by the Colonial Office thus became the new intermediaries between would-be emigrants and the governments of the destination colonies. These commissioners hired three vessels—one for British Guiana, one for Jamaica, and one for Trinidad—to serve as the official emigration transports from Sierra Leone. British authorities further proposed that a similar process of government-managed emigration should apply to the island of Saint Helena, from which the various West Indian governments had already begun seeking liberated African immigrants in 1842.[31]

The policy transformations of 1842 and 1843 meant the abandonment of the original focus on recruiting people who had been settled at Sierra Leone for some time. Attention shifted almost exclusively to Africans newly liberated from captured slave ships. This change in policy occurred largely as a result of negative reports that reached the West African colony concerning the arduous and restrictive nature of employment on Caribbean plantations. People already settled in and around Freetown naturally expressed reluctance to emigrate to such a questionable future. In contrast, newly arrived Africans had much less access to negative information. Indeed, it became standard practice to recruit these laborers directly from the Queen's Yard, where rescued slaves were first processed after they were removed from captured ships. The Queen's Yard was sometimes referred to as the Liberated African Yard.[32]

The incorporation of Saint Helena exemplified this new focus on Africans freshly rescued from Atlantic slave ships; the almost-desolate Atlantic island served as little more than a depot, not a settlement colony. At Saint Helena, British authorities never made anything but makeshift arrangements for liberated Africans, whom they came to envision as potential emigrants to the West Indies.[33] The increasing acceptance of emigration to the West Indies as standard British policy led to the abandonment in 1844 of actual government involvement in the emigrant transport process. According to Asiegbu, officials in London argued that the Colonial Land and Emigration commissioners had taken over the process mainly to reassure Africans in the face of reports of bad treatment in transit and in the Caribbean. The London officials contended that after a year of such reassurance, the government had fulfilled its mission and did not need to continue the expense of hiring emigration vessels. It is no surprise that British authorities did not formally concede that the recruitment of newly arrived liberated Africans had effectively removed any need to bolster the confidence of Africans in the emigration system. That is, they had shifted the emigration scheme toward a population that largely lacked both the knowledge and wherewithal to question the emigration process.[34] In the mid-1840s, while one official emigration commissioner remained in a supervisory capacity, the actual transport process returned to private vessels paid through a bounty system.

The late 1840s saw two final changes in the emigration system. Between 1847 and 1849, in addition to the existing operations at Sierra Leone and Saint Helena, the British government organized the use of a military vessel, H.M.S *Growler,* to recruit free African emigrants not only at Sierra Leone or Saint Helena but also elsewhere along the West African coast, most notably among the Kru people—the "Kroomen"—of modern Liberia. The *Growler* conveyed several groups of emigrants to the Caribbean, but the arrangement never functioned smoothly and ultimately ended in multiple disagreements among British officials about the operation of the program. Some officials claimed that the *Growler* scheme in fact encouraged kidnapping and virtual enslavement by the Africans who were asked to provide emigrants for the vessel.[35] By the end of the decade, new allegations were made of poor conditions aboard the private emigrant ships as they competed with one another to supply separate West Indian colonies with liberated African workers. The Colonial Office stepped in again with what would become their final solution to the management of emigration of liberated Africans. In 1849, the emigration commissioners decided to hire a single firm for the conveyance of liberated Africans to the Caribbean. They

awarded that contract to Hyde, Hodge and Company, which used five vessels over the next six years to transport approximately 6,000 emigrants
mostly to British Guiana, Jamaica, and Trinidad but also in smaller groups
to other colonies. The slave trade was declining in the mid-1850s, and the
emigration system faced a parallel decline. The British government finally
terminated the contract with Hyde, Hodge and Company in 1861. Emigration of some 6,000 liberated Africans occurred after 1860, especially in 1861
and 1862. After the end of the contract with Hyde, Hodge and Company
(and even as early as the late 1850s), private vessels began to participate in
the system once again.[36] Ultimately, a total of approximately 30,000 liberated Africans entered the Caribbean via these arrangements, along with several thousand other Africans from the Kru coast and its vicinity. At all stages
of this two-decade process, Trinidad played a prominent role as one of the
three major colonies to recruit labor. From 1840 through the early 1860s,
the island received over 7,000 immigrants from Africa.[37]

Trinidad's first immigrants from Sierra Leone arrived in May 1841
aboard the private vessel *Elizabeth and Jane* under the supervision of an emigration agent, W. Hamilton, who had been enlisted by Trinidadian planters
to procure such laborers. Consistent with the initial norms of the Sierra
Leone scheme, this group consisted largely of people who had already lived
for some time at Freetown before they agreed to voluntarily emigrate. The
lieutenant governor of Trinidad, Sir Henry MacLeod, described the group as
"much more advanced in every way, than [he] had expected; all speaking
good English, and many able to read and write."[38] At Sierra Leone, the Trinidad recruiter had posted the specific terms of employment workers could
expect to receive upon arrival in the Caribbean: a wage of half a dollar per
task, a house and provision grounds for subsistence cultivation, and a food
allowance of half a pound of fish for each task performed. Laborers would
also have the option of substituting a small quantity of rum or money in
place of the food allowance.[39] After the group of 181 people had arrived in
Trinidad and entered into arrangements with employers, the local agent
general of immigrants prepared a statement indicating prima facie compliance with these terms. According to the report of Agent General Thomas
Johnston, employers had also agreed to provide flour or something equiv-
alent as a part of the food payment and "medical attendance and medicines
. . . free of charge or deduction."[40]

In his report to the Colonial Office, Lieutenant Governor MacLeod explained that although these immigrants had full liberty to make their own
arrangements with individual employers, he had encouraged them to "hire
themselves in bodies of Eight or Ten" both for the purpose of easing their
social adjustment and for "a sort of mutual protection."[41] In his report

MacLeod mostly sought to demonstrate the promising nature of the new immigration, both for the Africans and for the Trinidadian economy. Nevertheless, with his comment about "mutual protection," he also indicated awareness of the potential for exploitation or mistreatment, although the Lieutenant Governor strongly implied that he would exercise vigilance to prevent any such problem. Presumably to facilitate official monitoring, MacLeod also attempted to direct the immigrants toward employers who owned plantations "nearest to the seat of Government" at Port-of-Spain.[42] No clear record exists of how well he succeeded in this effort. Unlike the liberated Africans transferred from Havana, these Sierra Leone immigrants selected their own employers. Lieutenant Governor MacLeod thus did not make lists of workers comparable to those prepared by Governor Hill years earlier. Nonetheless, MacLeod seemed to envision that the liberated Africans would remain an identifiable and specially treated group amid the wider laboring population.

To some extent, MacLeod valued the potential sense of community among the Africans; he hoped that a positive collective experience would lead them to encourage other liberated Africans from Sierra Leone to come to Trinidad. These first immigrants, as well as those in future years, had the option of paying for their return passage back to Africa at the end of whatever initial contract they had signed. MacLeod anticipated that the majority of this initial group would choose to return, but he hoped that good reports of their experiences would lead to a continuous series of other immigrants like them. The lieutenant governor explained: "We must not look to these people as settlers, but if this Island answers their expectation they tell me, great numbers of their Countrymen will come."[43] W. Hamilton, the emigration agent who had brought the group to Trinidad, expressed similar hope for continued immigration. However, he also reported that most of the initial group in fact wanted to stay in the Caribbean. In testimony before a subcommittee of the local Agricultural and Immigration Society, Hamilton claimed to have visited the majority of the newly arrived group at the plantations where they had taken employment. He testified that most of those with whom he had spoken had expressed satisfaction with their new situation and had encouraged him to "send their friends from Sierra Leone to join them."[44] Hamilton's report warrants some skepticism given the fact that he stood to gain financially from the continuation of the emigration scheme; he received a bounty for each immigrant delivered. Also, the Agricultural and Immigration Society consisted of Trinidadian planters who solicited testimony that would support their desire for an expanded program of immigration of liberated Africans. But Hamilton gains credibility from the fact that despite this biased environment, he did not paint a uniformly positive picture. Although describing general satisfaction among the immigrants, he also reported that some of the men who had held trade positions as carpenters or masons in Sierra Leone complained of their change to agricultural employment and wanted to return to Africa.[45] Most of this first group remained in Trinidad. However, the colony did not receive many more of "their friends" from among the settled liberated African population at Sierra Leone. Less than a year after the arrival of the *Elizabeth and Jane* in Trinidad, authorities in the Caribbean, London, and West Africa began to shift the focus of this labor recruitment effort toward liberated Africans more recently rescued from captured slave ships, both at Sierra Leone and at Saint Helena.

In 1842, Trinidad received one more group of immigrants from liberated Africans who were already established as settlers in Sierra Leone. The administrative discussions that surrounded this second cohort foreshadowed the policy changes on the horizon. Even as these immigrants arrived in Trinidad, arrangements had begun to bring the first group of newly rescued liberated Africans from Saint Helena. Emigration agent W. Hamilton had been commissioned by "several gentlemen in London connected with [Trinidad],"[46] but in early 1842 Lieutenant Governor Henry MacLeod hired a new agent, Andrew David, who would function in a similar role as Hamilton but under the formal supervision of the colonial government. MacLeod also engaged a private vessel, the *Cleopatra,* on which David traveled to Sierra Leone with the intention of transporting immigrants back to the Caribbean. David traveled with six African "delegates" who had volunteered from the *Elizabeth and Jane* group to assist in the recruitment of new immigrants by providing firsthand information of their experience in Trinidad. In July, David and the delegates returned to Trinidad with 128 new immigrant laborers.[47]

In a report on his experience, David devoted much of his writing to difficulties that confronted the emigration scheme. David explained that in the first place, the Trinidad government had acquired a reputation for bargaining in bad faith among some people in Freetown because of the behavior of the former agent, Mr. Hamilton. During his initial recruitment effort in 1841, Hamilton had promised that when he returned for new immigrants, he would bring delegates such as those who eventually accompanied Andrew David. When Hamilton returned to Sierra Leone without any representatives, residents had complained so extensively that they had forced him to abandon his position as a labor recruiter and in effect "compelled him" to leave the colony. Second, potential new emigrants had learned that three months after the *Elizabeth and Jane* immigrants had arrived in Trinidad, their employers had reduced the rate of wages originally promised and had terminated the allowances of rum and food. For obvious reasons, news of such reduced compensation and, perhaps equally important, broken promises prompted residents of Freetown to have second thoughts about the desirability of migrating to the Caribbean colony. Third, Andrew David cited several problems not specifically related to Trinidad. He complained, for example, that too many vessels arrived at once seeking emigrants for British Guiana, Jamaica, and Trinidad. This crowded competition made it difficult for any one ship to quickly recruit its full complement of passengers. David also criticized the fact that merchants at Freetown had developed the practice of extending almost unlimited credit to settlers, creating a large indebted population who could not emigrate unless they could pay off their typically substantial debts. Most telling, however, for the future of Sierra Leone emigration, David complained that "the higher and middle classes" of the colony viewed the emigration scheme with skepticism and spread "insinuations" about the poor treatment of immigrants on Caribbean sugar estates. Elsewhere in his report David cited even more bizarre rumors that he and the six delegates had to counter. For example, one false report alleged that Trinidadian authorities separated husbands and wives who emigrated together when they reached the Caribbean. Another rumor claimed that employers would require all immigrant laborers, both male and female, to shave their heads.[48] David did not recommend any radical change in the emigration scheme to overcome these various difficulties. He believed that Trinidad and other West Indian colonies could establish a smoother process that would still focus on liberated Africans and other people—some Kru migrants, for instance—from the settled population of Sierra Leone.[49] But even as David prepared this report, Trinidad had already received its first group of liberated African immigrants taken almost directly from captured slave ships at the island of Saint Helena.

By the summer of the 1842, the Sierra Leone scheme had brought just over 300 immigrants to Trinidad in two groups from the *Elizabeth and Jane* and the *Cleopatra*. In June 1842, on its first voyage to Trinidad from Saint Helena, the barque *Chieftain* delivered 232 liberated African immigrants. Once these Africans arrived in Trinidad, their employers agreed to pay "the sum of Ten dollars for each African (children excepted) towards defraying the expenses" of their journey to the island.[50] Where MacLeod had marveled in 1841 at the literacy of the first Africans brought from the settled populations of Sierra Leone, in the case of the *Chieftain* he expressed concern about the "extreme uncivilization" of the recently rescued Africans brought from Saint Helena.[51] In planning the settlement of this group, MacLeod looked to the arrangements made in the mid-1830s for similar groups of Africans transferred from the mixed commission at Havana. The lieutenant governor proposed that just as his predecessor Governor George Hill had arranged three-year indentures for the Havana Africans, he should have similar authority to arrange one-year indentures for the people from Saint Helena. When the *Chieftain* arrived at Port-of-Spain, MacLeod directed the Trinidad council to prepare "An Ordinance . . . for the protection of and the promoting the Industry of recently liberated Africans introduced into [the] Colony." The council modeled this measure on the similar legislation enacted in 1835 for liberated Africans from Cuba. The Colonial Office ultimately disallowed the new ordinance based on complaints about the process of its enactment. However, in April 1842 the secretary of state for the colonies advised Lieutenant Governor MacLeod that the central government approved of the principle of indenturing newly arrived Africans for a period of one year—"for their own benefit," given their untutored state as victims recently liberated from slave ships.[52] The legal and bureaucratic wrangling over the specific nature of such indentures would continue during the next fifteen years of liberated African emigration. The significance of the arrival of the *Chieftain* Africans and their enlistment as indentured laborers, however, lies not in the particular details but in the fact that this group marked the beginning of Trinidad's shift in policy to the most recently rescued Africans as the principal source of immigrant labor from the West African coast.

Although all groups of immigrants who came from Saint Helena belonged to this class of recently rescued liberated Africans, this demographic change would occur gradually for the emigrants leaving Sierra Leone. In 1843, for example, when the Colonial Office began its system of hiring one official emigration vessel for each major West Indian colony, MacLeod—now elevated to the post of governor—reported on more than one occasion that the ship assigned to his colony had returned with a disappointing number of immigrants. In May 1843, the *Senator* transported a group that consisted of only thirty-one people, all of whom MacLeod classified as "children." (It is not clear how any official could argue that a group entirely composed of children could have entered into the supposedly voluntary emigration agreement.) MacLeod noted that because they held the same right to voluntarily enter labor contracts as the previous literate adult immigrants from Sierra Leone, he had "no power to indent them." He explained that he would simply have to hope that they would receive proper treatment at the hands of their employers, who were subject to the scrutiny of the stipendiary magistrates.[53] Presumably, the difficulties described in 1841 by emigration agent Andrew David persisted in the labor recruitment process at Freetown two years later. Governor MacLeod speculated that the system of sending delegates from Trinidad to reassure potential emigrants might work more effectively if he could send representatives from each separate "tribe" to speak to their ethnic peers in Sierra Leone.[54] In September 1843, the *Senator* made its second journey to Trinidad, bringing back eighty-eight immigrants in what the governor characterized as a recruiting effort of "very partial success." MacLeod suggested to the Colonial Office that it might want to consider terminating the *Senator* enterprise rather than continue the expense for such minimal results.[55]

The governor gave no detailed account of the fate of the immigrants after their arrival in Trinidad. One can assume that, like the first Sierra Leone group brought by the *Elizabeth and Jane,* these eighty-eight people hired themselves to plantation employers of their own choosing. During the 1841 interviews conducted by the Agricultural and Immigration Society, several planters and other observers referred to the liberated Africans brought from Havana in the mid-1830s as a persistently distinguishable group within the larger African-descended working population. William Burnley, the chair of the interviewing subcommittee and himself a sugar planter, repeatedly asked witnesses to comment on their experiences with the liberated African laborers. Richard Darling, the attorney for seven local estates, described the liberated Africans from Havana as "steady workers and hardier in the field" than other working-class immigrants who had come to Trinidad from neighboring islands such as Barbados and Grenada. Frederick Maxwell, a former slave turned plantation manager, likewise praised the work of the three liberated African immigrants on the estate he supervised. But unlike Darling, Maxwell stated that he would prefer larger groups of immigrants from other Caribbean islands because he believed that they were "disposed to settle down more steadily."[56] These kinds of descriptions, notwithstanding their apparent contradiction, suggest that as the liberated Africans from Havana settled into Trinidadian society they remained an identifiable subgroup that maintained some level of similar behavior and perhaps also collective consciousness. One can surmise that the Africans who came in the first groups from Sierra Leone likely established some similar niche, reinforcing their identity as a separate and special community.

That community remained much smaller than the governor and local planters had hoped. The *Senator,* for example, made a third trip to Trinidad from Sierra Leone in December 1843 and a fourth in April 1844. These two voyages delivered 116 and 97 immigrants, respectively, making a total of just over 300 immigrants transported by the *Senator* during the course of a year.[57] In comparison to the almost 1,000 liberated Africans brought from Havana in only three voyages during the mid-1830s, this yield does seem minimal. In June 1844, Governor MacLeod hired an attorney, Robert

Guppy, to travel to Sierra Leone to investigate the reasons for the continuing difficulties in labor recruitment. Guppy's lengthy report in large part repeated the concerns expressed in previous years by emigration agent Andrew David. The report explained that as long as liberated Africans settled at Sierra Leone had multiple options for making a living within that colony—whether working for merchants in Freetown or even as agricultural laborers for more prosperous members of their respective ethnic groups—they would not choose to emigrate to the West Indies. Furthermore, the inclination to remain in West Africa often received encouragement from potential local employers and some Christian missionaries, who encouraged more recently settled liberated Africans not to leave.[58] Governor MacLeod described the Guppy report as "an interesting document as shewing the state of the liberated African at Sierra Leone" but lamented that the document "[did] not furnish any decisive data as to the causes of [Trinidad's] failure in obtaining laborers."[59] The report also did not offer any specific recommendations about how to increase those numbers. However, Guppy observed that

> [t]here is another source from which immigrants are at present occasionally derived, viz captured Africans obtained direct from the liberated yard before they are dispersed. By the present regulations these are allowed to stay a few days after they are declared free ... and an opportunity given them of enlisting in the African Corps, or emigrating by any vessel then in the harbour. (They are not however allowed to remain [in the yard] for any vessel not actually arrived.) ... It is possible that many emigrants may on future occasions be derived from this source, but it is subject to too many obvious contingencies to form the ground of a calculation.[60]

Guppy reported that the official emigration vessels for Jamaica and British Guiana had both obtained liberated Africans in this fashion during their last visits to Sierra Leone. The *Senator*, however, had never had the good fortune of arriving at Freetown at the same time as a newly captured slave ship. Thus, Trinidad had not had the opportunity to receive laborers through this process.[61]

Through all the policy machinations of the mid-1840s, no British official ever formally mandated detaining rescued Africans at the Queen's Yard to facilitate efficient recruitment of them as emigrant workers. The Queen's Yard was a specially constructed walled area in Freetown that was relatively close to the harbor and other government buildings. The site included offices for employees and other necessary structures, such as those for storing food and supplies. Newly arrived Africans remained there under the care of government workers until arrangements were made for their permanent settlement in Sierra Leone or elsewhere.[62] Some individuals argued for a policy of detaining liberated Africans at the yard until they could be recruited for a specific voyage to take laborers to the Caribbean, but proponents of this idea consistently met with opposition from other officials, such as the governor of Sierra Leone, who balked at the potential for coercion and exploitation inherent in such an arrangement. Instead of an explicit directive, British authorities at Freetown drifted into a practice of detaining newly rescued Africans for longer and longer periods and thus making a de facto policy change in the manner that Guppy had hoped. This practice evolved relatively smoothly, assisted by the fact that following their liberation from illegal slave ships, displaced Africans depended on their British rescuers both for daily maintenance and for information or direction concerning their new futures as British subjects. According to historian Christopher Fyfe, by the end of the 1840s, recently rescued Africans would remain literally locked in the Queen's Yard "with the public kept out,"[63] presumably awaiting the arrival of some emigrant vessel bound for the West Indies. In any case, after 1844 the Colonial Office discontinued the system of having only three designated emigration transports for the three major West Indian colonies. After the return to using multiple hired vessels for the emigration service, newly arrived Africans did not wait very long before some ship arrived seeking to recruit their labor. Such ships arrived in a steady stream for the next decade (and intermittently thereafter). Recently rescued Africans directly from the Queen's Yard became the overwhelming majority of emigrants taken from Sierra Leone and its environs during this period.

In the years immediately following 1844, descriptions of liberated African immigrants arriving in Trinidad often highlighted this change in the character of the incoming population. For example, in May 1845, Governor MacLeod reported that the *Senator* had recently delivered 247 immigrants, of whom all but twenty-seven had come directly "from the Liberated African Yard."[64] The *Senator* returned in September with 190 Africans, of whom 138 had come straight from a recently captured slave ship. In fact, in this case, the *Senator* had taken on board 160 people "just released from a captured vessel." They had departed for Trinidad ten days later, and twenty-two of the group had died en route, a mortality rate the ship's doctor blamed on their poor health coming from the slave ship.[65] The year 1845 proved particularly active for the vice admiralty court at Freetown. In December, the *Sierra Leone Watchman* reported that the court had condemned thirty-six slave ships that year, emancipating "not less than six thousand poor creatures." The *Watchman* discussed the departure of many of these 6,000 people to the Caribbean as emigrant laborers. The newspaper questioned the degree of "free will & choice" under which such Africans departed. Ultimately, however, the writer concluded that whatever flaws lay in the practice of taking liberated Africans directly from slave ships to become emigrant laborers, even that system held far greater benefits for the Africans than the Spanish or Brazilian slavery from which Great Britain had rescued them. The newspaper declared that it was preferable to "send them thousands of miles to a land of Freedom than let them perish in the 'Baracoon' or on board the Slaver, or die under the lash in the territories of Brazil."[66] With this justification for dispatching liberated Africans almost immediately to the Caribbean, the emigrant traffic out of the Liberated African Yard proceeded apace. Through the mid-1850s, Trinidad received on average about 200 such immigrants each year.

Johnson Asiegbu explains that, "[b]ecause of the ebb and flow, [and] the shifts and turns in policy," it is difficult to compile definitive statistics of emigrants.[67] Asiegbu's figures (derived from official British sources) list a total of almost 1,800 immigrants who entered Trinidad directly from continental West Africa (not via Saint Helena) between 1845 and 1854. While most of this number originated from the newly rescued groups taken from the Queen's Yard, this total also included small groups of Kru immigrants and people from the settled liberated African population of Freetown and its surroundings.[68] Beyond the aggregate totals, evidence of the flow of recently captured Africans into Trinidad appears most clearly in the steady reports of Lord Harris, who succeeded Henry MacLeod as governor of the colony. In June 1848, Harris advised the Colonial Office that the vessel *Persian* had arrived with 206 liberated Africans from Sierra Leone.[69] A year later, in July 1849, Harris reported the arrival of the ship *Agnes,* which brought "two hundred and fifty-five captured negroes" from Sierra Leone.[70] Trinidad's most infamous body of newly rescued liberated African immigrants arrived in the summer of 1850 aboard the vessel *Atlantic,* a very large ship of over 1,000 tons. The *Atlantic* appeared at Port-of-Spain with at least 490 liberated Africans in a group compiled from recently captured slave ships at both Sierra Leone and Saint Helena. This voyage gained its notoriety not because of the large number of Africans but because of a shipboard outbreak of smallpox that necessitated the quarantine of the vessel for six weeks before the Africans could come ashore. This quarantine led to months of recriminations concerning accusations of poor conditions aboard the *Atlantic* and requests from the owners of the vessel (Hyde, Hodge and Company) that they be reimbursed for costs incurred during the ship's detention.[71] Such matters, however, had no direct relevance for the future of the *Atlantic* immigrants. Because of their status as recently rescued refugees with little knowledge of the English language and, in the opinion of British authorities, no capacity to make their own labor agreements, these Africans were assigned one-year terms as indentured agricultural workers with local planters. The agent general of immigrants supervised this labor distribution with oversight from the governor himself.

These arrangements took as their model the system established for the liberated Africans transferred from Havana during the mid-1830s. However, the new, larger, and more continuous influx of liberated Africans from captured ships at Sierra Leone became routine enough that, unlike his predecessor George Hill, Lord Harris did not detail the disposition of each group in his dispatches to the Colonial Office. A few brief portraits of the entrance of such people into Trinidadian society appeared in the published writings of some private citizens who lived in or visited the colony during these years. For example, in his book *Five Years' Residence in the West Indies* (1852), Charles William Day described the arrival of H.M.S. *Growler* at Port-of-Spain in late 1847; it was carrying over 400 immigrants whom he described as "recaptured negroes," accompanied by fourteen African delegates "to see fair play."[72]

Day reported that as they arrived, the Africans each received a new checked shirt at government expense; women also received a head kerchief.[73] Local authorities—presumably under the direction of the agent general of immigrants—provided food, which consisted of rice and plantains, until the group was distributed among employers. In Day's account, each planter or employer made his selection of workers from the new arrivals, after which the Africans were "indentured to [them] for a period of one year."[74] Prior to receiving these indentured workers, employers paid a reimbursement fee of "about four dollars (sixteen shillings)" to the local government to cover the maintenance costs incurred on behalf of their new laborers during their time in government custody after arriving in the colony.[75]

Charles Day concluded his description of the dispersal of the *Growler* group with a brief commentary on the future of liberated African immigrants in Trinidadian society. According to Day, after their one-year indentures expired, most immigrants continued as hired laborers but "generally [sought] a new master." He reported that on the whole, liberated African immigrants "never return[ed] to Africa; and from the moment of their landing [might] be considered an integral part of the population."[76] Under the initial program of recruiting laborers from among liberated Africans who had already spent time settled in Sierra Leone, British authorities had explained to would-be emigrants that they would have the option of returning to West Africa at their own expense after completing any work contract which they signed in Trinidad. Also, during the years of administrative debate over the emigration scheme, some officials had unsuccessfully proposed that emigrants should receive return journeys to Africa free of charge. Even in the case of the educated Christian groups who arrived in 1841 and 1842, few people took the option of a permanent return to Sierra Leone. Discussion of the option of returning to Africa rarely arose regarding the immigrants taken directly from the Liberated African Yard. Thus, just as the 1,000 liberated Africans brought from Cuba had formed a distinctive and permanent presence largely in the plantation areas of the island, the thousands who arrived from Sierra Leone roughly a decade later began to form a similar presence.

Furthermore, during the 1840s and 1850s, as Trinidad received over 1,500 recently rescued Africans from Sierra Leone, the island welcomed even larger groups of liberated Africans from Saint Helena. The arrival of the *Chieftain* in 1842 with its 232 immigrants from Saint Helena commenced a period of over two decades during which Trinidad would receive some 4,000 liberated Africans who had been processed in its vice admiralty court.[77] Governor Harris and his predecessor Governor MacLeod filed a steady series of reports to the Colonial Office giving the size of each group of immigrants from Saint Helena and Sierra Leone and the ages and genders of each group's members, but they made comparatively little comment on the process of their distribution as indentured laborers. In March 1844, Governor MacLeod reported that the vessel *Margaret* had arrived at Port-of-Spain with a group of sixty liberated Africans from Saint Helena. In November 1846 the schooner *Arundel* brought 100 similar immigrants; in August 1847 the brig *Emma* brought 134.[78] Two years later, a larger group of liberated African immigrants from Saint Helena arrived than in any other single year. In April, the *Bathurst* delivered a group of 318 people. During the following month two ships, the *Reliance* and the *Sevenside,* conveyed 175 and 160 immigrants, respectively.[79] In July, the vessel *Janet* brought an additional 142. Amid the otherwise routine reports on this ship, a complaint appeared from the local inspector of health of shipping that the *Janet* immigrants "[were] not in as satisfactory a state as those brought by preceding arrivals." Twelve people died of dysentery during the transatlantic passage, and an additional twenty-five to thirty needed hospitalization upon their arrival. Dr. Thomas Anderson complained less of these problems than of the fact that many of those not sent to hospital "appear[ed] feeble and emaciated." Anderson recounted various criticisms made by the surgeon aboard the *Janet* concerning the health of the emigrants at the time of their embarkation and the quality of food and accommodation aboard the ship.[80] These problems apparently provoked no serious questioning by Governor Harris and certainly caused no interruption of the flow of liberated African immigrants from Saint Helena. In October 1849 the vessel *Euphrates* transported an additional 227 immigrants, and in November the *Sevenside* made a second voyage for the year with 168.[81] This last delivery made the total for 1849 almost 1,300.

The annual volume of the immigration from Saint Helena would never again reach this level. In 1850, Lord Harris reported the arrival of only 304 new immigrants aboard a single vessel, the *Tuskar,* which docked at Port-of-Spain in September.[82] But the Saint Helena route would continue to supply liberated Africans to Trinidad until the early 1860s. All such immigrants faced the same one-year indenture arrangement that Governor MacLeod had set in place for the first group brought by the *Chieftain* in 1842 and that prevailed for the groups from the Liberated African Yard at Sierra Leone. As had occurred with the Africans brought from Havana, Trinidadian authorities made somewhat different arrangements for immigrants they categorized as children. The arrival of the *Arundel* in 1846 prompted Governor Harris to propose some codification of procedures for dealing with liberated Africans younger than age fourteen. Harris characterized many of the 100 immigrants brought by the *Arundel* as "very young, varying from 5 to 14 years of age."[83] The governor suggested that he should have the authority to apprentice these children for periods of time determined at his discretion and under such conditions as he deemed appropriate. Governor Harris emphasized the idea that he could require individuals who received such apprentices to provide education "in reading, writing and arithmetic" in addition to whatever trade or generic laboring skills they would acquire.[84] In response to this proposal, in the spring of 1847, the Colonial Office agreed to extend to Trinidad the provisions of an Order in Council that had been prepared for dealing with liberated African children at the Cape of Good Hope. Under those provisions, liberated African immigrants below the age of fifteen would receive apprenticeships "as Household servants, or in Husbandry, or Gardening, or to any Trade . . . [requiring] peculiar art or skill" until they attained the age of either seventeen or eighteen.[85] Such arrangements in no way altered the overall character of the growing presence of liberated Africans in Trinidad: it was an immigrant class employed among the wider population of laborers of African descent that remained an identifiable subset within that larger group.

After the mid-1850s newly liberated African arrivals to Trinidad became increasingly rare. Between 1841 and 1855, in addition to the almost 6,000 liberated Africans who came from Sierra Leone and Saint Helena, Trinidad had also received at least 800 similar immigrants who had been transferred following proceedings against illegal slave ships at Rio de Janeiro.[86] In contrast to these large groups, during the decade after 1855, according to Johnson Asiegbu, the colony received only about 1,200 additional slave trade refugees (mostly from Saint Helena) before the scheme of liberated African immigration ended altogether.[87] This system ended in large part because of the decline of the illegal slave trade. Furthermore, as early as the late 1840s, Trinidadian planters had begun the transition to full dependence on indentured laborers brought from India as a more sizable, reliable, and predictable supply of workers for their sugar estates.[88] Interesting evidence of this transition appears in the records of two immigrant transport ships that brought to Trinidad passenger groups consisting of both African and East Indian immigrants. In June 1847, Governor Harris reported the arrival of the *Cornwall* bound from Madras with "282 Indian Immigrants and 97 Captured Africans put on board at Saint Helena."[89] The *Cornwall* had apparently stopped at Saint Helena for water or other supplies and had agreed to transport the recently rescued Africans in the absence of any other emigration vessel headed for the Caribbean. Almost six years later, in February 1853, the *Harkaway,* which was bringing 356 Indian immigrants from Calcutta, also took on a group of liberated Africans at Saint Helena. This group, however, numbered only four people, easily overshadowed by the 652 East Indians who also arrived that month.[90]

The illegal slave trade stumbled into decline in fits and starts rather than experiencing a steady diminution. This pattern may explain why in Johnson Asiegbu's figures—which are derived from periodic immigration returns published in parliamentary papers—show marked unevenness. Between 1855 and 1859, barely 1,000 recently rescued Africans were sent to all West Indian colonies combined, while between 1860 and 1864 the number climbed to almost 6,000 (most of whom were sent to Jamaica and British Guiana) before the liberated African immigration system ended entirely during the latter years of that decade.[91] Of the 926 African immigrants reported as entering Trinidad during this period, at least 695 arrived before the end of the year 1860. Seventy-eight of these arrived in early March aboard the *Tyburnia,* which had stopped at Saint Helena en route from Calcutta, having as its predominant mission the conveyance of several hundred Indian immigrants.[92] From Saint Helena, the *Ceres* brought 228 liberated Africans and the *Brookline* brought an additional 163 in mid-March.[93] The handling of these two cases clearly betrayed the fact that some years had passed since the last arrival of large groups of such African immigrants. Henry Mitchell, the new agent general of immigrants, reported to Governor Keate that he had separated the people from the *Ceres* into nineteen gangs and had distributed them to the first nineteen employers who had applied. Mitchell expressed some concern about the appropriate employment for individuals under age fourteen, including some under the age of ten. He also mentioned the possibility of using some special system of apprenticeship in the future, but on this occasion, he simply "distributed [the children] as equally as possible over the different gangs."[94] A week later Mitchell followed a similar procedure for the Africans from the *Brookline.* On both occasions the agent general distributed the immigrants to their employers "under no indenture."[95] Presumably this meant that the employers faced no binding requirements dictating how they should treat such laborers and that the Africans had no contractual obligation to remain with their assigned employers.

In early July 1860, Lieutenant Governor James Walker (acting after the departure of Governor Keate) questioned the wisdom of these arrangements and recommended that some form of indenture be instituted purportedly "for the advantage and security of the Africans themselves."[96] Less than two weeks after Walker expressed this concern in a letter to the Colonial Office, yet another liberated African transport, the barque *Mary Ann,* arrived at Port-of-Spain, bringing 226 immigrants from Sierra Leone. The Africans aboard the *Mary Ann* proved to be an interesting group in two respects. First, 220 were recently rescued Africans "from the Government Yard" at Freetown, and six people were described as longer-standing residents of Sierra Leone. Lieutenant Governor Walker offered no comment on the relationship between the six older settlers and the newly liberated Africans with whom they traveled. But he did comment on the apparent shipboard relationships formed between the liberated African adults and the five children included in their group:

> The older immigrants claimed the younger as their children; although there was no very reliable evidence of the reality of such ties; yet in the absence of any positive information to the contrary I deemed it prudent to admit the claims and allow the children to accompany their seniors.[97]

One can look at this simply as immigrant adults taking responsibility for immigrant children in new surroundings. But one must also see here some hint of early community formation among the new African arrivals.

Immigration Agent Mitchell assigned the Africans from the *Mary Ann* to employers without formal indentures, following the same procedure as he had done for the *Ceres* and the *Brookline,* explaining to Lieutenant Governor Walker that in his opinion, no law then in force authorized him to indenture such people. Walker repeated this viewpoint in a second communication to the Colonial Office. He referred to the 1847 Order in Council that addressed the apprenticing of children but noted that this granted no power to bind adults to plantation labor. Walker discussed a more pertinent ordinance of 1850 that he cited as the last local law that had "specifically provided for the indenture of Liberated Africans." He explained that a new

Consolidated Immigration Ordinance passed in 1854 superseded the 1850 measure and that this new law did not explicitly address the liberated African group.[98] In response, the Colonial Office authorized Walker to supervise the preparation of a new Trinidad law that would institute three-year labor contracts for any future African immigrants acquired through the system of slave trade suppression.[99] Such a law did pass in early 1861, but it would prove of almost no consequence as little more than 200 additional liberated Africans would enter Trinidad after its passage. With the new system of East Indian indentureship proceeding apace to fulfill the labor demands of local planters, over three decades of immigration of liberated Africans came to an unheralded close.

The efforts of Governor Keate in Trinidad to devise appropriate procedures for dealing with such late-arriving liberated African immigrants reflected more than the uncertainty of a colonial executive confronting a new situation during his administration. While he was unsure about which previous policies he could or should apply, Governor Keate—like Governor Bayley in the Bahamas in 1860—continued the practice of handling these people as unusual additions to the local population. The very category of persons termed "liberated Africans" had arisen from the first step in Britain's great nineteenth-century social experiment that had culminated in the dismantling of African chattel slavery in their West Indian colonies. The slaves who became free played the largest role in this drama, and one could even argue that the thirty to forty thousand liberated Africans who entered the Caribbean during this era constituted an almost incidental development. However, precisely because of their status as people who had not been slaves, these free immigrants became a population through whom British authorities would attempt to define new ideas about using African labor and even African cultural identity within the Caribbean context. In the labor-hungry sugar economy of Trinidad, the effort to use such immigrants as a post-emancipation work force entailed both greater deliberateness (and sometimes even urgency) and more intense management than the programs of apprenticeship, indenture, and (on a few occasions) subsistence settlement established in the Bahamas. But in both colonies, government authorities and private citizens, after some early reservations, sought to incorporate the liberated Africans into their economy and society as an idealized work force that they hoped would function with greater compliance and effectiveness than they believed possible from the poisoned and perennially failing relationship between employers and former slaves. It is no surprise that like the freedpeople—and also like enslaved people in previous centuries—liberated Africans worked to shape their relationship with a white-dominated society and economy into a far more mediated and complex association than that envisioned by the various officials who sought to manage their immigrant experience. In this fundamental respect, there was more similarity than difference between the experiences of these people in these two very different colonies.

But the entrance of the only large groups of free Africans brought directly from Africa to British colonies in the Caribbean had more consequence than simply adding their particular nuance to the ongoing social and economic struggles between people of African and European descent in these societies. Historians now take it as a commonplace that even during slavery, whites remained constantly aware of both the humanity and the Africanness of their human property.[100] With respect to the liberated African immigrants, such awareness became almost an official preoccupation. On the one hand, just as they held idealized expectations for the labor power of liberated Africans, many British authorities also articulated optimistic visions about the prospect of molding the cultural character of these immigrants through education and conversion to Christianity—both of which at various times were explicitly required of the employers who received such Africans as indentured laborers. Yet at the same time, both government and private voices expressed concern that the so-called savage customs and uncivilized behavior of the new arrivals might somehow negatively influence the culture and behavior of the existing black population who had lived for years under the socialization of British colonial society. Apart from their inherent racism and ethnocentrism, such concerns had validity inasmuch as they pointed to the fact that the African immigrants would inevitably bring their own cultures, ideas, and aspirations to the communities where they settled. For almost three centuries British West Indian colonies—as had all slave societies in the New World—had served as the crucible in which an African diaspora or African-Creole culture had begun to form. During the years of slavery, even Europeans who disdained the idea of African culture could not help but comment on the ways various African cultural inputs shaped the character of their slave communities. This kind of African-Creole culture formation continued with the arrival of liberated African immigrants. They were free people who had more liberty than slaves to choose where they would live, who they would associate with, and what they did during their free time. In the Caribbean colonies where they settled, these people brought an infusion of African inputs into a process of creolization that would flourish in new and dramatic ways. Late-nineteenth-century observers such as the French priest who in 1879 commented on the "queer customs" of Trinidad's most recent African immigrants or the travel writer William Drysdale who in 1885 made similar comments about "native Africans" in the Bahamas expressed no doubt that these latest African arrivals had significantly affected the wider African-Creole landscape in these two colonies.[101] Liberated African immigrants both stood out within that landscape and in many ways changed it. Yet even as they maintained this distinctiveness, they also became an African-Creole people.

3

"A fine family of what we call creole Yarabas":

African Ethnic Identities in Liberated African Community Formation

The story of liberated Africans in the Bahamas, Trinidad, and elsewhere in the Caribbean began in a fashion similar to the story of all Africans in the New World diaspora—in the cultural and demographic disarray of transatlantic slave ships. Historians have long speculated about how much research can determine about the identity of the Africans who arrived as slaves. Particularly in recent decades, as interest has grown in exploring the African influences on cultures of the African diaspora, numerous scholars have attempted to paint a more informed picture of the enslaved immigrants who created those cultures.

Historians have attempted to better understand the variety of West and Central African ethnic groups that made up this migration. Studies of the process of slave trading have shown that at different time periods and in different parts of the Americas, different regions of Africa played greater or lesser roles in the supply of slaves. Thus, for example, historians have discovered that heavy Dutch and English slave trading on the Gold Coast during the early eighteenth century led to the significant presence of Akan-Asante peoples among the slaves taken to British West Indian colonies in that era. Other studies have pursued the cultural consequences of this demographic pattern and have elucidated the dominant role this particular ethnic group played in shaping various aspects of West Indian slave folk culture, such as the well-known Anansi stories of Jamaica.

Akan-Asante peoples, termed "Coromantees" by the British, played predominant roles in British West Indian slave rebellions of the eighteenth century and in the founding of several communities of runaway slaves in Jamaica during this period.[1] Anthropologists and historians investigating the

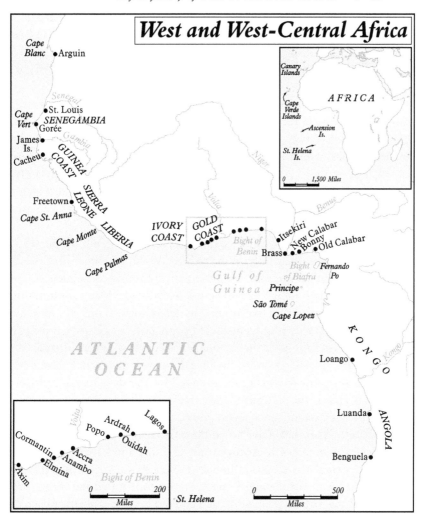

Map of West and West-Central Africa

African origins of Haitian vodun have traced the noticeable influences of Fon and Yoruba religious traditions. Scholars have connected the importance of these Fon and Yoruba ethnic traditions to the importance of these ethnic groups in the supply of African slaves to the island of Saint Domingue. The French colony received a significant percentage of its supply of slaves from the area around the kingdom of Dahomey, which was inhabited by Fon peoples, and from neighboring Yoruba regions in territory that lies in the southwestern part of contemporary Nigeria.[2] Most recently, historians of the slave trade into the southern United States have concluded that contrary to previous assumptions that emphasized the role of West Africa, as much as one-third of the North American slave supply originated in Central Africa among Kongo peoples. This information has fortified the work of other scholars who have found apparent Kongo influences on African-American folk culture in the U.S. south.[3]

Rarely have historians discovered that any single ethnic group formed a numeric majority in the supply of slaves taken to any particular colony. And even where one or two ethnic groups played very noticeable roles in the formation of local culture, other less-prominent ethnicities exerted influence as well. For example, even with the prominence of Yoruba and Fon contributions to Haitian vodun, historians and anthropologists have also identified Kongo cosmological aspects in the Haitian religious system.[4] The combination of ever-more-sophisticated studies of the slave trade with the cultural history of the African diaspora has thus entailed, not the pursuit of rigid African ethnic distributions in the New World, but rather the discerning of broad ethnic patterns or trends and their cultural consequences.

Making demographic linkages between liberated African communities in the Caribbean and the slave-trading patterns involves unique complications. The geographic origins of these people bore no relationship to the patterns of slave supply for the various British colonies where liberated Africans settled. As refugees from the illegal nineteenth-century slave trade, these Africans came from cargoes intended for the slave markets of Cuba and Brazil. Hence, the patterns of slave trading to these non-British territories had the greatest influence on the ethnic composition of the liberated African groups. Historians have noted the particular prominence of Yoruba peoples in the nineteenth-century trade to Cuba and have addressed the related importance of Yoruba influences in African-Cuban culture. It is recognized that both Yoruba and Kongo peoples constituted significant proportions of the African population that entered Brazil during the final half-century of its trade in humans. These two ethnic groups have also received attention for their noticeable contributions to Brazilian slave culture during the nineteenth century and to numerous aspects of African-Brazilian culture which continue in the present.[5]

Political and military developments in West and Central Africa during the first half of the nineteenth century provide explanations for the prominence of these two groups in the slave trade of this era. Beginning in the 1830s, several Yoruba kingdoms fought a series of wars both within and between themselves, which led to the formation of new political configurations during a long period of turmoil that would not really end until the establishment of settled British colonialism in the late 1890s.[6] During the same period the centuries-old Kongo kingdom likewise went through a series of wars and political dislocations that ceased only with the complete demise of the kingdom near the end of the century. These Kongo and Yoruba crises did not occur independently of the activities of European slave traders on the coast. But they did not occur solely or even primarily as a result of foreign activity. Most important, as had occurred in the region for over three centuries, conflicts such as these generated thousands of captives, who ended up sold as involuntary laborers into the transatlantic, trans-Saharan, and local slave trades. Herein lies the origin of the strong Yoruba and Kongo presence in the nineteenth-century slave communities of Cuba and Brazil. Any attempt to explore the demographic patterns that prevailed in nineteenth-century liberated African communities can thus logically begin with an effort to determine whether or not Yoruba and Kongo dominance also prevailed among this population of would-be slaves who by chance failed to reach their intended destinations in Cuba or Brazil.

It is not surprising that liberated African populations often prove more amenable to demographic study than do African populations under slavery. As the specially protected refugees of the British government, liberated Africans frequently received extraordinary bureaucratic attention. From the moment a British naval vessel seized a foreign slave ship, the Colonial Office, the Foreign Office, and even the War Office commenced a lengthy record-keeping process to chronicle the fate of the human cargo. The Liberated African Department at Freetown, Sierra Leone, produced the largest single body of such records because the majority of liberated Africans ended up in that West African colony. During the functioning of the system of mixed commission courts, the British-Portuguese court at Freetown processed more cases than any other site. The British-Spanish court at Havana generated a much smaller volume of data. However, during its period of peak activity in the mid-1830s, the Cuban operation produced a particularly rich collection of registers documenting the characteristics of each cargo of rescued Africans brought to that island, recording a level of human detail unprecedented in the history of the slave trade. The surviving registers contain descriptive accounts for forty-two slave ships carrying more than 10,000 African captives who constituted well over half of all liberated Africans processed in Cuba and almost one-tenth of the estimated total number of Africans rescued by the British navy throughout the nineteenth century. For each of these 10,000 individuals, the registers record an African name, an assigned Spanish name, measurements of age and height, and an ethnic designation. In many cases, entries also provide descriptions of physical features such as filed teeth or facial scarification related to ethnic rituals. Other entries provide descriptions of brand marks inflicted by slave traders to indicate particular claims of ownership.[7]

No obvious reason explains why the mixed commission at Havana should have produced such extraordinary records. At the mixed commission court and the vice admiralty court in Sierra Leone, the officials who managed matters related to liberated Africans seem to have paid greatest attention to assigning tracking numbers to the individuals they processed rather than to accumulating descriptive data. With hindsight, the idea of keeping track of individual liberated Africans after their settlement in Sierra Leone seems an impractical project that was destined to be minimally useful. However, many of the most ardent proponents of slave trade suppression feared that if that liberated Africans left the areas of Sierra Leone under British control they would run the risk of reenslavement either at the hands of unscrupulous traders or by becoming involved in local military conflicts once again. These British activists hoped that the system of unique assigned numbers would provide evidence of such reenslavement.[8] These kinds of concerns about reenslavement had little relevance in Cuba, perhaps giving the Havana mixed commission greater opportunity to compile more social information in their records. One might also speculate that the nature of record-keeping at Havana may have resulted in part from the extreme antislavery convictions of the British commissioners Richard Robert Madden and David Turnbull. As discussed in chapters 1 and 2, these men brought abolitionist zeal even to the routine administrative tasks of the mixed commission. These 10,000 records provide a fruitful source for demographic study of communities of liberated Africans.

This limited group from Havana does not constitute a random sample by any formal statistical standards. Nor does it provide even a rough cross-section of the liberated African group as a whole; it excludes entirely any slave ships that were bound for Brazil. Both Portuguese and Spanish traders participated in the Cuban slave market, but the presence of some Portuguese slave ships in the Havana group cannot serve as a proxy for a sample of the Brazilian trade. One might consider the possibility that the supply of slaves to Brazil involved a larger percentage of vessels from West-Central Africa—the broadly defined Kongo region—with which the Lusophone empire had conducted business since the sixteenth century. A sample of liberated Africans derived solely from Cuba-bound vessels might contain an underrepresentation of the Kongo ethnic group. No easy remedy exists for these kinds of concerns except for the unsatisfactory, albeit inevitable, conclusion that historians can only make use of the best available sources, whatever their limitations. For the purpose of discerning rough demographic trends as in this study, questions of over- or underrepresentation of one ethnic group or another have somewhat less weight than they might for a more rigorous quantitative analysis. And in any case, the Havana sample overall presents no major contradictions of the ethnic patterns that prior research has set forth for nineteenth-century slave cargoes. The greatest value of the Cuban registers lies in the nuances they provide concerning the nature of various African ethnic categorizations and the way such identities may have functioned in the lives of the Africans.

Of the 10,391 slaves listed, 2,755, or roughly 26 percent, identified themselves or were identified by others as Lucumí, the term used in nineteenth-century Cuban Spanish to refer to people of Yoruba background. Some 1,925 received the designation Congo and four the name Musicongo. An additional 388 people taken from the *Águila* received the label Luango. This term (more often spelled "Loango") referred to both a town and a region located just over 100 miles north of the mouth of the Congo River that lies within the area marked by anthropologists and historians as being inhabited by Kongo peoples if one understands that ethnic term as a broad one that includes many related subgroups. The number of Congo, Musicongo, and Luango therefore amounted to a total of 2,317 Kongo people, or approximately 22 percent of the whole group. Thus, consistent with the known composition of the nineteenth-century slave trade, Yoruba and Kongo peoples formed the largest individual ethnic populations and together constituted almost half of the mixed commission sample.

Among the remainder of the group, the designation Carabalí appeared with greatest frequency; it was attached to some 1,867 rescued slaves, or about 18 percent of the total. This name, however, seems to have referred to the town of Calabar rather than to any particular ethnic group or region. Throughout the era of the Atlantic slave trade, Europeans often labeled Africans according to their port of departure rather than using any known or imagined ethnic term. Two factors point to the port of Calabar as the probable location indicated by this unusual name. First, among the hundreds of terms used by Europeans—Dutch, English, French, Portuguese, and Spanish—to describe African ethnic groups from the seventeenth through the nineteenth centuries, no obvious linguistic cognate appears for this word. Perhaps most important, no word even close to Carabalí appears in Spanish atlases of West and Central Africa and the Atlantic islands of Sao Tome, Principe, and Cape Verde.[9] Calabar, the name of the busy port and trading center in southeastern Nigeria, emerges as the word most similar to Carabalí. This town and the Cross River region surrounding it served as a major transshipment point for slaves throughout the eighteenth and nineteenth centuries. Given the confusion that exists even among current scholars about the correct western orthography for various African names, it hardly seems surprising that a peculiar spelling and pronunciation existed in Cuba during the years of slavery.

The second factor that identifies the label as a reference to Calabar concerns the additional descriptive data provided in the registers. In most cases, individual entries did not simply identify slaves as having originated from Carabalí but rather used a system of suffixes that labeled each person more specifically with phrases such as "Carabalí elugo," "Carabalí suamá," "Carabalí Brincan," "Carabalí bony," "Carabalí Ibibi," or "Carabalí Ibo." Sorting out even a majority of these suffixes would prove difficult if not impossible and that task lies beyond the scope of this study. The Havana registers include over thirty such clarifying terms related to the Carabalí designation. The difficulties of transcribing from the handwritten documents compounds the problem of defining the terms. It is also likely that there are misspellings and other errors in the originals, which were prepared after all by harried employees of the mixed commission amid the confusion of each newly arrived cargo of rescued slaves. Such employees were responsible for feeding and sheltering these unique refugees in addition to attempting to gather their demographic data through the medium of interpreters. Nevertheless, several of the Carabalí suffixes point unmistakably to the Calabar hinterland or the area usually categorized in slave trade studies as the Bight of Biafra. In a confusing pairing, "Carabalí bony" seems to have referred to the town of Bonny, a coastal slave port in its own right 200 miles west of Calabar. This phrase therefore points to the correct region but offers no insight into the ethnic groups involved. More clearly, the terms Ibo and Ibibio refer to two major ethnic groups of the Calabar area, and in both the eighteenth and nineteenth centuries, these groups contributed significantly to the Atlantic slave trade. A more complete portrait of the ethnic groups represented under the Carabalí classification in the Havana sample would require a full etymological exploration of the numerous suffixes. But for the purpose of compiling broad ethnic and geographic patterns, one can conclude that in this sample of the liberated African population, the Bight of Biafra region contributed approximately 18 percent of the total.[10]

Even this modest conclusion requires some qualification. In one instance, for example, forty-one slaves of the Ibibio ethnic group appeared on a register separate from the Carabalí designation, although they formed part of a cargo otherwise linked to that town.[11] Those forty-one people do not figure into the calculation of 18 percent. Also, individuals may have existed among the Calabar slaves who by some unusual circumstance departed from Calabar but in fact originated from an ethnic group far away from the Bight of Biafra. However, because of the usual practice by slave ships of conducting their business within a limited geographic area, it seems unlikely that the number of such people would prove large enough to significantly alter the proportion. The Yoruba, Kongo, and Calabar totals thus account for approximately 66 percent of the sample.

Of the remaining 3,452 rescued slaves, 378 received the designation "Camaron," another geographic rather than ethnic name, which described a region southeast of the town of Calabar in the northern part of present-day Cameroon. Such people would in fact also fall within the scope of the Bight of Biafra as understood in nineteenth-century African history.[12] The regional label Camaron, however, might have involved several ethnic groups, and in this case the registers provide no additional detail.

In contrast, quite detailed entries appear for rescued slaves from the Ewe-Fon region around the Bight of Benin. Some 219 people, or 2 percent of the sample, received the designation Arara, one of several terms historians have considered to be proxy references for Fon people from the former kingdom of Dahomey, now largely the country of Benin and parts of Togo and western Nigeria. In various records from the slave trade era the terms Arara, Rara, Arada, Rada, and Allada have all appeared as supposedly ethnic identifications for Africans from Dahomey. The terms all in fact referred to the town of Allada, a virtual city-state within the kingdom. Fon ethnic prominence in Dahomey explains why scholars have come to accept the references to Allada as likely indicators for this ethnic group and some of its culturally related neighbors. Those neighbors included the Ewe who bordered Fon territory to the east. The largest entrance of these ethnic groups into the Atlantic slave trade occurred during the eighteenth century, but the Havana data suggests that such people continued to form a small but notable presence in the nineteenth-century trade and therefore also in liberated African populations. In addition to the 219 individuals labeled Arara, Fon, and related peoples likely also appeared among 127 people identified as Mina whose origins were presumably the port of Elmina. The heaviest years of slave trading of this port, which was located on the Gold Coast west of Dahomey, took place during the eighteenth century. That trade most often involved Akan-Asante peoples, but evidence suggests that almost half the 727 Mina departures delivered to Havana as rescued slaves in fact originated from the Fon ethnic area east of the port. A single group of 155 people appears in the records as "Mina Apapa," and a total of 188 appear as "Mina Popo." The terms Popo, Papa, Pawpaw, and Paupau all had similar associations with the kingdom of Dahomey. Some early-twentieth-century anthropologists conceived of the Popo as a distinct ethnic group, but in general scholars interpret this name as a reference that more loosely points to people within the Ewe-Fon region.[13] Taken together, the Rara and Popo references from the Havana registers amount to 562 people, or 5 percent of the group as a whole.

Like the kingdom of Dahomey, the heaviest years of slave trading along the Windward Coast of West Africa—which stretches from the Senegambia region southeast to the area of modern Liberia and Sierra Leone—took place during the eighteenth rather than the nineteenth century. Yet this part of the continent nonetheless contributed roughly 16 percent of the liberated African population represented in the Havana data. Some 792 people received the designation "Ganga," sometimes followed by various suffixes, while 892 people received the designation "Mandinga," also often followed by suffixes. At first glance, one might assume that this latter designation must have referred to people of the Mande (or Manding) ethnic group from the Senegambia area. However, in this case, the suffixes used provide evidence of some geographic and ethnic confusion, despite the apparent clarity of the ethnic term used. For example, in the phrase Mandinga Bambara, the word Mandinga seems to have served as a broad descriptor for the Upper Guinea coast, while the attachment Bambara denoted the particular ethnic group, in this case one of several major cultures inhabiting the area that has become modern Senegal and western Mali. A similar interpretation would apply to the phrase Mandinga Fula as a label for the Fula or Fulani of roughly the same geographic zone as the Bambara. Indeed, officials also used the phrase "Mandinga Mandinga," which presumably denoted Mande people; in this construction, the same word served first a geographic and then an ethnic purpose. The geographic range of the term Mandinga as used by British and Spanish authorities at the mixed commission seems to have stretched much farther south to the area of modern Sierra Leone and Liberia. The labels "Mandinga Temine" and "Mandinga Quisi," for example, almost certainly denoted the Temne and Kissi ethnic groups of these more southerly regions. On the one hand, this wide application of the Mandinga label reflects some of the uncertainty that existed (and still exists) about African ethnic groups. At the same time, in the period between the sixteenth and nineteenth centuries, patterns of migration and political change involved the wide spread of peoples and cultures now understood by anthropologists and historians as Mande or Mande-related. Thus, in his 1959 typology, *Africa: Its Peoples and Their Culture History,* anthropologist George Murdock categorized Nuclear Mande of the Senegambia region and Peripheral Mande of the Sierra Leone and Liberia region farther south.[14] Imprecision seems to be an inevitable feature of this ethnic term, even more so than others.

One can at some level define the entire Windward Coast area as a zone of similar and historically related cultures. Such a definition entails elision of differences between some quite distinct groups. But for the purpose of sketching ethnic patterns among liberated African populations, even an overgrown Mande classification serves to delineate a group of peoples that

Table 3.1. Distribution of African Ethnic Groups/Cultural Regions among Liberated Africans Processed by the Anglo-Spanish Mixed Commission at Havana, Cuba, 1828–1838

Ethnic Group or Other Designation	Number of People	Percentage of Group
Kongo	2,317	22.30
Yoruba	2,755	26.51
Carabalí (Calabar; includes Ibo and Ibibio)	1,867	17.97
Camaron	378	3.64
Mina (Elmina; includes many Ewe-Fon)	727	7.00
Arara (presumed mostly Fon)	219	2.11
Mandinga (Mande and Windward Coast)	892	8.58
Ganga (Windward Coast)	792	7.62
De Bisao (from port of Bissau)	146	1.40
Other	298	2.87
Total	10,391	100.00

Source: Derived from Records of the Anglo-Spanish Mixed Commission at Havana, FO 313/56–62. Calculations are by the author.

was markedly different in culture from the Yoruba, Kongo, and other ethnicities already represented. The Ganga designation seems to overlap and therefore further expand this broadly conceived Windward Coast representation within the Havana group. A review of atlases and anthropological and historical studies found only one term—"Gangaran"—that makes a close linguistic match with "Ganga." Murdock includes this term among his list of various ethnic groups represented among what he calls the "Nuclear Mande" of the Senegambia region. However, the phrases "Ganga cono," "Ganga Beré," and "Ganga Quisé," for example, all point to ethnic groups or subgroups around Sierra Leone: Kono, Bere,[15] and Kissi. Furthermore, at least one captured slaver carried a cargo that included a handful of people identified as Ganga among a majority labeled Mandinga. As with the designation Carabalí, a complete clarification of these Mandinga and Ganga relationships would require a minute exploration of all the clarifying suffixes used. Such an exploration would add nuances to the present general portrait of Mande and Mande-related representation in the Havana sample. But in any case, the overall portrait of Kongo and Yoruba prominence, as would be expected given the history of the nineteenth-century slave trade, remains intact.

Beyond the illustration of the numeric prominence of Kongo and Yoruba groups, the records of the Havana mixed commission provide much suggestive detail about the complex nature of these two enormous ethnic groupings, as understood by both the British rescuers and the Africans. Clarifying suffixes appear throughout the registers in relation to the designations Lucumí and Congo. Indeed, the scribes and their interpreters for *La Joven Reyna*, which carried 254 slaves identified as Kongo, recorded more than 100 different clarifying terms. In less extraordinary examples, the captured slaver *Amalia* brought 200 Kongo people for whom the Havana officials used eight descriptive suffixes, and the *Diligencia* carried ninety-four Kongo slaves for whom authorities used ten different suffixes. The Lucumí, or Yoruba, designation likewise almost always included the use of similar modifiers, although not as many as those used for the Kongo cargo of *La Joven Reyna*. The slave ship *Fila*, for example, carried 392 Africans, 333 of whom the mixed commission identified as Lucumí with approximately twenty added-on descriptive terms. These suffixes served to identify the many geographical and cultural variations that existed within these large ethnic groups. Contemporary anthropologists and historians often point out that while shared cultures existed over wide geographic areas, much local and regional distinctiveness existed within such comprehensive boundaries. These scholars further point out that for individual Kongo and Yoruba people, the broad identity—that culture shared with hundreds of thousands of other Kongos and Yorubas—had far less meaning in their local experience. Some anthropologists would even argue that the macro identity had no personal meaning at all. Much debate still exists about what exactly constitutes an African ethnic group beyond the basic concept of some group of people sharing significant and identifiable aspects of culture and history over time. Thus, when using even commonplace labels such as Yoruba, Ibo, or Kongo, one must work from the understanding that these categorizations have contested, changeable, and, often, ill-defined meaning. In considering so-called ethnic terminology, historians must also bear in mind that these labels had both cultural and political meanings in Africa. Therefore, their usage by Africans in the New World may have contained dual implications.[16]

Scholars such as Monica Schuler and Maureen Warner-Lewis have explored the role liberated African immigrants played in creating and/or strengthening Caribbean communities that defined themselves as Yoruba or Kongo, in what looked like unambiguous resistance to more subsuming modes of creolization.[17] However, scholars have shown little inclination to expand upon the conclusions of Schuler and Warner-Lewis, maybe in part because of the contrived nature of such broad ethnic categorizations. To be sure, in many cases these broadly conceived categories often successfully produced strong religious communities or even led to organized efforts by liberated Africans to return to specific African homelands.[18] Yet this kind of ethnically organized cultural resistance contained an inherent paradox. Even as Yoruba or Kongo groups demonstrably rejected erasure of their African past, the very adoption of such collective categories constituted a loss of significant elements of that past. In other words, if one takes into account the diverse particular cultural identities of Africans brought to the Caribbean, the adoption of collective "African ethnic" identities—although certainly an act of cultural resistance through maintaining African associations—must be viewed equally as an already creolized step along the path to becoming African-Caribbean.

The Havana registers provide two clues about the ways these matters of ethnic identification may have functioned in the experience of liberated Africans. As already mentioned above, individual slave ships usually conducted their business within a somewhat limited range along the African coast. Thus, for example, Mande slaves from the Senegambia area would most likely not end up on a slave ship with Kongo captives from West-Central Africa. However, groups from neighboring but ethnically different regions might find themselves together. Hence, in some cases from the Havana sample, Fon slaves from Dahomey who were classified as Mina Popo or Arara arrived on vessels that also carried Yoruba slaves from the territory east of Dahomey that has become modern Nigeria.[19] Such mixing of ethnic groups reflected not only the movements of slave traders but also some degree of intercourse between such groups within Africa long before their experience of shared community aboard foreign slave ships. A handful of marginal notations in the Havana registers provide evidence of such interaction. The slaver *Fila* carried a mostly Yoruba cargo but also brought two men designated as Mina Popo who were likely of Ewe or Fon ethnicity. Immediately following these Mina Popo slaves in the *Fila* list there appear three Yoruba males set apart with the following comment: "This man Number [386] and the two previous [boys], although they are Lucumí, understand only the language of Mina, to which nation they went when they were very young."[20]

But despite this example and other glimpses of interethnic experience, the mixed commission records prove most striking for the relative homogeneity of the many Kongo and Yoruba cargoes at the level of broad ethnic identity. Of the fifteen captured slavers that involved some Yoruba slaves, nine carried overwhelming Yoruba majorities, while a tenth had a 60 percent majority. Virtually all of the vessels involving Kongo slaves carried Kongo people exclusively. Eight ships fit this description, one ship carried a single Kongo person amid a largely Mandinga group, and another vessel carried only a single "Musicongo" slave, presumably having already delivered its cargo before being captured by the British. Such broadly homogeneous cargoes usually had the effect of drawing together people from different parts of the wide Kongo and Yoruba territories, forming pan-Kongo and pan-Yoruba communities in microcosm. Thus, for example, the 254 slaves of *La Joven Reyna* who required 100 different terms to describe their different Kongo identities found an environment aboard the slave ship in which their broad Kongo commonality did have salience—perhaps for the first time. Likewise, when thrown together aboard the *Fila,* the "Lucumí eyó," "Lucumí eva," "Lucumí ota," and other subgroups shared a collective Yoruba experience. Similar conditions may have prevailed for slave cargoes in previous centuries and for other nineteenth-century groups not intercepted by British naval forces. However, the unique status of liberated Africans gave them particular opportunities to nurture newfound ethnic communion. Perhaps most important, in all of the various processes through which liberated Africans settled in the Caribbean, large groups of people from individual cargoes of slave ships ended up remaining together at least until their arrival in the Bahamas, Trinidad, or some other location. Furthermore, once they arrived in such places, as free people, they had much wider opportunities to form their own communities than did slaves.

At the same time, however, despite the opportunities liberated Africans had to form intraethnic bonds within these large Kongo and Yoruba groups, at the time of their processing in Cuba, their local and regional identities clearly remained important to them. For some vessels, mixed commission authorities simply classified the whole group as Lucumí or Congo with no clarifying suffixes. It seems most likely that these cases reflected either disinterest or pragmatic reduction of bureaucracy on the part of authorities and translators rather than any attitude expressed by the liberated Africans. Conversely, the cases where the mixed commission recorded extensive Kongo and Yoruba details could only have arisen from the self-identification of the rescued slaves. Many of these extra descriptive terms had roots in towns and regions in Kongo and Yoruba territory. For instance, the designation "Lucumí Eyó," which occurred with particular frequency, very likely identified people with origins in the Yoruba kingdom of Oyo, a political entity very much at the heart of the social and military disruptions Yorubaland experienced in the mid-nineteenth century—the same disruptions that supplied tens of thousands of captives to the transatlantic slave trade. Similarly, the designations "Congo Luango" and "Congo Luanda" probably belonged to people with origins in these Kongo coastal towns. Other descriptive terms used with Congo and Lucumí may have indicated memberships in secret societies or other cultural groupings. Whatever the particular meanings of these many suffixed terms, it seems possible that when they were removed from their African local contexts, their significance decreased, especially with the passage of time. Indeed, one might even speculate that in the unique communities of liberated Africans created by the illegal slave trade, the broader Yoruba and Kongo macro identities would become more important. But given the evidence that individual Africans held clear attachments to their specific local identities, it also seems possible that they made some attempt to preserve them. The records of the Havana mixed commission, although they are detailed as demographic data, provide only a map with which to begin investigation of these and other questions relevant to understanding the function of African ethnic identity in the lives of liberated Africans.

An exploration of the nature of ethnic distinction within liberated African communities entails two separate, but related, paths of inquiry: first, an examination of the ways outside observers interpreted ethnic distinctions and used them as the basis for cultural and behavioral claims; and second, an analysis of the ways African immigrants understood, interpreted, and lived out such distinctions. Both lines of inquiry yield clear evidence that ethnic identifications retained long-term salience in the lives of these immigrants. In an essay entitled "Identity and Ideology: The Names Controversy," historian Sterling Stuckey addresses the debates that arose among African-American intellectuals about the use of the terms Negro and African to describe people of African descent in the nineteenth-century United States. With respect to the label African, Stuckey observes that for these intellectuals, more specific African ethnicity remained "largely abstract . . . especially for those who never knew the particular ethnic group or groups from which they sprang."[21] However, he speculates that for slaves of earlier generations who did possess such knowledge, individual African identities likely remained important in their American environment. He discusses at some length the significance attached to naming in various West African cultures and hypothesizes that slaves in the New World must have found similar ways to culturally label themselves through names that they used within their communities that were separate from their public or given names.[22]

For liberated Africans, at least in Trinidad, this kind of ethnic naming seems to have occurred, not only among themselves but also as a matter of public and official identification.

Evidence of this practice appears repeatedly in diverse legal notices from Trinidadian newspapers during the latter half of the nineteenth century. Some individuals bore the generic surname African, such as Robert African and Thomas African, who were identified in 1871 on a list of individuals who owed outstanding fees for receiving grants of crown land. Similarly, in an 1868 report from the San Fernando police court, a man named Manuel African served as a witness for the prosecution in an assault case involving a quarrel in a rum shop between the driver from Plaisance Estate and another man. In December 1887, Albert African found himself on the opposite end of a criminal matter, accused by police of having stabbed a constable who had attempted to arrest him for stealing chickens.[23] These three examples demonstrate a predictable singling out of people of African birth within the wider population. And by the 1860s the greater proportion of the African born would have come from the liberated African group. Police reported the age of the accused thief Albert African, for instance, as approximately forty years. Even allowing for significant underestimation in this figure, Albert African (or any man of age fifty or younger in 1887) could not have arrived in Trinidad as a slave. Still, it does not seem remarkable that nineteenth-century naming practices distinguished the African-born immigrants in this fashion, whether they instituted such surnames themselves or the names were assigned to them by other people. Recognition of differences between African-born and Caribbean-born people had formed a constant feature of Caribbean societies for centuries. The presence of specific ethnic surnames, however, proves somewhat more telling. Where historians such as Sterling Stuckey have speculated about the importance that separate African ethnicities held among slaves, the various mundane news items and notices from Trinidadian papers that included ethnic African names show that such distinctions existed as a very public and widely understood reality in the lives of liberated Africans.

During the 1860s and 1870s, people bearing African ethnic surnames made regular appearances at the Supreme Criminal Court in Port-of-Spain and before police courts throughout the island. For example, in November 1867, John Congo appeared at the San Fernando police court to face charges of stealing sugarcane and resisting a police constable. In June 1868, a Port-of-Spain jury convicted Jim Yaraba on a charge of burglary. During the same month the court acquitted James Congo and Allen Congo of a charge of "robbery with violence."[24] The fact that most such references concern criminal or other legal matters simply reflects the limited avenues through which ordinary people came to attention of the nineteenth-century West Indian press and does not at all imply any particular propensity among the African immigrants to engage in criminal activity or encounter legal problems. Indeed, the summary of Supreme Court proceedings published in June 1868 reveals a fair amount of nonwhite ethnic diversity among those accused and demonstrates how at least a crude understanding of the salience of ethnic subgroups within the African community formed a part of routine local knowledge. In addition to the cases of Jim Yaraba and the two Congos, the summary included four men identified as "Coolie," two as Chinese, and an accused arsonist, Eller Jean Baptiste, who was identified with the adjective African following his name.[25] The remaining ten names had no such qualifications and presumably belonged to people of African descent or perhaps, as with Antonio Daiva, to an immigrant from Venezuela or the Cape Verde islands. Most important for this study, the apparent Yoruba and Congo ethnicity of three of these prisoners warranted no particular attention in the published report but rather seemed to have formed an ordinary component of African immigrant identity in this era. As in the case of Albert African, the likely ages of such people accused of theft and assault all but confirms their status as liberated Africans and not former slaves. Indeed, in 1871, the *Trinidad Chronicle* described one accused murderer named Joe Yaraba as "scarcely more than a boy."[26] (I am assuming here that African-born people—and perhaps their children—were the people most likely to use such surnames.[27])

Beyond this basic evidence of ethnic identification, some of the more colorful cases reported in the press further demonstrate that these African cultural groups enjoyed not simply recognition but also an acceptance as nationalities like any other—European or African—that were understood to have unusual characteristics of their own. Such concepts of cultural identity arose twice in proceedings before the San Fernando police court during cases of alleged verbal abuse which, although informative for this study, also produced courtroom debates bordering on the absurd. In November 1867, Elizabeth Louis faced a charge of verbally abusing a police constable named Moorley. Specifically, Constable Moorley claimed that Elizabeth had called him a "d_____d Yaraba brute." He explained to the court that on the day in question a plantain seller had improperly brought his boat up on to the wharf. He, as a constable, instructed the vendor to remove the boat. Elizabeth, who was buying plantains from the seller, became annoyed at this order and thus allegedly hurled the "Yaraba" insult at Moorley. The newspaper account of the trial does not indicate whether the policeman was in fact a Yoruba, although the reporter noted that Moorley had required the assistance of an interpreter to make his complaint. Furthermore, a witness for the defense named Peter Irish claimed that Elizabeth had directed the offending words not at the constable but at him. The magistrate rejected this testimony when Irish admitted upon cross-examination that he was not a Yoruba.[28] This decision implied that the court would accept the integrity of the insult only if was properly directed at a Yoruba person. (Irish also damaged his credibility by giving contradictory details in his description of the altercation.) Ultimately, Magistrate Warner adjudged the offense as "not a great one" and fined Elizabeth two shillings.

The second case, which came before the same magistrate four months later, prompted an even more poignant and amusing commentary on the currency of separate African ethnicities in nineteenth-century Trinidad. In this matter, George Melville, the wharf master at the Guaracara dock in southern Trinidad, accused a boat captain identified only as Douglas of having called him "a d____d fool" and "a Congo fool" during an argument about the unloading of some barrels. In response to this testimony, Magistrate Warner inquired of Melville: "Is Congo famous for the stupidity of its fools?"—a question that seems to have remained unanswered! The court eventually dismissed Melville's complaint, apparently concluding that the two men had equally insulted one another, witnesses for the defense having testified that the wharf master had called Captain Douglas "a black son of a b____."[29] What is most striking is that neither the magistrate nor the newspaper reporter found anything worthy of comment in the fact that the participants in both of these incidents chose to assail one another with particularized African ethnic slurs. Acknowledgment of communities defined as Yaraba and Congo clearly formed a part of Trinidadian popular consciousness in this era. The prevalence of references to specifically Yoruba and Congo communities as opposed to other African ethnicities reflects the fact that people broadly defined as Yoruba and Congo made up the two largest ethnic groupings among the liberated African immigrants.

Further evidence that the Yoruba and Congo communities were distinct ethnic presences emerges from a comparison of the insult cases described above with a similar incident that occurred in June 1885. In this case, which was recounted in a letter to the *New Era* newspaper, an unnamed woman received a fine of seven shillings for calling a man "a Zulu thief" and using other obscene language toward him. Unlike the Yaraba and Congo incidents, this trial seems not to have prompted any discussion, facetious or otherwise, concerning the nature of Zulu personality or the ethnicities of the people involved in the dispute.[30] Rather, on this occasion the adjective Zulu seems to have carried a more vague implication, possibly referring generically to a person of presumed African birth. Where these former insults had made reference to groups that formed a part of Trinidadian society, the Zulu remark had no such salience. Zulu people did not form a part of the local population either of liberated Africans or former slaves.

More direct evidence of the reality of Yoruba and Congo communities among Trinidad's free African immigrants arises from newspaper reports of matters more serious than these exchanges of verbal abuse. For example, during an island-wide outbreak of smallpox in 1872, a correspondent from the southeastern district of Mayaro reported the death of a girl whom he described as "one of a fine family of what we call creole Yarabas."[31] One can only speculate about the specific meaning attached to the phrase "creole Yarabas." But even without such clarification, the remarks of the Mayaro correspondent add to the portrait of a society in which African ethnic divisions constituted significant social subgroups. A particularly striking glimpse of residential and social communities involving people of Kongo ethnicity emerges from reports of two murders committed near sugar estates in southern Trinidad in 1867. One morning in September a group of three Congos traveled to San Fernando to inform police that someone had killed a "countryman of theirs" in woods next to Cupar Grange Estate. In journeying to the reported scene of the crime, a group of policemen encountered a fourth Congo man whom they enlisted as a guide to direct them to the body. However, when the three original informants joined them, they singled out the guide as the person they suspected of the murder. The police arrested this man and upon further investigation discovered a newly fired gun at his house and learned through witnesses that he had previously threatened the victim. According to the testimony received, the alleged killer's daughter had recently died after accusing the murdered man of having poisoned her. The authorities thus interpreted the matter as a killing motivated by revenge. Two weeks after the arrest, in a preliminary inquiry, the San Fernando police court ruled that the arrested man, now identified as "Tony, an African," should stand trial for the murder of Simon Congo, the deceased.[32] The details of the murder reveal nothing remarkable, but the unfolding of the incident after the crime points to the existence at Cupar Grange Estate of at least a small and to some degree self-contained community of Kongo people. Non-Kongo people certainly lived around the Cupar Grange plantation, and anybody, perhaps most logically a person of authority, such as an overseer, might have reported the crime to the San Fernando police. The *Chronicle* account, however, implied that the three-man delegation that summoned the authorities took this responsibility as "countrymen" of the victim and in some way as representatives of the community most affected by the murder. By turning to the official authorities, the Kongo group demonstrated that they did not hold such an independent view of themselves as to have attempted to conceal the incident or to initiate retribution on their own. Or if they did hold that view, they recognized that, in pragmatic terms, their ethnic subgroup inescapably formed a part of the wider colonial society.[33]

Yet even in the context of entanglements with the New World environment, evidence exists not just of African ethnic communities but also of even finer cultural distinctions within such groups. In December 1867, a second murder occurred among people of Kongo ethnicity near an estate called Mount Pleasant outside the town of Pointe-a-Pierre, approximately three miles north of San Fernando. The *Chronicle* account explained: "William Grey, the murdered man, was a Congo, and the murderer is Jim or James Congo, one of his countrymen, but belonging to another tribe."[34] At first glance, this explanation of the motive for the crime seems confusing, given the typical western understanding of the concept of a tribe. Most popular definitions of the concept would construe the entire group of people called Congo as a single tribe. However, these broad ethnic collectivities usually encompassed thousands of people who shared similar but not identical cultural backgrounds and who viewed themselves first as members of their own local or regional variation of the broad group. This is why in response the inquiries posed by officials at the Havana mixed commission, liberated Africans identified themselves as Congo or Lucumí (Yoruba) and other broad ethnic labels but then modified those labels with the variety of suffixes.

Furthermore, as dramatically demonstrated in the nineteenth-century Yoruba wars and in the disintegration of the Kongo kingdom, the sharing of similar language and culture within these wide ethnic groupings did not at all preclude distrust, competition, or even violence between the different subgroups. Quite the contrary, their diverse cultural, social, and political associations with one another often provided the very basis for conflict. In the Caribbean, as elsewhere in the Americas, the broader African ethnic categories gained significance because of the new aggregations of people created by the slave trade. In other words, different Kongo peoples who may have never encountered one another in Africa became "countrymen" in Trinidad by dint of their new shared experience and their similar African past. However, the report of the murder near Pointe-a-Pierre offers a rare piece of evidence that among Trinidad's nineteenth-century free African immigrants, the more nuanced ethnic distinctions also remained salient. No available information directly states that an intra-Congo dispute provided the motive for the Mount Pleasant murder, and indeed the assailant and his victim may have quarreled over some mundane matter. Nevertheless, the newspaper description of the relationship between the two men gives a brief view of the ways that at least some African immigrants formed communities that remained attentive to ethnic complexities beyond a more generically understood status as the last major group of African-born arrivals in the West Indies.

British officials concerned with the effectiveness of liberated Africans as laborers in Trinidad also took some notice of the manifestations of ethnic differences among these immigrants. In 1851, during the height of organized recruitment of liberated Africans as laborers, Dr. Stephen Mitchell, the Trinidad superintendent of immigrants, prepared a report in which he outlined what he perceived as behavioral differences between Congo and Yoruba people already present in the island as imported agricultural workers. Mitchell did not complain of the performance of either group in their work but lamented the mixed success of efforts to provide them with religious and secular education and encourage them to adopt western social norms. He explained that a large part of the problem facing such efforts lay in the diverse and isolated locations of the plantations where the Africans labored. The superintendent also complained of "the character of the Yaribab [*sic*] Africans" who allegedly expected payment for attendance at church or school, just as they received compensation for the other activities (i.e. plantation work) required of them by their new colonial masters. The expectation of payment betrays the fact that although the British viewed themselves as the benevolent rescuers and civilizers of liberated Africans, the Africans understood their experience much differently. For them, it was an experience largely free of the coercion and violence of chattel slavery but nonetheless an involuntary experiment in life under European rule. Mitchell did not address this implied criticism of British policy. Rather, he continued his attempt to summarize different African ethnic behavior patterns as follows:

> The men of this [Yoruba] tribe are said to be fierce and intemperate and the women averse to marriage. Some of the children, however, especially Congoes are receiving instruction—a few at the parish school of Saint Paul's and others from persons in charge of the Estates or their families.[35]

While these descriptions seem stereotypical and would prove impossible to systematically verify or discredit, like most generalizations, they probably contained some degree of truth. Perhaps Yorubas did stand out as expressing greatest resistance to Christian conversion and attempts at their anglicization. At the very least, the Mitchell report indicates that among the immigrant Africans, people from different ethnic groups did not simply identify and perhaps live with one another but also sometimes behaved both collectively and distinctively as they determined how to respond to their new life in the Caribbean.

Another strong indication of the existence of significant African ethnic communities in nineteenth-century Trinidad comes from the continuing currency of such ethnic identifications well into the twentieth century. Although references to people of specific African ethnic backgrounds no longer appear in the Trinidad press or in the daily conversation of ordinary people, a few older Trinidadians still express familiarity with such categorizations and recall periods up to roughly the middle of the twentieth century when many people still identified themselves with such labels. For example, in an interview conducted in 1994, one resident of the village of Caratal, located in south-central Trinidad, used the ethnic adjective Araba or Yaraba in discussing the history of the local community during her lifetime. However, when asked directly what she knew about "different kinds of African people," she offered little further, explaining that other local inhabitants would possibly know more than she did about this subject.[36] Linguist Maureen Warner-Lewis has pioneered research on the persistence of the Yoruba language in Trinidad until the twentieth century. During the 1960s and early 1970s, Warner-Lewis interviewed elderly people who still used the language and identified themselves, their families, and sometimes their neighbors as descendants of Yoruba people.[37] It is not surprising that the people interviewed did not specifically discuss the schemes of liberated African immigration that occurred between the 1830s and 1860s. However since these twentieth-century people spoke of grandparents who had come to Trinidad directly from Africa, the roots of their family histories could only lie in the post-emancipation era and not during the years of slavery.[38]

Nevertheless, not all modern references to African ethnicity in Trinidad hearken back to this kind of differentiation among nineteenth-century liberated Africans. One example that illustrates this point appears in the work of a University of the West Indies student who conducted local history research in the south Trinidad villages of Lengua and Barrackpore during 1975. In Barrackpore, Andrew Ali found an area bearing the name Congo Hill. According to Ali, many people believed that "Africans [who had] run away from plantations" had settled at this location, thus the unique name. One of his informants even claimed to have known an elderly African man who had lived at Congo Hill and had corroborated this story. Other Barrackpore residents, however, contradicted this version of events and insisted that East Indians had named the area using the adjective Congo to refer generally to residents of African descent. The people in question did not have any particular history—they were not necessarily African-born or even descended from the most recent African immigrants, let alone members of the Congo ethnic group.[39] Ali accepts this explanation as the correct one, although he does not say why he arrived at this conclusion. The presence of the label Congo certainly seems suggestive, given the prominence of this group among the liberated Africans. However, Ali's account of the looser use of the adjective Congo among some Barrackpore residents illustrates the speculative character of many deductions made in the twentieth century about the origins of such naming patterns. All the same, a preponderance of evidence from both the nineteenth century and more recent times clearly points to the formation of significant ethnically defined communities by both Yoruba and Congo people within Trinidad's population of liberated Africans.

Contemporary Trinidad has also sustained a small but prominent community founded by liberated Africans from an ethnic group represented in somewhat smaller numbers than the Yoruba and Kongo: the Rada. During the seventeenth, eighteenth, and nineteenth centuries, Europeans and eventually some Africans used the terms Rada or Arada to refer to people from the area of the kingdom of Dahomey, which now roughly encompasses the southern half of Benin. Modern anthropologists would characterize such people as belonging to the Fon cultural group. Since at least the 1870s, outside observers have commented upon the presence of a community of people identifying themselves as Radas in the neighborhood of Belmont in eastern Port-of-Spain. These people have gained most attention because of their continued practice of African-derived religious rites, which are similar to Haitian vodun, Cuban santería, or Brazilian candomble. Nineteenth-century journalists and other observers called these practices obeah, or black magic. Since the middle of the twentieth century, both local and international scholars, including anthropologist Melville Herskovits, have attempted to study the group to better understand the African-derived content of their beliefs. Descriptions of the Radas of Belmont have portrayed them as a quasi-endogamous community that (like so many African societies) carried on their religion as a part of a holistic system. In addition to the sacred ceremonies for Fon spirits, various Rada social institutions guided their everyday life.

The most striking documented example of the partially self-contained secular life of the Rada community involved the conviction of two men for the theft of money from a kind of Rada community chest in 1874. A man called Cocombre and an accomplice stole the entire box of money containing the fund. The *Trinidad Chronicle* summarized the case in November 1876 in an article that covered the escape of Cocombre from a prison work gang on which he served. According to the newspaper, the Radas kept the community chest "as a mutual sick, lying-in and burial fund, built up of very small payments." The *Chronicle* reported that after the robbery, the people charged with supervising the fund adopted a policy of burying the collection box and changing its location frequently to prevent future trouble. In conclusion, the writer noted that the colony possessed a "savings bank" at the public treasury where the Radas might have secured their money. He speculated, however, that "in their ignorance they either [could] not understand or mistrust[ed] it."[40] Perhaps the Radas did mistrust the British colonial government and its institutions. They certainly had grounds for such an attitude given the prevailing system of labor exploitation and social discrimination, which was in large part dictated by white European racism. But very likely, the leaders of the ethnic enclave simply did not conceive of any external institution—even a trustworthy one—as an appropriate means of supervising a Rada community fund. Through this fund, as through their residential closeness and their religious rites, these liberated Africans (and later their descendants) demonstrated a commitment to maintaining the integrity of their particular ethnic identity within the cosmopolitan context of their life in the diaspora.

The Radas of Belmont provide an especially instructive example through which to consider the role of numeric predominance in the formation of ethnic African communities in the Americas. Some scholars of the African diaspora have speculated that during the years of slavery larger numbers of one ethnic group would have led to the prominence of their cultural inputs in the formation of various African-American cultures. While this argument has merit, even its proponents point out that under appropriate circumstances, African ethnic groups represented in smaller numbers within a given New World population also had the opportunity to leave a definitive cultural mark or to organize themselves collectively in ways similar to the groups most numerously represented.[41] The Trinidad Rada community dramatically illustrates this point, having been founded by liberated Africans among whom people from the area of Dahomey did not constitute one of the two largest ethnic groups. We can surmise that the formation of such a community required only a minimum number of founding members. In other words, Rada people did not have to dominate or permeate the liberated African population as the Yoruba and Congo apparently did—they simply had to exist in sufficient numbers to sustain their Belmont enclave. And using the records of the Havana mixed commission as a rough guide for speculation, people from Dahomey variously described as Arara or Mina Popo certainly formed a not-insignificant presence. However, historians and anthropologists still face a challenge in attempting to explain why this particular community—more than any other African ethnic enclave founded in the nineteenth century—has survived with such strength and visibility to the present day.

A large part of that explanation probably lies in the dedication and interest in history of the extended family that has led the Belmont group for most of its existence. The nineteenth-century newspaper references to the Radas of Belmont gave no clear indication of the size of the population, but they painted a picture of a community with meaningful leadership, not simply a loosely organized religious and residential collectivity. The most dramatic publicity surrounded a man called Robert or John Antoine, also known as Nannee, who served as a Rada spiritual leader from the 1870s through the 1890s. In 1886, a local court convicted Antoine on a charge of practicing obeah because of his pursuit of Fon-derived religious practices both for the Radas and for other people who sought supernatural assistance, for example in cases of illness. (According to the *New Era,* papers seized at the Antoine home included "lists of names of some of the leading citizens of Port-of-Spain.")[42] Antoine, however, won a reversal of this conviction on appeal. His lawyer argued that the Rada leader did not engage in black magic or supernatural chicanery for money but in fact functioned as a religious leader according to the beliefs of his followers. Historian Bridget Brereton explains that the law passed in 1868 to ban the practice of obeah defined it as "the assumption of supernatural powers for the purpose of making money."[43] Antoine's appeal contended that this law could not apply to the Rada leader any more than it could to a Christian priest.[44] Even without the surprising success of the appeal, this case demonstrated the role of Antoine as a leader for the Rada group in matters of supernatural practice. Subsequent oral history has portrayed him in an even richer role as founder of the community and its virtual headman until his death. It also confirms the creation of the community as a product of the migration of liberated Africans.

Led by folklorist Andrew Carr, whose article "A Rada Community in Trinidad" appeared in *Caribbean Quarterly* in 1953, scholars have studied Rada oral history from Belmont for over half a century. The material Carr collected in the early 1950s remains the most detailed source of information about the beginnings of the group. Carr interviewed diverse Belmont inhabitants, but most important, he spoke at length with Henry Antoine, the son of Robert, the founder. Henry provided Carr with details about his father's life in Africa prior to his coming to Trinidad and about his establishment as a Rada leader at Belmont. Henry estimated that Robert arrived in Trinidad directly from Africa during the mid-1850s, which fact alone—even allowing for a significant margin of error—would situate him within the liberated African population. Reputedly born in the town of Ouidah around the turn of the century, Robert served in the army of the kingdom of Dahomey. Henry's account implied, but did not state directly, that his father ended up among Africans transported to the Caribbean as a result of some failed military expedition. The broad details of his story thus fit well with known patterns of the nineteenth-century slave trade. After at first working on a plantation east of the capital, Antoine moved to Port-of-Spain, where in 1868 he purchased a plot of land in Belmont, constructed his home, took a common-law wife, and began his family.[45] He had not served as any kind of priest in Dahomey but did come from a "priestly class" and knew the art of divination. This background apparently helped to propel him to his status as a religious leader among people of his ethnicity in Trinidad. Also, if, as Henry reported, Robert arrived in Trinidad as a fully grown adult, perhaps as old as 50, he would have likely also gained stature by virtue of his seniority among the African immigrant population. (The statistics gathered at the Havana mixed commission suggest an average age between 18 and 20 years for those 10,000 liberated Africans as a group, with many children aged 16 and younger and very few people over the age of 30.)[46] Henry also explained that at the time his father arrived in Belmont, another group of Radas had already established a settlement, or "compound."[47] Thus when people in the late nineteenth century spoke of the Radas of Belmont, they most likely referred to both groups, not solely to the Antoine family and the people who eventually looked to Robert Antoine as a spiritual leader.

Precisely how Antoine's following developed is not clear. Carr explains that according to Henry, Robert Antoine gave his primary allegiance to one Fon spirit called "Dangbwe," while the other compound gave its allegiances to another called "Sakpata."[48] Such divisions exist in many West African cultures; individuals or groups have special relationships with particular spirits in the context of a single religious system. Alternately, the two Rada compounds at Belmont may have reflected some other cultural distinctions within the larger classification such as the various subgroups of the Yoruba and Kongo discussed above. Yet the portrayal of Robert Antoine at his trial and in other press reports consistently suggested that he alone served as the most prominent Rada leader in the capital.[49] Outsiders simply may not have known the details of intra-Rada relations inside Belmont, and a full exploration of those details lies beyond the scope of this study. But even without this exploration, it remains clear that free Africans of this ethnicity, like Yoruba and Kongo people elsewhere in the island, chose to form and maintain a community among themselves. There is no way to check the identity and origins of everyone who identified themselves as Rada and participated in religious ceremonies or other group activities, such as the bank, during the late nineteenth century. The community almost certainly did not remain the exclusive province of liberated Africans. With Trinidad's population of over 20,000 former slaves, some of Rada background who were not liberated Africans very probably also found their way to the Belmont compound. However, as demonstrated in the person of Robert Antoine, the African immigrants who arrived latest formed the core of the group. Andrew Carr also recorded the story of another well-known Rada woman named Ahoorloo who had reputedly used Fon spiritual powers to help sailors survive a storm during her voyage to Trinidad aboard an "English sailing ship." Because of this incident, Ahoorloo arrived in the island, and eventually in Belmont, with an already "established reputation" for having a powerful relationship with the Rada spirit world.[50] This description of her journey and arrival, along with the claim that she came from Dahomey "around the year 1855" clearly identifies Ahoorloo, like Robert Antoine, as a liberated African.

These free immigrants came to Trinidad with diverse African ethnic identities, and in a variety of situations they continued to so identify themselves—not often with the prominence and longevity of the Rada enclave but regularly enough to confirm the importance of such self-identification. The persistence of these ethnic divisions does not seem to have implied that they were isolated either from one another or from other segments of the African-descended population. By all accounts, Belmont was a bustling and ever-growing neighborhood made up of people of African descent with various social backgrounds. It is interesting that Carr labels other sections of the Belmont neighborhood as having been inhabited by "Mandingoes," "Iboes," or "Congoes" and their descendants.[51] No information exists with which to explore the origins of these enclaves in a manner similar to the explorations carried out for the Rada settlement. Although Carr's interview notes include some references to people of non-Rada ancestry, these other Belmont groups have not attracted much written attention either from nineteenth-century journalists or from twentieth-century historians and anthropologists because they apparently did not produce well-organized and lasting communities. The image of the different subneighborhoods on the Carr map, however, provides a visual metaphor that is useful for understanding the role of different African ethnic allegiances in the experience of many liberated Africans in Trinidad. These African immigrants lived both separately and together: separately according to their ethnic identification but together with other Africans of different ethnic groups and surrounded by the wider African-descended population, most of whose members no longer claimed any specific African ethnicity. The continued acknowledgment of particular African ethnicities by some liberated Africans functioned not as grounds for separatism but rather as an additional complexity in the way these unique free African immigrants fit into the African diaspora in the Caribbean.

In the Bahamas, similar evidence exists that shows liberated Africans expressing their membership in particular ethnic groups in a variety of ways, often many years after their arrival as immigrants. Some evidence arises from the work of late-nineteenth-century travel writers who sought through their publications to chronicle their journeys and provide amateur geographic and anthropological accounts that functioned at least in part as informational texts for other potential tourists. One indirect but very suggestive reference to the cultural behavior of immigrant Africans appears in an 1880 work entitled *The Isles of Summer,* written by New Haven lawyer Charles Ives. In describing the areas near the city of Nassau "occupied by colored people," Ives wrote: "Some [of these people], it is said, still use their native African dialects, and harbor some of their old superstitions."[52] Given that Ives wrote over seventy years after the end of the legal slave trade, one can only suspect that these speakers of African languages had arrived at some later period—in other words, that they had arrived as liberated Africans. Meanwhile the pluralization of the word "dialect" clearly implies that different groups of Africans maintained separate linguistic identities within the "colored" communities in question. And in fact, several years after the publication of *The Isles of Summer,* another North American travel account addressed this linguistic issue in more detail and left no doubt as to the liberated African origins of the Nassau residents who still spoke African languages. It explicitly described the presence of separate African ethnic groups among such speakers.

A Winter Picnic, published in 1888, described the experiences of four women visitors to the island of New Providence for several months between 1886 and 1887. In one of the many discussions of their encounters with the majority black population, the New England authors J. and E. E. Dickinson and S. E. Dowd explained:

> There are many native Africans here who distinctly remember the land of their birth. These speak their own language for the most part, and understand us but little better than we understand them. Nangoes, Congoes, Congars, or Nangobars, the Almanack calls them, but Nango and Egba are the only ones we have found.[53]

The comment here about the "Almanack" suggests that these travelers consulted a nineteenth-century reference text that listed different African ethnicities present in the Bahamas during the late nineteenth century. If such a work did exist, it would imply that in the Bahamas, as in Trinidad, the names of diverse African ethnic groups had some degree of popular currency, such that to speak of "Congoes," "Nangoes [Yorubas]," or "Egbas" did not constitute a novelty but was a normal feature of the local cultural landscape. It is possible that these authors read an African almanac or one that spoke in general of the presence of different ethnic Africans in the Americas. Whatever the case, the names of these different African ethnic groups certainly appeared with regularity in the experiences of the four women travelers, and their account presents a picture of language retention and hints at some sense of collective identification among these groups. In perhaps its most striking descriptions, the book highlights several individual African characters such as Aunt Peace, a Nango fruit vendor "brought from Africa long ago," and Ellen Darkholm, another Nango who still did not understand spoken English "very well." (Or at least she did not understand the English of the North American tourists!) Both of these women still bore their Yoruba scarification, which predictably fascinated the New England visitors: Aunt Peace with "parallel scars upon her cheeks" and Ellen Darkholm with "scarred on cheeks and forehead."[54] Dickinson and Dowd described similar markings on local Egba people and referred to one Egba woman "whose front teeth had each been filed to a point." Yet more significant than these physical observations, the authors reported evidence of group organization among the Egba. They described this ethnic class as seeming less numerous than others but explained that nonetheless the group had a woman whom they designated as a queen.[55] The authors did not elaborate about what functions, symbolic or material, this queen might have performed. In fact, they made light of her as more a "Queen of Rags." But whatever her role, the selection of such a figure demonstrates that even as Egba immigrants lived among the wider nonwhite population of Nassau and its environs they continued to view themselves as a specially defined subset of that larger whole.

Little question exists about the fact that these Egbas and the other "native Africans" described by Dickinson and Dowd belonged to the liberated African population. Their African birth alone suggests their membership in this category, given the late date in the nineteenth century at which the travelers encountered them. These authors characterized some of the Egbas as "wonderfully old," but almost eighty years after the end of legal slave importation, one would have to characterize anyone who had survived from that era as phenomenally or even implausibly aged. Perhaps a handful of former slaves might have had such longevity, but the account of Dickinson and Dowd and those of other travelers give a clear impression of many Africans, not simply a handful. Furthermore, one of the Yorubas interviewed actually spoke explicitly of having arrived in the Bahamas after a British man-of-war captured the Spanish slave ship that had taken him from Africa. *A Winter Picnic* provided an awkward transcription of his speech: "'Paniard 'teal me fum t'ibe; two ships; one T'under; man-wah take we fum 'Paniard. Lan' we cum fust, Jamaica; den take we Inagua; Inagua—we here."[56] No doubt if the authors had spoken more extensively with other Africans—ideally with a less haphazard arrangement for language translation and interpretation—they would have heard even more such tales.

Much more evidence exists of ethnic community-building among these people. Nineteenth-century accounts indicate that the selection of a queen, as the New England women reported for the Egba people, occurred in a variety of African ethnic groups in the Bahamas. L. D. Powles, who served as a circuit justice in the Bahamas during late 1880s, published his memoirs of this period in a volume entitled *Land of the Pink Pearl.* Under the heading "Manners and Customs" Powles wrote: "The Africans still retain their tribal distinctions, and are divided into Yorubas, Egbas, Ebos, Congos, &c. Every August some of these tribes elect a queen whose will is law on certain matters."[57] This description points to collective activity by several ethnic groups, and the concluding comment about the will of the queen suggests that such individuals may have provided meaningful leadership role for the groups involved, perhaps some lesser version of the role Robert Antoine fulfilled for the Belmont Radas in Trinidad. Unfortunately, Powles does not clarify which matters the queens may have presided over.[58] A more detailed sense of the annual activities related to the selection of queens emerges from a newspaper account of one election in February 1885 that was reported under the headline "Crowning of the Eboe Queen." The event took place on the morning of Mardi Gras, although nothing in the report indicates that this date had any particular significance. The overwhelmingly Protestant Bahamas had no major tradition of Mardi Gras street celebrations. The *Nassau Guardian* reporter did not specifically describe a procession but did refer to crowds of spectators gathering in the streets. The festivities culminated when the chosen queen arrived via carriage at the hall of the Grant's Town Friendly Society. A gentleman escorted her inside "and conducted [her] to [a] throne at the Eastern end of the building." After a half-hour ceremony, also not described in any detail by the reporter, the gathering switched over to celebratory dancing.[59]

Despite the sparseness of description in some respects, this newspaper account contains a wealth of significant detail about the process of community-building among liberated Africans in the Bahamas. The Grant's Town Friendly Society belonged to a group of similar "friendly societies" established in the Bahamas and elsewhere in the Caribbean during the decades following slave emancipation. Like lodges, burial societies, and similar organizations, these groups took collective responsibility for expenses such as funerals and medical care and even arranged pensions or savings accounts on behalf of their membership. They also sponsored social, religious, and civic

activities designed to strengthen the post-emancipation free black communities. In this case, the name Grant's Town referred to a village located on
the outskirts of Nassau that was known as an area where liberated Africans
settled. In fact, the government of the Bahamas had specifically developed
this settlement for the location of African immigrants. When liberated
Africans began arriving in the Bahamas in 1811, many worked in domestic
or other occupations in and around the Nassau capital. On the very small island of New Providence, even those with agricultural employment often
wanted to live near the town. As mentioned in chapter 1, the settlement of
Carmichael, seven miles south of Nassau, was settled in 1824 by a group of
liberated Africans apparently after they had completed their terms of indentured employment. The less rural Grant's Town emerged a year later. According to various accounts, Africans from Carmichael moved in order to
reestablish themselves closer to Nassau. They thus "migrated . . . to a rocky
tract of waste land located south of the town of Nassau, bordered by the
Blue Hills."[60] The outlying Carmichael Village allowed access to land for
subsistence cultivation, but this advantage failed to fully satisfy some of the
residents. Perhaps they sought more lucrative employment in domestic
work or trade in and around the capital. Most of the Carmichael settlers
would have worked at such pursuits for three to seven years after their arrival under terms of indenture. Perhaps some of these people had shipmates, friends, or other personal connections in the urban area. Whatever
the motivation, a significant group of the immigrants effectively initiated a
kind of African suburb; they formed a squatter community just outside the
town. Apparently in response to this initiative, local authorities decided that
it would be appropriate to establish a formal African settlement in that location. Thus, in May of 1825, Charles Poitier, the collector of customs, who
was officially responsible for the welfare of liberated Africans, purchased
400 acres of land at that site. Surveyor J. J. Burnside divided the parcel into
quarter-acre lots that liberated African immigrants could buy at a rate of ten
shillings per lot, or two pounds per acre.[61] So began the process of formal
settlement, not only by Africans migrating from Carmichael but also by the
addition of new arrivals from other captured slave ships through the early
1840s. This arrangement obviously provided fruitful grounds for community formation across various African ethnic lines. And the existence of the
Grant's Town Friendly Society suggests that this did indeed occur.

The 1885 *Guardian* report about the "Eboe Queen" also indicated that
Africans in the Bahamas formed such societies within their separate ethnic
boundaries. The authors of *A Winter Picnic* and *Land of the Pink Pearl* described the annual selection of queens by different African "tribes" without
reference to any specific "tribal" organization. However, the *Nassau Guard-*

ian account pointed specifically to an "Eboe Society" as the body responsible for making the coronation. In fact, newspaper reports during this period made many references to the activities of ethnically constituted friendly societies, often concerning their collective participation in religious celebrations. For example, in May 1886, the *Guardian* reported that "members of the Egba, Yoruba and Co-Operative Societies" had gone together to hear a sermon at Bethel Baptist Chapel. In January 1887, the paper reported that "members of the Congo societies" had "marched in procession" to attend service at Christ Church Cathedral. On one occasion in 1888, the *Guardian* even announced in advance that "the members of the Nangobar Friendly Society" would visit the cathedral on the following Wednesday.[62] These notices first and foremost give evidence of very deliberate ethnic association among liberated Africans in the Bahamas. The perfunctory tone of the announcements also suggests that, as in Trinidad, some understanding and acceptance of these African ethnic distinctions had become a part of the wider Bahamian culture in this era. Local British officials in the Bahamas also commented on the possible significance of ethnic distinctions among their nineteenth-century African immigrant population. In the mid-1870s a colonial secretary's report on the Bahamian colony included an abstract of census data (from 1861 and 1871) that commented specifically on the different "*races* [my emphasis] of native born Africans" in the territory, including seven groups: Yorubas (or Nangoes), Congoes (or Nangobars), Eboes, Mandingos, Fullalis (Fulas), and Hausas.[63] According to the report, only Yorubas, Congos, and Eboes were present in large enough groups to allow any generalizations about group characteristics. Like the analysis of the Trinidad superintendent of immigrants cited above, this census abstract set out a problematic series of traits supposedly attributable to these different cultural groups, comparing them both with one another and with the "native born Negroes." The Congo people, who had fared quite well in the Trinidad report, in this case ended up portrayed as "decidedly inferior . . . stunted in body, mind and morals."[64] The Yoruba, who had earned unflattering characterizations from Trinidad's Dr. Mitchell, received lavish praise in this Bahamas delineation of alleged ethnic behavior patterns:

> The Yorubas (or Nangoes) are very intelligent, hardworking and honest. The secret of their success is that they are industrious and self-denying i.e. will always spend a little less than they make. Quite the reverse of the Native Born negroes who is [*sic*] ignorant and most unthrifty. The Yoruba prefer huckstering to agriculture, delighting in selling in the market hawking about fowls and keeping shops. As traders their command of credit is better than that of any race. This race alone has organizations here.[65]

The author of this census abstract either made an error or a deliberate misrepresentation with the claim that only the Yoruba had their own social organizations in the Bahamas. However, this official description is interesting not because of the flawed quality of the generalizations but because the specific cultural or ethnic backgrounds of liberated Africans had a routine and presumed salience in the Bahamas of the late nineteenth century. Beyond stereotyping the Yoruba as models of industriousness, the census summary also characterized the Ebo as occupying a kind of middle ground physically and mentally, "as inferior in intelligence and physique to the Mandingo and Yoruba as they [were] superior to the Congo."[66] The writer also alluded to the potential for conflict among the African-born on the basis of their different ethnic backgrounds but reported that he knew of no "violence or faction fights" of this sort in the Bahamas. He suggested that one might find more information about "warlike" behavior between different African groups on the African continent,[67] yet he did not point out the obvious fact that within Africa different social and cultural groupings fought wars for economic, social, and political reasons similar to those that led to wars in other regions of the world. In fact, notable conflict between African ethnic groups seems not to have occurred within the liberated African community in either the Bahamas or Trinidad, according to available descriptive records. Assertions about their African ethnic identities were a peaceful and routine part of how these immigrants presented themselves and how others perceived them.

Like Trinidad, the Bahamas presents more recent legacies of this complex African cultural presence from the nineteenth century. While the Bahamian capital of Nassau does not boast an internationally studied community of liberated African descendants such as the Radas of Belmont, it does have two neighborhoods that have distinct reputations related to their historic settlement by specific African ethnic groups. According to oral history informants ranging in age between 50 and 90 years, up until the middle of the twentieth century, people referred to a small area south of Grant's Town by the unusual name of Conta Butta. According to the older informants, this name constituted a unique dialect pronunciation of the original name of the settlement, Congo Borough, which reportedly indicated the Kongo ethnicity of its original inhabitants in the nineteenth century, presumably liberated Africans, given the largely creole character of the Bahamian slave population at the time of emancipation. One informant asserted that he had heard that the name had formerly held negative connotations, because Yoruba people and other African ethnic groups looked down on their Kongo neighbors.[68] Such an attitude would prove difficult if not impossible to verify. But whether other people despised or admired the Kongos, the reputation of Conta Butta indicates that the town of Nassau had at least one self-identified and publicly identified Kongo ethnic community. It also seems important to note that the location of Conta Butta lay immediately south of Grant's Town, which placed it in the area of heaviest black middle- and working-class settlement on the southwestern edges of the capital. Thus, even as the Kongo identification remained important to the residents of the small enclave (and to their neighbors), they also lived within the wider African and African-descended community.

An even stronger demonstration of this demographic and social pattern emerges from the oral history regarding the village of Fox Hill, which is situated approximately five miles east of the town of Nassau. Some confusion exists in colonial records of land grants concerning the exact dates of earliest settlement of Fox Hill and the neighboring village of Sandilands. However, a combination of oral history and the correspondence of colonial governors and some missionary records indicates that in the middle of the nineteenth century Fox Hill saw significant growth and development with residents consisting of a mixture of Africans and recently emancipated slaves.[69] A series of neighborhoods (called towns) existed within the village—some of which residents can still point out today—bearing the names either of a prominent inhabitant or an African ethnic group: Congo Town, Nango (Yoruba) Town, Joshua Town, and Burnside Town.[70] Unfortunately, little evidence, either written or oral, speaks directly to the founding of the towns in the course of the growth of the village. One or two Methodist baptism records from the mid-nineteenth century explicitly identify liberated African individuals who moved to Fox Hill from other parts of the island.[71] The comparatively recent historical presence of African-born people also comes across dramatically in an interview conducted by historian Gail Saunders with an elderly Fox Hill resident (now deceased) in 1970. It is not surprising that Virginia Brice often expressed confusion when asked specific questions about the African names of the towns or the origins of their founders. However, she readily told a story of having heard "two old lady . . . talking in this different language what we just can't understand . . . saying 'A ree, a roo, a ree, a roo.'" Brice explained that she did not believe that the women had come from Africa but rather thought that their parents had arrived as immigrants.[72] Other oral history informants claim with some degree of certainty that in the nineteenth century the ethnically labeled towns consisted of the African-born and their descendants, while the other Fox Hill towns consisted exclusively of former slaves.

Similar to Andrew Carr's map of Belmont, the map of Fox Hill, with its separate but adjacent towns forming a single village, can serve as a symbolic representation for the settlement experience of liberated Africans in both the Bahamas and Trinidad. As some of the largest groups of free Africans ever to enter the Caribbean, these people had unique opportunities to publicly maintain separate African immigrant identities, particularly in the larger Kongo and Yoruba groups. They expressed those identities, however, in the context of lives lived very much within—rather than isolated from—the African-Bahamian and African-Trinidadian communities they had entered.

4

"Assisted by his wife, an African":

Gender, Family, and Household Formation in the Experience of Liberated Africans

Father Marie Bertrand Cothonay, a French priest working in late-nineteenth-century Trinidad, reported a powerful, although brief, tale of a liberated African he met who claimed to be a former member of the "royal family of Angola." This unnamed man told Father Cothonay the story of how he was captured in Africa during a war with a neighboring tribe around 1850. He ended up sold to Portuguese slave traders who intended to transport him to Brazil. However, the British navy captured the vessel, and after a brief stay on the island of Saint Helena, he ended up settled as a free man in Trinidad. Cothonay explained that the reputed prince "intended to marry a black woman, close to his own age, from the same country and transported on the same ship."[1] The prince did not know whether his future bride came from a royal bloodline but intended to proceed with the marriage all the same. One does not know whether the French missionary or the African bridegroom raised the issue of "royal blood" or other criteria for selecting a wife. The priest's journal entry implies that the prince valued his bride's Africanness and her Angolan origins and their shared experience as liberated Africans although he was apparently willing to compromise on the question of having a spouse with an appropriately royal lineage. Other observers during the nineteenth century alluded to the idea that newly arrived Africans may have preferred to marry among themselves.

This idea held interest for British officials. After the abolition of the slave trade in 1807, Great Britain embarked upon an unprecedented era of social experimentation for people of African descent in British colonies. The Africans rescued from illegally operating slave ships—especially those rescued in the thirty years before emancipation—came to be seen by both abolitionists and government authorities as a population with which Britain might rehearse for the realities of Caribbean colonial life after slavery.[2] This spirit of rehearsal involved not only considerations of how to exploit the labor of Africans without the abuses of slavery but also how to shape social relations between free Africans and Europeans and between Africans themselves, which included inevitable efforts to "civilize" the liberated Africans. It is not surprising that a significant element of these visions of social management focused on the household, and often specifically on the lives of women and children.

Historians of slavery all over the Americas have long noted that although slave masters recognized gender distinctions among black laboring populations, they rarely accorded women of African descent any special or protected status based on positive or palliative notions of womanhood. Thus, for example, women worked alongside men according to capability even in the heaviest or most onerous areas of plantation agriculture. And when women worked mostly in other areas, such as domestic service, their assignment to this work was understood as a matter of happenstance or white sufferance, not biological or social destiny.

The 1807 law abolishing the slave trade, specifically those provisions dealing with the treatment of liberated Africans, marked one of the first official ruptures in this pattern for the British Caribbean. The 1807 law and the Orders in Council for its implementation mandated that liberated Africans should serve terms of labor "apprenticeship" in the British colonies where they were settled. However, those 1807 mandates also declared that "females were in no instance to be employed in any of the labors of agriculture, except weeding, picking cotton and provisions and of assisting in the cultivation of the latter."[3] Predictably, this proposed restriction met with opposition from would-be employers and colonial officials assigned to supervise both the employees and the Africans. Reasons for opposition ranged from simple claims of "great inconvenience"[4] to far more elaborate arguments. One argument contended that there simply was not enough domestic work available for women who had only been trained as house servants. Another argument claimed that the exclusion of women from major agricultural labor would lead to their idleness, which would in turn lead to poor child-rearing and other failures of character.[5] The most basic (or cynical) interpretation of these objections would view them simply as rationalizations designed to extract more labor from liberated African women. Over the course of the nineteenth century, through broken and altered laws and regulations, liberated African women in fact performed all manner of extreme physical labor, including sugar cultivation. Nevertheless, the attempt to reserve a "gentler" sphere of women's work for women of African descent evinced an important change in the ideological and social paradigms that

Table 4.1. Gender Ratios among Africans Rescued from Forty-Two
Captured Slave Ships Processed at the Anglo-Spanish Mixed
Commission in Havana, Cuba, 1828–1841

Name of Captured Slave Ship	Male Africans	Female Africans	% Male	% Female	Total Number of Africans
Relampago	92	57	61.74	38.26	149
Isabel	6	4	60.00	40.00	10
Mágico	98	77	56.00	44.00	175
Fingal	40	18	68.97	31.03	58
Orestes	183	29	86.32	13.68	212
Nuevo Campeador	157	54	74.41	25.59	211
Gerges	272	113	70.65	29.35	385
Intrepido	65	68	48.87	51.13	133
Maria	1	—	100.00	—	1
Firme	355	128	73.50	26.50	483
Josefa (alias) Fortuna	124	78	61.39	38.61	202
Boladora	233	97	70.61	29.39	330
Midas	112	96	53.85	46.15	208
Gallito	104	31	77.04	22.96	135
Santiago	36	64	36.00	64.00	100
Emilio (alias) César	85	102	45.45	54.55	187
Planeta	183	53	77.54	22.46	236
Aquila	468	128	78.52	21.48	596
Indagadora	122	12	91.04	8.96	134
Negrito	367	110	76.94	23.06	477
Joaquina	236	82	74.21	25.79	318
Manuelita	412	65	86.37	13.63	477
Rosa	174	115	60.21	39.79	289
Carlota	102	61	62.58	37.42	163
Maria	271	69	79.71	20.29	340
Julita	238	98	70.83	29.17	336
La Joven Reyna	194	60	76.38	23.62	254
Chubasco	146	84	63.48	36.52	230
Marte	257	69	78.83	21.17	326
Fila	257	135	65.56	34.44	392
Amalia	198	2	99.00	1.00	200
Diligencia	70	24	74.47	25.53	94
Minfa (alias) Matanra	310	86	78.28	21.72	396
Ricomar (alias) Zafiro	85	101	45.70	54.30	186

Name of Captured Slave Ship	Male Africans	Female Africans	% Male	% Female	Total Number of Africans
Preciosa	224	66	77.24	22.76	290
Empresa	360	47	88.45	11.55	407
Matilde	155	100	60.78	39.22	255
Anta	150	33	81.97	18.03	183
Sierra del Pilar	100	72	58.14	41.86	172
Caridad Cubana	113	33	77.40	22.60	146
Jesus María	136	38	58.12	41.88	234
Segunda Rosario	207	74	73.67	26.33	281
Grand Totals	7,498	2,893	72.16	27.84	10,391

Source: Derived from Records of the Anglo-Spanish Mixed Commission at Havana, FO 313/56–62. Calculations are by the author. These forty-two ships are not a random sample, but are simply the vessels for which detailed registers were found in records related to the Anglo-Spanish court. The 10,391 Africans from these vessels constitute more than half of all rescued Africans processed in Havana, and almost ten percent of all liberated Africans rescued by the British navy. See chapter 3 for more discussion of this data.

shaped African-Caribbean experience. The labor and social experiences of liberated African women, while they were often harsh and undesirable, did not simply reproduce the negative experiences of their slave forbears. Furthermore, their special treatment under the abolitionist legal regimen illuminates the critical role of gender in shaping the lives of liberated Africans.

Historians have long commented on the gender imbalance that often existed in the transatlantic slave trade of the nineteenth century. In general, the groups of enslaved Africans who arrived in the Americas during this era consisted of approximately two-thirds men and boys and only one-third women and girls.[6] Most enslaved Africans of this period ended up in the slave societies of Cuba and Brazil. There the issue of gender imbalance played out within the context of each slave society. Once laws and treaties had been enacted prohibiting the human trade from Africa, many slaveholders expressed renewed interest in the natural reproductive capacity of their slave population. However, in the economically driven agricultural-export societies of Cuba and Brazil, such interest translated into coherent (let alone effective) demographic policies only rarely. Throughout the nineteenth century, both Cuba and Brazil remained committed to a system in which their enslaved populations maintained low fertility and high mortality; these systems continued to rely on the import of new Africans despite prohibitions against the trade. This state of affairs did not mean that women of African descent did not play distinctive roles in these societies or that the disproportionately male character of the nineteenth-century slave trade had no effect on their social structures and social policies. But much more dramatic debate and some of the most poignant crises over this gender imbalance occurred in the British Caribbean colonies during the settlement of liberated Africans. Data from the Havana mixed commission court readily illustrates the marked gender disparity of the nineteenth-century slave trade and therefore of the population of liberated Africans.

Because of this marked numeric dominance of males, questions of gender identity and the role of liberated African women as potential free wives and mothers often took center stage in the social drama around their settlement. First, the British preoccupation with encouraging western nuclear families among the Africans meant that colonial policies and practices often paid particular attention to inducing, encouraging, or helping African refugee women perform the roles of wives (and mothers). Second, because the gender imbalance produced a shortage of potential African-born wives for the African refugee men, African refugee women often possessed and manipulated a unique social capital that was valued by both liberated African men and colonial authorities who wanted to engineer marriage and family life for the refugee population. Economic indicators such as property ownership and access to more lucrative forms of employment (such as skilled trades) show that liberated African women predictably lagged behind their male counterparts, as did women from most social and racial classes both in the Caribbean and elsewhere. However, the gender imbalance combined with the social-management spirit of the emancipation age meant that in the lives of liberated African women, dynamics of gender and power often operated in ways that were significantly different from what one might expect for a group burdened with the double disadvantage of female gender and nonwhite race.

The question of gender imbalance played its clearest policy-determining role during the debates about the transfer of liberated Africans from the mixed commission court at Havana. The Colonial Office never made a definitive policy decision about which colonies should receive preference in receiving liberated African immigrants from Havana. Both labor-hungry colonies such as Trinidad and more economically marginal colonies such as the Bahamas received liberated Africans from this source. British officials ended up pursuing strict gender-management policies for the Africans formally distributed from Spanish ships, mostly because they did not want to exacerbate the preexisting predominance of males among nonwhite populations in some British Caribbean colonies. Some officials went so far as to argue that gender balance should be the principle criteria that determined the distribution of such immigrants. That is to say, they proposed that the disproportionately male groups of Africans should emigrate only to those British West Indian colonies that had a demonstrable surplus of nonwhite females.[7] The Colonial Office ultimately took a compromise position whereby imbalanced gender groups could emigrate to colonies with a reasonably balanced gender ratio. But liberated Africans could emigrate from Havana to colonies that already had a surplus of nonwhite males only in gender-balanced allotments with an equal number of males and females. The colony of Trinidad fell into this special category, in part because of the demography of its slave populations but also because in the early nineteenth century the island had received a sizeable group of all-male immigrants—disbanded African and African-Caribbean soldiers from the 3rd West India regiment.

For groups of liberated Africans bound for Trinidad from Havana, British officials carefully certified gender balance in the same documents they prepared guaranteeing the health and various other legal conditions relative to the emigrants. Authorities certified, for example, that the slave trade refugees had agreed to leave Cuba voluntarily and that no separations had occurred between husbands and wives or parents and children. These kinds of assurances sought to avoid any abuse of the emigration system for liberated Africans; the British wanted to avoid the inhumane attitudes toward Africans that characterized the slave trade. British officials in Cuba also guaranteed that before emigration each group of Africans had received, through interpreters, an explanation that they "would not be allowed to remain in idleness [in Trinidad]" but would have to perform "moderate and regular labor" in return for compensation.[8] Written guarantees of many of these issues seem logical, especially given the political backdrop of slavery and free labor surrounding the settlement of liberated Africans. The equally fastidious written guarantees regarding the question of gender balance seem a little more surprising. The issue of gender balance clearly held equal weight with the more predictable concerns of British policy at the Havana mixed commission. Thus, in August of 1835, as a group of 268 liberated Africans prepared to leave for Trinidad, a British secretary at the Anglo-Spanish mixed commission declared formally in a six-part affidavit: "And I do further certify that of the above mentioned 268 Africans—134 are males, and an equal number are Females."[9]

According to historian Barbara Bush, as early as the seventeenth century, British observers had speculated about the desirability of promoting western marriage and monogamy among African slave populations. In a work published in 1707, Sir Hans Sloane had suggested that plantations could be "kept in good order" only if slave owners promoted ties of marriage and "bought wives in proportion to their [male slaves]."[10] It is not surprising, as Bush and others have pointed out, that slave masters rarely responded with any seriousness to such recommendations. However, the concern over this issue by British colonial authorities bordered on obsession in the case of liberated Africans. British insistence on gender parity was sometimes so rigid that in January 1834, the Spanish governor of Havana made a direct plea to the governor of Trinidad asking him to accept more liberated Africans regardless of the proportion of their sexes. The Spanish official even proposed, to no avail, that he would keep in Cuba all "sickly and useless" Africans if Governor George Hill would only agree to accept larger groups of healthy emigrants even if they included a surplus of males.[11] Governor Hill seemed to have mixed feelings about this gender policy; he appreciated the marriage-oriented concerns that motivated the policy but also wanted to take maximum advantage of liberated African immigrants as a potential labor force. As a result, Hill made a unique suggestion in October 1835 that exemplified the crucial role this concern for gender balance played in British policy for liberated Africans in the Caribbean. Hill's report to the Colonial Office concerning the 268 Africans sent from Cuba in August of the same year that considered future similar arrivals proposed

> that with regard to equal numbers of Males and Females I should not require all the Females to be adults, but would, as on this occasion receive them ever so young. And when the number of Females could not be made up by sending Children, a debit account should be acknowledged to be paid on a future occasion and that the males in the mean time should be sent. [12]

Even taking into account the unfamiliar conventions of nineteenth-century British English that always sound peculiar to more modern readers, the analogy of deficit finance to maintain an appropriate number of African females sounds preposterous. Hill symbolically transformed African women, in their role as potential wives, into a measurable form of social capital that he could not buy and sell but that he and others clearly valued in a special way and hoped to accumulate over time.

Similar calculations of this valued capital of African females appeared in the correspondence of at least one Bahamian governor. During the mid-1830s, Governor William Colebrooke repeatedly advocated for the Bahamas as an ideal location for settlement of liberated African refugees from the nearby mixed commission court at Havana. While Colebrooke lobbied on numerous grounds, he explicitly boasted of "an excess in the number of females" that would permit the colony to receive without "objection" a disproportionate number of males.[13]

The promises and proposals of Colebrooke and Hill reveal much about British attitudes toward liberated African women, but they do not reveal how such attitudes did or did not translate into social power for these women. Exploring this matter runs into predictable problems of limited documentary evidence. In a stark statement of a long-accepted problem, Rosalyn Terborg-Penn declares that "historians cannot rely upon traditional, written historical sources in order to reconstruct black women's past totally."[14]

To be sure, in comparison to enslaved people, liberated African women in many respects have quite a rich documentary history. Because the rescue of such Africans constituted a core element of Britain's emancipation-era public policy, official records devote considerable attention to the everyday lives of these people in their special status under the protection of British antislavery "benevolence." All the same, women tend to appear in government and other records only at moments of difficulty or crisis that range from discussions of how to solve perceived shortages of African women to domestic disputes that reached the criminal courts. Historians can take two approaches to studying such moments of crisis. On the one hand, one can interpret them as exceptional circumstances and therefore unrepresentative or at least unreliable for determining any broad patterns in the experience of liberated African women. On the other hand, one can view such intensely scrutinized occasions as windows that provide some of the strongest evidence of broader trends. This chapter takes the latter approach.

Some indicators might lead one to conclude that the British preoccupation with gender imbalance and marriage patterns among liberated African populations had the potential to disempower both women and men from Africa. One of the earliest concerns Colonial Office staff expressed about the settlement of these African refugees was the possibility of so-called sexual immorality among them. Sometimes this referred to perceived sexual promiscuity among the women or to the simple possibility that (because of the demographic situation) the women could freely choose their sexual partners. At other times, officials hinted at the concern that gender disparity and competition over women would lead to bad behavior among the men. In the summer of 1836 the Legislative Council for the island of Trinidad met to discuss measures that might be adopted to encourage nonwhite female immigration. The council deemed some action necessary in order "to prevent all apprehension of the evil which might arise from the ... disproportion of the sexes."[15] Twenty years earlier, during the first decade of slave trade suppression, the collector of customs in the Bahamas had even more explicitly asked the Colonial Office what measures he should adopt when "female [African] apprentices violated all principles of good conduct, & pursue[d] an abandoned course of life."[16] As colonial authorities usually resorted to vague euphemisms in their discussions of these matters, historians can only spec-ulate about the exact behavior they feared. Perhaps they worried about the potential for (violent) conflict over access to a limited number of potential wives. Or maybe they feared the possibility of homosexual behavior among disproportionately male populations. From the tone of these comments, one might speculate that British authorities in both colonies wanted to in-stitute schemes to exercise as much direct control as possible over the social and sexual behavior of the African immigrants, in which case the imbalance among the sexes would have produced heightened interference in African immigrant lives rather than any social advantage for either men or women. However, in neither colony did authorities devise any extraordinary at-tempts to control sexual behavior. On the contrary, British officials often re-sponded to the perceived gender crisis in ways that gave at least some Afri-can women more rather than less control in shaping their lives, particularly as potential sexual partners, wives, and mothers.

The most striking example of the policy response of the British oc-curred between 1816 and 1826, when Trinidadian authorities contrived sev-eral schemes to transport groups of liberated African women from Antigua (and Barbados) to Trinidad not simply with the intention of alleviating the gender disparity in general but hoping to directly marry specific groups of imported women to eligible men. The first such scheme seems to have de-veloped as much by chance as by design. In November 1816, Trinidad gov-ernor Sir Ralph Woodford wrote to the Colonial Office describing the gen-der imbalance that existed in Trinidad's black population as a "serious Evil." (Woodford wrote in part as a result of a petition from a group of private cit-izens that expressed their concerns about the social consequences of the set-tlement of disbanded soldiers and other groups in Trinidad.) Governor Woodford suggested that in response to the gender imbalance problem, the Colonial Office might be able to arrange for Trinidad to receive liberated Af-rican women from other islands for "distribution" among its various groups of disproportionately male settlers. When Woodford wrote this letter, the British had recently captured an illegal French slave ship and had sent to Barbados a group of African refugees containing a larger than usual number of females. The Colonial Office instructed the relevant military authority at Barbados to "send down to Trinidad by the first convenient opportunity a considerable large number of [the] females lately captured on board [the] French ship." They then instructed Governor Woodford "to allow such of [his own] settlers as [were] willing to take any of these female Africans as wives who prefer such a marriage to being apprenticed as servants in the usual manner."[17]

In this instance, the African women from Barbados were offered an alternative to apprenticeship. Rather than years of service to some British West Indian employer, they could choose marriage to a free black settler in Trinidad. This is perhaps not the place to enter into a full discussion of the benefits of marriage versus indentureship/apprenticeship in the lives of these women, particularly as that discussion would have to negotiate both African and western understandings of these two forms of status. Suffice it to say that whatever subordination or subservience a wife might have had to her husband, a wife did acquire some sense of family and belonging that an apprentice to a British employer did not have. Additionally, in the age of emancipation, colonial authorities were actively entertaining the idea that free black women had the right to household responsibilities with the expectation that a husband's labor compensation should support the whole family. (This idea will be discussed in more detail below.) The African women from Barbados probably had only a limited choice of potential husbands among the men in Trinidad. But in all ways, after their enslavement in Africa and rescue from a slave ship, they faced lives of limited choice, and their gender in this case provided them with an option that was not available to male African refugees from the same French vessel. The records from Trinidad do not provide details of how authorities in Barbados presented this marriage option to the African women. Fifty-three of them did travel from Barbados, and within twelve months forty-two had entered into marriage relationships and seven had become formally engaged. Only the "four youngest" did not settle down in this way and presumably faced apprenticeship as a result.[18] All of the marriages apparently occurred with African-American men from the United States who had arrived in Trinidad after serving with the British against the United States in the War of 1812. The report of the forty-two marriages and seven engagements came to Governor Woodford from Robert Mitchell, the man charged with the superintendence of these "American refugees." It is interesting that throughout this correspondence no one discussed the idea that liberated African women should perhaps ideally marry liberated African men. The question of jealousy on the part of liberated African men did not arise, as in 1816 Trinidad had not yet received significant numbers of liberated African immigrants overall. In this case, therefore, the African women in question had a degree of social advantage not in relationship to fellow Africans in Trinidad but in relationship to male African refugees from the French ship at Barbados—liberated African men who had no choice other than apprenticeship and received no extra attention from the colonial authorities charged with managing their new Caribbean lives.

In December 1820, Governor Woodford apparently extended a similar opportunity to a group of sixty liberated African women from Antigua. Woodford expressed disappointment that the women came from the Gambia and Senegal Rivers of West Africa because Trinidad's population of disbanded soldiers and the island's population in general contained few Africans of similar ethnic background. He lamented that as a consequence of this lack it would "be more difficult to teach [the women] any principles of the Christian faith." He hastened to add that as governor he was grateful "to have received any [women] at all."[19] Five months later, Woodford reported that fifty-two of the women had been "distributed"; the remaining five were classified as either young, ill, or elderly.[20] The term "distribution" might have referred to assignments as apprentices or to distribution as wives. However, even if they were distributed as apprentices, the women had clearly been invited to Trinidad with the intention of alleviating a gender imbalance. Therefore, like the 1816 women from Barbados, these women from Antigua acquired an extra degree of opportunity as a result of the unusual demography of the nineteenth-century British Caribbean. All the same, a skeptic might argue that these African women possessed very little actual power or control given the fact that neither being indentured to white strangers nor married to black strangers constituted good or desirable options. And British authorities still determined what options the women did or did not have.

Yet on at least two occasions during the 1820s British authorities allowed that in the efforts at gender management of the non-white population, the much-valued liberated African women could exercise real choice about their fates. In August 1826, the collector of customs from Antigua, Mr. Wyke, brought six liberated African women to Trinidad, hoping that he might persuade them to remain in the new colony that so desired female immigrants. (Antigua, like the Bahamas, did not face Trinidad's particular problem of a disproportionately male population.) These women completely rejected the proposition of any life other than the domestic service they had already known in Antigua and promptly returned to that colony with their disappointed superintendent.[21] British pride in their treatment of Africans they had rescued from foreign slave ships precluded any possibility of coercing the women to remain in Trinidad against their will, despite Governor Woodford's almost obsessive concern with the island's need for African women. Correspondence suggests that colonial authorities hoped that the result of Mr. Wyke's mission would be that the liberated African women would choose to marry disbanded soldiers from the 3rd West India regiment, who constituted a major part of the disproportionately male population. One cannot help but wonder whether upon visiting the soldiers' settlement, the African women rejected not just the rural lifestyle but the men themselves! Whatever the case, the British authorities acceded to their wishes and continued their policy of seeking to persuade liberated African women to follow marital paths where they were most needed.

Also in 1826 Governor Woodford proposed an innovative solution that would have sent unmarried former soldiers to Antigua at government expense in the hope that the men would convince liberated African women to return with them to Trinidad as their wives.[22] Although this scheme never even received a trial run, the proposal provides suggestive evidence of the unique social climate liberated African women encountered in the Caribbean. That climate entailed at least three mores: first, nonwhite men (including but not limited to liberated Africans) should and must have wives; second, as newly arrived immigrants, liberated African women were valuable as potential wives; and third, colonial authorities and black men themselves should and must work to persuade African women to enter into the desired marital relationships. Many historians have pointed out that the definitions of most abolitionists of what "freedom" should mean for people of African descent included both western and Christian social expectations, particularly regarding family life. Liberated African women found themselves in the middle of varying quests on the part of the British to ensure that liberated Africans fulfilled that ideal, a set of circumstances that often worked to the African women's advantage.

Comparable efforts to the proposed marriage expeditions of Governor Woodford never materialized in the Bahamas. But in this colony as well the ideal of heterosexual monogamy for the black population had discernible consequences for liberated Africans. As in Trinidad, the most dramatic gender-related crises centered on prominent male populations of black soldiers. Incidents in the Bahamas arose around soldiers on active duty. This military population included a significant population of liberated Africans who had enlisted in the armed forces as an alternative to terms of indentured labor. Overall patterns suggest that the African soldiers preferred African wives and that among all soldiers there existed regular competition and tension over access to wives and/or sexual partners among the local population. Colonial authorities sought to minimize conflict as far as possible and to encourage the formation of monogamous family unions, perhaps especially among the Africans. In at least one instance it seems that a group of African women successfully took advantage of the British preoccupation with their potential role as ideal western wives and homemakers. This particular instance involved quite possibly the only group of women who can take full or partial credit for fomenting a near mutiny among a body of the British armed forces.

This near mutiny took place in the Bahamas in early 1816 and was reported on at length by Governor Charles Cameron, who commented on the role liberated Africans played. Cameron stated that he found the slave trade refugees "conscious of their power" that arose from their "peculiar situation."[23] According to Cameron, these Africans knew that they held a place of special attention among colonial authorities and whenever possible they consciously used this status to their advantage. This strategy was used by a group of African men enlisted in the 2nd West India regiment and their wives in January 1816. On January 3rd, small groups of soldiers left their barracks and went to Nassau to call on Collector of Customs Alexander Murray and Solicitor General William Martin. The soldiers brought a list of grievances mostly centered on allegedly incorrect wages and insufficient rations such as candles, bread, and firewood. The most immediate complaint, and the one that had provoked their action, was about the military issue of two required flannel shirts to each soldier at a cost of 2 dollars and 6 shillings. As a consequence of this charge, for their last payment the men had received the flannel shirts alone and no money, all of their wages having been used in the cost of the shirts. The soldiers who visited Customs Collector Murray warned that their comrades stood ready to mutiny if they did not win some redress. At least one of the men who spoke to William Martin intimated that the discontented soldiers might set fire to the town. No mutiny actually occurred and only six soldiers ultimately faced charges for their actions. The House of Assembly inquiry organized after the disturbance concluded that the incident might have been avoided had the army deducted payment for the flannel shirts in small installments over time rather than out of a single wage allotment, particularly given the fact that the wages the soldiers did not receive were those due on December 24, 1815, leaving the men with no money for festivities during the Christmas holiday period. The Enquiry Committee recommended an increase in the number of white troops stationed in the colony, noting that the black soldiers understood their power to threaten; nonwhite men in both the 2nd West India regiment and the local militia overwhelmingly outnumbered all white troops in the Bahamas.[24]

Neither Governor Cameron nor any other local official characterized the near mutiny as an exclusively liberated African affair. But significant evidence points to the conclusion that these African immigrants initiated and led the protest. The choice of Customs Collector Murray as the recipient of their complaints suggests that it was liberated Africans who were involved. For most liberated Africans in the Bahamas in 1816 (including those in the military), Customs Collector Murray constituted their first and most important official source of government assistance. Murray explained that the four soldiers who led the complaint probably selected him both because of his former military service and his role as superintendent of liberated Africans:

> [M]y having the superintendence of such Africans as may be brought into this Colony, many of whom were delivered over by me as Recruits to this Reg[iment], which many of the African Women having Husbands in the Reg[iment]: they are constantly in the habit of calling on me respecting them, which I have no doubt has made me rather popular with them.[25]

This explanation implies that the January disturbances were led by liberated Africans. Murray also hints that liberated African women played a special role. Although his sentence construction leaves room for ambiguity, Murray suggests that even more so than the soldiers, their African wives turned to him in search of information about their husbands' well-being. These kinds of inquiries would hardly cast the African women in any unique roles; they were simply exhibiting the predictable concern of any military wives. But where Alexander Murray remained vague in his observations, the commander of the Nassau garrison painted the liberated African wives in a far more definitive—and in his view sinister—light. The commander, Lieutenant Colonel Maclean, charged "that the discontent was occasioned and fomented by the women, wives to the soldiers, and particularly indented African women, under the guardianship and protection of Col. Murray . . . in consequence of their having no balance of Pay to receive at the end of the month on account of the flannel, and other necessaries furnished them."[26]

One might be tempted to dismiss this very pointed charge as the angry, and even sexist, rantings of the commanding officer against whom the soldiers had levied their principle charges. The soldiers not only blamed Maclean for some of their difficulties (such as insufficient supplies) but they also alleged that he essentially forced them to threaten mutiny because of his severe punishment of any soldier who expressed a routine complaint. However, neither Governor Cameron nor Customs Collector Murray accused Maclean of dishonesty or unfairness in this specifically gendered accusation. The governor had ample opportunity to correct any charges he viewed as specious in his various letters to London about the near mutiny. That Cameron did not comment gives strong encouragement to historians to consider the possibility that Maclean's charge had merit. One might even interpret Murray's vagueness about the women's role as an attempt by the advocate for liberated Africans to avoid being accused of encouraging a rebellious spirit among the women.

What did these liberated African women do when they complained to Murray about the treatment of their husbands and possibly encouraged those husbands to threaten mutiny? In a recent study of post-emancipation society in the United States, Amy Dru Stanley argues that in the age of emancipation, abolitionists and other allies of African-Americans believed that in the post-slavery world, men should be able to support wives and families with the wages they earned, allowing women to devote themselves to marital and household duties:

> [I]n exchange for hard work freed people would earn the right to maintain the traditional dependency relations of the household. They affirmed that wage labor would support wives' unpaid domestic work—unlike slave families, but like in idealized white families.[27]

Claire Midgely describes similar beliefs among British abolitionists in her work *Women against Slavery.*[28] The cumulative evidence from the 1816 military disturbance in the Bahamas suggests that the liberated African wives successfully sought to capitalize on similar idealized notions among the British authorities, who often saw liberated Africans as a kind of pre-emancipation experiment in free black experience. Lieutenant Colonel Maclean made an interesting grammatical choice when he referred to the African wives as being upset in consequence of "*their* having no balance of Pay to receive at the end of the month" (my emphasis). With his phrasing here, MacLean in effect gave the wives control over their husband's pay, or he at least implied that they claimed that right and that in so doing they received implicit sympathy and certainly no condemnation from colonial authorities (other than the garrison commander against whom the mutiny was directed).

Authorities in the Bahamas and elsewhere would debate for years about what work roles were appropriate for liberated African women. Should they or should they not have to work outside the home? Should they or should they not perform the most arduous labor such as sugar cultivation in Trinidad or salt-raking in the Bahamas? In practice, like most nonwhite working-class people, liberated African women rarely had the opportunity to rely solely upon the income of a husband. All the same, this near mutiny suggests that given the opportunity, these women understood that their role as wives possessed some strategic value to the British colonial actors who controlled such things as their wages or access to employment.

Many other scattered examples exist of liberated African women using their demographic and social position in strategic ways. Amid Trinidad's particularly severe problem of surplus male population, one observer reported in 1825 that in nine out of ten cases among both African and U.S. immigrants, when married couples separated, the women had "deserted" their husbands rather than the other way around.[29] This pattern clearly implies that African immigrant women had a great degree of control about whom they chose to retain as sexual or marital partners. In a similar example from the Bahamas in the mid-1860s, a special committee investigating quarrels between soldiers and civilians found that in Grant's Town—a settlement founded and heavily populated by liberated Africans—soldiers and seafaring men complained that other men were regularly "visiting" their wives while they were away. Although the committee focused on the fact that these romantic or sexual liaisons caused fights among the men, it is important to note that at least some of the married women involved must have permitted and indeed encouraged such extramarital affairs.[30] Liberated African women did not find radical ways to shape and define their experience in African or otherwise independently conceived ways. They did, however, find spaces where they could use their identity as women—and especially British perceptions of that identity—to some advantage. When African women used British perceptions of female roles to gain social benefits, did they engage in a form of feminist protest? Or did they become inevitably complicit in the British aim to "civilize" Africans and people of African descent according to western norms? Bahamas governor Charles Cameron did not necessarily intend a positive interpretation when he referred to liberated Africans in general as "conscious of their power." But through precisely that consciousness as it related to gender issues, liberated African women achieved small measures of power and success.

Beyond the arguably extraordinary sphere of British policies regarding gender management, scattered evidence also suggests that—as one would expect—liberated African women regularly negotiated both European and African expectations of gender and family, albeit within the special circumstances of liberated African settlement. The story of Yoruba widow Harriet Charles of south-central Trinidad offers an exemplary case study of such negotiation. The broad outlines of the life of Harriet (or Henrietta) Charles appear in an 1888 news report concerning the disposition of her estate following her death. Harriet died a widow, having had two husbands precede in her death: the first was known by the name George African and the second by the name Charles Yaraba (or sometimes Charles Baptiste). These details appeared in the *New Era* newspaper in the report of a hearing to determine the legitimate heirs to Harriet's land, which consisted of more than eighteen acres "planted in cocoa in the Ward of Montserrat."[31] In the context of the demographics of Trinidad's nineteenth-century black population, an African-born woman of Harriet's age was almost certainly a liberated African immigrant. The use of the surname Yaraba and family claims about its origin allows us to assume Yoruba ethnic background in this case—particularly given the representation of the Yoruba as approximately one-third of the liberated African population of the island.

As an independent female small proprietor engaged in commercial agri-culture, Harriet Charles led an unusual Caribbean life at the time of her death. Most of her female (and indeed male) nonwhite peers did not share that economic status. Although one would not describe Harriet Charles as wealthy—especially in the context of Trinidad's post-emancipation econ-omy, which was still dominated by owners of large sugar plantations—she was certainly a solidly successful female small proprietor of a cash crop. She left five living children, of whom four testified at the hearing concerning her land. It is interesting that their individual testimony offers very little indica-tion of whether any of them either wanted the land or considered themselves the most rightful heir to it. Their brief testimony reveals a great deal about how one African woman constructed a somewhat independent life and a very specific network of family and kin with complex connections based at times on blood and at times on other forms of social affiliation. As an Afri-can-born woman in British Caribbean colony, Harriet Charles also poses numerous challenges to those who would interpret her life and status in both western and African terms. In the absence of any self-conscious commentary from Harriet, historians can only speculate about whether she experienced notions of womanhood, widowhood, or family through primarily British or Yoruba lenses. One cannot presume that because British colonial norms held hegemonic social power they necessarily had greater weight in shaping Har-riet's life experience. In her provocative work *The Invention of Women: Making an African Sense of Western Gender Discourses*, Oyèrónké Oyewùmí asserts that western ideas of gender as an analytic category entered "contem-porary Yoruba discourse" when "Yoruba life past and present [was] trans-lated into English to fit the Western pattern of body reasoning."[32] Oyewùmí argues that precolonial Yoruba society, in contrast to most western societies, defined gender in ways that were not determined by the bodily reality of sex differences. The idea that gender meanings were translated from Yoruba to western idioms has clear resonance for those who would understand the ex-perience of African-born women in the Americas. Oyewùmí situates much of her analysis of precolonial Yoruba culture in the early nineteenth century, during the decades before settled British colonialism in Nigeria. The same people whose descendants "translated" Yoruba gender culture in colonial and post-colonial Nigeria had kin who engaged in similar processes of trans-lation in the Caribbean, having been transported there during the nine-teenth-century slave trade. Harriet Charles, then, took husbands and lost them, had children, purchased land, and even died with culturally compli-cated gender imperatives shaping her status as a woman and a widow.

The biggest caveat associated with using a so-called African perspective to interpret Harriet's life is the need to resist the temptation to view Harriet's economic success and relative independence as necessarily heroic or unique. Niara Sudarkasa notes that when exploring roles black women came to play in the Americas, "it is necessary to understand the tradition of female independence and responsibility within family and wider kin groups in Africa, and the tradition of female productivity and leadership in the extradomestic, or public domain in African societies."[33] Sudarkasa makes this observation in the context of considering possible ongoing cultural influences in generations of American-born people of African descent. Her observation holds even more weight for the life of an African-born woman in the nineteenth century.

Several factors about Harriet Charles's acquisition of her cocoa land mark her experience as being embedded in her new colonial environment. She received the land as a crown grant in 1871 and died sixteen years later. During the court proceedings regarding her case, Harriet's son Daniel testified that his mother "had lived on her estate twenty-six years" at the time of her death, which meant that she had lived on the land for ten years before receiving the grant.[34] Historians of nineteenth-century Trinidad, as of other parts of the Caribbean, identify the practice of squatting on public lands as a central feature of the post-emancipation environment. Bridget Brereton notes that by the mid-1860s, after numerous policies against squatting failed, "squatters included cocoa farmers, some of whom owned thousands of trees, especially in the Northern Range and the districts east of Arima and in the Montserrat area."[35] Harriet Charles clearly fell among this number. Brereton goes on to explain that in the late 1860s, Governor A. H. Gordon tried to alleviate the squatter problem by making it easier for squatters to legally obtain title to their land. He lowered the price of land and allowed the purchase of parcels as small as five acres. He also lowered legal fees and arranged for government officials to conduct land surveys at more affordable rates, choosing the ward of Montserrat to test out his new policies under the supervision of a particularly energetic warden and commissioner of crown lands.[36] It is almost certain that Harriet Charles purchased her land through these policies. Citing the 1868 report of Warden and Commissioner Robert Mitchell, Brereton notes that the inhabitants of Montserrat included Africans, immigrants from other West Indian islands, and Trinidad Creoles (that is, people of African descent born in Trinidad). She emphasizes that Governor Gordon's successors were not able to undo the lasting impact of his policies, which "had opened up the Crown lands to the small man."[37]

Brereton, who was writing in 1981, presumably used the "man" in its problematic nongendered sense; it does not necessarily indicate only or even principally male landholders. None of her discussion in the survey history gives a sense of the role individual women proprietors played in this proliferation of small landholders in central Trinidad. She does describe a tremendous cocoa boom which lasted from the 1870s until World War I; in creating prosperity out of cocoa cultivation on a smaller plot, Harriet Charles had many peers, including other liberated African immigrants. In Brereton's words, "the Trinidad cocoa industry was pioneered and built up by peasants."[38] This atypical pattern, by Caribbean standards, of small-scale success apparently prevailed as the norm in the community where Harriet Charles lived. Niara Sudarkasa would argue that in the context of such widespread success with cocoa, Harriet's gender may have seemed unremarkable from a West African perspective, "wherein women were farmers, craftswomen and entrepreneurs par excellence."[39] What seems more noteworthy from both African and western perspectives is the lack of clarity about who—if anyone—worked with Harriet Charles in the cultivation and care of the land. The testimony of her adult children at the inheritance hearing does not clearly indicate that any of them (or any other relative) lived with her on the property or helped in the cocoa enterprise.

While one always risks reductionism or oversimplification when pointing to the importance of kinship connections in African societies, it remains true that such ties proved critical in social and economic organization. Yet in Harriet Charles's case, one gets little sense that her property was any kind of family project. Four of her five surviving children offered testimony. One son, Thomas George, described himself as "a laborer residing at Milton Estate, Couva," which was many miles away from his mother's plot. Another son, Thomas Charles, lived at Indian Trail, again miles away from his mother's location. The other two children who testified did not identify where they lived, nor did they give any specific indication that they lived or worked on the Montserrat land. Thomas George described the nature of his mother's holdings in specific detail: "His mother owned eighteen acres of land at Montserrat, on which there were 1000 cocoa trees bearing and 1000 young ones."[40] But this information alone does not necessarily imply a working relationship with the property. The newspaper account was after all reporting summarized testimony and it seems that the person doing the questioning probably asked about the acreage and number of trees as a matter of course. Thus the same newspaper reported that the other son named Thomas—Thomas Charles—"[did] not know the quantity of land or the number of cocoa trees."[41] None of this means that her offspring did not work on the land. People in nineteenth-century Trinidad regularly traveled significant distances for various economic reasons. Nevertheless, the available evidence does not enable us to say what Harriet's children did for the farm.

Studies of social structures in colonial and postcolonial Africa have regularly shown how new economic formations can gradually change the ways people think about labor and property and the gender and familial roles attached to economic activities. Historians of slave societies in the Americas have long noted that under New World chattel slavery, Africans and their descendants had little opportunity to set gender or familial norms about the division of their labor. Even where enslaved people had the opportunity to cultivate their own provision grounds, responsibility for that work depended on who had the time to do it, and this depended on how slaveholders allocated work for various family members. So although most Africans came from societies with their own "explicit divisions of labor based on gender and age,"[42] in the slaveholding Caribbean they could rarely reproduce those patterns. One must ask what labor patterns Harriet Charles hoped to nurture in her environment, both before and after the death of two husbands? In the post-emancipation Caribbean, free people of African descent faced a range of new choices in the disposition and organization of their labor. Such people generally preferred independent cultivation over any form of labor on larger estates. Did the expansion of cocoa production as a cash crop produce different family expectations when contrasted with subsistence peasant farming, for example? Claire Robertson and Iris Berger offer the following generalization about gender and family labor divisions in precolonial Africa: "Women and junior males usually contributed a portion of the fruits of their labor to senior male lineage heads or political authorities, who allocated use rights to particular plots of land, which might be reallocated rather than inherited at a person's death."[43] They note the centrality of the "household [as] the most important unit of production," but in most African societies the term "household" usually incorporated several generations and multiple kinds of relations, rather than simply a nuclear family.[44] For the African-born, like Harriet Charles, transportation across the Atlantic disrupted all preexisting kin networks, and it was not possible to recreate the depth of such networks in the Caribbean. The Trinidad land commissioner, who noted Africans in the Montserrat ward sometimes cooperating to purchase plots of land, may have inadvertently glimpsed the construction of some new familial or extrafamilial networks.[45] But no specific evidence of that kind of network-building exists for Harriet Charles. The official records mostly portray her as a solitary commercial small proprietor with labor given or owed to her by no one. Curiously, the son Thomas Charles described the property as "his father's land." He also asserted that both his father and mother died on the land. Yet if the father, Charles Baptiste (or Charles Yaraba)—Harriet's second husband—in fact owned the cocoa property in any British colonial legal sense, that would have been reflected in the 1871 grant, which on the contrary awarded the land to Harriet. This fact argues against an interpretation that would portray Harriet Charles as taking over the role of commercial proprietor after becoming a widow for the second time.

At least one scholar has suggested that the idea of widows "taking over" has an explicit place in modern Yoruba religious understandings of the social order. Oyeronke Olajubu explains the use of various songs following a husband's death to remind a woman of her new status as a widow. He quotes one song as follows: "You do not have a husband anymore / So, when you see wives eating the yams of their husbands / Turn a blind eye / . . . /You do not have a husband anymore / So, when you hear wives calling their husbands / Turn a deaf ear."[46] Olajubu concludes that "[t]his song is an advice to the widow to be strong and take control of her life in the absence of her husband."[47] It is important to note that Olajubu explains that the yam reference is not principally agricultural. Instead, it refers more generally to "privileges that wives enjoy in their marital homes, including conjugal rights."[48] To use Olajubu's language, Harriet Charles had certainly taken control of her life as a widow but may have exercised much of that same control even during the lives of her first and second husbands. Additionally, although legal depositions tend to erase the emotions or analysis of the speakers, it still stands out that no voice in the 1888 court proceedings viewed her status or behavior as remarkable. This silence raises the possibility that independent female actors formed a significant fraction of the small-scale cocoa proprietors in Trinidad in this era. Or, more simply, Harriet Charles's behavior may have conformed to reasonable norms for a widow by either western or West African standards. Certainly in western societies, widowhood during the nineteenth century opened an avenue through which women could achieve economic and social independence in the context of social norms that often excluded married women from independent participation in nondomestic economies or other public spheres. Olajubu's analysis suggests that cosmologically, Yoruba widows could also be viewed as being to some extent on their own. Despite the very recent date of his fieldwork, the presence of such an idea within a ritual song for widows at least implies ideological roots long before the current era.

Still, this analysis sits uncomfortably, in part because marriage in precolonial West African societies generally entailed complex intertwinings of kin that did not necessarily end with the death of a husband. For example, drawing on a wide range of twentieth-century anthropological study, Judith Byfield offers the following evocative summary for Yoruba society up to the end of the nineteenth century: "Full Yoruba marriage . . . was a protracted process. Over its course lineages gave up their productive and reproductive rights over female members in exchange for bridewealth, goods, and services that were transferred from their husbands' kin. . . . Through marriage men and women expanded the pool of people from whom they could acquire economic resources."[49] Harriet Charles and the other African-born people in her social circles almost certainly entered the Caribbean as free Africans rescued by the British from some Portuguese or Spanish slave vessel. But even as free people, neither she nor her husbands George African or Charles Yaraba likely had much to bring to the marriage in terms of lineage connections or access to resources. One of the children she shared with Charles Yaraba reported his age as twenty-six in 1888. This means that Harriet's partnership with her second husband began no later than the early 1860s—a decade before she acquired formal title to the land in Montserrat, and also before the real takeoff of cocoa cultivation. Harriet's most significant prosperity occurred after her second marriage. Although she may have had other resources earlier in her life, earlier prosperity seems unlikely based on the testimony of Harriet's oldest surviving son, who was fathered by her first husband, George African. That son, Thomas George, was identified in 1888 as being thirty-four years old, and during his testimony he explained that he had been born at Friendship Estate. A child born to an African woman on a sugar plantation in Trinidad in 1854 was likely the son of a recently arrived indentured African laborer. Even though Harriet reputedly came from Grenada, she may have done so under arrangements with a sugar planter to serve the term on a Trinidad plantation. Or even if Harriet was working on Friendship Estate without a specific indenture, this place of residence and employment when she bore her first child strongly suggests that she did not yet have significant land or the independent life as a cultivator that she later achieved.

The network described by Harriet Charles's children gives some inkling of kinship ties and knowledge of family beyond the nuclear household but little indication that any of those ties were connected to economic activity. The testimony of the eldest son, Thomas George, offered some of the greatest detail: "He is the eldest son of his mother. . . . His father was George African; he was not married to his mother but was married to another woman in Grenada. Witness's mother died on 1st June, 1887, leaving five children living. She had ten children altogether, but five had died. With the exception of her children she had no blood relations in Trinidad. *Witness would have known if she had*" (emphasis added).[50] Thomas George boasted a very complete knowledge of his mother's marital and reproductive history and made a specific assertion that he knew of all relevant family ties. It is striking that he also testified that "she had no acquaintances in Africa."[51] The use of the term "acquaintances" here is perplexing, since mere acquaintances presum-

ably would have had no claim on the Charles estate, unless colonial authorities were asking questions which guarded against the possibility of family
relations defined in terms that were not necessarily recognized by British
law. After more than half a century of managing slave trade suppression,
some British authorities, either through goodwill or by necessity, prided
themselves on trying to take some aspects of African cultures into account.
Colonial correspondence dealing with the West Indies and the slave trade in
this era regularly contained claims of knowledge about African culture. One
way to interpret Thomas George's pronouncement about his family's history would view this son as embracing the importance of his mother's history and lineage and even her fertility in the mothering of ten children. One
might find particularly impressive his claims to be a definitive keeper of
family history—indicating that were there any relevant kin in either Trinidad he would know about them. However, a more cynical interpretation of
the same testimony might simply see Thomas George as the oldest living
male descendant who was solidifying a potential claim as heir by denying
the existence of anyone who might have competing claims.

One reason to eschew such cynicism—and consider the idea that the
George-Charles family did embrace a complex, even transatlantic, network
of kin—lies in the testimony of the last witness, daughter Victoria Charles.
Whereas her three brothers[52] testified principally about the amount of the
land, their ages, and the alleged absence of other relatives, Victoria testified
almost exclusively about a supposed uncle identified as "Tom Yaraba . . . her
mother's brother." Under questioning, she conceded that she did not know
if he was a "legitimate brother." Nevertheless, the court pursued his life history in some detail, despite the fact that by the time Harriet's estate hearing
took place in February of 1888, Tom had also died. Victoria described Tom's
household in great detail, explaining that he had married his wife, "Madam
Tom," in the Roman Catholic Church in Gasparillo and that they had borne
two daughters, both of whom had since died. Tom also had a son whom he
had fathered previously with a woman other than the wife. That son, Simon
Tom, a presumed nephew of Harriet Charles, still lived in San Fernando, the
largest and most important town in southern Trinidad. Victoria also told
the court that one of Tom Yaraba's daughters had married before her death
and left a surviving widower, identified only as "Philo," who was alive in
1888.[53] Did Victoria Charles view herself as presenting to the court relevant
matrilineal heirs to the Montserrat cocoa estate? Oyewùmí argues that in
precolonial Oyo-Yoruba society, "the single purpose of bride-wealth [paid
by the groom] was to confer sexual and paternity rights, not the rights to the
bride's person, her property, or her labor."[54] A full exploration of precolonial
Yoruba beliefs about property, gender, and marriage lies beyond the scope of

Family of Harriet Charles

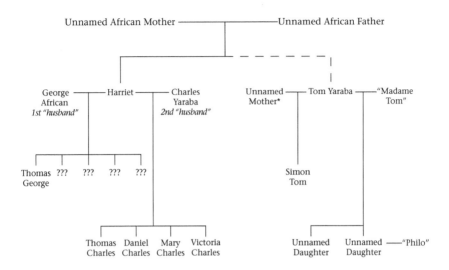

Notes

N.B. In the court testimony from newspaper records used here, it remains unclear whether or not Tom Yaraba was a "legitimate" (that is biologically related) brother of Harriet Charles.

??? Denotes unnamed sons or daughters who predeceased Harriet herself. These unnamed children are listed as possible full siblings of Thomas George because only he described his mother as having had a total of ten children, of whom five were still alive at the time of her death. No testimony specifically indicated with whom Harriet had mothered the children who predeceased her.

* According to the testimony of Victoria Charles concerning the disposition of her mother's estate, Tom Yaraba fathered his son Simon with a woman other than his wife "Madame Tom."

this study. Nevertheless, Oyewùmí's analysis offers one possible explanation for the genealogical assertions of Harriet's daughter. That is, was Victoria suggesting that her mother's family before her marriages had equal or greater claims to her land than any of the children she produced with her two husbands?

Victoria's testimony also points to the rich and complicating issue of "legitimate" versus "non-legitimate" kin and the role of African ethnic or cultural identification in shaping such bonds. As already explained in chapter 3, significant numbers of liberated Africans in Trinidad adopted African ethnic surnames, operating in British colonial culture in which surnames were expected. Decades of recent study about Africans in the Americas have shown that African ethnic labels served as the basis for community formation in diaspora among many black populations, not just liberated Africans.

Did that community formation also extend to an idea of kin? This notion hardly seems far-fetched. Karin Barber explains that in the context of migration within Nigeria, Yoruba groups that originated from the same town often resettled with ideas of themselves as kin because they had shared the same town of origin and experience of migration.[55] One can readily imagine similar ideas at work in the Americas, especially for the African-born people such as Harriet Charles and their first-generation children, in this case the daughter Victoria. Interpreting her claims through a lens of Yoruba kin rather than a lens of blood kin seems the only way to understand why the descendants of Tom Yaraba—the brother of the deceased widow—would hold so much importance, even when "the witness could not say if he was a legitimate brother."[56] In his work entitled *The Claims of Kinfolk,* Dylan Penningroth argues persuasively that African-influenced ideas about both family and property formed a part of African-American community consciousness in the southern United States well into the nineteenth century, including the period after emancipation. It seems even more likely that African ideas about family, property, and the relationships created by marriage would have in some measure shaped the worldview and behavior of an African-born woman who lived most of her adult life as a free person in the nineteenth-century Caribbean.[57]

Victoria's testimony and that of her siblings also highlights critical questions of family naming in the context of the multiple social and cultural imperatives that influenced how Harriet Charles constructed her life as a wife, mother, and widow and how her family and others understood the various relationships that surrounded her. Victoria, for example, noted the Roman Catholic formalization of the marriage of her reputed uncle, Tom Yaraba. Neither of Harriet Charles's marriages had such formalization. Indeed, in opening the inheritance case, the solicitor general had noted as a matter of course "[t]hat [the deceased] had never married and had had several natural children."[58] Thomas George explained that his father, George African, in fact "was married to another woman in Grenada" at the same time that he had fathered children (and presumably had some sort of stable partnership) with Harriet in Trinidad. And he described his mother as "living with" Charles Yaraba (the second "husband") after the death of George African. Another son described Charles Yaraba as having "co-habited" with his mother. It is clear that both the witnesses and the court recognized Harriet's status with these two men as something other than legal or Christian marriage. But the court and the children (and presumably, by extension, the society) viewed the households Harriet created with George African and Charles Yaraba as in effect nuclear families.

Even more intriguing is the way Harriet used an identifiable naming pattern in establishing these families; she granted her children surnames according to their respective fathers, yet in ways that departed from British or western norms for assigning surnames to children. Children fathered by George African received the surname George, while those fathered by Charles Yaraba (also known as Charles Baptiste) received the surname Charles. Harriet also carried the Charles surname, connecting her to the last of her two husbands. In an article on "Sexism in English and Yoruba," linguist Yisa Kehinde Yusuf notes that "[i]n normal Yoruba culture, children are not given surnames. Instead they are given only personal names."[59] Yusuf further explains:

> A Yoruba child carries their personal names throughout their life. In other words, marital re-naming does not take place in traditional Yoruba culture. The question of marking marital status as *Miss* and *Mrs* does not therefore arise. The wife may be described (not labeled) as the wife of X, while the husband may equally be described as the husband of Y. In other words, Yoruba naming practices . . . are, unlike those of English[,] non-sexist.[60]

Yusuf makes a critical point about the difference between some kinds of names—personal names or first names, which she views as more permanent "labels," and other kinds of names—including marital names or family surnames in general, which she views as more situational (and potentially transient) "descriptions." Using this perspective, one can conclude that Harriet Charles made distinctly creolized choices in giving herself and her children what were in effect British colonial surnames. But she assigned those surnames by privileging the "personal name" of each of her husbands, perhaps in some specifically Yoruba sense. Additionally, as a widow, Harriet retained her own "description" as the wife of Charles Yaraba (or Charles Baptiste) for the rest of her life. Nowhere do these particular court records identify Harriet as having used the either "George" or "African" as a surname after her first husband. But given the way she named her children, one can readily speculate that as the widow of George African, Harriet assumed a new name as Harriet Charles with her second "marriage," moving from the status of widowhood to a new status as wife. Harriet's naming system facilitated the means by which her offspring and colonial authorities could potentially mark the parameters of kinship and potential rights in property for this twice-widowed African woman at the time of her Caribbean death.[61]

This examination of one life seems a tenuous basis on which to draw any large conclusions about liberated African women as independent social actors following the death (or other departure) of their husbands. Nevertheless, for Harriet Charles the combination of two marriages followed by widowhood led to a life rich in economic opportunity and apparent prosperity. If one accepts the cautions of Oyèrónké Oyewùmí about the need for care in using "Western categories and questions" when examining African societies,[62] one might conclude that neither gender, widowhood, nor nuclear family structure are appropriate prisms through which to explore Harriet Charles's life experience. Numerous scholars have pointed out that in many African societies "wealth and age were the primary determinants of status."[63] Those scholars have often concluded that within Africa the consolidation of colonial power often meant the increasing imposition of western sexist norms in which "masculinity became another essential criterion for power."[64] That Harriet Charles had lost two husbands seems on its face a sufficient criterion to accept widowhood as a legitimate frame of analysis in this case. It seems far more difficult to definitively argue that her status as a widow specifically afforded her economic opportunities that were impossible for other women. One can, however, argue that Harriet Charles most certainly made use of African and western family norms and British colonial law to secure a successful life in both material and social terms. Such successful and often simultaneous negotiation of western and African norms characterized the experience of liberated African men and women in many areas of their lives.

5

Orisha Worship and "Jesus Time":

RELIGIOUS WORLDS OF LIBERATED AFRICANS

In 1994, in the village of Caratal in south-central Trinidad, a seventy-eight-year-old woman—the great-granddaughter of nineteenth-century free African immigrants—used the phrase "Jesus time" to explain her devotion to Christian Pentecostalism rather than the African-derived orisha worship brought to the Caribbean by her forbears and continued by many of her neighbors to the present day. Irene Joseph seemed to argue that at least for her, the time of African religious beliefs had passed. In earlier years, she had pursued Trinidad's African-derived religion, sometimes called Shango but in more recent times also widely referred to as orisha worship.[1] Irene would later explain that as an older woman, she met a Pentecostal minister and some of his followers during a hospital stay. She had received a poor prognosis from her medical doctors, and, convinced that the prayers of this minister had restored her health, she converted to his particular religious group.[2] She still remembered well the various Shango, or orisha, beliefs and practices and did not speak of them with any regret or criticism. Despite what official Pentecostal doctrine might teach, Irene gave no hint that she viewed her former African-derived religion as heathen or in any way bad. At most, she seemed to imply on occasion that the orisha worship might have less power than her newfound faith—at least in the late twentieth century! But on the whole, Joseph seemed to interpret her conversion to Pentecostalism as a kind of linear move from one form of religious or supernatural practice to another, neither condemning that which she claimed to have left behind nor overvalorizing that which she newly embraced.

Nonetheless, ideas of African cultural nationalism or folkloric preservation would seem to suggest that Irene Joseph's conversion represents some kind of loss. In both academic and popular discourse, African-derived religions have long served as favored examples of African cultural resistance in the face of European hegemony in the New World. The Shango, or orisha, worship of Trinidad has often received particular attention because it is the only example of a ritually structured African-based religion in the English-speaking Caribbean. Historians usually cite two factors to explain this anomaly. First, at the end of the eighteenth century, Trinidad received many French planters and slaves through the dispersion prompted by the Haitian Revolution. These slaves from Saint Domingue no doubt brought with them many of the vodun religious practices that existed in that colony from the earliest days of plantation slavery. Second, historians point to the presence of liberated African immigrants in nineteenth-century Trinidad, arguing that without the restrictions of slavery, free Africans could pursue the religious beliefs brought with them from Africa.[3]

With this history in mind, Irene Joseph's adoption of Pentecostalism—possibly the smallest of all Christian groups in Trinidad—becomes yet another interesting turn in a unique African diaspora religious journey begun by her African immigrant ancestors. More than this, however, Joseph's experience provides a paradigm for reexamining the very different religious paths of Africans and their descendants in the New World. Many Africans, including thousands of the nineteenth-century free immigrants, arrived at "Jesus time" long before the late twentieth century. Historians have carefully scrutinized both the introduction of Christianity to slave communities and the various continuations of African religious practices and beliefs in slave societies. The case of the liberated Africans, however, poses a somewhat different challenge. One might surmise that a majority of liberated Africans throughout the British Caribbean would have pursued organized African-oriented religion. Virtually all of them had sufficient (albeit not complete) freedom of movement and assembly to do so. Yet in many cases they did not. While Irene Joseph's forbears venerated Yoruba spirits in the hills of south-central Trinidad, liberated Africans in the Bahamas became active Baptists and Methodists with reputedly great fervor. No single factor will explain this stark contrast in the religious experience of the liberated Africans, who arrived in the Caribbean under similar circumstances and with a similar distribution of African ethnic backgrounds. But a comparison of these parallel but very different religious communities can distill factors of greater and lesser weight in the shaping of religious experience, not only for these free Africans but also for the African diaspora as a whole.

No single subject has received greater attention in the study of the cultural history of the African diaspora than the question of religious development. Scholars have explored at length both the African-derived religions

Irene Joseph with
obi seeds used for
divination, Caratal,
Trinidad (1994)

such as Brazil's candomble, Cuba's santería, and Haiti's vodun and the influence of African antecedents on the numerous varieties of African diaspora
Christianity. In many cases these two religious patterns have received separate treatment. The roots of this division, to a large extent, lie in the geographic distribution of the different religious practices. Well-organized (or
ritually structured) African-derived religions have occurred, and continue
to occur, for the most part in regions settled by the Roman Catholic countries of France, Spain, and Portugal. African-influenced forms of Christianity have been most prominent in the English-speaking and largely Protestant
territories of the United States and the formerly British Caribbean. Alfred
Métraux's classic, *Voodoo in Haiti* (1959), and Leslie Desmangles's more recent work *The Faces of the Gods* (1992) have explored how Fon and Yoruba

cosmologies interacted with Roman Catholicism to form Haitian vodun. Likewise, scholars such as Roger Bastide—*African Religions of Brazil* (1978) —and Joseph Murphy—*Santería* (1988)—have pursued similar explorations for Brazil and Cuba, respectively. The conversion of slaves in the British West Indies and in North America to Protestant religions has received parallel attention. These matters have formed a central place in all the broader studies of slave society and culture in these areas. Early works such as John Blassingame's *The Slave Community* (1972) for the United States and Elsa Goveia's *Slave Society in the British Leeward Islands* (1965) demonstrated how the Christianity promulgated by Protestant missionaries came to provide slaves with an important sphere in which to develop community values in many ways distinct from the society which enslaved them. These and other studies have pointed out the ways African traditions of religious singing, dancing, and, perhaps most notably, spirit possession became integral parts of the newly forming African-American Christianity. Other historians such as Mary Turner—*Slaves and Missionaries* (1982)—and Emilia daCosta—*Crowns of Glory, Tears of Blood* (1994)—have explored the spiritual and organizational role missionary Christianity came to play in slave resistance in Jamaica, British Guiana, and elsewhere. Mechal Sobel's *Trabelin' On: The Slave Journey to an Afro-Baptist Faith* (1988) broke critical ground in arguing that the Baptist faith, in particular, provided a unique terrain in which slaves from West and Central Africa could incorporate their understandings of the supernatural world. For the most part, the study of black Christianity in the Americas and the study of African-derived religions have existed as two halves of the same coin with relatively little comparison between the two.[4]

In a study now thirty years old, anthropologist Roger Bastide offered one of the few systematic attempts to explore religious comparisons across the Americas and the Caribbean with *African Civilisations in the New World* (1967). One might challenge Bastide's work for excessive rigidity in its attempt to divide societies according to greater or lesser degrees of obvious African influence. But even if one discards the specific categorizations, this text successfully delineates the wide range of factors that have affected religious and other differences across communities in the African diaspora. Like most historians of comparative slavery, Bastide cites the possible differences created by the nationalities of European colonizers. He proposes a distinction between Northern Europeans—the British and Dutch—and Southern Europeans—the French, Spanish, and Portuguese. This distinction parallels the distinction between Roman Catholicism and Protestant faiths.

Bastide also cites the uniqueness of the United States because of its high percentage of American-born people of African descent. He points to additional demographic factors such as the number of slaves held on individual plantations and the ratio between Europeans and Africans in the population as a whole. One presumes, for example, that hundreds of slaves housed on the same plantation had greater community-building opportunities than slaves held in units of ten, twenty, or even fewer than ten. Bastide notes the potential impact of particular concentrations of specific African ethnicities. That is, a significant number of people of the same ethnic origin would likely have an easier time maintaining their religious and cultural ideas and spreading them to people of other ethnicities who were present in smaller groups. For example, this subject has received considerable attention with respect to the influence of Akan-Asante peoples, who were a large presence in the trade to the English-speaking Caribbean during the late seventeenth and early eighteenth centuries.[5] It is also possible that certain African ethnic groups possessed religious systems that, for reasons of structure or doctrine, proved more amenable to a reorganized existence in the New World. In a given New World community, even if the Yoruba did not predominate, their religious notions might. Scholars have long noted that Yoruba and Fon beliefs provided the foundation for almost all of the major African-derived religions in the diaspora. All the same, ethnicity alone never proved sufficient to dictate particular religious developments. Thus one must ask which combination of factors proved sufficient to shape such determinations.

The experience of liberated Africans also provides an opportunity to challenge the divergence that exists between the scholarship on African-derived religions on the one hand and the scholarship on African-American (or African-influenced) Christianity on the other. At its most extreme, this divergence implies a framework of conceptual opposites: African cultural resistance exemplified, for example, by vodun or candomble, versus European cultural dominance, exemplified by widespread conversion to Protestant faiths. Few historians or anthropologists subscribe to such an absolute interpretation. This view perhaps remains the province of the most radical among the cultural nationalists of the African diaspora.[6] Nonetheless, much academic analysis still falls prey to a more nuanced version of this dichotomy. African-derived religions have come to represent greater assertion of Africanness, while African-influenced Christianity represents lesser assertion of Africanness. In other words, scholars imply, in varying degrees, that African-influenced Christianity marked a greater European victory in the admittedly two-way acculturation process.

It is not surprising that the language of Protestant missionary discourse tends to reinforce this perspective. The logic of so-called conversion presupposes knowledge and power on the part of the converter and ignorance and subordination on the part of the converted. Describing a bedside meeting with a free African immigrant, Methodist missionary John Brownell lamented: "Found him near death & as ignorant of God. . . . He knew not that he had a soul much less any proper idea of a future state. . . . [S]aid I to myself on leaving his hut, 'hath no man cared, thy soul to save!'"[7] Such a declaration leaves little opening for African agency or even input in the proposed conversion process. Quite the contrary, Brownell and most of his colleagues viewed their project as taking Christianity to the heathen. And even as historians have explored the ways Africans and their descendants reshaped that Christianity, the idea of an imposed religion has continued to raise the specter that those who converted ended up with less authentically African-Caribbean culture than those who did not. Although both orisha worship and African-influenced Christianity contain a mix of European and African elements, orisha practice is more obviously connected to African practices and beliefs. From this fact arise two related assumptions: first, that, given the opportunity, Africans in the diaspora would choose orisha worship over Christian practices; and second, that those who pursued Christianity did so mostly under duress (or at least because of the lack of opportunity to do otherwise). However, the comparative study of parallel liberated African communities in the Bahamas and Trinidad calls into question both of these assumptions. While the Trinidad community followed elaborate orisha practices, the Bahamian community became African-Christian-Protestants.

These two free African communities shared several characteristics that make them ideal for such an exploration. Perhaps most important, in both colonies the liberated Africans exercised much greater volition and control than their slave predecessors. As in most British colonies, especially during the years of slavery, colonial authorities discouraged (and sometimes legally prohibited) any non-Christian supernatural or religious practices viewed as akin to witchcraft. However, as free people who often lived away from their places of employment, liberated African immigrants had many opportunities to shape their religious life on their own. Second, the cases of the Bahamas and Trinidad provide opportunities to directly compare Roman Catholic and Protestant effects on similar populations. The Spanish held Trinidad until 1797, and although they left only a small population behind, they established Roman Catholicism as the primary European faith on the island, a fact that obtains to the present day. During their tenure they put in place a small number of missionaries and churches, some of which likewise persisted to the late twentieth century. But perhaps the greatest stimulus to Roman Catholic influence in Trinidad came from the influx of planters and slaves from the French Caribbean, both those who came in the wake of the Haitian Revolution and the significant number of francophone migrants who arrived even earlier during the 1780s. (The cedula of population issued by the Spanish crown in 1783 encouraged foreign, especially French, immigration as a way to transform the island into a more profitable colony.)[8] Historian Bridget Brereton writes that "[a]s early as 1784 . . . Trinidad had become virtually a French colony."[9] Many of the Francophone slaves arrived already baptized as Roman Catholics. Following the pattern typical of the Roman Catholic Caribbean, the missionary presence remained minimal, but at least some Roman Catholic observance occurred. Even after the switch to British control in 1797, francophone planters and their slaves remained prominent in both the size of their community and the persistence of their faith. By contrast, the Bahamas followed a Protestant pattern more typical of British West Indian territories. The Anglican Church launched only a minor missionary effort; dissenting Baptists and Methodists did most of the evangelizing of Africans and their descendants.

The Bahamas and Trinidad are also good places to reexamine African religious acculturation because both colonies received a large number of Yoruba Africans—the single ethnic group whose religious pantheon and worldview exercised the most dominant influence on the African-derived religions of candomble, santería, and orisha worship; it also had a significant impact on Haitian vodun. The partial demographic records from the mixed commission at Havana suggest that people of Yoruba ancestry constituted a significant percentage of the liberated Africans who arrived in both colonies. Although Yoruba people made up just over 25 percent of the Havana sample, one cannot predict that percentage for the colonies that received the immigrants. However, the mixed commission data provides a sound basis from which to conclude that people of this ethnicity would have enjoyed at least numeric prominence and probably predominance in any liberated African community. Furthermore, both Bahamian and Trinidadian oral historians identify the Yoruba as the most prominent African ethnicity to which their forbears referred. Yet as much as the Yoruba clearly shaped the development of Trinidad's orisha practices, the Yoruba in the Bahamas left no such inheritance. On the contrary, the strongest religious legacy of the Yoruba in the Bahamas lies not in any African-derived religion but rather in the well-known claim that a group of free Yorubas founded and dominated the largest and most prominent Methodist chapel to serve the African-descended community in and around the city of Nassau.[10] Such dramatically opposite paths provide obvious ground for a reevaluation of how Yoruba peoples participated in New World religious developments.

Finally, as a special immigrant population that was settled in the Caribbean as a part of Britain's "great free labor experiment," liberated Africans often received particular attention not only from government authorities but also from religious missionaries. Because of their unusual experience, these Africans have held a conspicuous place in the collective memories of their respective communities, and both written and oral sources yield rich material on their religious journeys.

Two communities in particular provide logical sites for comparison: in the Bahamas, the settlement of Grant's Town located on 400 acres less than one mile south of downtown Nassau, and in Trinidad, the collection of towns and villages scattered in or near the south-central range known as the Montserrat hills. Both are areas where liberated Africans settled in concentrated communities.

In her study of the Yoruba in Trinidad, Warner-Lewis includes the Montserrat-area villages of Caratal, Kanga Wood, Mayo, Poonah, and Tortuga as notable sites of African immigrant presence. She also includes the nearby town of Gasparillo, which several recent scholars have noted for its lasting evidences of a significant Yoruba (and other African) presence in the not-too-distant past—presumably the latter of half of the nineteenth century and the first few decades of the twentieth.[11] For example, in a 1969 essay, J. D. Elder contends that during the 1960s, Gasparillo not only had a strong community of orisha practitioners but also had several long-resident families who identified themselves as Yoruba descendants and continued to organize their households according to Yoruba kinship patterns. In the neighboring village of Mayo, Elder found people who self-identified as Congo descendants and a Hausa group that still had limited knowledge of Arabic language, the Koran, and several Arabic Muslim songs.[12] From the claims of Elders's informants and the chronology of the nineteenth-century slave trade in the British colonies, it seems almost certain that the majority of these people descended from liberated African immigrants rather than earlier generations of slaves.[13]

A resident of Caratal who was interviewed in 1994 confirmed the impression that the Montserrat area has long served as a major place of residence for free African immigrants and their descendants. Sylvia Ampson described orisha observances during her childhood (in the 1940s and 1950s) that would draw people from "all over the area." Twenty or thirty people formed the core participants; as many as two or three hundred, who ranged from fellow believers to the idle curious, would come to watch the core group's rituals and practices. When questioned about the ethnic ancestry of the central participants, Ampson responded that "all [their] parents came from Africa." (In this case, the term "parents" seems to refer to foreparents in a long-term generational sense rather than to immediate mothers or fathers.)[14] All diasporic Africans could accurately describe their ancestry in this manner. However, Ampson seemed to use this idea in a more specific and immediate sense to refer to people like herself who can trace their African origins to a specific immigrant generation of great- or great-great-grandparents. Ampson also echoed several of the patterns found thirty years earlier by J. D. Elder. For example, like Elder's informants, she too suggested that Mayo has long served as a particular home for the descendants of Congo immigrants: "I think Mayo has, they still have a lot of Congo people there.... [T]hey have some will remember.... [They] must."[15]

In addition to this evidence, which surmises backward from the twentieth century, nineteenth-century descriptions of Montserrat also characterize the area as having a concentration of liberated Africans. Liberated Africans tended to cluster close to areas with many sugar or other plantations, and the area around the Montserrat hills certainly constituted such a region. Descriptions of this area include references to at least five major plantations (Cedar Hill, Caracas, Philippine Edinburgh, and Bonne Aventure).[16] Furthermore, during the late nineteenth century the Montserrat ward received repeated attention from Trinidadian legislators because it was a haven for squatters, a category that included liberated Africans and other groups. During the late 1860s, the government appointed Robert Mitchell as Montserrat ward commissioner. He was charged with the task of completing a land survey and devising a plan for regularizing the status of the various squatters. In March 1868, an editorial in the *Trinidad Chronicle* reviewed and commended Mitchell's efforts. The editorial offered the following description of Caratal and other parts of the Montserrat hills region:

> The district known as Caratal and other districts are inhabited by negro-kind, from the Yaraba down to the Congo, who, though nominally Christians, live under the influence of Obeah superstition and who are, more or less, barbarous in their manners, and impatient of control.[17]

This description does not directly identify free African immigrants. However, during the latter half of the nineteenth century, liberated Africans constituted the overwhelming majority of the African-born population. The Trinidadian press of this era regularly—although not always—made distinctions between "negroes" born in Trinidad and those born in Africa. (Some writers used the term "creole" for the former while reserving "African" for the latter.) In most cases, references to specific ethnic African groups pointed to the African-born. Thus, this portrait of Caratal and its environs strongly suggests a region dominated by liberated African immigrants.

Comparable evidence exists to characterize the much smaller Bahamian neighborhood of Grant's Town. The government of the Bahamas had developed this settlement expressly for African immigrants in the 1820s and

1830s. Although newly freed slaves also became a part of the Grant's Town settlement after emancipation, both nineteenth-century descriptions and modern oral histories strongly suggest that liberated Africans—and later their descendants—remained the dominant component of the community's population. In fact, to accommodate demographic growth in the wake of emancipation, a second settlement was established immediately west of Grant's Town. This second suburb, known as Bain Town, emerged during the late 1830s.[18] Evidence suggests that here, too, liberated Africans played a prominent role. In an 1850 letter, a local Methodist missionary referred to these two townships as "comprehending" a single "District"; a logical union when one considers the fact that the towns together constituted probably less than a thousand acres. The missionary further described the area as "occupied by liberated Africans."[19] This description, with no qualification, seems to portray the area as virtually the sole province of African immigrants.

Bahamian local historian Cleveland W. Eneas reinforces this portrayal in his oral history memoir entitled *Bain Town*. Eneas based this work largely on his own recollections and those of his family and friends. He describes the original settlers of Bain Town as follows:

> The majority of them were actual Yorubas from Western Nigeria, or the immediate descendants of Yorubas. . . . The length of Meadows Street from Blue Hill Road to Nassau Street was owned and inhabited by Yorubas who called themselves N'ongas.[20]

Eneas also recalls—through his parents and grandparents and great-grandparents—descriptions of people with reputed Congo ethnicity who allegedly settled the area directly south of Grant's Town and Bain Town referred to as Conta Butta.[21] The Eneas family's oral genealogy traced their ancestors to a ship of liberated Africans that arrived in the Bahamas during the 1830s. The origin tale, passed down from one generation to the next, describes the arrival of a brother and sister from Africa who became the indentured servants of a British family named Eneas, and so began the story of a Yoruba-descended family with this particular English name. (In interviews conducted during 1993 and 1994, Eneas explained that since the publication of his book, he had successfully located in the Bahamas Department of Archives written evidence of an indentured African male bearing the uncommon name of "Briton Eneas," just as the oral history had always described.) Of even greater significance, Eneas points out that his forbears did not present the family history as a narrative of their uniqueness. On the contrary, the story always included the explanation that many other families in the Grant's Town–Bain Town area shared comparable origins.[22] Thus, a preponderance of evidence establishes Grant's Town and its environs as a locus of liberated African community in the Bahamas.

The Trinidadian and Bahamian locales clearly share many demographic and social parallels. Yet the histories of religious experience in these two communities could hardly differ more starkly. In the Trinidad case, African-derived religion was prominent. Beginning at least in the 1860s, nineteenth-century descriptions presented African-derived practices as a characteristic feature of the villages in the Montserrat area. Most such observations in the nineteenth century came from generally unsympathetic European observers, and one might rightfully question whether the portrayals of rampant African religious activity contained some exaggeration. However, the twentieth-century legacy observed by scholars and described by residents supports a vision of an area long steeped in the religion now referred to as orisha worship.

During 1869 and 1870, a British Anglican priest stationed in Trinidad devoted extensive and specific attention to the religious or spiritual state of the inhabitants of the Montserrat ward. At that time, the western coast of Trinidad between Port-of-Spain in the north and San Fernando in the south constituted four Anglican parishes. W. Bovell Laurie served as rector for the combined southerly parishes of Saint Philip and Saint Peter, which were situated northeast of San Fernando around the smaller town of Pointe-a-Pierre and directly east of the Montserrat hills. In the course of his mission work, Laurie became aware of the liberated African population of the neighboring Montserrat area. He found that many of them at some time in the past had received Christian baptism. However, they had lived without the supervision and guidance of a regular Christian minister for a long while. According to Laurie, these nominal Christians lived "without the privileges, and without a sense of the responsibilities of their Christian vocation."[23] These words seem mild in comparison to the *Trinidad Chronicle*'s description of "superstition" and "barbarous manners." Written only a year apart, both descriptions refer to the exact same region and apparently the same population. Analyzed together, these two portraits point to a situation that was perhaps ideal for the development of a syncretic but mostly African-derived religion. The region had a significant community of African-born people who had some introduction to Roman Catholicism but were left for long periods without a missionary or anyone else to supervise their religious lives.

Trinidad received most of its liberated African immigrants between the mid-1830s and the late 1850s. Thus, the Africans Laurie encountered in 1869 had most likely resided in the colony for at least ten years and possibly much longer. Given the presence of Francophone planters in Trinidad, the Africans may have received their Christian baptisms through a Roman Catholic missionary while they were working as indentured labor on local estates.[24] As Laurie speculates, missionary priests may have done little more than perform baptisms, either because the plantation they worked at discouraged anything further or because a shortage of local clergy precluded extensive teaching in any single place. (Such a pattern of baptism followed by relative neglect would be consistent with the experience that obtained in France's Caribbean colonies, most notably Haiti.) The African immigrants still possessed whatever culture and beliefs they had brought with them across the Atlantic. An outsider such as Laurie could hardly document the presence of such beliefs, but other nineteenth-century observers did at least note the persistence of African languages. For example, the *Chronicle* editorial complained of "a dozen African tribes who all speak different dialects."[25] Because language is perhaps the strongest outward cultural marker of inward orientations, the community at Montserrat seems to have been poised to nurture a religion of the African-derived model. That is, people still speaking African languages were also likely to be trying to continue other African cultural practices, including religion.

After evaluating the Montserrat situation, Rev. Laurie appealed to both Trinidadian and British sources for funds with which to establish a permanent Anglican chapel with its own attached missionary. His efforts to secure a building seem to have succeeded; several years later the Anglican Church of Saint Alban's was consecrated at Montserrat.[26] In addition, a survey of the region today reveals several Roman Catholic churches that date to the nineteenth century, among them Our Lady of Montserrat located in the village of Tortuga. All the same, no nineteenth-century account states or implies that the area acquired regular, permanent, or full-time missionary service. Thus, it is perhaps not surprising that the region seems to have produced an abundance of orisha practitioners—at least according to twentieth-century evidence.

Anthropologists, most notably George Simpson, have thoroughly described the basic character of orisha practice in Trinidad. The system accepts the existence of a supreme or creator god. However, the religion focuses not on interaction with this high or distant figure but on interaction with various spirits called orishas. Each orisha has special association with particular things such as iron or water, or with particular concepts such as war, love, or health. The orishas have African names that are based largely on Yoruba antecedents. Yet they also bear the names of Roman Catholic saints. That is, each orisha figure has at least two titles, one African and the other Roman Catholic. Like so many West African religions, orisha practice

Roman Catholic
Church, Gasparillo,
Trinidad (1994)

includes spirit possession or trance. Followers undergo possession or trance
when taken over in mind, body, and spirit by a particular orisha. While in
this state, devotees sing, dance, act, and speak not as themselves but as the
orisha by whom they are possessed, and a person in this state will often offer
guidance, warnings, or predictions for both individuals and the group.[27]

While these practices have occurred and continue to occur all over
Trinidad, certain locations have developed reputations as centers of concentration. Virtually the entire Montserrat area has had this characterization, as
J. D. Elder has demonstrated with his research of the 1960s. In particular,
Elder explored the religious practice of a group of Yoruba-descended families in the town of Gasparillo. He compiled a list of specific Gasparillo beliefs and practices that closely paralleled those of the Yoruba in Africa. Per-

haps most valuable is his probing of the conceptual foundations of the African and Trinidadian religious systems. He examines the intertwined notions of ancestors and spirits and collective ethnic identity. Elder concludes that even these abstract philosophical foundations persisted to a degree among Gasparillo followers of what he calls the "Orisha Work."[28]

In recent decades, the number of continuing practitioners has declined significantly, and it seems unlikely that present-day inquiries could yield results equal to Elder's depth. Several informants, however, paint a vivid picture of widespread orisha worship throughout the Montserrat region until relatively recent times. Sylvia Ampson of the village of Caratal makes a telling observation when she explains:

> You [didn't] have to invite [people], because they know . . . that . . . you having this [annual orisha observance], the first week in August. . . . [E]verybody used to take part.[29]

Like Irene Joseph, Ampson no longer follows the orisha religious system. But she readily explains at length that for much of her life, orisha devotions, both large and small, public and private, remained a common part of the cultural, social, and spiritual landscape of Caratal and its neighbors.

The great-great-grandchildren of liberated Africans in the Bahamas tell no such orisha tales. The religious narrative of the Grant's Town settlement paints a picture of regular, intense, and productive Protestant evangelism for over 150 years. During this period African immigrants and their descendants became active members of Anglican, Baptist, and Methodist congregations. Like many missionaries, evangelicals in the Bahamas during the nineteenth century bemoaned the insufficiency of both money and manpower. As an archipelago, the Bahamas posed particular challenges; missionaries had to travel to over fifteen inhabited islands. But in the island of New Providence and around the capital of Nassau, concentration of missionaries who often competed for the population's attention developed. Since the 1840s, the Grant's Town–Bain Town area has either encompassed or bordered at least five major churches of the three Protestant denominations: Saint Agnes Anglican, Bethel Baptist, Saint John's Native Baptist, Zion Baptist, and Grant's Town Wesley Methodist. All of these congregations claim distinctive and distinguished histories that intertwined in various ways with the social and political struggles of people of African descent. Therefore, to single out any one church perhaps runs the risk of inaccurately making that one church seem more important than others in the history of this neighborhood. But, in terms of the specific history of liberated Africans, Grant's Town Wesley holds a special place.

Wesley Methodist Church, Grant's Town, Nassau, Bahamas (2004)

Wesley is distinctive because it is a chapel originally established for the specific and virtually exclusive use of free African immigrants. This mission began late in 1831, seven years after the establishment of Grant's Town but two years before emancipation. In other words, the mission began at a time before freed slaves had joined the settlement en masse. It seems most likely that British missionary Charles Penney entered the Grant's Town community late in 1831 or early in 1832. During this period, the Methodists had already established three significant chapels on the island of New Providence: a town congregation apparently dominated by white Methodist converts; an eastern chapel, also dominated by whites but including some "Black and Coloured" inhabitants; and a western chapel, founded in the late eighteenth century by a freed Loyalist slave from the United States and attended thereafter by "Black and Coloured" people both slave and free. In a report to his London supervisors in January 1832, Penney noted two major developments. One was that he had begun a special Monday-evening meeting "for the Black and Coloured people." At these Monday events, Penney sought to provide this special group with extra teaching "in a plainer manner," consistent with what he viewed as either their weaker comprehension or lesser education in comparison to the "large mixed congregations." Penney thus clearly had specific pedagogical plans for his black and colored converts. He did not mention liberated African immigrants as a subset of this group. Rather, they received separate attention in his second major announcement. Penney explained: "I have been invited to extend my labors to a Company of Coloured people who are settled in a place called 'Grant's Town.'"[30]

Although he made this announcement with some pride, Penney at first used it as an opportunity to document his extreme overwork, making a typical thinly veiled plea for further assistance. He pointed out that even without this new task, he had scheduled mission events six nights of the week. Saturday night remained free, but he needed that to prepare his three Sabbath sermons. Such distress notwithstanding, Penney concluded his letter: "I must and will by God's blessing, embrace this [Grant's Town] opening, as it is too important to be neglected."[31] Future records indicate that Penney did indeed find time to begin a regular evangelizing mission for the liberated Africans. Penney's successor, John Corlett, reported that the Grant's Town work had begun with a single evening service held on alternate weeks. This would hardly seem to constitute an intensive missionary presence. All the same, the community demonstrated sufficient receptiveness to construct a makeshift meeting place at their own expense.[32] Under Corlett's guidance, the group grew in numbers and built more permanent structures; this community would later become the most populous and most powerful community of African-descended Methodists in the Bahamas, a compelling symbol of creative and self-determining African diaspora Christianity. In the words of a Methodist youth minister penned in 1993:

> Wesley is the Jewel in the Methodist Church crown. It is the church with the largest congregation and the most potential for growth. Out of Wesley have come three [new] congregations. . . . Yes Wesley is still the jewel in the crown.[33]

Over a century before this grand declaration, missionary John Corlett focused his Grant's Town efforts on the liberated African core of that community. By 1839, newly emancipated slaves had also joined the settlement, but according to Corlett's descriptions, immigrant Africans continued to predominate. In fact, during 1838, more liberated Africans entered the Bahamas than in any other single year. Corlett quotes a figure of 1,000 settled on New Providence alone. (This figure may overlook the fact that several hundred of the Africans ended up settled on other Bahamian islands. But even an influx of 700 would have made a significant increase in the African immigrant group.) Corlett divided his work between instructing this population and seeking the financial resources to build a proper chapel and school. In 1847 the church acquired property and construction began. The congregation grew enormously, led largely (albeit not exclusively) by the devotion and energy of liberated African converts. In the commemorative booklet Wesley produced for its centenary in the 1947, Rev. William Makepeace cites several notations from both missionary letters and synod reports affirming the critical participation of this unique population: "Rescued from the foul entrenchments of the slave-ship . . . by British power and philanthropy, they have also in many instances been rescued by the influences of the Gospel from the moral slavery which enchained their souls."[34] One might reasonably question this melodramatic claim of missionary success. After all, might not a minister have exaggerated such claims either to improve his stature or for some other ulterior motive? However, as many as one-third of several hundred letters written by Methodist missionaries report difficulty or failure rather than the success. (For example, John Corlett noted that the Grant's Town mission had largely collapsed for almost a year after a hurricane in 1837 destroyed their makeshift meeting place.) Given the forthright tone of this correspondence, it seems reasonable to presume accuracy in the later portrayals of increasing success.

Grant's Town's popular history further reinforces the image of Wesley Chapel as the special province of liberated African people and their descendants. The commemorative centenary booklet of 1947 includes a special segment entitled "Leaders and Church Officers" that presents a brief description of the earliest leaders of the Wesley Church community. The text describes at least half of such people as Africans and identifies several as being of "Nango" (Yoruba) ethnicity.[35] This essay combines several family histories to establish a genealogy of liberated Africans for the Wesley Church community. While much of this genealogy has arisen from the orally transmitted recollections of members of the community, documentary sources from throughout the nineteenth century support this portrayal of church history. For example, the early Wesley activists described by the commemorative booklet included a carpenter and musician named Domingo Weir. According to the brochure, Weir established the first Wesley choir and served as its choirmaster for forty years. In a 1994 interview, Gaspare Weir—great-grandson of Domingo—reiterated these details concerning the choir and explicitly asserted that his African Methodist ancestor had arrived in the Bahamas as a rescued slave taken from a captured foreign vessel.[36] For many, perhaps most, descendants of reputed liberated Africans, such an assertion would prove difficult to verify. But in this case, the name of Mingo Weir does in fact appear on an 1843 list recording land grants for the village of Adelaide in southwestern New Providence,[37] a community established in 1831 expressly for the settlement of a group of liberated Africans rescued from the Portuguese slave ship *Rosa* in June of that year. In his account of Domingo's background, Gaspare Weir also refers specifically to a Portuguese vessel. Thus, a confluence of relevant details seems to confirm the historical assertions of the 1947 commemorative brochure.

Another life history that illustrates the role of liberated Africans in the development of Wesley Church involves a man named Alliday Adderley. Like Weir, Adderley received mention in the 1947 document as one of the early leaders of the Grant's Town chapel. The booklet describes him as "an African gentleman of the Nango [Yoruba] tribe . . . a Christian in word and deed."[38] Such an individual would seem to exemplify African immigrant espousal of Protestant Christianity. The clearest verification of Adderley's identity as a converted liberated African immigrant arises from his obituary, which appeared in the *Nassau Guardian* in September 1885. The brief but detailed announcement describes the participation at the funeral of the Bahama Friendly and Yoruba Societies along with other friends and mourners, "large numbers forming the procession which marched, from the residence . . . first to Wesley Chapel, Grant's Town, and from there to Potter's Field Cemetery."[39] The funeral procession to Wesley would seem to confirm Adderley's membership in that congregation. The presence of the Yoruba Society implies at least some affiliation with a specific African ethnic group. These deductions prove secondary, however, as the newspaper notice in fact directly identifies the deceased as "a native of Africa [who] came [to the Bahamas] in a captured slaver."[40] It thus seems clear that liberated Africans and their descendants not only dominated the founding of Wesley Chapel in the late 1830s but remained a notable presence in the church through the nineteenth century.

Perhaps even more significant, nineteenth-century descriptions indicate that the Wesley congregations practiced a style of Christian worship that had such pronounced African influences that the Grant's Town chapel stood out even among other local missionary churches with predominantly black and colored memberships. A North American author, William Drysdale, visited the Bahamas and Cuba in the early 1880s and published a narrative of his journey entitled *In Sunny Lands: Out-Door Life in Nassau and Cuba*. Drysdale includes a description of a visit he and other tourists made to a Grant's Town "church known as 'The Shouters.'"[41] While Drysdale does not identify this church as Wesley Methodist chapel, no other church stood in the midst of Grant's Town at that time. Several churches existed in the immediate vicinity of the liberated African village, but only Wesley lay properly within it. According to Drysdale, this church enjoyed such a reputation for its unique and ecstatic worship style that North American travelers regularly visited the congregation to observe and be entertained. In fact, Drysdale reports that the interest of tourists had grown so significant that some Wesley members allegedly took payments in exchange for promising visitors a good "shouting" performance during the services they attended. He explains: "For the shouters do not always shout, but only when the spirit moves, or when Americans want to invest a few dollars in seeing the fun."[42] Drysdale concedes that he could not verify the occurrence of such payments, but even a fabricated legend about such transactions would serve as evidence of Wesley's particular reputation in this regard.

The term "shouting" has usually referred to a combination of African-influenced ecstatic singing, dancing, clapping, and stamping of feet, often but not always in ring formation. From the eighteenth through twentieth centuries observers have described this phenomenon in various Protestant churches throughout the African diaspora, although most commonly in the United States.[43] Drysdale describes in some detail the behavior he observed at Wesley chapel during his visit. He characterizes the hymns he heard as "curious" but reports that he found the sermon "quite sensible enough" until its closing passages. At that point, the minister "warmed up . . . till he had some of his women hearers excitedly rocking their bodies to and fro, crying amen, and giving the other signs of religious excitement often seen in 'revival' meetings."[44] Nevertheless, Drysdale complains that on the whole, during his visit "[t]here was no more commotion than . . . in any lively Methodist meeting, and the shouting part was a miserable failure."[45] Drysdale does not indicate what precisely he understood to be the "shouting part" of the service. However, it seems reasonable to assume that he referred to some version of the several factors usually associated with the term. Drysdale's disappointment notwithstanding, his narrative offers testimony of the distinctive reputation of Grant's Town Wesley for the performance of this particular African-influenced practice. After all, there were other churches with African-descended congregations within easy traveling distance of downtown Nassau which might have satisfied the curiosity of foreign tourists or the voyeurism of white local residents. Among such churches, the Baptist chapels would almost certainly have had some kind of charismatic and African-influenced elements in their services. But according to Drysdale's account, outsiders expressly selected Wesley. Popular opinion apparently portrayed the chapel that had been founded and dominated by liberated Africans as the place that manifested the most potent and most dramatic examples of African-influenced charismatic Christianity.

A brief corroboration of this image of Wesley appears in a letter written by a British Baptist missionary who was also present in the Bahamas during the 1880s. In a letter to the *Nassau Guardian* in April 1885, Rev. Daniel Wilshere wrote: "The emotional nature of the services of the African Methodist Episcopal church is well-known in Nassau as one of the Sunday attractions of northern visitors to this island."[46] As no American Methodist Episcopal church existed in the Bahamas during this era, it seems almost certain that Wilshere referred here to Grant's Town Wesley, the only Methodist church in the town of Nassau with an exclusively African-descended population. Wilshere offered this comment in response to reports of an outbreak of religious "hysteria" on the island of San Salvador (now Cat Island) in the central Bahamas. Between the months of March and June numerous people on that island experienced violent seizures followed by periods of trance. Many members of the local community interpreted these experiences as "Visitations of the Lord." A kind of ongoing religious revival ensued that included daily singing and public processions followed by nightly gatherings that sometimes involved more seizures and trances.[47]

The first report of these events apparently came from the rector of the Anglican church at Port Howe, Cat Island, although the *Guardian* published the report without identifying an author. This account not only condemned the experiences as "ridiculous" but also suggested that the "midnight meetings for dancing and shouting [would] lead to greater immorality than already exist[ed]."[48] In the letter he wrote in reply to this report, Rev. Wilshere accused the Anglican rector of painting an unfair portrait of the residents of Cat Island during this affair. Wilshere made mention of the "emotional" services at Grant's Town in order to buttress this critique. He seems to have wanted to use the example of Wesley to demonstrate two points: first, that Cat Island hardly had a monopoly on ecstatic religious behavior; and second, that if the well-known ecstatic behavior at the Wesley Methodist chapel did not automatically produce "immorality," one should not cast aspersions on the Cat Islanders, however "hysterical" their religious activities had become.[49] In the late nineteenth century, Grant's Town Wesley had thus clearly become a kind of local exemplar of African influence in Bahamian religious culture. Observers such as William Drysdale and Rev. Daniel Wilshere did not necessarily highlight the role of liberated Africans in molding the nature of religious practice at the Grant's Town chapel. However, the influence of these latest-arriving African immigrants clearly lay at the roots of Wesley's cultural prominence.

Never once does the author of Wesley's 1947 commemorative essay consider the irony of mixing an embrace of African origins with a celebration of Christian conversion. Yet therein lies a clue to reevaluating the interpretation of African religious experience in the diaspora. The comparison of Grant's Town with the Montserrat hills suggests that two factors above all others shaped the different religious developments. First, the Montserrat experience clearly reinforces the long-established proposition that Roman Catholicism, with its pantheon of saints, proved uniquely conducive to syncretism with West African religious systems. Second, and more important, however, the comparison suggests that the single greatest influence was the volume and nature of interaction between missionaries and Africans.[50] Limited contact with missionaries left African immigrants to govern their own spiritual lives to a large extent. Hence, they crafted a system that was most heavily based on the systems of their former societies. Conversely, intense missionary teaching presented African immigrants with a new set of propositions and practices for the governance of spiritual life. Perhaps from their perspective, it represented a new spiritual order for the radically changed existence of life in the diaspora. Thus, liberated African Methodists in the Bahamas were no less free, no less Yoruba, and no more European-dominated than their orisha-practicing counterparts in Trinidad. Most likely, like Irene Joseph, they viewed their transition to "Jesus time" as a transition that had equal cultural integrity with any other New World experience.

The cases of Grant's Town in the Bahamas and the ward of Montserrat in Trinidad represent only part of the New World spiritual experience of liberated African immigrants. The practice of orisha worship, in particular, merits attention beyond the confines of the limited district around Caratal, Tortuga, and Gasparillo. One student of the University of the West Indies who conducted research in 1970 asserted that at that time there existed "at least one hundred [orisha worship] centers in Trinidad" that claimed thousands of full members and "additional thousands of marginal participants."[51] During the nineteenth century, Christian proselytizers visited the ward of Montserrat—and many other areas of Trinidad—infrequently. In 1859, a Methodist missionary assigned to the colony complained plaintively to his superiors in London of the geographic challenges he faced in his mission. John Richardson described the population as being "scattered over the whole country" with travel to diverse locations made particularly difficult by the poor condition of the roads, many of which by his account became "almost impassable" during the six-month wet season.[52] Richardson also complained of the fact that the French presence in the colony had resulted in the prevalence of "popery"; the Roman Catholic Church constituted the sole Christian foothold in many areas. He especially bemoaned the fact that under arrangements made when Britain had acquired Trinidad from Spain in 1797, the British government had actually paid to support the local Roman Catholic archbishop and no less than thirty priests.[53] However, this Roman Catholic presence by no means meant intensive missionary education or close supervision. Richardson accused the priests of drunkenness and other laxity in their work. And, derelict or not, such priests would have faced the same geographic obstacles of which the Methodist had complained. During the 1880s, a French priest—not a Protestant critic—provided testimony of the Roman Catholic Church's pattern of baptism with little follow-up. In a diary entry for October 1880, Abbé Armand Massé made the following complaint about an African immigrant he visited near the town of Oropouche (now South Oropouche) in southwestern Trinidad: "He is only Christian by baptism, and since he has been baptised he has barely made any act of religion. He does not know his prayers or rather he . . . mixes up in the most sadly strange way some words of the Pater, of the Ave Maria and of the Credo."[54] Commentaries such as these provide ready justification for the impression that liberated African immigrants all over Trinidad experienced an environment that was almost ideal for the pursuit of a syncretic religion such as orisha worship.

Just as Sylvia Ampson, Irene Joseph, and others point to the most recent African immigrants and their descendants as having had prominent roles in the practice of African-derived religion in Caratal and Tortuga, twentieth-century residents from other parts of the island allude to the probable influence of liberated Africans in shaping local orisha worship communities. Most important, such allusions do not seem to occur in a random pattern but rather tend to follow areas otherwise noted for significant liberated African settlement. For example, in her study of the persistence of Yoruba cultural influence in twentieth-century Trinidad, Maureen Warner-Lewis includes the valley of Diego Martin in the northwestern part of the island as a site of significant free African settlement during the previous century.[55] And in interviews conducted in 1994 for this study, Diego Martin residents repeatedly suggested that some particular Africans and their descendants— whom they distinguished from the wider population of African descent —would have had the greatest involvement with the conduct of orisha ceremonies and related religious practices.[56] Predictably, such ordinary residents, who were speaking almost a century and a half after the arrival of the last liberated Africans in Trinidad, did not specifically refer to the migration of free Africans rescued from slave ships. However, these nineteenth-century settlers and their descendants provide the only logical population segment to whom such special references would apply. None of this evidence suggests that liberated Africans held sole or even dominant responsibility for the development and perpetuation of Trinidad's vodun-like religion. Rather, in conjunction with the presence of former slaves from the French Caribbean (who possibly followed vodun) and the particular theology and conversion practices of the Roman Catholic Church, these free African immigrants, whose numbers included a significant population of Yorubas, became key participants in molding and perpetuating the Trinidad variant of a Yoruba-derived syncretic religion of the African diaspora.

Trinidad has also stood out in British West Indian religious history for having produced an autonomous and obviously African-influenced form of Christianity during the nineteenth century: the "Spiritual" or "Shouter" Baptists. Anthropologist Stephen Glazier has described the modern Spiritual Baptist faith as "an amalgam of many beliefs and practices . . . [with borrowings] from the four major world religions (Christianity, Islam, Hinduism and Buddhism) and from African-derived tribal religions."[57] He modifies this description with a notation that "Christianity and African-derived religions seem to have had the greatest impact."[58] Spiritual Baptist theology upholds the major tenets of Christianity, while its practice incorporates a variety of charismatic and symbolic performance rituals, the most well known of which involves an extended period of trance-like meditation known as mourning. This particular experience may last anywhere from seven to twenty-one days and involves the isolation of the participant or participants in a special room adjacent to the main place of worship, where a spiritual guide called a pointer supervises a process of meditation, partial fasting, and possible trance, usually accompanied by visions or dreams that the mourner and church leaders later interpret in order to determine their spiritual significance.[59] It is important to note that this mourning ritual is not in any way related to the mourning after a death or other loss. Many aspects of the Spiritual Baptist faith have parallels both with orisha ceremonies and with various forms of the charismatic African-American Christianity that has been studied at length in the United States but is also present in parts of the Caribbean, perhaps most notably in the Revivalism movement of Jamaica.

As a result of the perceived parallels with orisha worshippers, the Spiritual Baptist church has often received the misnomer of Shango Baptist in popular Trinidadian discourse. Despite the error of this name, the label demonstrates some general understanding that these two religions—one avowedly Christian and the other mostly African-derived—share similar African cultural roots. In the analyses of historians and other scholars, virtually all aspects of African-American culture throughout the hemisphere share a cultural legacy at some level. However, the case of the Spiritual Baptists requires us to look for the possibility of particular influence from liberated Africans. Anthropologists and other scholars who have studied the religion do not agree about the origins of the Spiritual Baptist church. According to one theory, the faith did not develop in Trinidad until the early decades of the present century when immigrant laborers from Saint Vincent brought the beliefs and practices of the Vincentian "Shaker" church when they came to the larger island. Like the Spiritual Baptists, the Shakers combine Protestant Christianity with African-influenced singing, dancing, and variations of possession trance, including the mourning ritual. Although some members of the group cite their origins in the Methodist conversion of slaves during the eighteenth century, many Shaker worshippers also "refer to themselves as 'Spiritual Baptists' or 'converted people.'"[60] Because of the sometimes shared name and the similarities in practice, especially the unique mourning, some scholars and laypeople have credited the Vincentian immigrants with creating the Trinidad church. Stephen Glazier notes with some skepticism that this interpretation holds greatest sway with church members of Vincentian descent.[61] Glazier, however, also cites the work of a fellow scholar, Charles Gullick, who bases his support of the Saint Vincent hypothesis on the fact that the Trinidadian and Vincentian churches seem unique in their conduct of the distinctive mourning period. Gullick concedes that similar meditative and trance practices occur elsewhere in the Caribbean and beyond the region,[62] but he claims that the specific and unusual terminology—"mourning"—remains unique to these two islands.[63] At least one piece of nineteenth-century evidence, however, proves Gullick incorrect in this linguistic assumption and provides grounds for speculation concerning a possible connection between liberated African immigrants and the development of the Spiritual Baptist faith. The 1888 travel account about the Bahamas of J. and E. E. Dickinson and S. E. Dowd reports the use of the term "mourning" by a Bahamian of African descent to describe certain religious behavior carried out by worshippers at the Wesley Methodist Church.

One Sunday in late March these three women attended the service at "a Methodist church in Grant's Town that [was] familiarly termed 'The Shouters.'"[64] Such a reference could only refer to Grant's Town Wesley, the only Methodist church in that particular community. The women describe the sermon on that day as "a very disjointed talk" based on a passage from the Revelation of Saint John which read in part "I was in the Spirit on the Lord's day."[65] In the course of his exegesis, the minister complained of the apparent loss of "the Spirit" within his congregation. He recalled more enthusiastic behavior of the past as follows:

> [I remember] a revival when the floor was covered with people *mournin'*, but now there's no fire in the island. Folks come into church as cold as water, and go out like ice-blocks.[66] (emphasis added)

The citation here clearly does not refer to the more standard kind of mourning associated with grief or loss. At the same time, however, this description does not imply anything like the lengthy and semi-private Spiritual Baptist mourning retreat. Perusal of other nineteenth-century records could conceivably reveal additional references to charismatic, meditative, or trance-like mourning in communities that had no connection with liberated African immigrants. In her study of Afro-Baptist Christianity in the United States, Mechal Sobel produces a single source that variously uses the terms "sinner," "seeker," and "mourner" to describe people not yet fully converted to the Christian faith.[67] The possibility of multiple undiscovered references to trance-like mourning in early sources seems unlikely given the apparent absence of the mourning concept in most scholarship on African-American religion to date except in reference to Trinidad or Saint Vincent.[68]

In any case, this study does not propose that the use of this term and the patterns of trance behavior associated with it are unique to liberated African immigrants. (According to various sources, the biblical origin of the term is the book of Daniel, where the prophet describes a period of fasting and meditation that resulted in divinely inspired visions.)[69] The word alone is less important than the concept of extended or elaborate trance-like behavior in the course of Protestant Christian worship, whether during a single service or "revival," as described in the Grant's Town Methodist Chapel, or for several days, as in the Trinidadian Spiritual Baptist faith. Just as liberated Africans did not introduce orisha worship to Trinidad but encouraged and reinforced such practices, so too the presence of free African immigrants probably encouraged particularly elaborate articulations—"mourning"—of already-existing trance-like behaviors as a part of Protestant Christian practice in both Trinidad and the Bahamas.

In many respects the charismatic behavior of the Grant's Town Methodists seems minor alongside the diversity of African-influenced ritual in Spiritual Baptist practice. Spiritual Baptist services regularly include the use of candles, water libations, bell ringing, chalk markings similar to the vevers of Haitian vodun, and various forms of ecstatic verbal expression that believers interpret as the power of the Holy Spirit. Based on twentieth-century accounts from the Herskovitses during the 1940s to the more recent work of Stephen Glazier and the Rev. Eudora Thomas, it seems likely that such activities have constituted a part of Spiritual Baptist ritual for considerable time and very possibly since the origins of the church. Perhaps the earliest accounting of such details occurred as a result of the 1917 Shouter Prohibition Ordinance; Melville and Frances Herskovits cite the 1936 edition of the *Trinidad Constabulary Manual*, which itemized different Spiritual Baptist behaviors in order to assist police officers in the enforcement of the law.[70] The explanation for the elaborateness of these rituals and unique nature of the Spiritual Baptist church is almost certainly the same isolation and relative missionary neglect that influenced of evolution of the orisha worship communities. One might argue that the Spiritual Baptist church constitutes a kind of midpoint on a continuum of African-influenced religious development, with various forms of African-American Christianity toward one end and the New World orisha-worshipping religions toward the other.

The second major theory of the origins of the Spiritual Baptist church prioritizes not the role of immigrants from Africa or Saint Vincent but rather the influence of former slaves from the United States. Following the War of 1812, Trinidad received almost 1,000 black refugees who had sided with the British during that conflict. During the war, the British formed African-American defectors into a group of segregated companies of Royal Colonial Marines. Most of these immigrants were members of disbanded special marine units and their families. Several of the Trinidadian towns that these refugees founded still bear the military names of Third Company and Sixth Company. Most of these refugees arrived in Trinidad as already-converted Christians, having worshipped as Baptists in the United States. Their religious communities earned the label of American or 'Merikan Baptists to distinguish them from other Baptist communities founded or directed by missionaries from the United Kingdom. One school of thought has proposed that the roots of the Spiritual Baptist church lie with these North Americans. Glazier, however, offers strong grounds for discounting this proposition; perhaps his most salient point is the fact that in the late twentieth century, the "'Merikan Baptists and their descendants no longer exert[ed] direct influence in the religion."[71] Glazier also points out that although some nineteenth-century observers recorded behavior described as religious "shouting" in the marine villages, the modern 'Merikan Baptist churches lack anything like the elaborate ritual practices of their Spiritual Baptist counterparts. And they certainly have no rite of mourning. Glazier also notes that many contemporary Spiritual Baptists who support the hypothesis of American origins seem to do so as a means of "protesting what they perceive as Vincentian domination of their faith."[72]

Some nineteenth-century evidence exists of other Baptist churches that were founded by British missionaries but composed almost exclusively of liberated Africans. The Baptist Missionary Society began its work in Trinidad during the 1840s. According to a mission history published in 1866, a woman of African birth had the dubious distinction of becoming the first recorded Baptist Missionary Society convert. In his 1866 text, the Rev. W. H. Gamble describes this woman as a former slave converted by missionary George Cowen. Gamble portrays Cowen's first chapel as a place where the missionary "gathered the sons and daughters of Africa together [and] taught them . . . the truth as it is in Jesus."[73] Located in Dry River, a neighborhood in the eastern part of Port-of-Spain, this congregation most likely included a mixture of former slaves and liberated African immigrants. Although nineteenth-century authors tended to use the adjective "African" to refer to the African-born, the phrase "sons and daughters of Africa" seems most likely a more generic (and sentimental) reference to the entire African-descended population to whom he and other missionaries directed most of their efforts.

Elsewhere in his text, however, Gamble speaks somewhat differently of a "small church" in southern Trinidad "chiefly composed of Africans."[74] This congregation existed during Gamble's missionary tenure in the island during the late 1850s and early 1860s. In this period, liberated African immigrants would have almost certainly constituted the majority of the African-born population.[75] In his descriptions of these and other Africans, Gamble repeatedly implies that the people in question had the status of relative newcomers. For example, Gamble wrote: "They are obedient, industrious, liberal and simple-minded people. They have raised a considerable sum of money *considering their position*, and have built themselves a neat little chapel" (emphasis added).[76] This chapel functioned not under the direct supervision of Rev. Gamble but rather under the leadership of a Brother William Carr, himself the son of former slaves.[77] A church such as this, "chiefly composed of Africans" and subject to only periodic visits by its designated British missionary, would seem to have constituted an ideal site for the development of a heavily African-influenced and relatively autonomous Protestant religious practice—a religious practice such as the Spiritual Baptist faith.

Stephen Glazier concludes his exploration of Spiritual Baptist history with a declaration of his belief that "it will [never] be possible to trace the 'true' origins" of the faith.[78] One can, however, draw at least two major conclusions about those origins. Firstly, given the nineteenth-century presence of both North American and other Baptists in Trinidad, it seems unlikely that the only roots of the Spiritual Baptist lie with the early twentieth-century immigrants from Saint Vincent. Second, given the evidence of the impact of liberated Africans on Protestant religious practice in the Bahamas and Rev. Gamble's testimony about the existence of at least one Trinidadian Baptist congregation dominated by African immigrants, it seems highly probable that newly arrived Africans played some significant role in the development of this church.

The religious experience of liberated Africans in these two colonies reflected a pattern of various African cultural influences on prevailing religious practices. Specific outcomes were determined by environment and the degree of input by missionaries. Despite the distinctive practice of the Wesley Methodist community, nowhere in the relatively confined and more intensively covered missionary territory of New Providence—where most liberated Africans made their home—did there ever exist the combination of autonomy and missionary neglect that facilitated orisha worshiping and the practices of the Spiritual Baptist church in Trinidad. Nevertheless, it bears mentioning that a small number of suggestive twentieth-century references to the possibility of some kind of more-organized African-derived religious practice in the Bahamas exists. Perhaps predictably, these comments have arisen in descriptions not of the island of New Providence but of other outlying islands that received far less intensive missionary attention. For example, in an account of a journey to the Bahamas during the late 1930s, Rosita Forbes, a travel writer from the United States, described people she encountered in the interior of the island of Andros as follows:

> Inland, there are "bush blacks" primitive as their blood brethren in the Congo. These still hold to the fetishes and taboos of a tribal system which did not survive the original crossing of the Atlantic. They know a few words of the African dialects . . . but they have lost all sense of their meaning.[79]

Although elsewhere Forbes seems to hypothesize that these people and their ancestors had lived in relative isolation since eighteenth-century slavery, their continuing knowledge of some African language strongly suggests that she may have in fact encountered the descendants of liberated Africans who would have had a more recent link to their African linguistic past. As for the "fetishes and taboos," Forbes's choice of language in describing what she called "bush blacks" implies that she almost certainly harbored stereotypical and condescending views of African and African-derived cultures. But these prejudices do not automatically discount her descriptions. Forbes does not portray all Bahamians of African descent as following unclear "tribal systems"; she contrasts the apparent beliefs of the inland population of Andros with the less-African-seeming lifestyle of the "colored people and negroes" in coastal parts of the island who had presumably experienced greater interaction over time with various inhabitants of European descent.[80] Forbes's allusion hardly constitutes definitive evidence of a Bahamian religious system in any way comparable to Trinidad's orisha worship. If an organized practice did exist in the comparatively isolated interior of Andros Island, this fact would only confirm the role of geographic and cultural isolation in determining the nature of religious practices shaped by liberated Africans.

An additional passing reference to the possibility of an organized African-derived religious system in the Bahamas appears in the work of French author Max Deslèves. During his travels through the Bahamian islands in the early 1960s, Deslèves heard tales of supernatural creatures called chickcharnies who could interfere in the lives of human beings, presumably to cause mischief or misfortune.[81] Stories of such beings are a part of Bahamian folklore to this day; perhaps most often associated with the island of Andros. Based on the stories he heard, Deslèves describes the chickcharnies as "a kind of sylvan elf, little men with white skin and ruby-red eyes which shine in the darkness."[82] He interprets these figures as being "without doubt the survival of an ancient African cult involving albino monkeys."[83] Research into African anthropology, or perhaps into French misperceptions thereof, might further elucidate this curious interpretation made by Deslèves. However, this reference, which is derived from folk tales, seems even more tenuous than the information provided by Rosita Forbes. The consideration of creatures such as chickcharnies is not strong evidence of a particular organized African-derived religion, although such references clearly point to other things. Like the distinction between religion and magic in the study of many societies, the study of supernatural matters in Caribbean life and history involves forms of organized religious practice on the one hand and more ad hoc supernatural practices—usually called obeah in the anglophone Caribbean—on the other. In matters of obeah, as in matters of more organized religion, nineteenth-century liberated African immigrants exerted a significant and discernible influence.

6

"Powers superior to those of other witches":

NEW AFRICAN IMMIGRANTS AND SUPERNATURAL PRACTICE BEYOND RELIGIOUS SPHERES

In the study of African-influenced culture in the Caribbean basin, perhaps no area has received greater attention than the sphere of religion and other supernatural practice. Anthropologists, historians, and sociologists have explored at great length the origins and nature of diverse phenomena, including the highly organized African-derived systems of vodun, santería, and other orisha worship; the somewhat looser systems of myalism, kumina, saraka feasts, and "big drum," or "jombee," dances; and the many different varieties of African-influenced Christianity.[1] Alongside this body of literature that addresses formal religious systems, the study of obeah and other Caribbean practices of magic, healing, and divination has held a somewhat secondary place. The most obvious reason for this imbalance lies in the very nature of obeah. As an ad hoc and most often secret practice, obeah gives rise to an exceedingly sparse body of resources from which historians may attempt to gain insight into the craft. Many scholars point to the definition posited by Orlando Patterson in his 1975 work *The Sociology of Slavery:* "Obeah was essentially a type of sorcery which largely involved harming others at the request of clients, by the use of charms, poisons, and shadow catching."[2] While in some societies, similar types of sorcery have involved the use of texts that scholars or other outsiders might examine, Caribbean obeah has existed and continues to exist largely (albeit not exclusively) as an oral system, which constrains historians to rely upon a combination of chance anecdotes on the one hand and sporadic descriptive evidence from anti-witchcraft court cases on the other. But even with such patchwork sources, British West Indian historiography has established the presence of obeah as a consistent feature of the African-Caribbean cultural fabric over three centuries.

Patterson's definition requires one significant modification. While it accurately synthesizes the necromantic nature of obeah, the definition errs in construing the practice as an activity used largely to achieve negative ends. The cumulative evidence amassed prior to and since Patterson's work yields a more comprehensive portrait of obeah as a magical art used for the supernatural pursuit of both help and harm. Anthropologists Basil Hedrick and Jeannette Stephens cite the twentieth-century research of psychiatrist Timothy McCartney, who has studied obeah beliefs among mental health patients in the Bahamas: "Obeah is the phenomenon of the supernatural. It renders evil or good. . . . It can cause one to become rich or it can make one poor. It can cause an illness, either physical or mental . . . or can cure."[3] In this sense, obeah shares an arguably universal character with magical systems across many cultures. However, in the context of the Caribbean, the specific content of that system has remained predominantly African-derived. And liberated African immigrants exerted a noticeable influence both on the practice of obeah and on the public perceptions of that practice.

In his 1932 study of the history and nature of obeah, Joseph J. Williams cites a variety of evidence indicating that during the eighteenth century, observers often pointed to African-born slaves as the primary culprits in the practice of this craft. For example, in 1789, in testimony before a privy council committee investigating Britain's overseas plantations, a British official from Jamaica reported as follows:

> [T]he professors of Obi are, and always were, natives of Africa, and none other, and they have brought the science with them from thence to Jamaica. . . . [W]e believe there are few of the larger Estates possessing native Africans, which have not one or more of them. . . . The Negroes in general, whether Africans or Creoles, revere, consult, and abhor them.[4]

Some liberated Africans earned a similar reputation.

European observers in nineteenth-century Trinidad regularly pointed to African-born immigrants as followers and particularly powerful practitioners of obeah. In his lengthy cultural study of the island, published in 1858, Louis de Verteuil lamented "the continued belief in sorcery" among what he labeled "the more ignorant classes of the population," including people of both East Indian and African descent.[5] De Verteuil followed this complaint with a brief description of prevalent obeah activities such as the poisoning of people or livestock and the use of incantations for purposes of romantic seduction or other influencing of human relationships. He concluded his description by bemoaning the supposed credulity of obeah followers and condemning the practitioners of the art, singling out "Negroes from Africa" as the predominant guilty parties.[6] European authors did sometimes use the adjective "African" in ambiguous ways that might have referred to all people of African descent rather than only the African-born. However, by using the phrase "Negroes *from* Africa" de Verteuil left little doubt of his intention to cast blame upon African-born immigrants. During the 1850s, when de Verteuil wrote, the population of Trinidad still included some elderly former slaves of African birth. However, liberated African immigrants constituted the majority of the African-born. It seems almost certain that they were the group de Verteuil accused.

An even more dramatic reference to immigrant Africans as notorious obeah practitioners emerges from the published journal of a Roman Catholic missionary who worked in southern Trinidad near the end of the nineteenth century. In an entry made in January 1884, Marie Bertrand Cothonay described an apparently obeah-related figurine—"a frightful idol"—which he had discovered in the home of one his parishioners. The doll-like figure had a head fashioned as "half-bird and half-human, an enormous body and animal hooves!"[7] Cothonay berated the man and insisted that he destroy the offending image. Indeed, the missionary himself aided in the destruction, crushing the arms and legs before discarding them. Cothonay explained his "horrific" discovery: "These *African blacks* still retain certain pagan practices of their countries, and they transmit [such things] from father to son" (emphasis added).[8] Like de Verteuil, Cothonay assigned to African immigrants —people with memories of their own countries—the primary blame for the maintenance of obeah.

Given the fact that such practices existed in the Caribbean long before the arrival of nineteenth-century African immigrants, skeptics might suggest that the assertions of Cothonay and de Verteuil reveal nothing more than the biases or paranoia of the two authors. During the initial considerations of settlement of liberated Africans in the West Indies, several British colonial officials openly expressed concern that the "barbarism" of new African arrivals might somehow contaminate the creolized culture of former slaves—people who, in the opinion of the Colonial Office, had already spent many "civilizing" years under European influences. It certainly seems possible that Cothonay and de Verteuil harbored similar beliefs, which could have led them to distort or exaggerate the importance of African immigrants within circles of obeah practice. Perhaps liberated Africans actually had no greater propensity for obeah involvement than any other members of the community. Yet the implication that liberated Africans had a special relationship to obeah arises from sources other than the texts of European observers. In subtle ways, the idea also appears in the oral traditions of African-Trinidadian society, an arena hardly shaped by European fears about contagious African barbarism.

During the 1950s, Andrew Pearse, a folklorist from the United States, and Andrew Carr, his Trinidadian partner, made several collections of stories and folk beliefs in the community of Belmont, a neighborhood of Port-of-Spain. Pearse and Carr paid particular attention to the Rada community, an extended family whose members descended from a group of Fon people brought to Trinidad as liberated Africans during the 1860s. As they interviewed these people, the two scholars discovered a discourse that implied that at least some African immigrants had superior magical powers over other people. The Radas have maintained to the present day a well-organized religious community, based on Fon beliefs similar to those expressed by Trinidad's orisha worshippers. But this community religious practice stands separate from the more ad hoc and individualized activities of obeah. The Rada descendants interviewed by Pearse and Carr clearly defined the necromancy practiced by other people as something occupying a different (and perhaps less honorable) conceptual space than their own organized sacred activities. In particular, Henry Antoine, the lead drummer of the Rada community in 1951, recounted with great relish the Belmont collective wisdom about a man known as Daddy Sargeant. Although he had been dead for a long time by the mid-twentieth century, Sargeant apparently continued to enjoy a vibrant life in popular memory. Pearse and Carr transcribed the following excerpt from one of their interviews with Antoine:

> "Congo people are bad people. Laugh at them and you die." Such a man was Daddy Sargeant—a Congo man who used to live on a hill in Belmont Valley Road. . . . Whenever he wanted to kill anyone he just did it and such was the power of his magic, it couldn't be pinned on him.[9]

Nothing in this brief comment directly identifies Daddy Sargeant as a liberated African immigrant or the descendant of such a person, but during the late nineteenth-century, references to specific African ethnic groups usually referred to the African-born. A more thorough investigation of the life of Daddy Sargeant would prove fascinating. However, even without such an investigation a powerful cultural message emerges from Antoine's story. The fact that a specific legend developed concerning the particular power of Congo obeah strongly implies the existence of a significant public perception that liberated African immigrants possessed exceptionally potent skills in the practice of magic.

A more detailed exploration of this perception would prove almost impossible, except for the fact that during the latter half of the nineteenth century, colonial authorities in the island engaged in a series of much-ballyhooed obeah-related prosecutions. Three of these cases in particular illustrate the actual and symbolic roles liberated Africans played in the practice of obeah.

The first of these incidents unfolded in April and May 1868. During the month of April, two women, Jessie Williams and Mary Irish, became involved in a convoluted legal dispute with a third woman identified as Sarah Cassidy. According to reports in the *Trinidad Chronicle*, Williams and Irish had unsuccessfully attempted to rent a room from Cassidy in a dwelling she had inherited. The newspaper reports do not explain why Cassidy refused these particular tenants, but for whatever reason, the women became embroiled in a public disagreement with one another. One evening during this state of declared rancor, Williams and Irish discovered a miniature coffin deposited at their gateway in an apparent attempt to cause them harm or misfortune through supernatural means. In the words of the *Chronicle* reporter: "The coffin . . . was a perfect little miniature, about a foot long, in which were the legs of a fowl tied up with some feathers."[10] Even without attempting to deduce the meaning of these particular objects, it seems obvious why Williams and Irish would interpret this act of vandalism as some kind of witchcraft. Believing Cassidy to have arranged this attack, the two women reported the incident to the police, who accompanied them to Cassidy's home, where a confrontation ensued. Williams and Irish did not accuse Sarah Cassidy of having planted the coffin herself. Rather, they alleged that Cassidy had enlisted the services of her "Yaraba" housekeeper to engineer the sorcery. As a crowd of spectators surrounded Cassidy's house, a Sergeant Haynes demanded the name of the Yoruba housekeeper so he could arrest her. However neither Cassidy, Williams, nor Irish would produce the name. While Cassidy denied any involvement in the matter, Williams and Irish seemed more interested in confronting their nemesis Cassidy than in pursuing her alleged obeah assistant. At one point Williams even suggested that she might force open Cassidy's door and "drag [the woman] to the Police Station" herself. Despite such threats, no violence transpired, and eventually Sergeant Haynes, assisted by a Constable St. Philip, managed to disperse the crowd and take the coffin to the police station for possible use as evidence.[11]

As a result of the disturbance at her home, however, Sarah Cassidy brought rioting charges against Williams, Irish, and another woman who had participated in the mob. During the trial, Cassidy even suggested that Williams and Irish had prepared the coffin themselves and had fabricated the accusations against the Yoruba housekeeper as a devious escalation of the preexisting feud concerning the rental property. Although evidence on both sides exhibited error and contradiction, the judge ruled in favor of the prosecution and sentenced Williams and Irish to "one month's imprisonment with hard labor." (He did, however, acquit the other woman from the mob.)[12] Regardless of whether one believes Sarah Cassidy or the two defendants, this tortuous case gives testimony to the role liberated African immigrants had come to play within the world of obeah. Given Trinidadian demography, historians can reasonably assume that the Yoruba maid in question belonged to the liberated African population. If Sarah Cassidy used this woman as a hired sorcerer, the incident would seem to at least implicitly reinforce the hypotheses advanced by Cothonay and de Verteuil concerning the role of African immigrants as dominant and specially valued actors in the practice of obeah. Yet even if the incident was in fact an elaborate plot by Williams and Irish, it would still prove illustrative. After all, why would the two conspirators explicitly pick out Cassidy's Yoruba housekeeper to become the target of their fabrication? They might have selected her solely because it was convenient to do so, but this simple explanation is not persuasive. If they had simply wished to escalate their feud, they could have accused Cassidy herself of masterminding the plot. They did not need to provide details of who had actually prepared the coffin or placed it in the gateway. If Williams and Irish did indeed contrive the whole affair, it seems more likely that they accused the Yoruba maid not by chance or caprice but because, in the context of nineteenth-century Trinidad, they viewed the recent African immigrant as a particularly plausible candidate for the role of obeah villain. Regardless of the truth, the fact that the housekeeper's ethnicity was mentioned repeatedly throughout the discussions of the case strongly suggests the existence of an accepted public belief concerning the special relevance of African-born immigrants in matters involving obeah.

For reasons that are not clear in the published reports, neither side in the court case ever summoned the Yoruba housekeeper as a witness. The alleged obeah woman never spoke for herself. Did she or did she not place the coffin in the gateway? Did she or did she not practice obeah as a regular enterprise? Perhaps she prepared the coffin simply because her employer had asked her to do so. Perhaps the infamous "Yaraba woman" actually knew nothing about magical practices. Here again historians confront the possibility that the study of the role of new African immigrants in obeah practice becomes study not of immigrant behavior but of public perceptions. However, the second prominent obeah prosecution of 1868 left little doubt about the fact that at least one liberated African woman did indeed establish herself as a particularly powerful practitioner of African-derived magical arts.

In October 1868, a woman named Phillis Shower, who lived near Milton Estate in central Trinidad, appeared at Couva police court charged with the illegal practice of obeah. Shower faced these charges along with her son, Thomas Emmanuel Shower, and an acquaintance, Thomas Cole. The case against the Shower family and Cole arose from a complex police operation contrived explicitly to entrap and apprehend them. Phillis Shower had developed "great notoriety . . . as an obeah or witch woman," prompting a constable from Couva to plan her arrest. Constable Harley arranged with the proprietor of Milton Estate that he should masquerade as a laborer in order to visit Phillis without arousing suspicion. According to his testimony, as presented in the *Trinidad Chronicle,* Harley went to the Shower house and asked Phillis whether or not she could use her supernatural powers to find him a job. He embellished his request by claiming that he had a sick wife to look after. Phillis assured him that she could help but requested a payment of eight dollars for her services. Harley offered to pay five dollars at once and the remaining three dollars at a later time. After conferring with her son and with Cole, Phillis agreed, and she and the two men began their work. Phillis mostly gave instructions while her son and Cole performed the actual rituals. They mixed a combination of water and an unidentified substance which Phillis kept in a special mortar. The two men then escorted Constable Harley out of the house and into the yard, where they washed his head and face with the mixture. Phillis then joined the men outside and washed Constable Harley's neck. She told the constable that he should "not wash his face for ten days, and wherever he went he would get work."[13]

While this incident arguably provided ideal and sufficient material for an obeah prosecution, the accusations against Phillis Shower did not end here. Leaving no margin for error, Constable Harley constructed a case composed of multiple charges that (perhaps intentionally) presented a strikingly balanced portrait of the different aspects of obeah. In addition to the charges related to the ritual to end Harley's feigned unemployment, the Couva defendants faced a second charge related to claims they had allegedly made about their ability to cure the illness of Harley's fictitious wife. The testimony concerning these secondary claims yielded the first direct reference to Shower's African ethnicity—specifically Yoruba—as a part of her obeah practice. According to Harley's evidence, on the same day that he received the solution for his unemployment, he also paid the trio a fee of eight dollars to obtain a cure for his wife's illness. Phillis provided Harley with a quantity of "black stuff" enclosed in a piece of paper. She instructed him to take the substance home and "blow it upon [his] wife" in order to make her well. Phillis did not simply hand over the product. As had occurred during the first transaction, she and her assistants acted out a series of apparently ritual steps. Phillis brought the "black stuff" to the yard in a calabash. She poured some of the substance into the folded paper, passed the calabash to her son, "and spoke to him in Yaraba [*sic*]."[14] Thomas Shower repeated his mother's action, also pouring some of the "black stuff" into the paper. He passed the objects to Thomas Cole, who did the same thing. Only after this serial performance did Harley receive the paper packet containing the curative substance.

No one at the trial provided any information about what Phillis Shower might have said when she spoke in the African language. Whatever she said, Harley's reference draws a clear link between manifest Africanness and the practice of obeah. And this link would become increasingly pronounced as the legal troubles of the Shower group progressed. One might speculate that the police constable invented the "Yaraba" conversation to embellish his case. Some parts of Harley's testimony do indeed seem not only implausible but in fact specifically calculated to provoke outrage from the judge and jury. For example, the constable claimed that during his visit to the Shower house, he had at one point exclaimed, "My God!" in response to something Phillis Shower had said. According to his testimony, the alleged obeah woman had rejoined, "Don't call God's name in my house!"[15] Like most anti-witchcraft legislation, the laws against obeah rested at least in part upon the understanding of paganism as the antithesis of Christianity. A conversation such as the one Harley reported would have clearly dramatized the alleged evil nature of the accused witch. However, if Harley wanted to concoct a fraudulent story in which use of the Yoruba language was a marker of African paganism, it seems probable that he would not have restricted himself to a single instance of Phillis speaking in the African tongue. Because he referred to the Yoruba language only once, it is probable that Harley in fact spoke the truth, at least with respect to this detail. The idea that Shower's Yoruba identity constituted a crucial component in her role as an obeah practitioner certainly resonated with the editors of the *Trinidad Chronicle,* who, in a commentary on October 6, 1868, labeled Shower, who had by that time been convicted as an obeah woman, as the "Queen of the Yarabas."[16]

The convictions of Phillis and Thomas Shower and Thomas Cole were preceded by the presentation of three additional charges unrelated to the operation engineered by Constable Harley. These cases accused the elder Shower of "practising the surgical art without being duly licensed." Two individuals, a man and a woman, testified that they had sought care from Phillis because they suffered with "sore legs." A third individual, David Solomon, had sought relief from "a troublesome disease." (This euphemism may have referred to some form of venereal infection.) In this case, the patient paid Phillis "$20 in cash" along with quantities of rum, olive oil, sperm candles, a goat, and two fowls as remuneration for a potential cure. In exchange, Shower had provided Solomon with "3 bottles and 2 pans of stuff."[17] From the newspaper accounts of the trial, it seems that the court made no effort to identify this supposedly curative substance. Legally it was not required to do so. The prosecuting authorities needed only to demonstrate that Shower had attempted to sell her services as a medical practitioner. If successful, the court could convict the three accused subjects of engaging in all the different aspects of obeah practice: using charms or spells to achieve social consequences such as a job for Constable Harley; using charms or spells to cure illnesses such as that of Harley's imaginary wife; and providing herbal or otherwise unconventional substances for use as medicine.[18]

Constable Harley and his colleagues achieved mixed success in their effort. The magistrate refused to convict on any of the charges concerning the illegitimate practice of "the surgical art." With respect to one of the "sore leg" patients, the judge dismissed the charge because the court had not heard any evidence that the patient had actually proffered money or goods in return for Phillis Shower's assistance. In the case of the second leg patient, the court concluded that this man had only paid an appropriate price for his room and board while he stayed at the Shower home during his convalescence. Finally, the third accuser, who suffered from the "troublesome disease," had not appeared at trial but had sent an acquaintance who had witnessed his interactions with Phillis to give testimony on his behalf. As a result of this weakness in the evidence, the court once more declined to convict. Constable Harley's entrapment scheme, however, proved fully convincing to the magistrate, and for her actions in those two matters—the unemployment and the wife's illness—Phillis Shower received two consecutive sentences of six months' imprisonment, of which a total of two months would be served in solitary confinement, enforced in three-day segments. Thomas Shower and Thomas Cole likewise each received two six-month sentences, with the extra penalty of hard labor. In addition, each defendant received a sentence of thirty lashes for each conviction.[19] With the conclusion of the case, the police prepared to transfer the prisoners to the Royal Gaol at Port-of-Spain, where they would serve their sentences. According to the *Trinidad Chronicle,* "an enormous crowd" assembled at the Port-of-Spain wharf on the evening of Saturday October 3 in anticipation of the arrival of the elder Shower by steamer from Couva following her conviction earlier that day. The adjective enormous on this occasion seems to have referred to at least several hundred people, as elsewhere in same column the *Chronicle* described the "many thousand eyes" that awaited the obeah woman.[20] Even supposing some degree of hyperbole on the part of the author, one can reasonably presume that the crowd consisted of at least several hundred onlookers, and probably many more.

Even stronger evidence of Shower's reputation arises from the preventive actions the police took to avoid problems with the crowd during the transfer of the prisoner. Anticipating that a large crowd would assemble to see the Couva woman, the authorities did not transport Phillis to Port-of-Spain until the day after her conviction, "when no one expected her." They also elected to use a private police vessel rather than the public steamer and thus succeeded in avoiding any encounter with large groups of either supporters or spectators, although Shower nonetheless arrived "escorted by a strong detachment of Sergeants and Constables."[21] That the police made this effort—in effect sneaking the prisoner into town—betrays something beyond routine prudence or concern about crowd control. The *Chronicle* contended that the police feared that supporters might attempt to rescue the obeah woman either at Couva or at Port-of-Spain. While such fears perhaps reflected a measure of paranoia on the part of the police, the newspaper account leaves little doubt that Phillis Shower enjoyed enormous public recognition. In fact, according to the *Chronicle* report, knowledge of Phillis's skills as a practitioner of obeah extended even as far as the Venezuelan mainland, with which Trinidad exchanged both goods and itinerant laborers.

The most striking piece of evidence in this case is the allegation in the newspaper that Phillis Shower "professed to be a witch with powers superior to those of other witches."[22] Of course, a newspaper statement can hardly serve as definitive evidence illuminating the mindset of the famous woman from Couva. Did Phillis Shower ever in fact make that claim about her superiority? More important, did she portray her African birth or perhaps specifically her Yoruba background as the explanation for her supernatural strengths? While answers to these questions remain elusive, it seems clear that the nineteenth-century journalists reporting the case wanted to emphasize a linkage between Shower's Africanness and her obeah-related notoriety. The moniker "Queen of the Yarabas" not only drew attention to the convicted woman's African ethnicity but also implied that Shower's clientele and other members of the public attached importance and even fealty to the power they associated with that ethnic identity.

The celebrity of the Shower case would linger for months, and even years, after the imprisonment of the three offenders during the first week of October 1868. In November of that year, the police unearthed a coffin containing a human skeleton on the property of the Shower home, which the *Chronicle* referred to in a sinister tone as the "House in the Woods."[23] The newspaper report, although brief, raised suspicion that Phillis Shower had some malevolent involvement in the death of the person discovered. British author Charles Kingsley, who visited Trinidad in 1869 and 1870, reported that according to his sources, the body belonged to that of a "rival Obeah-man, who . . . [had] challenged [Phillis Shower] to a trial of skill." This man had allegedly ventured into the Shower home one evening for the purpose of engaging in the proposed competition and had never emerged.[24] Kingsley, however, is a questionable source of information because his travel narrative also presents an apparently erroneous account of the events that led up to the Shower trial and conviction. According to Kingsley's sources, the undercover police constable had not sought assistance in finding a job and curing an imaginary wife but rather had approached the reputed obeah woman in search of a love potion that would "win [him] the affections" of an otherwise uninterested woman.[25] Such an altered version of the entrapment scheme suggests a possible tendency toward salacious embellishment on the part of Kingsley's informants. Or perhaps Kingsley took some creative license in his rendition of Phillis's story. Suspicions of obeah-related murder with possibly African culprits were not unique to the case of Phillis Shower. This theme would appear repeatedly in prominent obeah investigations during the final decades of the nineteenth century.

The most publicized of these cases involved the apparent murder of a three-year-old boy named Luther Barrow in December 1888. The Barrow family lived in the Port-of-Spain neighborhood of Belmont, a community that consisted of liberated Africans, their first-generation descendants, and other segments of the African-descended population. Luther Barrow went missing on the morning of December 3 after his mother had sent him on a brief errand to a corner store accompanied by an older child. Margaret Barrow had instructed the older child, a girl identified as Fredericka Gulston, that when the two returned from the shop, Fredericka should accompany Luther as a far as a cashew tree outside the Barrow home. The house apparently lay some distance from the street, but when questioned, Margaret Barrow emphasized the fact that "the tree [described] was nearer to the house than to the road." When the child did not appear after a reasonable time, Mrs. Barrow went in search of him. She approached a Sergeant Corbin from the nearby police station and asked him to speak to Fredericka concerning Luther's whereabouts. The girl claimed that she had left Luther on a bridge near the Barrow home. A search of Belmont and the adjacent neighborhood of Laventille failed to produce the child, although at least one witness claimed to have seen the boy after the time Fredericka left him. Almost three weeks later, a resident of Laventille, the neighborhood bordering Belmont on the east, discovered the partially decomposed remains of a child. Police and medical personnel identified these remains as those of Luther Barrow.[26]

One month after this gruesome discovery, local authorities convened a coroner's inquest to investigate the circumstances of the child's death and, if appropriate, determine which person or persons were responsible. The formal inquiry before coroner Llewellyn Lewis lasted a total of three days between mid-January and early March 1889. Much of the testimony focused on medical and biological matters concerning the decomposition of the body and the means by which doctors had made their identification. Other witnesses, however, provided information and opinions that attempted to piece together the activities of the boy between the time Fredericka had left him on the bridge and the time of his death. According to the editors of the *New Era* newspaper, the inquest took place with the presumption that some "savage necromancer" had murdered the child for purposes connected with obeah.[27] Although the coroner did eventually conclude that a murder had taken place, the evidence shed very little light on what exactly might have happened. Witnesses presented a variety of details that implied that the death had not occurred naturally but provided no clear hypotheses about the circumstances of the presumed homicide. Some details seem to have subtly implied supernatural practices of African origin; two witnesses specifically cast suspicion on a resident of Belmont whom they identified as "the old African."[28]

One detail which suggests that supernatural beliefs from Africa affected this case is the repeated appearance in the testimony of references to a silk-cotton tree. George Barrow, Luther's father, made the first mention of this tree as he described his efforts to find his son on the morning the boy disappeared. Mr. Barrow recounted in some detail his traversing of Belmont and Laventille and his questioning of various residents on that first day. During the course of this account, Barrow noted that "[t]he morning was fine, but it commenced to rain when he was up by the silk cotton tree."[29] In the context of a thorough description that included numerous references to landmarks such as buildings and street names, this notation might appear as a simple geographic reference with no particular significance. However, in the modern Caribbean, widespread beliefs exist concerning the supernatural characteristics of silk-cotton trees. People often claim that spirits inhabit such places. Like so much of African-Caribbean folklore, such beliefs have their roots in various cosmological systems of West and Central Africa. In his twentieth-century study of the BaKongo of Zaire, anthropologist Wyatt MacGaffey explains:

> The silk cotton tree . . . which so dominates the forest that vultures . . . perch in it, resembles the chief . . . but is also a haunt of witches. . . . [L]ike power itself the tree is ambivalent.[30]

References to the supernatural importance of trees in general and silk-cotton trees in particular appear in numerous studies of West and Central African anthropology.[31] It thus seems not only reasonable but imperative to consider the repeated appearance of the silk-cotton tree during the inquest as a meaningful allusion by those who gave evidence. No other tree appears repeatedly as a landmark in the descriptions of those who had searched for the missing boy. Mrs. Barrow did refer to the cashew tree near her house. However, the silk-cotton tree her husband referred to appears no less than twelve times in the descriptions of six separate witnesses. (It is interesting, but perhaps not surprising, that the girl Fredericka who had escorted Luther to the store claimed in her testimony that she and Mrs. Barrow had never discussed the cashew tree as a meeting place for the little boy.)

On at least one occasion, the reference to the silk-cotton tree arose largely as a result of directed questioning from the coroner or some other official, who presumably recalled the landmark from previous evidence. This elicited reference occurred in the testimony of a young man identified as Emmanuel Lemacy, a resident of Belmont who had seen and spoken to some of the adults involved in the search on the morning of Luther's disappearance. The *New Era* account of Lemacy's turn on the witness stand stated in part: "He told Mr. Barrow, the Sergeant and another policeman that he had heard Waldron speaking to a child. This was the day after he was lost. He knows Laventille Hill and has been up to the silk-cotton tree. He knows none of the paths leading from it."[32] This style of prose, which was often used in nineteenth-century reporting of court proceedings, indicated that the journalist or other transcriber had recorded only the statements of the witness, omitting any prompting questions. In this instance, as the mention of the tree does not form a part of any logical narrative sequence, it seems probable that the coroner had specifically inquired about Lemacy's familiarity with the landmark George Barrow and others had pointed out. This case of an elicited reference constituted an exception during the Barrow inquest. The coroner did not prompt the other eleven citations which, at the very least, indicate that in the minds of these Belmont residents, the silk-cotton tree stood as a particularly prominent feature of the landscape in the area where the child had vanished. Given the anthropological and folkloric evidence cited above, it is likely that this prominence resulted not simply from size or location but also from African-derived connotations with the supernatural. The repeated references to the tree during the inquest may in fact have constituted a subtle indication from the witnesses that, like the newspaper reporters who sensationalized the case, they too believed that some obeah activity had led to the death of Luther Barrow.

Even if one could confirm such a belief in the minds of those who testified, the allusion by itself would not automatically imply the involvement of liberated African immigrants. Almost the entire population of both Belmont and Laventille consisted of people of African descent, any one of whom might have engaged in the practice of obeah. However, considered in conjunction with the singling out of African immigrants in other nineteenth-century obeah cases, these recurring references to the suggestive silk-cotton tree seem to be part of a pattern. During the Barrow investigation, witnesses specifically identified an "old African"—presumably an immigrant—among the potential suspects in the case. Most suspicion seemed to focus around a man identified as Jean Baptiste Walter (also called Waldron) who claimed to have seen Luther running through Belmont crying after he and Fredericka Gulston had concluded their shopping trip. According to Walter, the little boy did not respond when spoken to but instead stopped only briefly before running away. Several witnesses at the inquest had heard of this encounter and seemed to doubt Walter's veracity concerning the incident. Indeed, at one point the coroner admonished Walter to "divulge all he [knew]" and "warn[ed] him that strong steps would be taken if he kept anything back."[33] Other characters, however, also emerged in a questionable light. Both the unnamed African and another man called Sandy seem to have lived in the upper reaches of Laventille Hill, closer than any other residents to the site where Luther's body was found. Jean Baptiste Walter claimed to have visited Sandy's house (a short distance past the silk-cotton tree) on the day of the child's disappearance. According to Walter's testimony, he had asked Sandy whether or not he had seen the missing boy, to which Sandy had replied "No." Walter had in fact observed a child on Sandy's property, but he described this boy as bigger than Luther Barrow.[34]

Both Walter and the young man Emmanuel Lemacy discussed the mysterious figure of the "old African" in their testimony. While explaining his familiarity with Laventille Hill and the area beyond the silk-cotton tree, Lemacy stated that "[h]e had been as far as the old African's garden pretty often to see the old man." He did not know the man's name, nor did he know any of the other residents in the area. However, he had visited the site periodically to check on the man because the African rented his land from Mrs. Deeble, with whom Lemacy lived. Jean Baptiste Walter had no formal connection with the African recluse. Nonetheless, he too reported to the inquest that he "[knew] the old African." He further testified, however, that he had not ventured as far as the African's property during the Barrow search.[35] Neither of these witnesses explicitly pointed a finger of accusation at this particular man. Yet they both cast suspicion around him by implying that he, rather than any other random resident, might have relevance to the case. After all, Jean Baptiste Walter had drawn suspicion to himself as a result of his admitted conversation with the missing child. Similarly, the vaguely identified Sandy earned his notoriety at least in part because Walter had sighted an unknown boy on his property. The "old African" seemed to acquire his cloud of suspicion for no obvious reason beyond the location of his house and his apparent immigrant ethnic identity.

Perhaps more similar to the 1868 coffin incident than to the Phillis Shower case, the Barrow inquest clearly illustrates the perceived cultural role occupied by African immigrants (and the idea of Africanness) in nineteenth-century understandings of obeah practice in Trinidad. This particular case seems to have never moved beyond the realm of suggestive innuendo. Although the coroner eventually ruled that "some person had [probably committed] a felony,"[36] subsequent newspaper accounts yield no information concerning the arrest and trial of anyone in the case—neither Jean Baptiste Walter nor Sandy nor "the old African." However, public perceptions, such as those expressed during the inquest, arguably reveal as much as any other type of evidence about the distinctive position occupied by African immigrants within the wider African-descended community.

Nineteenth-century news reports by no means suggest that liberated African immigrants exclusively dominated the world of obeah or the alleged crimes associated with the practice. For example, twenty years before the Barrow murder, during the same decade as the sensational Shower case, the *Trinidad Chronicle* reported several other instances of suspiciously missing children without any allusions to the possible or probable participation of specifically African malefactors. In one case in October 1866, someone murdered a child on Hope Estate in the ward of Diego Martin. The *Chronicle* reported that "suspicion [was] fixed upon a man who [had] recently threatened the boy's father." This presumed assailant heightened his appearance of guilt because after the child's disappearance, he too "disappeared from his usual haunts."[37] This incident proves illustrative for the study of obeah practice in several ways. First, this murder exemplifies the ambiguity that not only plagued the investigations of police authorities during the nineteenth century but continues to plague the analysis of historians. To murder a child as an act of vengeance against a parent seems a particularly cruel act. Both historians and police officers would seem justified in their speculations that some ritual or supernatural motive must have lay behind the crime. This hypothesis perhaps gains additional plausibility from the fact that the child's throat was cut. Yet in the absence of explanatory statements from the murderer or his associates, suspicion needs remain only suspicion. As for the strength of the obeah powers of liberated Africans compared to those of the rest of the population, the Hope Estate murder, which made no mention of Africans, demonstrates the complex challenge of understanding the role of these immigrants in African-Caribbean society. As with the study of organized religious practice, the study of the practice of obeah demonstrates the virtual impossibility of exclusively crediting liberated Africans with the creation or sole control of any cultural practice. In the midst of an African-descended population, their impact seemed destined to be composed of the magnification or variegation of forms and patterns whose roots lay in the earlier African migrations of the years of slavery. Obeah constituted one of the most obvious and ubiquitous African-derived practices formed in that era. Hence it should seem no surprise that the new African immigrants would acquire a particular niche in the practice of obeah. The Cassidy, Shower, and Barrow cases demonstrate that nineteenth-century African-Trinidadians and other observers interpreted the newest Africans in their midst as having greater potential "powers" in this sphere. They viewed the immigrant obeah experts as having stronger—or to some minds more pernicious—power than other practitioners because the newly arrived immigrants had a more recent connection to the African sources of their craft.

Evidence from nineteenth-century Bahamian records does not yet yield a comparable pattern of involvement of liberated Africans in these kinds of supernatural practices. (For example, the Grant's Town–Bain Town area boasts its own silk-cotton trees, inviting tantalizing speculation in light of the discussions above. However, this study found no particular allusions connecting those trees to beliefs or practices of liberated Africans.) This lack of written records, however, may simply reflect the nature of obeah. Such ad hoc curative and magical activities rarely received formal notice from authorities or other outside observers. In Trinidad, it seems likely that the significant media coverage from the 1860s through the 1880s occurred at least in part because of changes in the colony's laws that strengthened the power of the courts to convict and impose severe sentences for obeah-related crimes. During the Shower matter in particular, much of the newspaper coverage expressed praise for the institution of stricter anti-obeah measures.[38] Whatever the reasons for the comparative lack of discussion of liberated Africans and obeah in the Bahamas in the nineteenth-century, both countries link liberated Africans and obeah in twentieth-century understandings of the practice in their respective societies. Numerous modern scholars of Caribbean culture point to the persistence of obeah through the present century, although as in previous eras the practice remains largely clandestine or at least takes place away from wide public scrutiny. African-descended people themselves now control both the legislative and police authorities in these territories, but for various reasons common to many postcolonial societies, political and social change has not led to official acceptance of African-derived magical arts. (Even the self-consciously religious practices of Spiritual Baptists and orisha practitioners did not receive official sanction until the late twentieth century.)[39] Nevertheless, since the mid-twentieth century, significant legal pursuit of alleged obeah offenders has ceased, and it is widely accepted that obeah men and women form a part of the regional cultural landscape, resorted to for assistance in varying de-

Silk-cotton tree, Grants Town, Nassau, Bahamas (2004)

grees by representatives of many segments of the population, despite periodic condemnations by some mainstream Christian leaders. Furthermore,
as with the case of Phillis Shower during the nineteenth century, obeah
practitioners whose reputations far exceed those of their peers continued to
emerge during the twentieth century. And, like Shower, a few figures have
achieved a notoriety that has extended not only to their clientele but also to
wider populations. In both the Bahamas and Trinidad, an individual has
emerged who has come to serve as virtually the representative of obeah people of the twentieth century: Papa Neezer of Moruga in southern Trinidad
and Pa Bay of the village of Fox Hill. Both of these men—who are now deceased—originated from and established their reputations in areas known
for having significant populations of liberated Africans in their histories.

Papa Neezer arguably had the greater notoriety of the two, having
achieved recognition even beyond Trinidad with his mention as a character
in the calypso song "Obeah Wedding," sung by the internationally renowned
performer Slinger Francisco, who is more commonly known as the "Mighty
Sparrow."[40] In a 1969 undergraduate thesis for the Caribbean Studies program at the University of the West Indies, Jack Warner cited Neezer's place
of residence as Moruga, which in this case referred not to the town on
Trinidad's southern coast but to the Moruga Road area located south and

A former residence of reputed obeah man Papa Neezer, Trinidad (1994)

east of Princes Town.[41] Neezer lived near the town of Lengua. While not as noted as the Montserrat hills as a site where liberated Africans settled, Moruga, which included several major plantations, received large groups of such immigrants. The Montserrat ward, which includes Caratal and Gasparillo, centers where many liberated Africans settled, lies less than ten miles away from Lengua and all of these towns effectively encompass a single small district of less than thirty square miles. In an interview conducted in March 1994, Joseph Hudlin, one of Neezer's former neighbors, asserted that "most of the people" who visited the Lengua obeah man came from Caratal.[42] As an example of the confusion that has always surrounded obeah practice, this neighbor described Papa Neezer not as an obeah man but as a "Shango person," or leader of orisha worship. Hudlin referred to the fact that Neezer "[kept] feasts," thus using much the same language that residents of Caratal, Gasparillo, and other towns use to describe the African-derived religious celebrations in their communities.[43] In a similar vein, Hudlin's sister, Priscilla Taylor, described Neezer as the "only Shango person" in their immediate vicinity at Lengua.[44] On the one hand, these descriptions raise the possibility that Trinidad's most famous obeah man did not practice obeah at all. On the other hand, it seems unlikely (although not impossible) that so many other observers, both casual and scholarly, could have misunderstood or misrepresented Neezer's identity. More likely, the blurred portrayal of Papa Neezer that emerges from the recollections of these neighbors simply reflects the blurred boundaries that have always existed between the religious and the extrareligious in African-derived supernatural practices. For example, numerous interviews reveal that contemporary Trinidadians have resorted to both orisha rituals aimed at specific Yoruba spirits and to less-formal assistance from obeah when seeking medical relief outside the parameters of modern health care.[45] Papa Neezer's notoriety as an obeah man thus both accords with and enhances the wider ethnohistory of the region. While Papa Neezer is not a known descendent of nineteenth-century African immigrants, it seems as likely as not that the demographic and cultural presence of liberated Africans played some role in shaping the life of this prominent obeah man and in producing Moruga's reputation as the "home of obeah."[46]

The village of Fox Hill, home of the Bahamian obeah man Pa Bay, has not earned as strong a reputation as a place where obeah is practiced. However, like that of Moruga and Montserrat, the history of Fox Hill includes significant settlement by liberated Africans and their descendants. Also, like the memory of Papa Neezer, in the late twentieth century the name of Pa Bay enjoyed fairly widespread public recognition, even among Bahamians who have had no involvement with obeah, including many who dismiss the practice as ineffective or even heathen superstition. Pa Bay has also made an appearance in Bahamian artistic culture, although without the international celebrity of Papa Neezer's calypso. Bahamian award-winning poet Marion Bethel twice mentions a figure named Pa B in a religious piece entitled "The Passion." The poem invokes various Christian images and engages in a none-too-subtle questioning of the efficacy of Christianity in improving the lives of ordinary Bahamians. Bethel proclaims: "There is no victory / in the palm Pa B. No balm for / your daughters and sons nailed / to the cross every day. And Mary's / son, well, he died in vain."[47] The name Pa B is almost certainly an allusion to the obeah man of Fox Hill, whom Bethel positions as a more authentic spiritual figurehead for African-descended Bahamians than either Jesus Christ or the Virgin Mary. Pa Bay has also consistently appeared in explorations of Fox Hill community history conducted during the past two decades, although he died during the 1960s.

In a 1974 teaching-certificate thesis prepared for the College of the Bahamas, Jacqualine Rahming includes a chapter entitled "The Obeah Man" that summarizes various beliefs of residents of Fox Hill concerning the identity and life history of Zechariah Adderley, otherwise known as Pa Bay. According to Rahming's account, Pa Bay lived in an ordinary house much like his neighbors, inspiring curiosity and fear solely based on his reputation rather than on anything overtly peculiar or sinister about his home. She explains that some children would even avoid walking near the house as a result of this reputation, although others with more bravado would shout teasing remarks or songs directed at the old man.[48] To some extent, the description suggests that Pa Bay may have served a more mythic or symbolic role for Fox Hill inhabitants without actually engaging in supernatural or healing activities. The scenario Rahming portrayed, particularly the antics of the children, exhibits a pattern of behavior that may occur in any community in response to a person with reclusive habits, a strange appearance, or any other mundane peculiarity. Rahming inadvertently encourages this line of speculation with a subsequent chapter that provides an apparently fictionalized and certainly stereotypical narration of a death caused by sorcery performed by Pa Bay. (In the tale the obeah man uses "straight pins" to pierce a crudely fashioned doll, thus causing the death of a man who had attempted to lure away another man's girlfriend.)[49] Yet if Rahming's thesis casts some doubt on the actual behavior of Pa Bay, other sources provide quite specific evidence that Zechariah Adderley (Pa Bay) conducted business as a kind of diviner and possibly as a healer.

During an interview in 1994, Rev. Dr. Phillip Rahming, pastor of a Fox Hill Baptist church, asserted that Pa Bay had achieved his greatest popularity during the boom years of the Hobby Horse Hall race track during the mid-twentieth century. Located in western New Providence, Hobby Horse Hall attracted a large betting business. According to Rev. Rahming, would-be bettors visited Pa Bay seeking his help in making successful wagers: "Whether they won big or they won small, they wanted to win. And Pa Bay facilitated them to a great extent."[50] However, even as the pastor emphasized this gambling angle, he also alluded to other obeah-like services reportedly performed by Adderley. Rahming sought to explain Pa Bay's reputed success as a healer by stressing the probable "psychosomatic" nature of many of the illnesses cured. Rahming claimed that Pa Bay had denied the use of obeah or magic in his practices.

> I spoke with him myself. . . . Pa Bay said he had no magic about . . . working on any . . . anybody. . . . But he was good in cutting cards . . . he cuts cards for people, and they . . . he tells them things. . . . You know . . . he doesn't order to you, but he will show you something, and then you, you tell yourself certain things. . . . [H]e cut cards, and came up with some answers. And people believed he was doing something. But he was telling me he did nothing.[51]

The minister thus portrayed Adderley as a man who used playing cards for divination and the power of suggestion to provide both physical and psychological healing to his clientele. It seems logical that a Christian pastor might not wish to declare knowledge of and acceptance of obeah—even a pastor such as Rahming who, elsewhere during the same interview, expressed his appreciation for the various African influences on Caribbean culture. Nonetheless, the activities he described fit a classic obeah profile.[52] Thus, like the district of Moruga in Trinidad, the village of Fox Hill also gave rise to a particularly prominent obeah practitioner.

The Fox Hill community originated during the eighteenth century but saw its greatest growth during the mid-nineteenth century with large influxes of recently freed slaves and liberated African immigrants, who formed separate neighborhoods, some delineated by African ethnicity and others by the names of individual prominent inhabitants. Even without making a connection between Pa Bay and specific liberated African ancestors, it seems more reasonable than not to suspect the influence of liberated Africans on an African-derived practice such as obeah. Furthermore, according to an amateur local historian, the name Adderley belongs to a group of Fox Hill surnames historically associated with the area of the village known as Congo Town.[53] More in-depth genealogical research might succeed in clarifying a linkage between the family of Zechariah Adderley and liberated Africans from the Kongo region. However, even without such clarification, the emergence of both Papa Neezer and Pa Bay from areas where considerable numbers of liberated Africans are known to have settled is significant. In the nineteenth century, the arrival of liberated Africans sustained and perhaps strengthened the practice of obeah, and in the twentieth century, legacies of their impact on this supernatural practice apparently remained.

7

"Deeply attached to his native country":

Visions of Africa and Mentalities of Exile in Liberated African Culture

In August of 1888, the leadership of Congo No. 1 Society, Nassau, Bahamas, drafted a letter to "His Majesty Leopold II, King of the Belgians and King of the Congo Free State." President John O'Brien, his chairman, William Higgs, and member Samuel Ranch described themselves as "Natives of the Congo" and explained that they wrote on behalf of a larger community of such natives living in the Bahamas. They further explained that they had come to the Bahamas from a Spanish slave-trading vessel captured by the British, who liberated the Africans on board. O'Brien and his comrades described the difficulties of their experience as small-scale cultivators in the Bahamas; they had exhausted the soil of lands they had received by grant and other tracts they had purchased. They expressed their belief that they and their children would fare better were they allowed to return to the land of their birth, which was then under the sovereignty of His Majesty King Leopold.[1] In the context of Caribbean and wider African diaspora history, this petition represents a remarkable though not unique moment. There are other examples of extraordinary efforts made by former slaves to return to the African continent. However, both the terms and the circumstances of the appeal to King Leopold offer particular insight into the nature of the community of the Congo No. 1 Society.

The organization belonged to the Bahamian community of friendly societies discussed in chapter 3. These friendly societies often jointly attended Christian services at the churches of their members. On symbolic colonial occasions such as the queen's birthday, the societies would join other local organizations in presenting written "memorials" of loyalty and good wishes to the governor. They used these gestures both to assert their faith in the goodness of British government and to remind the governor of their desire for support in matters such as land acquisition or equal ecclesiastical rights between the Anglican church and their own Methodist or Baptist congregations.[2] In these activities, the friendly societies—including Congo No. 1— exemplified the acculturation of African people in diaspora. Scholars have speculated that such bodies had at least some ideological and structural roots in the traditions of the secret societies of West and Central Africa. Yet British authorities and apparently some missionaries encouraged such formations, and the groups shared similarities of structure and function with freemasonry. (It is interesting that during the first half of the twentieth century most of these groups in the Bahamas transformed themselves into chapters of international masonic bodies.) The societies professed Christianity and in some instances even discouraged African-derived religious practices. At the same time, their members almost invariably belonged to Protestant congregations whose doctrine and practice exemplified the merging of African and Christian elements. Thus, from many appearances, these "Natives of the Congo" had become citizens of the diaspora and people whose culture and identity reflected that experience.

In fact, John O'Brien and his associates selected their British Baptist minister as the means by which they would transmit their petition to the Belgian government. The Rev. Daniel Wilshere arrived in the Bahamas during the 1870s under the auspices of the London-based Baptist Missionary Society (BMS). Like most missionaries of this era who belonged to dissenting traditions, he served as a kind of itinerant, supervising several Baptist congregations founded by his BMS predecessors in the island of New Providence. Like his predecessors, Wilshere also attempted to work with the several churches of non-BMS, or "native," Baptists founded by African-American preachers who arrived from the United States as a part of the Loyalist migration of the late eighteenth century. From Wilshere's papers it seems most likely that the Congo Society membership belonged to the Baptist Missionary Society community in Fox Hill in eastern New Providence. This community formed Mount Carey Baptist Church in the 1840s; the church is active to the present day.[3] On more than one occasion prior to the letter of 1888, Wilshere described his interactions with Africans from the Congo who belonged to his congregation "in the east." Furthermore, the presence of gravestones for both Wilshere and his wife Charlotte in the Mount Carey churchyard suggests that the missionary may have had a particularly close relationship with this congregation.[4]

Additional evidence that the Congo No. 1 Society belonged to Mount Carey Baptist Church arises from an obituary published in the *Nassau*

Monuments to
Reverend Daniel
Wilshere and
Charlotte Wilshere,
Mount Carey
Baptist Church,
Fox Hill, Nassau,
Bahamas (1994)

Guardian for Guilliam Rahming of Fox Hill, who died in 1898 leaving five
sons. The brief citation describes Rahming as "a native of Africa ... [who]
was deeply attached to his native country and [had] made two attempts to
return."[5] Nothing in the newspaper links this man specifically to Mount
Carey. However, people who share his surname and claim ties of kinship
with one another have served as prominent members of both the Fox Hill
and Mount Carey communities for the past hundred years. A Moses Rahming, possibly one of the five sons, served as the first non-European pastor
of Mount Carey from 1877 until his death in 1900. Some residents of Fox
Hill today claim in jest that only a known member of the Rahming family
can ever hold the pastorate of the church.[6] None of this is conclusive proof of
the relationship between the Mount Carey congregation and the would-be
Congo emigrants, but the Rahming genealogy strengthens the assumption
derived from Wilshere's notes. In any case, the petitioners certainly belonged
to an Afro-Baptist congregation and demonstrated sufficient commitment

to their faith to earn them not simply the approval of their missionary leader but also his special attention and assistance in a matter only tangentially related to the church. Indeed, one might argue that Wilshere must have had great confidence in the strength of their Christianity to not only sanction but in fact promote the idea of their return to their still largely "heathen" homeland.

Whatever the strength of their New World religion or their other commitments to their life in the African diaspora, the group represented in the Congo Society appeal maintained a relationship that was both primal and primary with their specific homeland. The deceptively simply opening statement of their letter immediately betrays that relationship: "We were born in the Congo Land beside the Great River." At first glance, this seems at best a vague statement of their origins in the vast region of Central Africa known as the Congo. To describe the world's sixth longest river as "the Great River" hardly seems remarkable or even particular. However, anthropologists and historians of Central Africa have long noted that references to the Congo River hold more than basic geographic significance for the peoples who inhabit the river basin. Based on field work conducted during the last decade of the nineteenth century, John Weeks explains that the BaKongo word Nzadi, which describes the Congo River, "simply means 'the river.' . . . [A]ll other rivers and streams . . . have separate names to distinguish them from each other and [from] *the* river."[7] In more recent work, Wyatt MacGaffey goes beyond this to explore the cosmological significance of Nzadi in BaKongo religious belief and in regional oral history.[8] The signatories of the 1888 letter, or those who wrote on their behalf, certainly knew the colonial name of the territory in question. Elsewhere in the text they not only refer to the "Congo Free State" but also make other explicit references to the new sovereignty of the Belgian king over the land.[9] In the context of a painstakingly crafted letter whose authors had learned the political details necessary to best make their appeal, we can reasonably assume that all words they used were carefully chosen. The reference to the "Great River" and its attendant cultural meanings therefore seems deliberate.

Such deliberateness seems all the more likely given the evidence that suggests that O'Brien, Higgs, and Ranch did not themselves draft the English text. The Baptist Missionary Archives holds a hand-copied version of the letter. (The original found its way to the Brussels office of the Department of the Interior for the Congo Free State.) According to this archive copy, President O'Brien lacked even the ability to sign his name except with an X. Even if Ranch and Higgs could sign their names in English—which the copy suggests—the body of the letter describes them all as only speaking the "British" language. They explained that their children had received English-language education. These children or perhaps Daniel Wilshere seem the likely authors of the actual English words; a phrase such as "Great River" was probably reproduced (and noticeably capitalized) at the bidding of the substantive authors—the people of Nzadi in exile.

The notion of exile has always loomed prominently yet awkwardly in the African diaspora experience. In the introduction to their collection of essays on African-American culture in the Caribbean, Margaret Crahan and Franklin Knight point out that the study of African people in the New World has focused heavily on "slaves" rather than on "migrants."[10] To be sure, the institution of chattel slavery dominated the lives of the majority of Africans who entered this hemisphere between the seventeenth and nineteenth centuries. However, these people, at least conceptually, shared much with all immigrants. That is, they entered a new society in which they would craft new lives while at the same time retaining both cultural and emotional relationships with the societies they had left behind. In many ways, the system of New World slavery tried to sever such relationships, defining Africans either as chattel without culture or as savages with no culture worthy of note. In later years, more sympathetic arguments have been made that although African people did possess cultures of their own, the trauma of the Middle Passage and the process of enslavement stripped them of any significant cultural memory—made them tabulae rasae on which a New World experience would write. Herskovits and other scholars have long since overturned such notions, and the African contributions to African-American culture have received volumes of attention. Yet even historians who explore such contributions rarely conceptualize New World Africans as immigrants. The Africans these historians describe incorporated African culture into the New World as a form of self-determination in defiance of presumed European hegemony. However, scholars rarely envision a sense of deliberateness in this process. They describe syncretism almost as if it were a natural phenomenon without human agency. In many, perhaps most, historical portrayals, Africans seem to make their cultural contributions to New World society as a matter of course. They do not demonstrate any forceful sense of loss or nostalgia toward their origins, no conspicuous, aggrieved consciousness of a ruptured connection with their past.

To a large extent, many cultural developments do occur as a matter of course, without specific calculation by human actors. Furthermore, the sources available for the study of slave societies—diaries, letters, and other records written by slaveholders or other whites; materials written by Christian missionaries; a few slave narratives; African diaspora folklore; twentieth-century oral history—provide a particularly complex and piecemeal basis for evaluating the desires, intentions, or understandings of immigrant

Africans. All the same, it seems unreasonable to presume that such Africans did not maintain a deliberate consciousness of their relationship to their homelands. The liberated African experience in both the Bahamas and Trinidad yields clear evidence of precisely this consciousness, not only among the immigrants but also to some extent among their descendants.

Far more so than slaves, liberated Africans had the opportunity to consider and engage their status and identity as migrants. They did not arrive with the designation of chattel. Nor did they face attempts to "break them in," make them submissive, or otherwise mold them as slaves. Nonetheless, during the nineteenth century, British opinion continued to view African cultures as at best inferior and more often as savage or barbaric. Therefore, although liberated Africans entered the Caribbean as free people, they too faced a European society bent on de-Africanizing them. Indeed the project of settling liberated Africans in the West Indies had always included the civilization, or cultural "improvement," of Africans as one of its aims. The rigors of indentured labor or other aspects of working-class survival dominated the existence of African immigrants in much the same way that coerced labor defined the lives of slaves. And unlike true free immigrants, these Africans had made no decision to leave one society in exchange for another. At the same time, however, much of their experience involved official acknowledgment of their status as immigrants rather than slaves.

This acknowledgment occurred in British policies that offered some liberated Africans the option of repatriation; that is, a formal, and in some cases subsidized, return to the African continent. This option affected only a small minority of immigrants to the Bahamas and Trinidad. The contracts of some of the Africans brought as indentured labor to Trinidad during the 1840s included the option of return to Sierra Leone. However, very few people took advantage of this option, at least in part because of the expense involved in such an undertaking. (Although one of the responsibilities of the subsidized immigrant transport H.M.S. *Growler* was return voyages for liberated Africans, the returnees themselves had to pay for their passage.) Also, for most of the indentured Africans, the prospect of a return to Sierra Leone had only limited meaning and no automatic attraction. Most had never lived in or even near this territory constructed by the British. They had merely passed through the port of Freetown after being rescued by the British from various illegal slave ships.[11] In any case, only a minority of the Trinidad contracts offered the option of repatriation. The Africans who entered the Bahamas as refugees, not as planned immigrant labor, had no such choice at all.

In both the Bahamas and Trinidad, some African soldiers were given the option of traveling to Sierra Leone or elsewhere in British West Africa, either after their terms of service had expired or following the dissolution of various West India regiments. (These African-born soldiers included both liberated Africans and other Africans who had entered military service as slaves.) During May 1844, Methodist missionary John Corlett encountered one such returning soldier on a transatlantic voyage from the Bahamas: "Peter Nicols of the 3rd West India Regt and who has a Bill on the Treasurers is returning with me to England. He has got his discharge and wishes to return to Sierra Leone." Corlett suggested that the Methodist Missionary Society help Nichols complete his voyage.[12] In a similar instance, in June 1874, the *Trinidad Chronicle* printed a brief and somewhat cryptic notice concerning the "DISBANDING" of the "last of the Houssa [*sic*] men."[13] This short news item reported that the men had reached Lagos where, led by "Lieutenant John Jumbo of the Bonny River," they had "been received with all honours."[14] The report does not specifically say that the disbanded soldiers came from a West India regiment. However, it seems plausible to assume that they did, given the fact that the notice appeared in a Trinidadian newspaper that concerned itself largely with matters of local or West Indian relevance. Whatever the specifics of this Hausa case, such instances were the exception rather than the rule. Like the indentured laborers, few disbanded soldiers ever actually made a repatriation journey. Indeed, most never had the option.

Yet even such slim formal prospects of return gave liberated Africans a different New World perspective than that of their slave predecessors.[15] Their status as immigrants from their homelands was explicitly acknowledged in official policies, and the idea of return lay at least within the realm of plausibility. For these communities, the notion of exile perhaps loomed even larger (or fit more comfortably) than it did for communities of slaves. Antonio Benitez-Rojo has described the slave plantation as a "deculturating regimen that took direct action against [African] language . . . religion . . . and customs."[16] Not only did liberated Africans avert the power of such a regimen at its height, they in fact faced an alternate regimen: one that, although it did not embrace African culture by any means, at least conceded to Africans their condition as people that had been both literally and culturally displaced.

An understanding of liberated Africans as exiles requires a critical consideration of the notion of "Africa" as homeland. The prospect of "return" to Sierra Leone had no automatic meaning for people who had originated from different regions. Even Africans who shared an ethnic or regional origin most likely considered their identity in terms of narrow locales or even specific towns or villages. Nation-states came to Africa as a twentieth-century postcolonial concept. Various kinds of empires had existed in previous centuries, but these entities, even at their most expansive, rarely exercised intimate cultural influence over local communities. The Kongo kingdom, for example, held one of the widest spheres of influence of any precolonial entity. Covering much of present-day Congo, Democratic Republic of Congo (formerly Zaire), and Angola between the fifteenth and nineteenth centuries, this kingdom incorporated tens of thousands of people who shared similar, but not identical, indigenous cultural systems. During the late fifteenth century, early Portuguese explorers persuaded the Kongo court to convert to Roman Catholicism. This conversion at the center led to the widespread development of Christianity in the Kongo kingdom during the era of the slave trade. Conversion to Christianity, however, hardly reached all parts of the kingdom, and even Christian converts differed widely in their exact beliefs and practices. Thus, despite cultural similarities and a shared political entity, people did not necessarily hold a comprehensive Kongo identity. Besides, during the nineteenth century, most BaKongo people who ended up as export slaves came to that fate as a result of multiple wars that disrupted the long-standing empire. Parallel experiences—of similarity yet diversity, commonality with division—characterized most regions of West and Central Africa during the era of the slave trade. Anthropologist Karin Barber has described pan-Yoruba identity as a by-product of nineteenth-century British activity in Nigeria.[17]

Needless to say, the even wider idea of Africa as a single place or concept likewise had its roots in the actions of Europeans. In the New World, Africans of various origins very quickly began to construct pan-African identities and communities. Liberated Africans obviously had this experience. Indeed, they developed a specific identity as newly arrived Africans who were distinguished from other people of African descent. For example, in Trinidad in 1825 during an inquiry into the condition of the laboring population, almost every witness faced a series of questions asking them to differentiate between the behavior of Africans and the behavior of other members of the black population. On one occasion, chairman William Burnley asked witness Robert Mitchell: "Amongst the Settlers do you find the Americans generally more moral than the Africans?"[18] In this case, the term Americans referred to free African-American immigrants from the United States. Elsewhere Burnley would request similar comparisons between liberated African settlers and other people of African descent, both slave and free. In response to this particular question, Mitchell reported that in fact, he found the Africans more moral than the Americans. He described them as being "steady and quiet and . . . [faithful to] their Word." Despite this testimony, Mitchell was not biased toward Africans. During other parts of his testimony, he was equally willing to praise the Americans and criticize the Africans.[19] One European observer specifically described liberated Africans as a group with some degree of collective consciousness or identity. John Dougan, a commissioner sent to the West Indies during the 1820s to examine the condition of liberated Africans wrote the following from Tortola in 1823: "The African Apprentices in this Island have with few exceptions, kept themselves distinct from the slave population; they have always considered themselves a superior class and have a perfect knowledge of their freedom."[20] To a large degree, this description simply reflects an outsider's characterizations of a class of people whom he viewed as a social collectivity. That is to say, the observations of John Dougan do not necessarily reveal anything about the development of a pan-African exile consciousness among liberated Africans.

The themes of exile and repatriation for liberated Africans and other people of African descent fall into two broad categories. The first category includes symbolic, spiritual, or mythic ideas about returning to the African continent. The second category encompasses actual plans or attempts to make such a journey. In the symbolic, spiritual, and mythic experiences, the idea of flying back to Africa has played a prominent role. Descriptions of this concept have emerged in virtually every New World society that received African slaves during the years of the Atlantic trade. According to European accounts of slave society, many Africans (and even their descendants) believed that after death their souls would return to Africa. They expressed this belief in language that described traveling back to Guinea. This European term (which was used in Spanish, Portuguese, French, and English) referred to West Africa in a generalized sense rather than to any particular location.[21] Some accounts explained that a person's soul or spirit would make the return; most descriptions proved more ambiguous. Slaves simply alluded vaguely to the belief that their dead returned to Africa. Observers tended to interpret this belief as being analogous to the Christian view of souls traveling to heaven. However, it seems equally possible that the Africans might have envisioned a more bodily reincarnation.

Authorities repeatedly complained that this unique understanding of death hindered their ability to control their slaves. If slaves believed that death would return them to their homelands, the threat of death as an ultimate punishment became no threat at all. On some occasions, to counter this belief, authorities mutilated the bodies of executed slaves. In several extreme instances, planters resorted to gruesome decapitations. They beheaded the corpses of slaves who had been executed for the most serious offenses such as marronage or rebellion. Slaveholders hoped that displaying the heads of the deceased on pikes would inculcate an idea of ultimate mortality and therefore their own murderous power. Such displays no doubt inspired fear and succeeded to some degree in discouraging acts of resistance. However, these atrocities did not succeed in dispelling the belief in an African afterlife. Indeed, similar beliefs persisted in the Caribbean and parts of the United States into the twentieth century.

During the era of slavery, planters complained that these kinds of beliefs led some slaves to suicide. Only a tiny percentage of slaves ever took their own lives. But when suicides occurred, white observers often cited the belief in a return to Africa as part of the motivation. In more than one slave society, Europeans claimed that Ibos, in particular, found the option of suicide attractive. At the site now designated Ibo Landing in South Carolina, folk history claims that a group of Ibo slaves walked eastward into the Atlantic bound for the African continent. In their view, drowning and mortal death proved no obstacle to their intention of return.

In some versions of this tale, the Ibos flew rather than simply walked into the sea. But flight does not seem to constitute a necessary element in this particular body of folk belief in the diaspora. Nor in fact does death itself; Africans in the New World also incorporated the theme of repatriation into the powers they ascribed to various supernatural agents. Evidence from both organized religious communities and the practice of obeah suggests that African people believed that in the context of certain religious experiences, both leaders and ordinary devotees might make spiritual (or perhaps out-of-body) journeys to Africa. This might occur, for example, during the course of spirit possession. In addition, African diaspora folklore includes several varieties of ghost-like beings who regularly fly back and forth between Africa and the New World. Perhaps most intriguing is the role salt plays in these return-to-Africa beliefs. Time after time the consumption of salt appears as a taboo for those who want to return to Africa. For example, when they were asked if everyone returned to Africa after death, slaves would sometimes explain that those who ate salt could not do so. Even the supernatural beings who allegedly flew back and forth would sometimes lose their powers if they interacted with salt. African diaspora societies, both with and without liberated Africans, clearly produced a rich symbolic discourse around the concept of returning to Africa. Liberated Africans in both the Bahamas and Trinidad shared this discourse with the wider community of people of African descent. They also contributed trajectories of their own.

For these free immigrants, hopes or plans for physical return perhaps played an even greater role. Still, their experience in this regard also shares characteristics with broader African diaspora history. In that larger history, actual schemes for return tended to develop around a collection of issues. The first, and possibly most important, issue concerned dissatisfaction with life in the New World. In the United States, during the early nineteenth century, white philanthropists founded the American Colonization Society. This group proposed an emigration scheme that would help free blacks leave the United States to form an initially subsidized settlement in West Africa. From the outset, many free blacks viewed the project as a cynical attempt to deport them in order to evade the dilemma of how to give them equal rights. This criticism held more than a grain of truth. All the same, some free blacks embraced the idea as a reasonable opportunity to begin a new life apart from the economic and social discrimination of the United States.[22] In the end, only a tiny fraction of the free black population actually emigrated to establish the colony of Liberia. But virtually all of these colonists cited discrimination as a driving factor in their decision to depart. Liberated Africans in the nineteenth-century Caribbean also faced a complex series of obstacles in seeking to establish themselves economically in their new societies. Even though they arrived as free immigrants, most of this group had limited access to quality land, and the perquisites of the dominant white community greatly circumscribed their opportunities to become trades people or pursue other economic endeavors. In all cases where liberated African immigrants sought repatriation, they too cited discrimination and material hardship as critical motivating factors in their course of action.

Many of the African Americans involved in the Liberia debate viewed the whole of West Africa as a culturally alien or even barbarous place. Such alienation points to the second major feature that characterized so many of the back-to-Africa projects conducted by African Americans. On the one hand, any attempt to relocate in Africa presupposed a rejection of the New World. However, many returnees in fact viewed that rejection in a selective or partial way. That is, they embraced large parts of western culture as they had experienced it and sought to transplant many of its norms to their resettlement locations. Returnees born in the New World had little choice in this matter; they had had no first-hand experience of any African societies. When they went to Liberia or Sierra Leone, they set out to establish farms, shops, or other enterprises based on models they had seen in the United States or the Caribbean. Even more notably, however, many nineteenth century African Americans viewed the African continent as an ideal mission field for spreading the Christian gospel they had learned in the New World. They did not condone the system of slavery through which their conversion had occurred, and they did not argue that Christianity in any way compensated for the horrors of that system. But they described their conversion to Christianity in terms of an enlightenment that they might share with denizens of their ancestral homeland. Indeed, many church leaders—both black and white—argued that African Americans had a special obligation to carry Christianity to their "heathen" kin.

Several Protestant denominations (perhaps most notably the Baptists) sought to recruit African-American missionaries to lead a unique project of evangelism. This kind of evangelism did not require group repatriation. Individual missionaries could travel to Africa alone or with their families, establishing new churches in the fashion already begun by their European counterparts. Many African-American missionaries followed exactly this pattern. However, virtually all attempts at collective return to Africa incorporated the evangelical impulse. People from the diaspora who traveled to Liberia or Sierra Leone viewed their emigration as both self-serving and altruistic. They hoped to leave behind the hardships of European-dominated societies, but they also hoped to spread economic improvement and religious or moral education to the African continent. It should come as no surprise that European sponsors involved in back-to-Africa projects emphasized and encouraged these goals. Hardly anyone questioned the hierarchical cultural assumptions of such designs. Few people, either of African or European descent, defended the integrity of various African cultures in their own right. Almost all accepted the preferability of western norms in general and Christianity in particular.[23]

To a certain extent, these attitudes originated in the fact that African Americans born in the New World had no direct connection to or understanding of individual African cultures. For most African-descended people in the diaspora, the opportunity to consider repatriation did not occur until the second generation. Liberated Africans, however, could consider this idea almost from the moment of their arrival. One might therefore expect that when they spoke of Africa or thought of return, they would not espouse a western cultural agenda or ambitions of converting African peoples to Christianity. And in most cases, liberated Africans' thoughts of returning to Africa did indeed focus more on a desire to reclaim their societies of origin rather than on plans to alter them. Yet even immigrant Africans sometimes included proselytizing goals in their plans for repatriation. And their ideas often reflected other social, cultural, or economic priorities learned through their experiences in the New World. Thus, even as they expressed the mentality of exiles and articulated the idea of return, many liberated Africans also expressed creolized and Christian sensibilities that they shared with other people in the African diaspora. As one might expect, such sensibilities played their greatest role during the later decades of the nineteenth century, in cases such as that of the Congo Society that involved liberated Africans who had spent most of their lives in the Caribbean. These people combined their desire to return to Africa with a clear creole consciousness. They demonstrated what one might describe as a classic immigrant identity—they belonged to and yearned for a distant place while at the same time they were molded by their new world.

In this respect, the liberated African experience of exile shared many characteristics with the experience of all Africans and their descendants in the Americas. But for these nineteenth-century free immigrants, that experience had a unique intensity. The idea and prospect of return loomed large from the earliest days of their arrival in the Caribbean. The very authorities who organized liberated African settlement repeatedly acknowledged the displaced status of these people. Pragmatic considerations dictated that for most liberated Africans, actual return to Africa remained out of reach, but the idea retained a powerful and persistent resonance throughout these communities.

While literal return generally seemed unlikely, liberated Africans clearly espoused the notion of returning to Africa by spiritual or supernatural means. Suggestive evidence points to their belief in the "return to Guinea" through death. The term Guinea itself appears only rarely in the historical records of the Bahamas and Trinidad related to liberated Africans. In the Bahamas, a small village east of the town of Nassau that was inhabited by "free Negroes" was known by the name New Guinea. The use of this term for the African continent thus did have some currency. However, this particular village existed at least a quarter-century before the arrival of liberated Africans, and the settlement in question also seems to have had a more common name, Creek Village, or simply The Creek.[24] A possibly more pertinent reference to Guinea appeared in the 1833 trial of a West India Regiment soldier for the murder of one his comrades. A jury in the Bahamas General Court convicted Private William John Peters of the murder of Private John Thunder. In his testimony for the prosecution, a third soldier, John Williams, offered the following explanation as to why apparently simple fisticuffs may have resulted in Thunder's death: "Peters [the assailant] was very drunk. Thunder was a small boned man, a boy might have knocked him down. He was old *before he came from Guinea*" (emphasis added).[25] The Bahamas-based 2nd West India Regiment, like its counterparts throughout the West Indies, included both liberated Africans rescued from slave ships and other Africans acquired as slave soldiers before the abolition of the slave trade in 1807. It seems likely that the soldier who made this statement belonged to the liberated African group, which was recruited after 1807. According to the trial record, Williams required an interpreter in order to make his testimony understandable to the court. This strongly suggests a soldier who had recently arrived. Africans who had arrived before 1807 would almost certainly have achieved proficiency in English after twenty-five years. The words of

Private John Williams with respect to the idea of Guinea cannot serve to represent the thinking of a majority of the liberated African population. However, Williams's statement provides evidence that this generalized notion of Africa—most often associated with thoughts of repatriation after death—formed a part of the conceptual system of at least some liberated Africans in the Bahamas.

Mere reference to Guinea does not necessarily point to beliefs about returning there after death. Evidence of this specific belief emerges elsewhere in both the Bahamian and Trinidadian experiences. Well into the twentieth century, descendants of liberated Africans in Trinidad explained that their ancestors "did not remain in [the island], rather they flew back (returned) to Africa."[26] When asked to clarify such statements, informants either offered no explanation or indicated that flying back to Africa took place after people had died. Maureen Warner-Lewis, who has written extensively about Trinidad's Yoruba community, collected a diverse assortment of such accounts when she interviewed the descendants of Yorubas and other liberated Africans during the late 1960s. She records the following oral history account of a work stoppage that took place at Harmony Hall Estate during the late nineteenth century: "A work stoppage of three days occurred among Africans . . . when a man, returning to his hut to discover his wife had been raped by the overseer, called his countrymen together and, in their midst, flew back to Guinea."[27] Warner-Lewis does not expand on the possible details of this incident. One might speculate, however, that upon learning of the rape, the aggrieved husband murdered his wife—in a response possibly of anger, possibly of shame, or possibly related to some more complicated sense of community mores concerning appropriate behavior in such a situation. The husband then perhaps committed suicide. Not only did this tragedy provoke the three-day strike, but the African immigrant community memorialized these deaths in the tale of returning to Guinea that was recorded by Warner-Lewis almost a century later.

In the decades since Warner-Lewis conducted her research, scholars have continued to encounter descendants of liberated Africans who make similar references to their ancestors flying back to Africa. In 1989, an undergraduate at the University of the West Indies documented the existence of that belief in her own family history with respect to her great-great-grandparents, a Yoruba man and a Congo woman who purportedly arrived in Trinidad as liberated African immigrants. Charmaine Fletcher's thesis focuses on a biography of her great-grandmother, Emily Scope, the daughter of these immigrants. Based on interviews with older relatives, Fletcher describes Scope's belief in and acceptance of "the 'myth' that her parents flew back to Africa."[28] The various informants involved in 1989 evidently did not enlarge upon the nature of this so-called myth. Fletcher interprets Scope's belief as a reference to her parents' death. Similarly, in an interview conducted in 1994, Winifred Lendore, another probable descendant of liberated Africans, implied that some of her ancestors had spontaneously returned to Africa.[29] She too offered no explanation, leading once more to the presumption that this return referred to an act effected through death.

Maureen Warner-Lewis has explored such interpretations beyond the straightforward understanding of them as myth or metaphor. She considers the possibility that African immigrants used the idea of flying back to Africa to specifically explain (untimely) deaths such as those "by suicide or public execution." She also suggests that the notion of flying back to Africa may have expressed a "death- or escape-wish" on the part of the African immigrants.[30] Historian Monica Schuler makes similar allusions in her study of liberated African immigrants in Jamaica. Schuler does not present specific instances of suicidal or escape-oriented behavior by liberated Africans. However, like Warner-Lewis, she suggests that the persistence of the idea of flying back to Africa in these communities might have had suicidal content. Schuler cites the autobiography of Cuban slave Esteban Montejo, who speaks at length about the beliefs of Africans in Cuba concerning return to Africa in death. According to Schuler, in Montejo's account, such beliefs provoked a significant occurrence of suicide.[31] Warner-Lewis makes one general reference to liberated Africans attempting suicide on ships bound for the Caribbean; she says they threw themselves overboard.[32] She also cites the work of nineteenth-century Trinidad historian Louis de Verteuil, who described immigrant Africans attempting to return home by walking eastward on the island of Trinidad.[33]

Several specific instances of liberated Africans threatening, attempting, or committing suicide also exist, although in these cases, the individuals did not explicitly state an intention to return to Africa through their own demise. For example, in 1871, an African immigrant in the Trinidad town of Arouca hanged himself in jail after a seemingly trivial arrest for drunkenness. The press at the time reported that no one knew of any direct reason that might have "[driven] him to the desperate act."[34] British officials on the island of Saint Helena also reported suspiciously self-destructive behavior among liberated Africans stationed there before emigration to the West Indies. The collector of customs on the island complained that some of the Africans had either drowned or nearly drowned by "falling into the sea."[35] This seems a peculiar problem given the fact that Africans at Saint Helena sometimes resided on British ships in the harbor but most often inhabited makeshift barracks on shore. Neither of these situations posed an undue risk of falling accidentally into the sea. One might therefore speculate that these drowning victims had a deliberate hand in their fate. Perhaps they intended to take their lives as a means of escaping the uncertain and certainly unattractive predicament in which they found themselves. Perhaps through such suicide they hoped to achieve some kind of supernatural repatriation to their communities of origin. Perhaps they hoped to literally cross the water and return to the African continent. In any case, their behavior seems to demonstrate the "suicide- or escape-wish" posited by Warner-Lewis.

An even more explicit account of this wish emerges from the liberated African community in the Bahamas. Early in the nineteenth century, when the first groups of liberated Africans began to arrive in the Bahamas, the collector of customs was responsible for the welfare of this population. In September 1815, Collector Alexander Murray wrote a letter of complaint to the governor, indicating that he found this responsibility overly burdensome. He recommended that the Colonial Office appoint a separate individual to oversee the African immigrants. Murray wrote that his role as ombudsman for liberated Africans seemed destined to fail. If he responded solicitously to every complaint, even more complaints ensued. However, complaints left "unattended to, [had] caused attempts at suiside [sic]."[36] Needless to say, Collector Murray had no access to the spiritual or conceptual expectations of those African immigrants who allegedly took their own lives in response to hardships he failed to correct. Even though their actions clearly manifested a rejection of the New World and a desire to escape, one cannot say for certain that they envisioned that escape as a return to Guinea. Yet this possibility seems at least as likely as not, given the documented prevalence of that belief in so many eighteenth- and nineteenth-century communities of the African diaspora.

The most noticeable legacy of this belief lies in the various religious and folkloric traditions that invoke the idea of supernatural return to Africa as a part of their conceptual systems. Liberated Africans did not create these traditions. However, at least in Trinidad, they seem to have nurtured or reinforced them. One of the more striking examples of such traditions occurs in the beliefs and practices of Trinidad's Spiritual Baptist Church, which include a periodic time of exclusion called mourning during which a member or members isolate themselves in a kind of contemplative trance for approximately a week supervised by a church leader. Many mourners describe trance journeys during which their spirit departs from their body and travels according to instruction from a guide figure they meet in the trance. In some experiences of mourning, the spirit travels to a relatively nonspecific location such as a river or field, at which place the guide offers some kind of advice to the mourner on how to conduct his or her Christian life.[37] Most interesting, however, is the fact that in the majority of cases the mourning spirit travels to an identified location, often (although not always) Africa.

In his study of the Spiritual Baptists, folklorist Stephen Glazier does not link this spirit travel with ideas of exile or nostalgia in the minds of Trinidad Baptists whose ancestors arrived under duress from elsewhere. However, this link is made in the research of at least one University of the West Indies undergraduate who studied Spiritual Baptists as a part of the local history requirement of the curriculum. Based on his interviews conducted in the mid-1980s, Ian Anthony Taylor writes:

> The spiritual places most often mentioned by Baptists in their mourning visits were Africa, India and China. Of course this is noteworthy since these are the nations from which three of Trinidad's main ethnic groups originate.[38]

Taylor notes that although Africans came as slaves and East Indians and Chinese came as indentured laborers, all three groups had low social and economic status as poorly compensated agricultural workers for generations.[39] Taylor does not expand upon the role an immigrant consciousness might have played in shaping the evolution of the mourning ritual. Yet it seems clear that this spiritual discourse of return likely reflects a desire that was important to the African immigrant population present in Trinidad during the formative years of the Spiritual Baptist faith in the nineteenth century. Not until well into the twentieth century did people of non-African descent—those of Indian or Chinese descent—become a significant presence in this church. Does the inclusion of China and India in the mourning visions simply reflect the spiritual imaginations of these new participants? One argument against this interpretation lies in the fact that mourners' experiences do not fall along tidy ethnic lines. That is, people of African descent report visionary journeys to China or India, and Chinese and Indian followers report mourning journeys to Africa.[40] On the one hand, such mixing might seem to negate the suggestion that trance journeys to Africa contain any meaning related to repatriation desires of liberated Africans. On the other hand, one can equally interpret the inclusion of China and India as a confirmation of the repatriation theme. That is, the Africans who most likely developed the ritual first situated their Old World homeland as the desired place of enlightenment—an inspiring and strengthening escape from their New World exile. The incorporation of other Old World locales remains consistent with this conceptual scheme and in no way detracts from what was probably a focus on Africa during the ritual's earliest days.

The Spiritual Baptist Church does not have a monopoly on the idea of spirit flight to Africa. The idea has retained perhaps its most vibrant life in folklore that is far less bounded by any organized religious rubric. Monica

Schuler explores this folklore in some detail in the case of liberated African communities in Jamaica. She focuses on the belief among Africans that common salt had supernatural properties that could affect the possibility of a spirit's return to Africa. Schuler explains: "[S]pirits do not eat salt, and abstention from it was believed to confer special powers like those of the spirits, making people 'come like a witch,' 'interpret all things' and powerful enough to fly back to Africa."[41] In this exposition, the notion of spirit travel to Africa has two possible meanings. The term "spirit" seems to refer to supernatural entities as opposed to human souls. Such supernatural beings (who remain nameless) could apparently travel back and forth at will between Africa and the Caribbean. Human beings might obtain such ocean-crossing power by denying themselves salt. One presumes, however, that humans who could cross the Atlantic would do so in soul or spirit rather than in body, hence the appearance of a double meaning. Schuler traces these ideas to various aspects of BaKongo cosmology, in which people often view the ocean as a barrier between the worlds of the living and the dead. They view Kongo territory in Africa as the world of the living and the Americas and the Caribbean as the world of the dead. Spirits of those who die cross from the former to the latter. After death, the spirits of some unique people "such as prophets" allegedly cross back and forth. Other kinds of spirits (or perhaps people) traverse the water through the power of witchcraft.[42] As Schuler indicates, these ideas have myriad implications for understanding how the BaKongo have interpreted the nature of the transatlantic slave trade in their history. Among liberated Africans in the Caribbean, the presence of such ideas—even in fragmented form—points to the enduring cultural significance of the prospect of mythic return.

The Bahamas and Trinidad do not yield a discourse quite as coherent as the one Schuler documents for Jamaica, but similar concepts and motifs repeatedly appear in the African diaspora folklore of at least one of these two countries, namely Trinidad. Schuler has speculated that the origins of the significance attached to salt may lie in the behavior of Roman Catholic missionaries who proselytized in the Kongo kingdom as early as the fifteenth century. Portuguese priests sometimes placed salt on the tongue rather than sprinkling water as the sign of Christian baptism. Schuler suggests that among the BaKongo, salt might have come to symbolize an embrace of the European world. If this symbolism continued in the Caribbean, it would make sense that only the spirits of those who abstained from salt could return to Africa.[43] In Trinidad, however, the significance attached to salt appears consistently in religious practices derived from Yoruba (or at least West African) traditions, not from Kongo cosmology. According to many followers of Trinidad's orisha worship, the sacrificial foods for their religion must be prepared without the use of salt. Orisha practitioners and their descendants described this restriction almost casually in the course of interviews conducted during 1994. Even though they regarded the interviewer as an outsider, they mentioned the prohibition on salt as a matter of course, in a tone that suggested they considered it an unremarkable feature.[44] Documentation of this restriction exists in several recent folklore studies of the orisha faith. One informant explained to an interviewer in the early 1980s:

> Salt was not an African product. It was only introduced by the English when they conquered Nigeria. The Yorubas knew nothing about salt. . . . If anyone wished to salt their food at a Shango [orisha worship] ceremony in Trinidad, they must walk with their own salt.[45]

Another orisha practitioner simply stated that "Africans never used to salt."[46] The salt prohibition has also appeared in connection with "saraka" or "sakara" feasts. These celebrations, though not connected to any specific or formal religion, also included killing, cooking, and sharing food as a part of the propitiation of supernatural spirits. And here too, tradition required saltless preparation.[47] None of these occasions directly link the abstention from salt with notions of returning to Africa. These examples do however connect Africanness with saltlessness in the same fashion Schuler described in the case of liberated Africans in Jamaica.

Furthermore, at least one orisha practitioner interviewed in 1994 explicitly linked a refusal to eat salt with the ability to mysteriously leave Trinidad. Winifred Lendore of the village of Tortuga recounted an exceptional tale about the departure of some of her ancestors from the island. She described a family of five that consisted of an African man and woman and their three daughters. According to Lendore, the mother of the family repeatedly counseled her children to refrain from eating salt. One of the daughters failed to follow this advice, and when "the mother went, the father went [and] the two sisters went," but this third daughter who had eaten salted food "couldn't go." Lendore depicted this departure as having taken place next to a body of water, following some kind of ceremony that involved drumming. She did not actually state that the family flew away, but at one point in the story, she described the mother coming "back down" to reassure the daughter they had left behind,[48] a phrase that implies aerial flight. Given the cultural diffusion of the notion of flying back to Africa, it seems only logical to interpret this tale as a part of that tradition. On this occasion, Lendore did not directly mention Africa as a destination for the family. But in a separate interview with Lendore and her niece, Naomi Toby, the specific matter of African repatriation did indeed arise. At that time, while Lendore spoke of people returning to Africa by ship, Toby made a distinctive series of gestures intended to indicate flight.[49] These two women—who claimed direct ancestry from liberated Africans—thus provide evidence that the concept of flying back to Africa (and the related significance of salt) had specific resonance for free African immigrants and their descendants.

Specific evidence of similar beliefs does not emerge in the oral history or folklore of the Bahamas. However, a vague allusion to these ideas about avoiding salt and flying back to Africa possibly exists in Bahamian beliefs about hags or soucouyants. Holm and Shilling's *Dictionary of Bahamian English* defines a hag in the Bahamian context as "a witch (male or female) who leaves [his or her] SKIN at night to haunt victims by tormenting them or sucking their blood." This definition accords with other cross-cultural descriptions of such figures, who most often attack their victims in bed, leaving the person with a sense of paralysis, unable either to rise and flee or confront the hag.[50] One can compare the hag of the Bahamas with Trinidad accounts of soucouyants. One researcher, Claudia Harvey, describes this character as "a natural born woman who by the possession of some special powers is able . . . to fly, enter people's houses and suck their blood." According to Harvey, accounts do not agree about the "changes that take place in [the soucouyant's] body," but many informants have referred to the removal of her skin. Even more important, some tales have asserted that "slaves [assumed] the form of soucouyants and [flew] home to Africa."[51] Despite the similarities between the Trinidad soucouyant and the Bahamian hag, one cannot automatically assume that the hag figure had conceptual linkages with the notion of African return. But given the other parallels between the two figures, one must consider the possibility that such linkages did exist. Furthermore, the hag of Bahamian folklore has a very suggestive connection to the idea that salt is supernaturally powerful. Some older Bahamians claim that if one encounters a hag, one can neutralize its powers or even destroy it by pouring salt onto its exposed, skinless flesh.[52] This curious allusion does not come close to the specificity of the Trinidad references cited above. All the same, there do seem to be grounds for speculation that some version of the fly-back-to-Africa myths also developed in the Bahamas.

During the latter half of the nineteenth century, both colonies exhibited signs that liberated Africans and their descendants had developed an understanding of a generically defined Africa as the homeland to which they properly belonged (and perhaps wished to return to). In studying the experience of East Indian immigrants to the Caribbean, sociologist Arnold Itwaru has described this kind of broadly expressed immigrant identity as a "means for the maintenance of psychic strength under the atrocity of oppression."[53] Itwaru focuses on East Indian collective identity in the Caribbean, but to a large extent, his conclusion seems equally apt for Africans.

That is, claims of Africanness just as much as claims of Indianness are evidence of a collective rejection of the largely negative experience of the New World and a casting of cultural and geographic allegiances elsewhere. European West Indians and even government officials nurtured this identification as exiles by dealing with liberated African immigrants as a separate and collective group. But more than the simple reality of collective experience, during the late nineteenth century public dialogues developed in both the Bahamas and Trinidad that engaged notions of "Negro nationality" or "African nationality."

In Trinidad, this discourse developed in a broadly encompassing tone that included all people of African descent rather than specifically liberated Africans. However, the presence of African-born Africans in the colony almost certainly gave added impetus to the unfolding of such ideas, among both Africans and the non-African elites who observed them. During the 1870s, for example, *The New Era* ran a series of articles about the establishment of a "West African University" in colonial Sierra Leone. The paper's colored middle-class editors published this material because they felt that the subject had particular salience for their colony and its significant population of so-called African nationals.[54] In the initial notice about this matter, they explained: "The subject [of a University in Western Africa] is one of great importance, and offers so many subjects for consideration that we have decided on devoting one or two of our next numbers to it."[55] The *New Era* statement also presumed and indeed encouraged a persistent identification with Africa on the part of Trinidad's African-descended residents. In a subsequent feature that followed the progress of the West African University, the editors explicitly espoused this viewpoint. On April 28, 1873, they summarized the contents of correspondence between West Indian intellectual Edward Blyden and John Pope Hennessy, the British administrator in chief of West Africa. Blyden expressed to Hennessy his belief that any educational projects in West Africa would have to incorporate both African culture and African leaders in order to achieve success. The liberal *New Era* editors not only expressed their agreement with Blyden's opinion but also recommended his writings on this subject as "a work of great value and momentous interest to all men of color."[56] The newspaper thus recommended the ideas of a pan-Africanist and African cultural nationalist to Trinidad's African-descended population.

The interest in Edward Blyden had particular relevance for questions of African identity and the idea of diasporic Africans returning to an African homeland. Born in the Danish Virgin Islands in 1832, Blyden chose to emigrate to Liberia after education and travel in the Caribbean, Latin America, and the United States. According to Blyden's biographer Hollis Lynch, he made this choice as a young man of only eighteen years after observing the enslaved or otherwise oppressed condition of people of African descent throughout the New World. Through connections with Presbyterian clergy, Blyden learned of the colony of Liberia. Despite the controversy surrounding this project, the idea of founding such a nation appealed to Blyden, and he emigrated in December 1850. He devoted the remainder of his life to educational, political, and religious service first in Liberia and later in nearby Sierra Leone, a British colony founded upon similar principles.[57]

The *New Era* newspaper seems to have had a particular interest in this intellectual champion of repatriation (or at least of pan-African nationalism), even beyond the question of the proposed West African University. Months before the advent of the university issue, the paper ran an article in August 1872 concerning *The Negro,* Blyden's newspaper founded that same year in Freetown, Sierra Leone. The *New Era* article quoted at length from Blyden's explanation of why he chose the name "Negro" for his publication rather than "West African" or some other title. He preferred "Negro" as a term because it encompassed all members of the African diaspora in the New World as well as Africans on the continent. In the course of this explanation, Blyden offered perhaps his most famous statement on the persistent African identity of Africans in the diaspora and their descendants: "Every Negro is an African."[58] He did not directly advocate repatriation in this text or in any of his other statements quoted by the *New Era.* However, the editors of the Trinidad newspaper clearly recognized Blyden's symbolic significance as a man from the African diaspora who returned to Africa as the location from which he could best promote the interests of African people materially, socially, and politically. Although somewhat indirectly, the *New Era* situated the notion of return to Africa within the constellation of ideas shared by literate Trinidadians of African descent during the late nineteenth century.

The *New Era* editors, who Bridget Brereton describes as having mixed African and European ancestry, did not belong to the population of liberated Africans or their descendants. However, by the 1870s at least some members of the liberated African group had attained sufficient literacy, education, and income to be included among the "black and coloured middle classes" identified by Brereton as the *New Era's* reading public.[59] In fact, it seems possible that the newspaper's most prominent reader and a regular contributor of letters may have had liberated African ancestry. John Jacob Thomas, an educated Trinidadian of African descent, gained attention and later prominence in both England and the Caribbean with his publication in 1869 of a work entitled *The Theory and Practice of Creole Grammar,* which explored the development and nature of Trinidad's French-based

Creole, a unique mixture of African and European linguistic antecedents. During the 1870s and early 1880s, Thomas moved from his life as a rural teacher to various civil service and educational posts in Port-of-Spain, where he became a well-respected intellectual and public figure both among liberal whites and in his own ethnic community.[60] Historian Donald Wood characterizes Thomas's childhood as "obscure" but describes him as "a man of pure African descent . . . born of humble parents in or about 1840."[61] Wood does not cite a specific source for this information, nor does he explain his use of the phrase "pure African." This term may simply indicate the absence of any European mixture or it could suggest that Thomas's parents arrived directly from Africa. In that case, they would most likely have arrived as free African immigrants. This single, albeit striking, example by no means demonstrates that literate liberated Africans or their descendants played a unique role in the public discussion of African nationalism and its linkages to the idea of repatriation. However, the participation of a man such as Thomas at the very least confirms that this type of discussion held a prominent place in the communities to which literate liberated Africans would have belonged.

This discourse also took place among educated people of African descent in the Bahamian colonial capital, the town of Nassau, where liberated Africans seem to have played a major role in *The Freeman*, a news paper that was published for slightly more than a year between 1887 and 1888 and concerned itself with the economic, social, and political development of people of African descent, mostly in the Bahamas but also throughout the New World diaspora and in Africa. Articles appeared concerning discrimination African Americans faced in the United States, the looming question of slave emancipation in Brazil, and, occasionally, the activities of various European colonizers on the African continent. Much like Trinidad's *New Era*, the editors did not specifically promote the idea of repatriation. But the idea surfaced as part of the dialogue of African "progress" their paper advanced. In the manner of so many nineteenth-century newspapers, *The Freeman* published the following brief paragraph extracted from an "American paper" in March 1888:

> We think that the Negro can have all his rights in this country if he will contend and fight righteously for them. We can hardly see the real necessity of American negroes leaving their native country to obtain their rights in a foreign land.[62]

On the one hand, this statement clearly dismisses the notion of emigration to Liberia, Sierra Leone, or anywhere else as an appropriate course of action for people of African descent who were unhappy with their social, economic, or political status in the New World. On the other hand, the editors of *The Freeman* neither endorsed nor criticized the "American paper's" pronouncement. Indeed, by publishing the extract without comment, the newspaper seemed to encourage debate on the back-to-Africa question. As in Trinidad, this idea clearly formed a part of the African-Bahamian consciousness.

The work of Edward Blyden made at least one appearance in this Bahamian newspaper. In December 1887, *The Freeman* printed a review of Blyden's work *Christianity, Islam and the Negro Race* (1887). The review originally appeared in a London paper under the title "The Future of Africa." Blyden's book was a series of essays dealing not only with questions of religious conversion (and the relative merits of Christianity and Islam for people of African descent) but also with broader issues such as the history of Liberia and Sierra Leone or the vagaries of post-emancipation developments in the United States. Many times throughout the text Blyden endorses the idea of repatriation. He describes the Caribbean, the United States, and Latin America as "countries of exile" for "the Negro" and portrays the notion of return to an "ancestral home" as natural, human, and even "irresistible."[63] The review reprinted by *The Freeman* focuses precisely on this back-to-Africa argument. The reviewer neither agrees nor disagrees with Blyden but suggests that Liberia and Sierra Leone should continue to serve as experiments through which to measure the merits of repatriation and to assess the ability of African people to educate and govern themselves. Nonetheless, the tone of the review leans toward support for Blyden's case; the reviewer describes Blyden's book as "reasonable, thoughtful and full of matter which deserves serious consideration."[64] Thus, once again *The Freeman* provided a forum for the positive evaluation of the idea of returning to Africa.

Considerable evidence suggests that liberated Africans and their descendants would have formed a significant part of any such discourse promoted by this paper. In a popular history entitled *The Other Bahamas,* Hartley Saunders identifies "James Carmichael Smith, an African man of fair complexion" as the founder and principal editor of *The Freeman.*[65] Here, as elsewhere in his text, Saunders uses the adjective "African" to describe any person of African descent regardless of their place of birth or any European or other ethnic mixture in their ancestry. From this description of Smith's complexion it seems reasonable to assume that the newspaper founder did not belong to the nineteenth-century African immigrant group. And because the paper did not print a masthead, it proves difficult to identify other major participants. The name "J. F. Aranha" appears in several issues under the title of "Secretary," responsible for collecting subscriptions and investments. His particular ethnic or social identity remains unknown. Although the identities of the directors and writers of *The Freeman* remain somewhat anonymous, the content of the newspaper provides many clues about the journal's presumptive audience. The paper offered liberal coverage of an organization that called itself the Anglo-African League. Reports of League meetings regularly constituted the major item of local news. These reports provided a level of detail more akin to secretarial minutes than to a journalistic account of a particular event. One might almost speculate that *The Freeman* served as a kind of unofficial chronicle for this organization, notwithstanding the fact that the articles concerning Anglo-African League meetings appeared under the byline "From our Reporter." At the very least, one can conclude that *The Freeman* believed that a significant proportion of its readers were League members. And that membership included a substantial number of liberated Africans and their descendants.

The Anglo-African League functioned as an administrative and social umbrella for the various friendly societies, including those with ethnic African names and others. The League was formed in October 1887 at the initiative of the president of the Bahama Friendly Society, who believed that collectively the groups could have greater impact in pursuing various public issues for their mutual benefit. According to the reports contained in *The Freeman*, the League focused its efforts on lobbying the local and colonial governments for electoral, economic, and social reforms they believed would aid the majority population of African descent. For example, during the early months of 1888, the League petitioned members of the Legislative Council and the Colonial Secretary in London to adopt a "Ballot box" system of voting rather than the system of verbal "naming" at the polls. On an economic front, the organization sought an alteration in the government proposal to subsidize the expanding Bahamian sisal industry. The legislature had proposed that premiums be offered to sisal exporters at a rate of five pounds per ton. The Anglo-African League suggested that the government instead offer a smaller premium to individual sisal growers, as the export bonus "would only benefit the mercantile portion of the community"—which presumably meant mostly white or European Bahamians.[66]

This activist confederation of all friendly societies included men of African descent from a variety of origins: former slaves, liberated African immigrants, and others. Confirmation of strong involvement of liberated Africans exists in the composition of the friendly societies. The groups represented included a specific trade organization, the Ship Carpenters' Union; the United Burial Society; and the Bahama Friendly Society. Historian Howard Johnson describes the Bahama Friendly Society as "a creole organisation . . . composed entirely of ex-slaves."[67] Other groups indicate liberated African roots. The Grant's Town Friendly Society (G.T.F.S.) had emerged from the Grant's Town neighborhood. In 1835, Thomas Conyers, president of the G.T.F.S., described his group's membership as follows: "natives of Africa . . . Torn from our Native country and Connections by Evil Men, and . . . rescued from Slavery by [His Britannic] Majesty's brave Seamen." The latter phrase clearly refers to their status as African recaptives.[68] The society's membership certainly must have changed during the half-century which passed between Conyers's statement in 1835 and the formation of the Anglo-African League in 1887, but it seems fair to presume at least some continuity through the presence of elderly founding members and the possible membership of their sons. (The works of Howard Johnson and Hartley Saunders both strongly imply the existence of generational succession in these groups.)

Likewise, the ethnically specific friendly societies of the Anglo-African League also probably originated with liberated Africans.[69] The Congo No. 1 Society referred directly to its liberated African roots in the 1888 petition that requested their return to Kongo lands in Africa. In an especially striking connection of the Yoruba and Egba Societies, Johnson cites an 1884 statement from Governor Henry Blake that described the membership of these two groups as being largely comprised of "the children and grandchildren" of over 1,000 liberated Africans who were rescued from two Portuguese slave ships and settled in the Bahamas in 1838. The remainder of the membership consisted of "a few [elderly people] of the original [immigrant] number."[70] Indeed, on May 8, 1888, *The Freeman* omitted its own editorial in favor of a description and celebration of the history and events surrounding the "Jubilee of the Landing of the Yoruba and Egba Tribes on the Free Shores of Nassau."[71] This occasion commemorated the fiftieth anniversary of the 1838 arrivals.[72] Thus, when *The Freeman* styled itself as a forum for issues relevant to people of African descent in the late-nineteenth-century Bahamas, liberated Africans and their descendants clearly formed a large part of the newspaper's expected audience and therefore its presumed discursive community. And, as the examples cited previously demonstrate, this literate discourse included not only a generic identification with Africa but also specific consideration of the notion of repatriation. This notion had a diverse and long-lived influence in the liberated African experience.

For the immigrants, the notion began with their self-identification as expatriates and a deliberate and continued association with their particular African homelands even as they went about the business of becoming participants in diverse New World communities. Unlike their slave predecessors, liberated African immigrants often found that the society around them accepted their self-characterization as specific African nationals rather than homogeneously or vaguely defined immigrants. In other words, they often successfully resisted even the implicit erasure of their status as foreign exiles.

These liberated Africans sometimes delineated their expatriate identity in terms of geographic locations and at other times in terms of a more broadly stated regionalism or ethnicity. The trial of Private William John Peters provides several striking examples of ethnically defined nationality on the part of such Africans. Following Peters's conviction, his attorney, T. M. Matthews, appealed for relief to the Bahamian attorney general, Lewis Kerr. Matthews raised technical questions about the nationality of Peters and whether or not the court had treated him as a British citizen or as a foreign national. Matthews also questioned the nationality of some of the witnesses who had testified against Peters. He further questioned the citizenship of some of the jurors, who may not have been eligible to serve in that capacity. These inquiries produced a series of telling statements concerning the civil and personal identity of various African immigrants.

One juror, for example, explained himself as follows in a post-trial affidavit: "I John Laing of the Island of New Providence, Free black man, do hereby certify that Culmantee [sic] on the coast of Africa is the place of my nativity, and that since my arrival at the Island of New Providence aforesaid, I have not been naturalized."[73] Evidence does not reveal Laing as a liberated African immigrant, although there is at least a 50 percent chance that he belonged to that group. According to Michael Craton and Gail Saunders, by 1834 African-born slaves constituted less than 10 percent of the total slave population in the Bahamas.[74] Given the fact that the free nonwhite population included both "blacks" and "coloureds" of mixed race, one might assume that, excluding liberated Africans, this free segment had an even smaller percentage of the African-born. Thus, if Laing claimed African "nativity" he quite likely arrived as a liberated African immigrant. Laing's statement demonstrates how free Africans could and did understand themselves to be foreign citizens of non-British, non-Caribbean places. In this case, the locale transcribed as "Culmantee" most likely referred to the term Coromantee, a word used during the eighteenth and nineteenth centuries to refer to parts of the Gold Coast and the Akan-Asante peoples who lived there. According to most scholars, the British used this term rather broadly to describe the area that now constitutes roughly the southern and coastal zone of modern Ghana. In his work *Africa in America*, historian Michael Mullin pursues somewhat greater specificity. Citing African anthropologist D. Kiyaga-Malindwa, Mullin describes the Coromantee as a specific ethnic "subgroup of [the] Twi," or Akan-Asante, peoples.[75] Thus, although Laing made his declaration in response to an unusual legal inquiry, his markedly specific statement reveals a continued personal relationship with a particular African community. Such a relationship would seem to constitute the root of any exile sensibility.

During the course of the legal proceedings, defense attorney T. M. Matthews produced comparable statements regarding nationality for his client, William John Peters, as well as one of the witnesses, Frederic Walker, who also served as a solider in the 2nd West India Regiment. Both Peters and Walker began their military careers as liberated Africans who enlisted at Sierra Leone after rescue from slave ships by the British navy. One officer from the 2nd West India Regiment at New Providence cited Peters's date of enlistment as the February 16, 1823, while another cited the date as September 16 that same year. In any case, Peters arrived in the Bahamas within two years of his enlistment and had served eight years in New Providence at the time of his arrest.[76] The trial records do not provide parallel details for Walker, although his statement indicates that he and the defendant had followed a similar career path. More significant, Walker's statement details the fact that he and Peters had shared the same ethnic homeland in Africa prior to the beginning of their journey into the diaspora. Walker's deposition, made in August 1833, explained

> that he [was] well acquainted with William John Peters . . . that he saw him first in a part of Africa where Deponent [Walker] was born called Eboe; and that from the circumstance of Peters speaking the Eboe language, Deponent considered him to be a countryman of his.[77]

Walker said that this first meeting took place before either man was captured and sold into the Atlantic slave trade. Both men ended up on slave ships which were captured by the British navy and taken to Sierra Leone, where the two acquaintances met again. Shortly after arriving in Freetown as a liberated African, Walker enlisted in the 2nd West India Regiment, only to discover Peters already enrolled.[78]

Walker's claim of connection with Peters clearly rests as much in their shared Ibo background as in any bonds of common experience as African recaptives or as soldiers. This specific ethnic and territorial background continued to have salience for Walker despite the ten years that had intervened since his departure from that place. The law required only that Walker confirm Peters's status as a person born outside of any British colony, either Sierra Leone or the Bahamas. The defense lawyer and the public secretary no doubt encouraged the deponent to provide details that were as specific as possible in his statement. Nonetheless, it seems almost certain that Walker himself chose to indicate his ethnically defined birthplace and to elucidate Peters's status through an explanation of their relationship as Ibo "countrymen." According to anthropologists, the term Ibo includes roughly 200 smaller ethnic groups who speak a common language and share cultural similarities but have never had any overarching kingdom or state structure. They have inhabited a region that now encompasses the southeastern corner of Nigeria.[79] Walker and Peters seem to have shared a regional homeland rather than a local one, but all the same, it was a precisely defined homeland that remained a meaningful memory to them.

Evidence indicates that Peters claimed his exact birthplace as the area of Calabar at the southeastern edge of Ibo territory. A document provided by the commanding officer of the 2nd West India Regiment listed Peters's birthplace only as "Eboe Africa." However, another officer described the accused murderer as "a native of Calabarian Eboe county [*sic*]."[80] Peters may or may not have been born in or even near the town of Calabar. It seems possible, even likely, that the name of this major trading site arose as a matter of course during formal communication between a British army official and an African private who originated from the general area of Ibo territory. During the nineteenth century (and indeed well into the twentieth) the term "Calabar" referred not only to the town but also to a much wider area surrounding the Cross River estuary.[81] Whatever the geographic particulars, the inclusion of the adjective Calabarian adds further weight to the perception that these liberated Africans understood and valued very specific understandings of their nativity, albeit translated into western terms.

Even more striking, in both the Bahamas and Trinidad, evidence shows that some liberated Africans expressed specific preoccupation with their places of origin. For example, in 1826, a Methodist missionary in the Bahamas made a telling entry in the baptism register for the island of New Providence. William Dowson recorded the case of a newly baptized infant as follows: "Thomas Philip Bayong/Wallace . . . the son of Philip Bayong of Nassau . . . and of Phebe [*sic*] Roker his wife." In his asterisked footnote Dowson added: "Or rather [the son of] Philip Wallace, this being the true name. The former is the name of the country in Africa from whence he came."[82] As discussed in chapter 3, in Trinidad other liberated Africans similarly used their ethnicity or place of birth as a surname. However, they seem to have done so routinely without the kind of opposition expressed here by William Dowson, who wanted Philip Bayong to use his "true [English]" surname. In fact, in some cases colonial officials or other British people may themselves have given newly arrived Africans such ethnic or geographic names.[83] Bayong, in contrast, clearly adopted the name of the "country from whence he came" as a deliberate and self-defining act. Historical atlases yield no direct match for the word that Dowson transcribed as "Bayong," but the Wolof state called "Baol" in the Senegambia region seems a likely possible cognate.[84] This area also is a strong candidate as Wallace's place of origin, given its role in the export of slaves through the mid-nineteenth century. The Methodist register does not specifically identify Bayong-Wallace as a liberated African, but if one assumes that the new father was between fifteen and thirty years old, demographic probability would place him almost certainly in this group. And indeed a man with the English name "Phillip" and African name "Bayong" does appear in an 1828 list of Africans settled in the Bahamas from the Spanish slave ship *Isabella*.[85] During the eight years that followed 1826, this African man and his Bahamian-born wife baptized five more children in the Methodist Church. However, in these later records the father's name appears only as "Philip Wallace" with no mention of the alternate self-identification used at the baptism of Thomas. Did Philip Bayong, come to accept his English surname, moving away from his earlier gesture of nationalism or nostalgia? On the other hand, Bayong may very well have insisted upon his chosen name—and its significance—for many years to come. Three new missionaries, not William Dowson, performed the later baptisms. It seems very possible that the change in the register reflects not a change in the attitude of Philip Bayong but rather differences in the policies of various Methodist pastors.

A similar example of defiant self-naming based on nation of origin emerges from the 1888 probate case of the widow Harriet Charles explored in chapter 4. Charles's genealogy included a deceased first husband, George African, and a surviving brother, Tom Yaraba, both of whom apparently used their ethnic surnames in public records. However, the newspaper summary of the court proceedings cited Charles's second husband as "Charles Baptiste *alias* Charles Yaraba" (emphasis added).[86] One can certainly draw some conclusions about the mindset of liberated Africans who carried ethnic or geographic surnames without any dispute from the society around them. But when individuals such as Charles Baptiste and Philip Wallace explicitly chose an African birthplace name despite external legal or other objections, they manifested even more clearly an important and continuing sense of connection to their homelands. Sociologist Arnold Itwaru explains that "to be in exile is considerably more than being in another country. It is to live with [oneself] knowing [one's] estrangement."[87]

In his meeting with the elderly African man who claimed to have belonged to the royal family of Angola, Father Cothonay alluded to precisely this knowledge of estrangement among the liberated Africans he encountered in late-nineteenth-century Trinidad. The rough outline of this Angolan's life story has already been discussed in chapter 4: he was captured in warfare in Africa, sold into slavery, and ended up on a Portuguese slave ship seized by the British navy. The particulars of that story have less relevance here than the French missionary's evaluation of the African storyteller:

The poor black man of whom I speak, and who hardly has the appearance of a prince, is now a fine household servant. He remembers his *country powerfully,* because he was already twenty years old when he left.[88] (emphasis added)

The French-speaking Cothonay wrote in his own language: "*Il se souvient fort bien de son pays.*" A translator seeking the simplest possible English version might have arrived at the phrase "remembers his country very well" rather than the more suggestive expression "remembers his country powerfully." However, Cothonay clearly seems to intend multiple connotations in his use of the adjective "*fort,*" which means not only "very" but also "strongly," rather than the simpler term "*tres*" which does not have this additional implication. (That is, he could have written: "*Il se souvient tres bien de son pays.*") The more nuanced term seems intended to modify not only the detail or clarity of the African's recollections but also the nature or quality of his remembering process. The missionary's comment implies that in telling of his past, the African expressed a deep connection, or perhaps even affection, for the country he remembered. Cothonay concludes this discussion by noting that he knew "a good number of black people" brought to Trinidad under conditions similar to those quoted from this individual. He does not comment on whether or not these other liberated Africans also spoke with detail or passion of their countries of origin. But neither does he make any suggestion that his single quoted informant possessed a unique attitude. Taken with other evidence from the Bahamas and Trinidad, Cothonay's observations solidify a portrait of a liberated African community that did indeed "remember powerfully" the homelands from which it had come.

Conclusion:

AFRICAN CREOLES AND
CREOLE AFRICANS

The members of Congo No. 1 Society never succeeded in their attempt to return to Kongo lands beside the Great River in Central Africa. Although Reverend Daniel Wilshere did succeed in having their letters sent to Belgium, the proposed return seems to have fallen apart in the face of logistical questions from both Belgian authorities and the British Colonial Office.[1] In September 1888, the *Nassau Guardian* published a brief article about the Kongo petition under the cynical headline "What Next?" The newspaper cited a report on the repatriation effort that had appeared in the New York *Weekly Tribune.* The Bahamian editors commented on the extract as follows: "In the language of our American cousins, we do not 'see the point,' but publish it to show how far sensational reports may be carried."[2] The adjective "sensational" does not seem entirely inappropriate in reference to the request submitted by the Kongo group. Although ideas about returning to Africa formed a part of the diaspora experience from its beginnings under slavery, actual attempts to return occurred only rarely and successful repatriation even more infrequently. Indeed, the largest groups of Africans or African-Americans—and these were usually people born in the New World—who emigrated to the African continent went to Sierra Leone or Liberia, not to their ancestral homelands. Thus, the people of Congo No. 1 Society had proposed a truly exceptional project.

However, the tone of the *Guardian* report implied that there was something preposterous in the very idea that a group of Africans should wish to leave the Bahamas for such a return journey. The brief commentary even suggests that the Bahamian journalists may not have believed the existence or legitimacy of the petition. Perhaps they found it unreasonable that Africans should wish to leave the security of a British Caribbean colony for a dubious fate in Africa. Or perhaps, like so many scholars of future generations, they doubted the depth of the connection displaced Africans felt for the communities and cultures they had left behind. The very real Kongo petition illustrated just such a connection beyond any doubt. While no scholar can claim a full understanding of the consciousness of liberated African immigrants or their offspring, it seems fair to conclude that this 1888 group negotiated at least a dual identity as Kongo people with a past they wished to reclaim and as integrated immigrants in an African-Bahamian world. Their relationship to that new world was most clearly expressed in their Baptist Christianity and their relationship with their pastor, Reverend Wilshere.

This Kongo immigrant group occupied an unusual space within the wider history of the African diaspora. As African-born people and their first-generation descendants, they shared much with African-born enslaved people of previous centuries who ran away soon after their arrival and formed maroon communities in places such as Jamaica or Suriname or found less radical or dramatic ways to claim and assert their Africanness. Yet in its conversion to Christianity and expressions of missionary designs this Kongo-born group also shared things with second- and third-generation members of the African diaspora who looked upon Africa more as a symbolic homeland and as a place where they could spread some of the western culture and/or resources they had acquired in the Americas.

Many scholars have demonstrated that, for slaves and their descendants, collective experience as Africans in the New World gave birth to a sense of group reminiscence for a broadly conceived Africa—an Africa to which they might, in theory, return. Based on their shared New World experience, liberated Africans also developed collective notions of exile vis-à-vis an Africa made meaningful solely by the fact that they had all left it behind. In addition, as demonstrated by the Congo Society, these Africans also expressed exile sensibilities with respect to more particular ethnic or regional locales. But, like the invented notion of Africa, such regional identities had meaning largely as a result of the immigration experience. Only in the diaspora did Kongo, Yoruba, or Manding peoples consider the salience of their cultural commonalities and the prospect of return to a regionally imagined homeland. Herein lies the paradox of all African repatriation discourse. On the one hand, persistent identification with Africa as home evinced a clear consciousness of alienation and a sense of cultural non-belonging. The idea of return—whether it was envisioned or actually attempted—implied the deepest possible rejection of New World society. At the same time, all scenarios of return required diaspora ways of thinking, and actual attempts to return inevitably worked through governments or civic or religious organizations based in the Americas. For all their expression of an exile mentality, back-to-Africa projects arose from the very process of new culture formation in the African diaspora.

In their essay first published twenty-five years ago entitled *An Anthropological Approach to the Afro-American Past: A Caribbean Perspective,* Sidney Mintz and Richard Price attempt to conceptualize the beginnings of African-American culture with a discussion of how African slaves on a random Caribbean plantation might have responded when first faced with situations such as birth, death, or illness "which would have required specialized ritual attention" according to the norms of the West and Central African cultures from which the slaves originated. Mintz and Price hypothesize that on such occasions, anyone with even a small amount of ritual knowledge from their own particular society would have become a de facto expert, and whatever procedures he or she employed would have formed the foundation for new African-American norms.[3] Mintz and Price argue that such combinations of memory, improvisation, and creativity likely formed the basis for all cultural development by Africans and their descendants in the New World. They further point out, however, that given the nature of slavery and the kinds of sources left behind by slave societies, scholars can obtain few direct portraits of that development process in motion. Hence their engagement in the speculative exercise described above.[4]

While the unusual case of liberated Africans cannot serve as a basis for generalizations about the African diaspora experience writ large or cultural processes under slavery in particular, the unique and uniquely documented lives of these immigrants clearly inform some larger questions about the genesis of culture in the African diaspora. Perhaps most striking is the way the liberated African experience in the Bahamas and Trinidad challenges many conventional models of cultural development, cultural change, and creolization in African-Caribbean history. The experience of these immigrants in both colonies suggests that creolization should not be viewed as a progression from Africanness to African-Americanness but rather that diasporic Africans and their descendants simultaneously and over long periods of time could and did negotiate a dialectical experience of simultaneously remaining African and becoming African-American.[5]

The liberated African experience also has particular relevance because of its place within the history of British interaction with Africa and with people of African descent in the Caribbean in the nineteenth century. This era included both the end of British West Indian slavery and the rise of British colonialism on the African continent. In fact, for Britain and for other European nations, the latter half of the nineteenth century became a period in which relations between Europeans and Africans were redefined. For over three centuries, slavery and the slave trade had dominated those relations, but many Britons hoped that emancipation would usher in the dawn of new cultural, economic, and social mores. Most scholarship now looks back with a combination of criticism, cynicism, and regret over the fact that this revolution failed to materialize. Furthermore, Africans themselves likely did not view the late nineteenth century as the beginning of any new age and certainly not as an age that held special promise for new relationships with the British or other Europeans. But during this time, Great Britain did end, and even came to denounce, its own Caribbean slave system; took the lead in policing the illegal international slave trade in the Atlantic and Indian Oceans; launched the beginnings of modern colonialism with experiments in plantation agriculture and nonslave commerce on the West African coast; and began to campaign against Africa's own systems of slavery. Even after the period of intense slave trade suppression and liberated African immigration had ended, Colonial Office authorities continued to view the experience of liberated Africans in the Caribbean as a part of these new patterns in British policy.

Many late-nineteenth-century observers—missionaries, public officials, and private travelers—who described the lives of liberated Africans in the Bahamas and Trinidad conceived of their descriptions as important contributions to the expansion of British understanding of darker races. The second half of the nineteenth century became an age when the genre of published travel journals and amateur anthropological texts proliferated among the British middle and upper classes, and much of this literary production concerned Africa and African peoples or the British West Indies and its black population. Where current historians can to some extent use the liberated African experience to speculate about African acculturation under slavery, nineteenth-century observers examined liberated African communities with a view toward devising new ways for Britons to institute cultural, economic, and social control in their interactions with Africans and black West Indians. It is ironic that this kind of effort, while it was often plagued with stereotypes, did have some merit. Many of the ways these African immigrants resisted labor domination and developed hybrid cultural patterns would in various forms characterize both Caribbean and African colonial experience into the twentieth century. As is particularly evident from the labor struggles shared by liberated Africans and former slaves, the arrival of liberated Africans in the Caribbean did not lead to dramatic innovation in British-African or white-black interaction. Rather, the experience of liberated Africans became a part of a long-unfolding African-Caribbean social history. Most important, these unusual free African immigrants demonstrated in their behavior how they (and other Africans or their descendents) could function with both African and western identities and mores, while also responding to diverse situational constraints.

This study only begins to explore the potential instructiveness of the liberated African experience for African diaspora cultural history as a whole. Unlike the hypothetical plantation of Mintz and Price, the lives of liberated Africans and their descendants provide historians with many specific and distinct looks into the process of culture-building in the African diaspora.[6] While much about the lives of these people still remains hidden from both oral and written documentation, the diverse public examinations of their lives as newly arrived Africans in the Americas sets them apart from most populations in the African diaspora prior to the twentieth century.

The richness and particularity of their history is exemplified in the experience of a group of Africans taken from the Portuguese slaver *Vigilante* and settled in the Bahamas in 1836. British officials conducted interviews with this group to record the particularly violent abuse that had occurred during their transatlantic crossing. Through the medium of interpreters from the appropriate African ethnic group, Bahamian authorities called upon the new immigrants to testify under oath about cases of assault and about two murders that had occurred aboard the vessel. In these already-novel circumstances, the swearing of oaths for this testimony provoked a striking cultural crisis. Having only recently emerged from the hold of a slave ship, the Africans had little experience with either British civil procedure or Christianity. Anxious to obtain properly sworn testimony, the British authorities asked the witnesses how people swore oaths to tell the truth in the African "country" from which they had come:

> [The Africans] stated that their form was to lay their hands upon a certain bush, while they were taking the oath, and then, if what they said was not true, they believed they would certainly die. The interpreter stated that the bush did not grow in this country. They were then examined as to their belief in God, and replied that they believe in the Great Spirit who had delivered them from the Portuguese, and that if they told an untruth after kissing the book, they would, after death, go into the fire. They were then sworn according to the usual form, the words being interpreted to them.[7]

Beyond the sense of fascination provoked by the image of people discussing the use of a bush to determine truthfulness in the context of a British colonial court, this anecdote illustrates both the intrigue and the importance of the liberated African experience. These Africans did not function as passive recipients of British cultural norms. But neither did they, nor could they, retreat into insular African immigrant worlds. Rather, they and their British rescuers—not always knowingly or willingly—went about the process of inventing functional African-Caribbean cultures. The environmental factors that determined what worked and what did not naturally differed between the Bahamas and Trinidad. But the experience of liberated Africans in both colonies repeatedly displayed the dynamic and often paradoxical mixture of enduring African influence and New World adaptation.

APPENDIX 1

Reports of Liberated African Arrivals in the Bahamas from Governors' Correspondence

Date of Arrival	Name of Slave Ship	Details of Slave Ship Seizure	Name of Transport Ship	Site of Legal Proceedings	Number of Africans	Comments
June 1809	*La Sentinelle*	Captured by *H.M.B. Elk* and *H.M.B. Variable*	N/A	Nassau	6	
August 1809	*Little Dick*	Seized by searcher of customs in Nassau	N/A	Nassau	—	Unspecified number of Africans alluded to in records of this seizure.
September 1809	*San Rafael*	N/A	N/A	Nassau	6	Records indicate "Six Negro Slaves" seized after being illegally sold from this vessel. Ship itself never captured.
March 14, 1811	*El Atrevido* (or *South Carolina*)	Captured by *H.M.B. Colibre*	N/A	Nassau	204	
June 1811	*Sancta Isabel*	Captured by *H.M.S. Rattler*	N/A	Nassau	115	
August 1811	*Joanna*	Captured by *H.M.B. Decouverte*	N/A	Nassau	120	
June 1816	*La Rosa*	Shipwrecked near Abaco	*H.M.S. Bermuda*	Nassau	221	Sometimes referred to in records as "Pakenham's Seizure" after the captain of *H.M.S. Bermuda*.
May 1818	*Experiencia*	Captured by an "Insurgent Privateer" whose crew landed the Africans at Inagua Island	—	Nassau	96	Sometimes referred to in records as "Boyd's Seizure" after the collector of customs at Caicos Islands who arranged transport of the Africans to Nassau.

Date of Arrival	Name of Slave Ship	Details of Slave Ship Seizure	Name of Transport Ship	Site of Legal Proceedings	Number of Africans	Comments
February 1826	*L'Hyppolite*	Shipwrecked near Mayaguana Island	*Lively* and *Diana*	Nassau	93	Sometimes referred to in records as "Bethel's Seizure" after the searcher of customs at Nassau.
June 30, 1831	*Rosa*	Captured by H.M.S. Pickle	N/A	Sierra Leone	157	
July 27, 1832	*Hebe*	Captured by H.M.S. Nimble	N/A	Sierra Leone	401	
June 15, 1834	*Despique*	Captured by H.M.S. Firefly	N/A	Sierra Leone	205	
August 26, 1834	*Felicidad*	Captured by H.M.S. Nimble	N/A	Sierra Leone	162	
March 17, 1836	*Vigilante*	Captured by H.M.S. Racer	N/A	Sierra Leone	231	
April 6, 1836	*Creole*	Captured by H.M.S. Gammet	N/A	Sierra Leone	314	
November 17, 1836	*Empresa*	Captured by H.M.S. Vestal	*Cuba*	Havanna	393	
April 6, 1837	*Flor de Tejo*	Captured by H.M.B. Wanderer	N/A	Sierra Leone	417	
June 23, 1837	*Antonio*	Captured by H.M.B. Racer	N/A	Sierra Leone	183	
July 1837	*Esperanza*	Shipwrecked near Caicos Islands	—	—	220	
October 7, 1837	*Nepal*	Captured by H.M.S. Comus	N/A	—	79	
October 27, 1837	*Invincible*	Shipwrecked near Harbour Island	—	—	53	
January 25, 1838	*Washington*	Shipwrecked at Cherokee Sound, Abaco	—	—	151	
May 6, 1838	*Diligente*	Captured by H.M.S. Pearl	N/A	Sierra Leone	474	
May 7, 1838	*Camoens*	Captured by H.M.B. Sappho	N/A	Sierra Leone	569	
December 6, 1838	*Scorpion*	Captured by H.M.B. Wanderer	N/A	Sierra Leone	190	
February 4, 1841	*Jesus María*	Captured by H.M.S. Ringdove	*Meg Lee*	Havana	223	

DATE OF ARRIVAL	NAME OF SLAVE SHIP	DETAILS OF SLAVE SHIP SEIZURE	NAME OF TRANSPORT SHIP	SITE OF LEGAL PROCEEDINGS	NUMBER OF AFRICANS	COMMENTS
March 2, 1841	*Segunda Rosario*	Captured by H.M.S. *Cleopatra*	*Meg Lee*	Havana	275	
March 31, 1841	*Trovadore*	Shipwrecked at Breezy Point, East Caicos Island	—	—	177	Transported to Turks Island. The Turks and Caicos Islands were a part of the colony of the Bahamas from 1766 until 1848.
July 28, 1860	*Heroina*	Shipwrecked near Abaco Island	*Expeditious, Try* and *Syp*	—	389	
TOTAL					6,124	

Source: Bahamas Original Correspondence, 1808-1864, CO 23/53-174, Public Records Office of the United Kingdom. See also, "Copies of the Several Returns Annually Made by the Collectors of Customs, in the Several West India Islands, Of the Names Numbers, State and Condition of all Negroes that have been apprenticed, in pursuance of the directions of the Order in council, for carrying into effect the Abolition of the Slave Trade," Secretary-at-War: Office of Army Accounts: In-Letters relating to Accounts ('A' Papers) 1820-1822, WO 41/74, Public Records Office of the United Kingdom.

Note: In this table and in appendix 2, the number of Africans indicates the number of living Africans who arrived in the Bahamas or Trinidad. This number excludes people, for example, who died en route from Cuba, Sierra Leone, or Saint Helena, but does count those who died shortly after arrival at their British Caribbean destination. The date of arrival indicates the date that the rescued Africans arrived at a port in the Bahamas or Trinidad for disembarkation. The transport ships described in both appendices are ships which were used to remove Africans from one location (such as the site of a Mixed Commission Court or the site of a shipwreck) to the place of their intended settlement.

For further details on most of the arrivals listed above see chapter one. This appendix presents a near complete accounting of the liberated Africans who settled in the Bahamas, but does not pretend to be an exhaustive list. It is based almost entirely on information reported in correspondence from the office of the governor of the colony. For arrivals prior to 1820 information was also derived from the records of collectors of the customs concerning liberated Africans, compiled for the House of Commons in July 1820 and printed in 1821. Some information on liberated African arrivals before 1820 was also taken from the *Vice Admiralty Court Minutes* at the Bahamas Department of Archives. The earliest arrivals have some of the more complicated records. For example, the printed report of 1820 lists two groups of enslaved people liberated in 1809—apparently the groups from *La Sentinelle* and *San Rafael* noted above. However, the report mentions neither vessel by name; nor does it mention the case of the *Little Dick*. Also, in these three early cases those liberated included some people born in Africa and some born in the Caribbean. Four of the twelve people identified above who arrived in 1809 were born in Africa. This fact reduces the tabular total of true "liberated Africans" from 6,124 to 6,116.

This appendix also makes use of: Peter T. Dalleo, "Africans in the Caribbean: A Preliminary Assessment of Recaptives in the Bahamas 1811-1860," *Journal of the Bahamas Historical Society* 6, no. 1 (October 1984): 15-24. Dalleo's list of Africans landed from illegally operating slave ships includes 27 vessels, all of which appear above. See note 98 in chapter one for a discussion of some differences between Dalleo's data and the information gathered for this study, especially concerning the slave ship *Nepal*.

APPENDIX 2

Reports of Liberated African Arrivals in Trinidad from Governors' Correspondence

Date of Arrival	Name of Slave Ship	Details of Slave Ship Seizure	Name of Transport Ship	Site of Legal Proceedings	Number of Africans	Comments
1808	—	—	—	Tortola	107	Sir Alexander Cochrane's apprentices
June 22, 1833	*Negrita*	Captured by *H.M.S. Nimble*	N/A	Havana	189	No Africans from this ship landed in Cuba due to cholera fears.
February 8, 1834	—	—	*Manuelita*	Havana	207	
March 26, 1834	*Rosa*	—	*Maria Christina*	Havana	193	Transport ship also known as *Reyna Christina*
March 1835	—	—	*Montan*	Havana	—	Sir George Hill made note of this arrival with no further detail.
September 14, 1835	—	—	*Las Siete Hermanas*	Havana	262	
May 1841	—	—	*Elizabeth. and June*	Sierra Leone	181	Immigrants who had spent significant time settled in Sierra Leone
June 1842	—	—	*Chieftan*	Saint Helena	232	
June 1842	—	—	*Cleopatra*	Sierra Leone	128	Immigrants who had spent significant time settled in Sierra Leone
October 1842	—	—	*Warwick*	—	114	Cited only from annual report of immigration without details.
November 1842	—	—	*Chieftain*	Saint Helena	239	Possibly a duplicate record of June voyage already noted.

Date of Arrival	Name of Slave Ship	Details of Slave Ship Seizure	Name of Transport Ship	Site of Legal Proceedings	Number of Africans	Comments
February 1843	—	—	*Chieftain*	—	119	Cited only from annual report of immigration without further details.
April 1843	—	—	*Louisa*	—	112	Cited only from annual report of immigration without further details.
May 1843	—	—	*Senator*	Sierra Leone	31	
June 1843	—	—	*Fairy Queen*	Saint Helena	195	
September 1, 1843	—	—	*Senator*	Sierra Leone	88	
December 18, 1843	—	—	*Senator*	Sierra Leone	118	
January 7, 1844	—	—	*Earl Gray*	Rio de Janeiro	216	
February 10, 1844	—	—	*Lancashire Witch*	Rio de Janeiro	288	
March 8, 1844	—	—	*Margaret*	Saint Helena	60	
April 6, 1844	—	—	*Senator*	Sierra Leone	97	
October 16, 1844	—	—	*Senator*	Sierra Leone	154	
April 25, 1845	—	—	*Senator*	Sierra Leone	247	
September 1, 1845	—	—	*Senator*	Sierra Leone	190	
November 30, 1846	—	—	*Arundel*	Saint Helena	100	
February 1847	*Flor da Loando*	—	—	Rio de Janeiro	—	Lord Harris noted in April 1848 that such a group had arrived. No further details.
June 1847	—	—	*Emma*	Saint Helena	134	
June 16, 1847	—	—	*Cornwall*	Saint Helena	97	Mainly brought 282 East Indian immigrants from Madras
December 5, 1847	—	—	*Growler*	Sierra Leone	395	
May 19, 1848	—	—	*Bangalore*	Sierra Leone	1	

Date of Arrival	Name of Slave Ship	Details of Slave Ship Seizure	Name of Transport Ship	Site of Legal Proceedings	Number of Africans	Comments
May 31, 1848	—	—	Persian	Sierra Leone	206	
April 10, 1849	—	—	Bathurst	Saint Helena	318	
May 6, 1849	—	—	Reliance	Saint Helena	175	
May 16, 1849	—	—	Sevenside	Saint Helena	160	
June 22, 1849	—	—	Agnes	Sierra Leone	255	
July 19, 1849	—	—	Janet	Saint Helena	242	
September, 28, 1849	—	—	Euphrates	Saint Helena	227	
October 3, 1849	—	—	Sevenside	Saint Helena	168	
December, 21, 1849	—	—	Marion Leith	Rio de Janeiro	110	
December 26, 1849	—	—	Viscount Hardinge	Rio de Janeiro	213	
August 20, 1850	—	—	Atlantic	Sierra Leone and Saint Helena	490	
September 4, 1850	—	—	Tuskar	Saint Helena	304	
January 1852	—	—	Clarendon	Sierra Leone	105	
February 1853	—	—	Harkaway	Saint Helena	4	Mainly brought East Indian immigrants from Calcutta
March 4, 1860	—	—	Tyburnia	Saint Helena	78	Mainly brought East Indian immigrants from Calcutta
March 20, 1860	—	—	Ceres	Saint Helena	228	
March 31, 1860	—	—	Brookline	Saint Helena	163	
July 15, 1860	—	—	Mary Ann	Sierra Leone	218	
TOTAL					8,158	

Source: Trinidad Original Correspondence, 1807-1868, CO 295/19-247, Public Records Office of the United Kingdom.

Note: For further details of most of these arrivals see chapter two. Although this table provides a near complete accounting of liberated African arrivals in Trinidad, it is not exhaustive. It does not for example attempt to review records from all relevant government departments, but uses only communications from the office of the governor of Trinidad concerning this class of immigrants. The table also does not include groups of rescued Africans who arrived under extraordinary circumstances, such as fifty-three liberated African women transferred from Barbados in 1817 (CO 295/44) or sixty African women and girls brought from Antigua in 1820 (CO 295/51). Nor does it include any liberated Africans who may have been among demobilized soldiers of the Third West India Regiment settled in Trinidad between 1818 and 1825.

NOTES

Introduction

1. Armand Massé, *The Diaries of the Abbé Armand Massé, 1878–1883,* translated by M. L. de Verteuil (Port-of-Spain: Scrip-J Printers, 1980), 4: 66–67. This quotation substitutes the adjective "lively" where Maureen De Verteuil uses the term "volatile." Given the tone of the passage where this description occurs, the adjective "lively" seems more appropriate, and it seems highly probable that de Verteuil chose the English word "volatile" as the simplest translation of its French cognate *"volatile."* According to *The Concise Oxford French Dictionary* (1977), contemporary French language does not use the adjective "volatile" in any figurative sense. However, it seems most likely that the nineteenth-century priest did use the term in this non-literal fashion. My assumptions about this translation are strengthened by the occurrence of similar disputable translations throughout the four volumes translated and compiled by Maureen de Verteuil. De Verteuil's collection does not to attempt present a complete or straightforward translation of the Massé diaries; the four volumes forego the priest's original chronology in favor of thematic groupings of diary extracts.

2. Ibid.

3. Records from the Special Liberated African Department that existed at Freetown, Sierra Leone, in the nineteenth century cite 476 captured vessels and rescue of a total of 94,329 liberated Africans. See Richard Meyer-Heiselberg, *Notes from Liberated African Department: Extracts from Sources on the Trans-Atlantic Slave Trade 1808–1860 from the Archives at Fourah Bay College, the University College of Sierra Leone, Freetown, Sierra Leone* (Uppsala: The Scandinavian Institute of African Studies, 1967). These figures do not include captured ships processed at Havana or Rio de Janeiro after Britain had concluded mutual enforcement treaties with Spain and Brazil. And the Freetown numbers do not include liberated Africans rescued from illegally operating slave ships that wrecked or otherwise became disabled in British Caribbean territories. In his economic analysis of the effectiveness of suppression of the slave trade by the British, E. Phillip Leveen quotes a total figure of "almost 160,000 slaves" rescued by the British navy. The records from Freetown total roughly 94,000 people; Leveen's estimate presumably includes a total of approximately 66,000 liberated Africans processed at sites other than Sierra Leone, but he does not indicate the source of his estimate. See Leveen, *British Slave Trade Suppression Policies, 1821–1865* (New York: Arno Press, 1977), 59.

4. The phrase "new negroes" is from an early-nineteenth-century report by a British colonial official. In a letter commenting on the kinds of procedures thought necessary for the successful settlement of Africans or other enslaved black people rescued from illegally operating slave ships, James Stephen wrote: "*Africans or new negroes as they are called,* neither being intelligent enough to protect their own free-

dom, nor able immediately to work for their own subsistence . . . it was necessary in respect of them to give [government officials] . . . the power of enlisting [them in the armed forces] or apprenticing [them to employers]. But the same necessity did not exist in respect of Creole Negroes, i.e. negroes born in the West Indies" (emphasis added). Under Secretary of State James Stephen, Colonial Office, to the Earl of Liverpool, Principal Secretary of State, Colonial Office, July 11, 1811, CO 23/58.

5. The act included very complex provisions that not only outlawed the trade in enslaved Africans within Africa and across the Atlantic and Indian Oceans but also forbade British subjects to transport Africans or people of African descent for use as slaves anywhere except within British territories in the Caribbean and the Americas. See *The Statutes of the United Kingdom of Great Britain and Ireland, 47 George III, 1807, Sess. 1 & 2* (London: Printed by His Majesty's Statute and Law Printers, 1807), 140–148.

6. There is obviously great irony in the phrase "African recaptives," because although British authorities emphasized the fact that they were rescuing such Africans from enslavement, the use of the term "recaptives" highlighted the fact that the Africans involved still faced involuntary displacement from their former homes and lives, albeit at the hands of the British government rather than private slave traders. It is perhaps not surprising that the term "liberated African" was used much more often, and that is the term I use throughout this study.

7. Johnson U. J. Asiegbu, *Slavery and the Politics of Liberation, 1787–1861: A Study of Liberated African Emigration and British Anti-Slavery Policy* (New York: Africana Publishing Corporation, 1969), 20–21. Some liberated Africans also spent time on Saint Helena island, which served as a transitional processing point for seized slave ships. The island hosted what became in effect a refugee camp for rescued Africans, but all of them ended permanently settled elsewhere, either in Sierra Leone or in the British Caribbean.

8. For the most comprehensive overview of these demographics, see "Appendix VI: The Place of Origin of Liberated Slaves and other Africans introduced into the West Indies between 1841 and 1867 (as far as known)" in Asiegbu, *Slavery and the Politics of Liberation,* 189. For this period of labor immigration organized by the British government, Asiegbu has compiled a total list of 36,120 people. My estimated total of between forty and forty-five thousand derives from a combination of Asiegbu's figure plus several thousand liberated Africans transferred from an Anglo-Spanish slave trade court at Havana during the 1830s and all other liberated Africans settled in British Caribbean colonies through various other circumstances prior to 1841.

9. This Anglo-Spanish mixed commission court was established under an 1817 treaty signed between Great Britain and Spain for the suppression of the slave trade. British officials did not take up their appointments at the mixed commission court until 1819. See David Murray, *Odious Commerce: Britain, Spain and the Abolition of the Cuban Slave Trade* (New York: Cambridge University Press, 1980), 76.

10. See Leslie Bethell, *The Abolition of the Brazilian Slave Trade: Britain, Brazil, and the Slave Trade Question, 1807–1869* (New York: Cambridge University Press, 1970).

11. I am thinking here of works in literary and/or cultural studies that attempt to address broad themes in the formation of cultures in the African diaspora; these works often deal with historical events and documentary evidence in addition to literary texts and sometimes make significant use of postmodern and/or postcolonial theoretical frameworks. See for example Antonio Benitez-Rojo, *The Repeating Island: The Caribbean and the Postmodern Perspective,* 2nd ed., translated by James Maraniss (Durham, N.C.: Duke University Press, 1996); Maria Diedrich, Henry Louis Gates, Jr., and Carl Pedersen, eds., *Black Imagination and the Middle Passage* (New York: Oxford University Press, 1999); and Paul Gilroy, *The Black Atlantic: Modernity and Double Consciousness* (Cambridge, Mass.: Harvard University Press, 1993). I am also thinking of recent edited collections of a less theoretical bent that attempt to draw together the myriad new approaches in a variety of fields that include but are not limited to anthropology, ethnomusicology, history, literature, and sociology. See for example Isidore Okpewho, Carole Boyce Davies, and Ali A. Mazrui, eds., *The African Diaspora: African Origins and New World Identities* (Bloomington: Indiana University Press, 1999); Darlene Clark Hine and Jacqueline MacLeod, eds., *Crossing Boundaries: Comparative History of Black People in Diaspora* (Bloomington: Indiana University Press, 1999); and Joseph E. Holloway, ed., *Africanisms in American Culture* (Bloomington: Indiana University Press, 1990).

12. I use the term "African Atlantic world" to refer loosely to communities of African people and people of African descent in those regions of Africa, Europe, the Americas, and the Caribbean that were linked from the fourteenth through the nineteenth centuries by their relationship to the transatlantic slave trade and to Caribbean and American slave societies.

13. Sidney W. Mintz and Richard Price, *An Anthropological Approach to the Afro-American Past: A Caribbean Perspective* (Philadelphia: Institute for the Study of Human Issues, 1976). Price and Mintz published a revised edition of this work as *The Birth of African-American Culture: An Anthropological Perspective,* rev. ed. (Boston: Beacon Press, 1992).

14. Price has recently published a retrospective consideration of the various ways scholars have responded to the challenges he and Mintz articulated a quarter-century ago. See Richard Price, "The Miracle of Creolization," *New West Indian Guide/Nieuwe West Indisch Gids* 75, nos. 1 and 2 (2001): 35–64.

15. Philip D. Morgan, *Slave Counterpoint: Black Culture in the Eighteenth-Century Chesapeake and Lowcountry* (Chapel Hill: University of North Carolina Press, 1998), 658.

16. See for example the local history *Bain Town* (Nassau, Bahamas: Cleveland and Muriel Eneas, 1976), published by Bahamian community historian Cleveland W. Eneas, or the numerous works of linguist Maureen Warner-Lewis on Yoruba language and culture in Trinidad, particularly *Guinea's Other Suns: The African Dynamic in Trinidad Culture* (Dover, Mass.: The Majority Press, 1991). Some scholars and laypeople have implied that because of their arrival in the mid- to late-nineteenth century and their special free status, liberated Africans maintained such identifications more commonly, more successfully, or more publicly than earlier enslaved populations in the British Caribbean.

17. In considering monograph-length studies specifically on the liberated African experience, the work of John Eric Peterson should also be mentioned. In 1963, Peterson completed a Ph.D. dissertation at Northwestern University entitled "Freetown: A Study of the Dynamics of Liberated African Society, 1807–1870," which was published as a somewhat broader study of the Sierra Leone colony entitled *Province of Freedom: A History of Sierra Leone, 1787–1870* (Evanston, Ill.: Northwestern University Press, 1969). Despite the broader title, the majority of this book deals with liberated Africans as opposed to other populations of Sierra Leone.

18. See Asiegbu, *Slavery and the Politics of Liberation,* 189; and Patrice Williams, *A Guide to African Villages in New Providence* (Nassau, Bahamas: Department of Archives, 1979), 13.

19. See for example Louis A. A. de Verteuil, *Trinidad: Its Geography, Natural Resources, Present Condition and Prospects* (1858; London: Cassell & Company, Limited, 1884).

20. See Williams, *Guide to African Villages in New Providence.*

21. Colonial Department to Spedding, Foreign Department, May 2, 1836, CO 318/127.

22. "Minute on the Condition and Disposal of the Captured Africans at the Havana, 24 October 1835," in Removal of Liberated Africans from Cuba, 1835, vol. 4, CO 318/123.

23. Governor James Carmichael-Smyth, Bahamas, to Lord Viscount Goderich, Principal Secretary of State, Colonial Department, February 5, 1832, CO 23/86.

24. See William Green, *British Slave Emancipation: The Sugar Colonies and the Great Experiment, 1830–1865* (Oxford: Clarendon Press, 1976); and Thomas C. Holt, *The Problem of Freedom: Race, Labor and Politics in Jamaica and Britain, 1832–1938* (Baltimore, Md.: Johns Hopkins University Press, 1992).

In *British Slave Emancipation,* a work of British colonial history prepared without particular attention to the lives of former slaves, Green demonstrates that, as they had feared, planters did indeed face declining economic fortunes in the years after slavery. He does not blame these problems entirely on the behavior of the freedpeople but he does demonstrate how the reluctance of the newly emancipated to continue regular plantation work and the end of preferential sugar tariffs undermined most West Indian sugar economies.

In *The Problem of Freedom,* Thomas Holt, in contrast, devotes much less attention to the economic details of the post-emancipation decline and instead focuses on the different expectations white West Indians, colonial officials, and former slaves had for a free Jamaica. According to Holt, although some colonial officials often spoke in progressive terms about the rights of freedpeople, the Colonial Office ultimately joined forces with planters in a lengthy and often stalemated struggle to balance their desire for cheap wage labor with the desire of Jamaica's black majority to live as independent cultivators on their own small plots.

25. Governor Carmichael-Smyth to Lord Viscount Goderich, February 5, 1832, CO 23/86.

26. Governor William Colebrooke, Bahamas, to Under Secretary of State James Stephen, Colonial Department, August 19, 1835, CO 23/94.

27. Report on the State and Conditions of Liberated Africans in the Bahamas, 1828, CO 23/80.

28. Ibid.

29. Enclosures in Lieutenant Governor Cockburn to Lord Glenelg, Principal Secretary of State, Colonial Department, May 19, 1838, CO 23/102.

30. Lord Glenelg to Lieutenant Governor Cockburn, August 10, 1838, and enclosures, CO 23/102; Lieutenant Governor Cockburn to Lord Glenelg, October 4, 1838, CO 23/103.

31. Lieutenant Governor Cockburn to Lord Glenelg, November 8, 1838, and enclosures, CO 23/103.

32. C. R. Nesbitt, Public Secretary [of the Bahamas, writing on behalf of Lieutenant Governor Cockburn] to One of Her Majesty's Justices of the Peace, November 2, 1838, enclosure in Lieutenant Governor Cockburn to Lord Glenelg, November 8, 1838, CO 23/103. Stipendiary magistrates supervised newly freed people after they were emancipated.

33. Governor James Carmichael-Smyth, Bahamas, to Lord Viscount Goderich, Principal Secretary of State, Colonial Department, July 23, 1831, CO 23/84; Williams, *Guide to African Villages in New Providence,* 3. This village of Adelaide and another (southwest of Nassau) named Carmichael in honor of the governor have received considerable attention in Bahamian local histories that address liberated Africans. A group of Africans apparently founded Carmichael in the early 1820s, presumably after the conclusion of apprenticeships served during the first decade of liberated African settlement. In later years, Governor Carmichael-Smyth and others drew on public funds to provide both religious and secular education for this community. In 1836, Governor William Colebrooke sent Africans from two Portuguese slave ships to join the Carmichael settlement. In December 1838, Lieutenant Governor Cockburn also sent "twenty to thirty Children" from a Portuguese vessel to this village. The majority of liberated Africans did not have this experience of independent settlement. Also, as noted elsewhere, some of the Africans there initially served terms of apprenticeship in the wider economy and in later years, other village residents took employment elsewhere on the island to supplement their subsistence community. See Governor James Carmichael-Smyth, Bahamas, to Lord Viscount Goderich, Principal Secretary of State, Colonial Department, February 5, 1832, CO 23/86; Governor William Colebrooke, Bahamas, to Lord Glenelg, Principal Secretary of State, Colonial Department, December 15, 1835, and enclosures, CO 23/94; Governor Colebrooke to Lord Glenelg, April 25, 1836, and enclosures, CO 23/96; Williams, *Guide to African Villages in New Providence,* 5–7.

34. Lieutenant Governor Cockburn to Lord Glenelg, December 21, 1838, CO 23/103.

35. Letter of Rev. Thomas Gilbert, Rector of Saint Paul's Parish, Trinidad, June 3, 1850, enclosure in Governor George Harris, Trinidad, to Earl Grey, Principal Secretary of State, Colonial Department, July 3, 1850, CO 295/170.

36. Ibid.

37. Ibid.

38. Right Rev. Thomas Parry, Bishop of Barbados, to Earl Grey, Secretary of State for the Colonies, August 19, 1850, enclosure in Governor George Harris, Trinidad, to Earl Grey, Principal Secretary of State, Colonial Department, August 26, 1850, CO 295/171.

39. Letter of Rev. Gilbert, June 3, 1850.

40. Governor George Harris to Earl Grey, September 11, 1850, CO 295/171.

1. Potential Laborers or "Troublesome Savages"?

1. "Memorial to His Excellency Charles Cameron Esquire Captain General and Governor in Chief and over These Islands Chancellor Vice Admiral and Ordinary of the Same &c. &c. &," enclosure in Governor Charles Cameron, Bahamas, to Earl Bathurst, Principal Secretary of State, Colonial Department, July 12, 1816, CO 23/63. These memorialists wrote to the governor in response to the seizure of a Spanish slave ship off the island of Abaco in a case that became known as Pakenham's seizure, which I discuss in more detail below.

2. See Asiegbu, *Slavery and the Politics of Liberation;* and Monica Schuler, *"Alas, Alas Kongo": A Social History of Indentured African Immigration into Jamaica, 1841–1865* (Baltimore, Md.: Johns Hopkins University Press, 1983) and *Liberated Africans in Nineteenth-Century Guyana,* Elsa Goveia Memorial Lecture Series (Kingston, Jamaica: Department of History, University of the West Indies, Mona, 1992).

3. On the diplomatic history, see for example Leslie Bethell, *The Abolition of the Brazilian Slave Trade;* Murray, *Odious Commerce;* and Suzanne Miers, *Britain and the Ending of the Slave Trade* (New York: Africana Publishing Company, 1975). Miers focuses on the final three decades of the nineteenth century and therefore devotes the majority of her attention not to the transatlantic trade but to the establishment of British colonialism on the African continent and the suppression of the trade from East Africa. A more recent contribution to the historiography of legislation and diplomacy offers a comparative study of British and French experiences; see Paul Michael Kielstra, *The Politics of Slave Trade Suppression in Britain and France, 1814–1848* (New York: St. Martin's Press, 2000).

In addition to the literature on diplomacy, some mid-twentieth-century works focused on naval history. See Christopher Lloyd, *The Navy and the Slave Trade: The Suppression of the African Slave Trade in the Nineteenth Century* (London: Frank Cass and Company Ltd., 1968); and W. E. F. Ward, *The Royal Navy and the Slavers: The Suppression of the Atlantic Slave Trade* (London: George Allen & Unwin Ltd., 1969).

4. "An Act for the Abolition of the Slave Trade," 47 Geo. III. c. 36, sess. I, Mar. 25, 1807, *The Statutes of the United Kingdom of Great Britain and Ireland: 1807–1869* (London: His Majesty's Statute and Law Printers, 1807–1869).

5. Asiegbu, *Slavery and the Politics of Liberation,* 22–23.

6. Laird Bergad, Fe Iglesias García, and María del Carmen Barcia, *The Cuban Slave Market, 1790–1880* (New York: Cambridge University Press, 1995), 38–39.

7. Murray, *Odious Commerce,* 50–51, 65–71, 100–101.

8. Ibid., 40–41.

9. Chief Justice William Munnings, Bahamas, to the Earl of Liverpool, Principal Secretary of State, Colonial Department, November 25, 1811, CO 23/58.

10. W. E. B. Du Bois's study published in 1904 remains the most comprehensive study of the behavior of the U.S. government and its citizens in the abolition and suppression of the Atlantic slave trade. Like Great Britain, the United States made the slave trade illegal beginning in 1808. For discussion of illegal slave trading by U.S. vessels, see Du Bois, *The Suppression of the African Slave-Trade to the United States of America, 1638–1870* (New York: Longmans, Green, and Co., 1904), 109–118, 128–130.

11. Murray, *Odious Commerce,* 41.

12. Governor Charles Cameron, Bahamas, to Lord Castlereagh, Principal Secretary of State, Colonial Department, February 10, 1808, CO 23/53.

13. Summary of hearing before the Vice Admiralty Court of Revenue, Nassau, Bahamas, with William Webb, Searcher of His Majesty's Customs for the Port of Nassau, appearing on behalf of the King, to Determine the status of Six Negro Slaves, October 31, 1809, enclosure in Chief Justice William Munnings, Bahamas, to the Earl of Liverpool, Principal Secretary of State, Colonial Department, August 6, 1811, CO 23/58.

14. For information on the schooner *Little Dick,* see summary of hearing before the Vice Admiralty Court of Revenue, Nassau, Bahamas, to determine the status of the schooner *Little Dick,* December 19, 1809, enclosure in Munnings to Liverpool, August 6, 1811, CO 23/58; Minutes of Vice Admiralty Court Hearing with William Webb, Searcher of His Majesty's Customs, appearing on behalf of the King, to Determine the Status of the schooner *Little Dick,* her Tackle, Apparel &c., December 19, 1809, in Court of Vice Admiralty Minutes, August 27, 1809–February 7, 1810, 191–192, Department of Archives, Commonwealth of the Bahamas, SC (Supreme Court) 4/3. For information on *La Sentinelle,* see "A List of Negroes, Seized, Adjudicated and Condemned to the Crown, in the Vice-Admiralty Instance Court of the Bahama Islands, since the year 1807 to the 6th of November, 1832," enclosure in Governor James Carmichael-Smyth, Bahamas, to Lord Viscount Goderich, Principal Secretary of State, Colonial Department, November 6, 1832, CO 23/87.

15. Minutes of Vice Admiralty Court Hearing before Surrogate Judge Peter Edwards to Determine the Status of the vessel *San Carlos,* de Oca, Master, July 17, 1811, in Court of Vice Admiralty Minutes, January 11, 1810–July 7, 1812, 62, Department of Archives, Commonwealth of the Bahamas, SC (Supreme Court) 4/4.

16. Minutes of Vice Admiralty Court Hearing before Surrogate Judge Peter Edwards to Determine the Status of the vessel *San Carlos* (for Sentence on Second Assignation), August 14, 1811, in Court of Vice Admiralty Minutes, January 11, 1810–July 7, 1812, 71–72, Department of Archives, Commonwealth of the Bahamas, SC (Supreme Court) 4/4.

17. Abstract of Suits instituted in General Court and Court of Vice Admiralty in New Providence, by Virtue or in consequence, of the Acts of Parliament made for the Abolition of the Slave Trade, between the 4th Day of October 1809, and the 4th Day of October 1811, enclosure in Munnings to Liverpool, October 6, 1811, CO 23/58.

18. Ibid.

19. Minutes of Vice Admiralty Court Hearing before Surrogate Judge Peter Edwards to Determine the Status of the vessel *Bom Amigo,* Cardozo, Master, November 29, 1811, in Court of Vice Admiralty Minutes, January 11, 1810–July 7, 1812, 96–97, Department of Archives, Commonwealth of the Bahamas, SC (Supreme Court) 4/4.

20. Minutes of Vice Admiralty Court Hearings before Surrogate Judge Peter Edwards to Determine the Status of the vessel *Alerto,* Haneiro, Master, December 2, 1811, and December 3, 1811, in Court of Vice Admiralty Minutes, January 11, 1810–July 7, 1812, 98–99, Department of Archives, Commonwealth of the Bahamas, SC (Supreme Court) 4/4.

21. Abstract of Suits instituted in General court and Court of Vice Admiralty in New Providence, by Virtue or in consequence, of the Acts of Parliament made for the Abolition of the Slave Trade, between the 4th Day of October 1809, and the 4th Day of October 1811, enclosure in Munnings to Liverpool, October 6, 1811, CO 23/58.

22. Minutes of Vice Admiralty Court Hearing before Surrogate Judge Peter Edwards to Determine the Status of the vessel *Volador,* de Ferrity, Master, July 26, 1811, in Court of Vice Admiralty Minutes, January 11, 1810–July 7, 1812, 66, Department of Archives, Commonwealth of the Bahamas, SC (Supreme Court) 4/4.

23. Ibid.

24. For biographical information concerning the public career of Attorney General William Wylly in the Bahamas, see Michael Craton and Gail Saunders, *Islanders in the Stream: A History of the Bahamian People,* vol. 1, *From Aboriginal Times to the End of Slavery* (Athens: University of Georgia Press, 1992).

25. Minutes of Vice Admiralty Court Hearing before Surrogate Judge Peter Edwards to Determine the Status of the vessel *Volador,* de Ferrity, Master, October 1, 1811, and December 3, 1811, in Court of Vice Admiralty Minutes, January 11, 1810–July 7, 1812, 84, Department of Archives, Commonwealth of the Bahamas, SC (Supreme Court) 4/4.

26. Minutes of Vice Admiralty Court Hearing before Judge Henry Moreton Dyer to Determine the Status of the vessel *El Atrevido*, de Leon, Master, March 25, 1811; Minutes of Hearing before Judge Dyer concerning the vessel *El Atrevido* (for Sentence), April 15, 1811; Minutes of Hearing before Judge Dyer concerning the vessel *El Atrevido* (for Sentence on Second Assignation), May 3, 1811; all in Court of Vice Admiralty Minutes, January 11, 1810–July 7, 1812, 36-37, 44, 47, Department of Archives, Commonwealth of the Bahamas, SC (Supreme Court) 4/4; Abstract of Suits instituted in General Court and Court of Vice Admiralty in New Providence, by Virtue or in consequence, of the Acts of Parliament made for the Abolition of the Slave Trade, between the 4th Day of October 1809, and the 4th Day of October 1811, enclosure in Chief Justice Munnings to Earl of Liverpool, October 6, 1811, CO 23/58.

27. Minutes of Vice Admiralty Court Hearing before Judge Henry Moreton Dyer to Determine the Status of the vessel *El Atrevido,* de Leon, Master, May 4, 1811, in Court of Vice Admiralty Minutes, January 11, 1810–July 7, 1812, 48, Department of Archives, Commonwealth of the Bahamas, SC (Supreme Court) 4/4.

28. Minutes of Vice Admiralty Court Hearing before Surrogate Peter Edwards to Determine the Status of the vessel *Sancta Isabel,* Alves, Master, July 30, 1811, in Court of Vice Admiralty Minutes, January 11, 1810–July 7, 1812, 67, Department of Archives, Commonwealth of the Bahamas, SC (Supreme Court) 4/4; Abstract of Suits instituted in General Court and Court of Vice Admiralty in New Providence, by Virtue or in consequence, of the Acts of Parliament made for the Abolition of the Slave Trade, between the 4th Day of October 1809, and the 4th Day of October 1811, enclosure in Munnings to Liverpool, October 6, 1811, CO 23/58.

29. Minutes of Vice Admiralty Court Hearing before Surrogate Peter Edwards to Determine the Status of the vessel *Joanna,* Correa, Master, September 3, 1811, in Court of Vice Admiralty Minutes, January 11, 1810–July 7, 1812, 79–80, Department of Archives, Commonwealth of the Bahamas, SC (Supreme Court) 4/4; Abstract of Suits instituted in General Court and Court of Vice Admiralty in New Providence, by Virtue or in consequence, of the Acts of Parliament made for the Abolition of the Slave Trade, between the 4th Day of October 1809, and the 4th Day of October 1811, enclosure in Munnings to Liverpool, October 6, 1811, CO 23/58.

30. "The Petition of the Undersigned Inhabitants of the Island of New Providence to His Honor William Vesey Munnings Esquire President and Commander in Chief in and over the said Islands, Chancellor, Vice Admiral and Ordinary of the same," enclosure in Chief Justice William Munnings, Bahamas, to the Earl of Liverpool, Principal Secretary of State, Colonial Department, August 23, 1811, CO 23/58.

31. "Petition of the Legislative Council and the House of Assembly, Bahama Islands, in General Assembly to the King's Most Excellent Majesty in Council," November 22, 1811, enclosure in Munnings to Liverpool, November 25, 1811, CO 23/58.

32. Ibid.

33. Ibid.

34. Ibid.

35. Munnings to Liverpool, November 25, 1811, CO 23/58.

36. The Earl of Liverpool, Principal Secretary of State, Colonial Department to Chief Justice William Munnings, Bahamas, January 31, 1812, CO 23/58.

37. Governor Charles Cameron, Bahamas, to Earl Bathurst, Principal Secretary of State, Colonial Department, July 12, 1816, and enclosures, CO 23/63; Minutes of Vice Admiralty Court Hearing concerning the seizure of Certain Natives of Africa by Captain John Pakenham of His Majestys Sloop *Bermuda* (for Sentence on Second Assignation), September 10, 1816, in Court of Vice Admiralty Minutes, September 10, 1816–April 25, 1826, 2, Department of Archives, Commonwealth of the Bahamas, SC (Supreme Court) 4/5. For identification of the name of the vessel on which Captain Pakenham found these Africans, see Peter T. Dalleo, "Africans in the Caribbean: A Preliminary Assessment of Recaptives in the Bahamas 1811–1860," *Journal of the Bahamas Historical Society* 6, no. 1 (October 1984): 24. For the case of the *Experienca* see William Vesey Munnings, Chief Justice, President of the Council and Administrator of Government, Bahamas, to Earl Brathurst, Principal Secretary of State, Colonial Department, July 12, 1818, CO 23/67.

38. Attorney General William Wylly, Bahamas, to Governor Charles Cameron, Bahamas, October 29, 1816, enclosure in Governor Cameron to Earl Bathurst, Principal Secretary of State, Colonial Department, November 16, 1816, CO 23/63.

39. Ibid.

40. "Memorial of the Inhabitants of New Providence and Other Islands to Governor Charles Cameron," June 1816, enclosure in Governor Charles Cameron, Bahamas, to Earl Bathurst, Principal Secretary of State, Colonial Department, July 12, 1816, CO 23/63.

41. Records thus far consulted from both the Colonial Office and the Bahamian vice admiralty court do not explain the outcome of this appeal. Evidence of its result appears in a letter from the collector of customs, Alexander Murray, who assumed responsibility for the Africans once the new court ruling made them legal prize of war. Murray wrote to Governor Charles Cameron: "The Africans lately seized at Green Turtle Key by Captain Pakenham . . . having been delivered over to me as Collector of His Majesty's Customs at this Port, *in consequence of an Appeal interposed against the sentence of His Honor the Judge Surrogate* of the Court of Vice Admiralty. . . . It becomes my duty pursuant to the Acts of Parliament for the Abolition of the Slave Trade . . . to place out, as apprentices all the females and such of the men as shall not be taken into his Majesty's Naval or Military service" (emphasis added). Alexander Murray, Collector of Customs, Bahamas, to Governor Charles Cameron, Bahamas, September 16, 1816, enclosure in Alexander Murray to Earl Bathurst, Principal Secretary of State, Colonial Department, September 27, 1816, CO 23/63.

42. "Memorial of the Inhabitants of New Providence and Other Islands to Governor Charles Cameron," June 1816, enclosure in Governor Charles Cameron, Bahamas, to Earl Bathurst, Principal Secretary of State, Colonial Department, July 12, 1816, CO 23/63.

43. Ibid.

44. On the relatively common practice of hiring out enslaved people in Bahamian slave society, see Howard Johnson, *The Bahamas from Slavery to Servitude, 1783–1933* (Gainesville: University of Florida Press, 1996). Chapter 2 in this collection of essays specifically addresses "The Self-Hire System and the Transition to Contractual Relations in Nassau."

45. Alexander Murray, Former Collector of H. M.'s Customs at New Providence, to Viscount Howick, Under Secretary of State, Colonial Department, August 18, 1832, CO 23/87.

46. Many historians have noted that slaves throughout the New World remained ever vigilant for any sign of political, legal, or military weakness among the master class that might have provided the opportunity for some kind of resistance. See Michael Craton, *Testing the Chains: Resistance to Slavery in the British West Indies* (Ithaca, N.Y.: Cornell University Press, 1982).

47. Alexander Murray to Viscount Howick, August 18, 1832, CO 23/87.

48. Governor James Carmichael-Smyth, Bahamas, to Lord Viscount Goderich, Principal Secretary of State, Colonial Department, November 2, 1832, CO 23/87.

49. Alexander Murray, Collector of Customs, Bahamas, to Earl Bathurst, Principal Secretary of State, Colonial Department, August 10, 1816, CO 23/63.

50. Ibid.

51. "Queries submitted to His Majesty's Secretary of State in August 1816 by His Majesty's Collector for the Port of Nassau, & which he is anxious to receive Earl Bathurst's answer respecting," enclosure in Alexander Murray to Earl Bathurst, August 10, 1816, CO 23/63.

52. Ibid.

53. Ibid.

54. Ibid.

55. Alexander Murray, Collector of Customs, Bahamas, to Earl Bathurst, Principal Secretary of State, Colonial Department, September 27, 1816, CO 23/63.

56. Dalleo, "Africans in the Caribbean," 24.

57. Leslie Bethell, "The Mixed Commissions for the Suppression of the Transatlantic Slave Trade in the Nineteenth Century," *Journal of African History* 7, no. 1 (1966): 79–82.

58. Ibid., 84.

59. Murray, *Odious Commerce*, 271–281.

60. "Treaty between His Majesty and the Queen Regent of Spain . . . for the Abolition of the Slave Trade, Signed at Madrid, June 28, 1835," in Removal of Liberated Africans from Cuba, 1835, vol. 4, CO 318/123.

61. Bethell, *The Abolition of the Brazilian Slave Trade*, 114, 380–383.

62. Murray, *Odious Commerce*, 120–121.

63. "Minute on the Condition and Disposal of the Captured Africans at the Havana, 24th October 1835," in Removal of Liberated Africans from Cuba, 1835, vol. 4, CO 318/123.

64. Ibid.

65. Several British Caribbean officials included in this study served in different British colonies during the mid-nineteenth century. Both Carmichael-Smyth and Cockburn also held administrative posts in the Bahamas.

66. "Minute on the Condition and Disposal of the Captured Africans at the Havana, 24th October 1835," in Removal of Liberated Africans from Cuba, 1835, vol. 4, CO 318/123.

67. Ibid.

68. Ibid.

69. Ibid.

70. Cited in ibid.

71. Ibid.

72. Ibid.

73. Ibid.

74. Murray, *Odious Commerce*, 280.

75. These 900 refugees came from three separate Spanish vessels condemned at Havana: 393 from the *Empresa* in 1836, and 233 from the *Jesus María* and 282 from the *Segunda Rosario*, both in 1841. See Murray, *Odious Commerce,* 281; Governor William Colebrooke, Bahamas, to Lord Glenelg, Principal Secretary of State, Colonial Department, November 19, 1836, CO 23/97; David Turnbull, Superintendent of

Liberated Africans at Havana, to Governor Francis Cockburn, Bahamas, January 21, 1841, enclosure in Governor Francis Cockburn, Bahamas, to Lord John Russell, Principal Secretary of State, Colonial Department, February 8, 1841, CO 23/109; David Turnbull to Governor Francis Cockburn, February 23, 1841, enclosure in Governor Cockburn to Lord John Russell, March 6, 1841, CO 23/109.

76. Murray, *Odious Commerce,* 281.

77. "Minute on the Condition and Disposal of the Captured Africans at the Havana, 24th October 1835," CO 318/123.

78. Dr. Richard Robert Madden, Superintendent of Liberated Africans at Havana, to Lord Glenelg, Principal Secretary of State, Colonial Department, November 6, 1836, in Removal of Liberated Africans from Cuba, 1836, vol. 4, CO 318/127.

79. John Corlett, Missionary, Nassau, Bahamas, to the General Secretaries, Wesleyan Methodist Missionary Society, November 22, 1842, MMS 4C: West Indies (Various) 1833–1906, Box 218, File 1842, Wesleyan Methodist Missionary Society Collection, School of Oriental and African Studies, University of London (hereafter cited as WMMS Papers).

80. Murray, *Odious Commerce,* 281.

81. Various descriptions in official correspondence indicate that these facilities seem to have included both a hospital for the most gravely ill and a convalescent building of some sort.

82. "Medical Report of the State of Health of the Liberated Africans at Their Embarkation on Board the Bark 'Cuba' Till Their Landing at Nassau, N.P. from Havana during the Period of Six Days" enclosure in Dr. Richard Robert Madden, Superintendent of Liberated Africans at Havana, to Lord Glenelg, December 12, 1836, in Removal of Liberated Africans from Cuba, 1836, vol. 4, CO 318/27. In addition to the deaths that occurred between Havana and Nassau, Madden notes elsewhere in his correspondence of the death of no less than fourteen people during the temporary stay in Cuba.

83. "Superintendence and Removal of Liberated Africans—Particulars—The Empresa Slave Ship" and *The Bahama Argus,* Saturday, November 19, 1836, enclosures in Madden to Glenelg, December 12, 1836, CO 318/127.

84. "Superintendence and Removal of Liberated Africans—Particulars—The Empresa Slave Ship," CO 318/127. In examining these various records of the arrival and settlement of liberated Africans from the slave ship *Empresa* in the Bahamas, it is also important to note that the figures prepared at Havana by Richard Madden also presented detailed age and gender breakdowns for the group. These are discussed in more detail below.

85. Governor James Carmichael-Smyth, Bahamas, to Lord Viscount Goderich, Principal Secretary of State, Colonial Department, July 22, 1831, CO 23/84.

86. Ibid.

87. Ibid.

88. Governor James Carmichael-Smyth, Bahamas, to Lord Viscount Goderich, Principal Secretary of State, Colonial Department, August 2, 1832, CO 23/86.

89. C. R. Nesbitt, Bahamas Acting Public Secretary, to James Walker, Collector of Customs, Nassau, May 25, 1833, enclosure in Governor James Carmichael-Smyth,

Bahamas, to E. G. Stanley, Principal Secretary of State, Colonial Department, May 25, 1833, CO 23/88.

90. "Return of Africans received from on Board the Portuguese Slave Trader 'Hebe' prize to His Majesty's Schooner Nimble . . . 4 March 1835," enclosure in Governor William Colebrooke, Bahamas, to Earl of Aberdeen, Principal Secretary of State, Colonial Department, March 23, 1835, CO 23/93. Governor Carmichael-Smyth wrote at length about the arrangements he made at Highburn Cay to set these Africans up under a system of supervised subsistence agriculture. The governor made preparations for the Africans to grow their own food at Highburn Cay, which he described as having "fresh water in abundance" and a good supply of fish. During the setup period, the government provided the Africans with daily rations of Indian corn and salt fish. He complained in 1832 that medical supervision of liberated Africans had become especially challenging, with over 1,000 immigrants—who had arrived from different vessels over time—receiving medical care. Yet nothing in the governor's reports points to any specific factor that may have led to the particularly high mortality rate among the Africans from the *Hebe*. The doctor who looked after liberated Africans in and around Nassau (mostly at the convalescent establishment) also traveled to Highburn Cay. See Governor James Carmichael-Smyth, Bahamas, to Lord Viscount Goderich, Principal Secretary of State, Colonial Department, August 1, 1832, and October 4, 1832, CO 23/93.

91. Lieutenant Governor Blaney T. Balfour, Bahamas, to E. G. Stanley, Principal Secretary of State, Colonial Department, June 21, 1834, CO 23/91.

92. Lieutenant Governor Blaney T. Balfour, Bahamas, to T. Spring Rice, Principal Secretary of State, Colonial Department, September 8, 1834, CO 23/91.

93. Ibid.

94. Governor William Colebrooke, Bahamas, to the Earl of Aberdeen, Principal Secretary of State, Colonial Department, March 12, 1835; and Governor William Colebrooke to the Earl of Aberdeen, March 23, 1835, CO 23/93.

95. "Minute on the Condition and Disposal of the Captured Africans at the Havana, 24th October 1835," CO 318/123.

96. Earl of Aberdeen, Principal Secretary of State, Colonial Department, to Governor George F. Hill, Trinidad, January 14, 1836, CO 295/106.

97. Lieutenant Governor Francis Cockburn, Bahamas, to Lord Glenelg, Principal Secretary of State, Colonial Department, May 19, 1838, CO 23/102. For one attempt to comprehensively list these vessels, see Dalleo, "Africans in the Caribbean," 24. However, as Dalleo indicates in a footnote, there does not yet exist precise agreement between scholars about the exact number of ships or their names and nationalities. Dalleo himself incorrectly identifies the Spanish slaver *Jesus María* as a Portuguese ship. Also, his list cites no nationality for a vessel using the name *Creole*, which was seized in April 1836 with 314 Africans aboard. The *Creole* was one of the seven ships captured in this period sailing under Portuguese colors. See Governor William Colebrooke, Bahamas, to Lord Glenelg, Principal Secretary of State, Colonial Department, April 25, 1836, CO 23/96. Dalleo also incorrectly lists the Portuguese vessel *Antonio* as a shipwreck. The *Antonio* was captured by *H.M.B. Racer* in June 1837. See Joseph Hunter, President of the Council and Acting Administrator of

Government, Bahamas, to Lord Glenelg, Principal Secretary of State, Colonial Department, June 30, 1837, CO 23/99. The current figure of seven Portuguese ships received between 1836 and 1838 does not include a vessel named *Nepal,* which Dalleo cites as having arrived in the Bahamas in 1837 carrying seventy-nine African slaves. Colonial Office records consulted for this study have produced no reference to this vessel by name or nationality. However, the *Nepal* was probably the slave ship described by Lieutenant Governor Francis Cockburn as having been captured by the *H.M.S. Comus* in October 1837. According to Cockburn the slave ship proved unseaworthy and was abandoned after her capture. The *H.M.S. Comus* brought the Africans rescued from this vessel to Nassau. See Lieutenant Governor Francis Cockburn, Bahamas to Lord Glenelg, Principal Secretary of State, Colonial Department, October 27, 1837, CO 23/100. Dalleo lists this group as numbering seventy-nine people.

Concerning the nationality of slave ships, it is important to remember that the tactics of illegal slave traders often deliberately confused this issue. They regularly used false flags or false papers in an attempt to evade the terms of various treaties or national laws. Thus, for example, Lieutenant Governor Francis Cockburn first described the slave ship *Washington* (wrecked near Abaco in 1838) as being "under Portuguese colours but commanded by a Spaniard." However in later correspondence Cockburn referred to the same ship as "the Spanish schooner *Washington.*" See Lieutenant Governor Francis Cockburn, Bahamas to Lord Glenelg, Principal Secretary of State, Colonial Department, February 11, 1838 CO 23/102 and Cockburn to Glenelg, July 3, 1838, CO 23/103. Peter Dalleo's work and this study leave the shipwrecked *Washington* classified among the Portuguese vessels.

98. Governor Charles J. Bayley, Bahamas, to the Duke of Newcastle, Principal Secretary of State, Colonial Department, March 15, 1860, May 3, 1860, May 31, 1860, and June 26, 1860, and enclosures, CO 23/162; Governor Bayley to the Duke of Newcastle, Principal Secretary of State, Colonial Department, October 15, 1860, CO 23/163; John Wodehouse, Under Secretary of State, Foreign Office, to Sir Frederic Rogers, Colonial Office, July 31, 1860, and August 17, 1860, and enclosures, CO 23/164.

99. See for example Rachel Wilson Moore, *Journal of Rachel Wilson Moore, kept during a tour to the West Indies and South America in 1863–1864 with Notes from the Diary of her Husband together with His Memoir by George Truman, M.D.* (Philadelphia: T. Ellwood Zell, 1867), 27–31. Moore reproduced an account allegedly provided to her by another traveler from the United States who had witnessed the clandestine disembarkation and sale of a group of African slaves: "I will give relation, as nearly as I can, in his own words. 'They went,' he says, 'in the darkness of the night, to a certain point on the island [of Cuba], where slave-ships generally unload their cargoes'—it being an isolated spot. 'We there saw a large number of planters on the shore waiting for the arrival of the anticipated slave-ship.... On reaching her moorings, the cargo was hurried out of the ship, with all the rapidity possible.... The many planters who had been waiting for the arrival of the ship, were now making purchases of such as suited them best. In the course of an hour or two, all

were gone, not a vestige being left of the blackened crime and shameful exhibition we had been witnesses to. The ship was then towed out into the sea and scuttled; which is the custom with the owners of slave-ships after discharging their cargoes, so that no trace shall be seen that such a ship has brought a cargo of slaves to the Island.'"

100. Governor Charles J. Bayley, Bahamas, to the Duke of Newcastle, Principal Secretary of State, Colonial Department, August 22, 1860, and enclosures, CO 23/163.

101. Ibid.

102. Governor Charles J. Bayley, Bahamas, to the Duke of Newcastle, Principal Secretary of State, Colonial Department, August 24, 1860, CO 23/163; Major & Brevet Lieutenant Colonel James R. Travers, 1st West India Regiment, to Governor Charles Bayley, November 20, 1860, enclosure in Governor Charles J. Bayley, Bahamas, to the Duke of Newcastle, Principal Secretary of State, Colonial Department, December 6, 1860, CO 23/163.

103. T. F. Elliot, Under Secretary of State, Colonial Department, to Governor Charles J. Bayley, Bahamas, September 29, 1860, CO 23/163.

104. Governor Charles J. Bayley, Bahamas, to the Duke of Newcastle, Principal Secretary of State, Colonial Department, November 16, 1860, CO 23/163. Under Secretary Elliot wrote his initial complaint about indenturing liberated Africans as agricultural laborers in the erroneous belief that one of the Orders in Council related to the Abolition Act restricted the practice. In a comment in the margin on this November 16th letter that Governor Bayley sent in reply to the complaint, a second Colonial Office functionary noted Elliot's mistake. Of course, this acknowledgment in no way addressed the concern about the propriety of apprenticing such Africans in the unpleasant work of the salt ponds.

105. Governor Bayley to the Duke of Newcastle, August 22, 1860, CO 23/163. Bayley even claimed in this report that the Bahamian-born blacks referred to the new Africans as "niggers"—a term of obvious disdain, although it did not carry the same context or connotations that it did in the United States during the nineteenth and twentieth centuries. For a recent exploration of the etymology of this word, see Randall Kennedy, *Nigger: The Strange Career of a Troublesome Word* (New York: Vintage Books, 2003).

106. Governor Bayley to the Duke of Newcastle, August 22, 1860, CO 23/163.

107. Because Britain ended its legal slave trade in 1807 and ended slavery in its Caribbean colonies in 1834, there would have been very few African-born people who had arrived in the Bahamas as slaves by 1860. According to historians Michael Craton and Gail Saunders, at the time of emancipation in 1834, only 938 African-born slaves remained in the colony, and most of them were older than 40 years. See Craton and Saunders, *Islanders in the Stream,* 1:274–275.

108. "An Act to Provide for the Care of Africans Brought in or Otherwise Arriving in the Colony from Vessels Engaged in the African Slave Trade," (24 Vic: Cap. 2). For the full text of the act, see Colonial Office and Predecessors and Successors: Bahamas Acts, 1729–1973, vol. 24, 1859–1863, CO 25/24. The Colonial Office explic-

itly directed Governor Bayley to pursue such legislation in October 1860. See C. Fortescue, Under Secretary of State, Colonial Department, to Governor Charles J. Bayley, Bahamas, October 23, 1860, CO 23/164. For negotiations about the details of the act between authorities in the Bahamas and London, see for example Acting Governor Charles R. Nesbitt, Bahamas, to the Duke of Newcastle, Principal Secretary of State, Colonial Department, September 14, 1861, and enclosures, CO 23/166.

The debates among colonial officials leading up to this law included preparation of an extensive report by a crown legal expert who attempted to reconcile Bayley's actions with forty years of law and policy related to settlement of liberated Africans. See "Report of H. C. Rothery, Registrar, Admiralty Registry to the Lords Commissioners of Her Majesty's Treasury Relative to the Disposal of Africans from a Slaver Which Had Been Wrecked on the Island of Abaco, Bahamas," October 9, 1860, enclosure in Treasury Department to Frederic Rogers, Under Secretary of State, Colonial Department, October 12, 1860, CO 23/164. Rothery included in his examination the 1847 Order in Council that addressed the treatment of liberated African children in Trinidad, which he cited as "the last Order in Council on the subject [of apprenticing such people.]" For discussion of the history of law and policy related to apprenticeships of liberated Africans in the Bahamas, see Johnson, *The Bahamas from Slavery to Servitude*, 62–83.

109. In December 1860, another slave ship bound for Cuba carrying an estimated 500 Africans wrecked on reefs near Cay Lobos in the southern Bahamas. Before Bahamian authorities or civilians could initiate a rescue, a Spanish vessel came from Cuba and took the group away. According to the lighthouse keeper and other Bahamians on Cay Lobos at the time, the captain and crew of the slave ship forcibly commandeered both the lighthouse boat and two private vessels, one of which the captain used to travel to Cuba and arrange for the collection of the slaves from his disabled ship. See Governor Charles J. Bayley, Bahamas, to the Duke of Newcastle, Principal Secretary of State, Colonial Department, December 22, 1860, and enclosures, CO 23/163.

2. "Binding them to the trade of digging cane holes"

1. "Copies of the Several Returns Annually Made by the Collectors of the Customs, in the Several West Indian Islands, of the Names, Numbers, State and Condition of Negroes that Have Been Apprenticed, in Pursuance of the Directions of the Order in Council, for Carrying into Effect the Abolition of the Slave Trade," February 19, 1821, 101–102, WO 41/74.

2. For example, in contrast to many lengthy Bahamian census returns that included both an African name and a newly assigned English name for each person, the Trinidad returns included only English names, which the fourteen rescued slaves presumably already possessed at the time of their seizure. The case of two slaves, Apollon and Charley, seems typical of this early Trinidad experience. These two teenagers constituted the sole seizure from a vessel called *Fame* that was detained in May 1812. Not only did the two boys already possess non-African names but the

certificate of apprenticeship prepared for Charley described him as a "Mulatto lad" and therefore almost certainly a slave born in the Americas. Samuel Chollet, Collector of Customs, Trinidad, to Lord Castlereagh, Principal Secretary of State, Colonial Department, May 1813, and enclosures, CO 295/31.

3. See for example "Copies of the Several Returns Annually made by the Collectors of the Customs" and Memorandum for R. Wilmot Horton, Under Secretary of State, Colonial Department, from John Moody, Commissioner of Enquiry into the State of Captured Africans in the West Indies, with Colonial Office responses and enclosures and Memorandum Relative to the Duties Still to be Performed by Commissioners for African Apprentices in the West Indies, both in Memoranda 1826–1827, CO 320/5.

4. A. McKenrot to William Wilberforce, November 17, 1813, enclosure in A. McKenrot, Late a Magistrate of the Island of Tortola, to Earl Bathurst, Principal Secretary of State, Colonial Department, June 11, 1814, CO 295/34. McKenrot claimed that Cochrane had taken "at least 200." However, in 1808 Trinidad Governor Thomas Hislop had identified Cochrane's apprentices as totaling "one hundred and seven." See Governor Hislop to Lord Castlereagh, Principal Secretary of State, Colonial Department, July 1, 1808, CO 295/19.

5. A. McKenrot to Earl Bathurst, June 11, 1814, CO 295/34.

6. A. McKenrot to William Wilberforce, November 17, 1813, CO 295/34.

7. Ibid.

8. Ibid.

9. Captain General Mariano Ricafort, Havana, to Governor George F. Hill, Trinidad, January 16, 1834, enclosure in Governor George F. Hill, Trinidad, to E. G. Stanley, Principal Secretary of State, Colonial Department, February 12, 1834, CO 295/101.

10. "Summary of the 'Negrita' case & of the preceding correspondence with reference to captured Negroes. 2 Septr [1833]," responses bound with Governor George F. Hill, Trinidad, to E. G. Stanley, Principal Secretary of State, Colonial Department, July 1, 1833, CO 295/98. The case of the *Negrita* constituted the sole incident of unorchestrated liberated African immigration to Trinidad from the Anglo-Spanish Commission at Havana. In February 1833, H.M.S. *Nimble* captured this Spanish slave ship and took it for prosecution to Havana. However, due to an outbreak of cholera in the port, Cuban authorities did not want the newly arrived Africans to come ashore. At first they proposed that the British naval vessel should escort the slave ship to Sierra Leone for prosecution there. But British officials in Cuba opposed this suggestion on humanitarian grounds, citing the length of the journey between the Caribbean and the West African coast. As a compromise, they agreed to send the vessel to Trinidad, which had expressed an interest in receiving liberated African immigrants. Governor Hill willingly accepted the 189 Africans from the *Negrita* and reported to the Colonial Office in London that local residents had shown great enthusiasm for hiring them both as plantation laborers and as "domestics." Governor Hill in fact used the "avidity" of the attention paid to the *Negrita* immigrants as evidence to strengthen his request that liberated Africans from the

Cuban mixed commission be channeled into the Trinidadian economy. See Governor Hill, to E. G. Stanley, July 1, 1833, CO 295/98.

11. Governor George F. Hill, Trinidad, to E. G. Stanley, Principal Secretary of State, Colonial Department, March 9, 1834, CO 295/101.

12. Mintz and Price, *The Birth of African-American Culture*, 43.

13. "Distribution of the 207 Africans from Havana per Schr. Manuelita in Lots and to Whom Distributed, with the Receipts of the Parties for the Same, 15th February 1834," enclosure in Governor George F. Hill, Trinidad, to E. G. Stanley, Principal Secretary of State, Colonial Department, March 9, 1834, CO 295/101.

14. "Return shewing the distribution and location of the Africans who arrived here from the Havana on the 14th of September 1835 on board the Spanish Brigantine Las Siete Hermanas," enclosure in Governor George F. Hill, Trinidad, to Lord Glenelg, October 6, 1835, CO 295/108.

15. Governor Hill to E. G. Stanley, March 9, 1834, CO 295/101.

16. Ibid.

17. Ibid. In the case of the vessel *Las Siete Hermanas*, which brought liberated Africans from Havana in September 1835, Governor Hill provided details on the employment of fifty-four girls. He listed all of these girls as "domestics," almost all of whom received placements in the service of married women. "Return Shewing the Distribution and Location of the Africans Who Arrived Here from the Havana, on the 14th of September 1835, on the Spanish Brigantine, 'Las Siete Hermanas' [7th October 1835]," enclosure in Governor George F. Hill, Trinidad, to Lord Glenelg, Principal Secretary of State, Colonial Department, October 6, 1835, CO 295/108.

18. Governor Hill to E. G. Stanley, March 9, 1834, CO 295/101. The implication that the Colonial Office had prescribed the terms of such employment arises from Governor Hill's language in his dispatch to Secretary of State Stanley. The governor reported to his superior that "the others were distributed in 20 lots upon 20 different Estates in the capacity of *free laborers* [emphasis in original] *pursuant to Your Instructions* [emphasis added] for Six Months, and were delivered to the Parties direct from the Spanish Schooner by the Captain Don Salvador Castello."

19. "Minute on the Condition and Disposal of the Captured Africans at the Havana, 24th October 1835, CO 318/123."

20. "Distribution of 193 Africans arrived in the Spanish Schooner 'Reyna Christina' from the Havana, on the 26th March 1834, Divided into Lots of 6 each, with the receipts of the parties, 31st March 1834," enclosure in Governor George F. Hill, Trinidad, to E. G. Stanley, Principal Secretary of State, Colonial Department, June 27, 1834, CO 295/102.

21. "Return Shewing the Distribution . . . of the Africans who arrived here from the Havana, on the 14th of September 1835," enclosure in Governor Hill to Lord Glenelg, October 6, 1835, CO 295/108.

Of the six apparently duplicated names, three appear with only an initial on one of the two lists, precluding verification based on these documents alone. However, it seems unlikely that there would have been several local planters with identical names. The list for the *Siete Hermanas* includes the names of the plantations involved, but the list for the *Manuelita* does not.

22. "Return Shewing the Distribution . . . of the Africans who arrived here from the Havana, on the 14th of September 1835," enclosure in Governor Hill to Lord Glenelg, October 6, 1835, CO 295/108.

23. "An Ordinance Enacted by the Lieutenant-Governor of the Island of Trinidad by and With the Advice and Consent of the Council of Government Thereof, for the Protection of and the Promoting the Industry and Good Conduct of Africans Transferred to this Island," enclosure in Lord Glenelg's Circular Despatch, Downing Street, January 15, 1836, Removal of Liberated Africans from Cuba 1835, vol. 4, CO 318/123.

24. Governor George F. Hill, Trinidad, to Lord Glenelg, August 20, 1836, and enclosures, CO 295/112. Governor Hill enclosed with his dispatch a copy of the *Royal Gazette of British Guiana* for August 2, 1836, which published a letter written by Commissioner Edward Schenley at Havana stating that he found the terms of the Guianese ordinance "infinitely more advantageous to the Africans" than the terms offered by either Trinidad or British Honduras.

25. Murray, *Odious Commerce*, 281. According to Murray, this reduction occurred largely because slave traders increasingly turned to the dishonest use of Portuguese or U.S. flags.

26. Earl of Aberdeen, Principal Secretary of State, Colonial Department, to Governor George F. Hill, Trinidad, April 29, 1835, CO 295/106.

27. Taylor to James Stephen, Under Secretary of State, Colonial Department, April 19, 1835, CO 295/106.

28. The British Emancipation Act required the newly emancipated population to serve as "apprentices" to their former masters for a period of six years, until 1840. The British government ended this mandatory "apprenticeship" two years early in 1838 following extensive criticism that West Indian employers—former slaveholders—persisted in treating the apprentices almost as poorly as slaves.

29. Asiegbu, *Slavery and the Politics of Liberation*, 42–43.

30. Bethell, "The Mixed Commissions," 89–92. On the question of the jurisdiction of British vice admiralty courts over foreign slavers, Bethell explains that some ship captains would sometimes discard their papers upon capture by the British navy. British authorities would then treat the vessel in question as a "stateless" entity. Unlike the earliest years of Britain's suppression campaign, by the 1840s, most nations involved had completely outlawed the African slave trade, and no ship found carrying slaves could claim protection under foreign laws.

31. Asiegbu, *Slavery and the Politics of Liberation*, 69–71.

32. Ibid., 71.

33. See Saint Helena, Original Correspondence, 1842–1849, CO 247/65-72.

34. Asiegbu, *Slavery and the Politics of Liberation*, 80.

35. Ibid., 93–118.

36. Ibid., 136–139, 145–150, 189–190.

37. Ibid., 189–190.

38. Lieutenant Governor MacLeod, Trinidad, to Lord John Russell, Principal Secretary of State, Colonial Department, May 20, 1841, CO 295/133.

39. "Notice to Emigrants to the Island of Trinidad," enclosure in Governor MacLeod to Lord Russell, May 20, 1841, CO 295/133.

40. "Statement of the Terms on Which the Immigrants from Sierra Leone Have Been Engaged," enclosure in Governor MacLeod to Lord Russell, May 20, 1841, CO 295/133.

41. Lieutenant Governor MacLeod to Lord Russell, May 20, 1841, CO 295/133.

42. Ibid.

43. Ibid.

44. "Present Condition of Trinidad as Exhibited by the Evidence Taken by the Agricultural and Immigration Society of the Colony, Pursuant to a Resolution of that Society, Passed at a Special General Meeting of the Members Held on the 11th day of February, 1841.—Revised by the Chairman, The Honourable W.H. Burnley," enclosure in Governor MacLeod to Lord Russell, August 20, 1841, CO 295/134.

45. Ibid.

46. Ibid.

47. Acting Governor Thomas Fuller, Trinidad, to Lord Stanley, Principal Secretary of State, Colonial Department, July 9, 1842, CO 295/137.

48. Andrew David, Special Trinidad Emigration Agent for Sierra Leone, to the Honorable Arthur White, Trinidad Colonial Secretary, July 6, 1842, enclosure in Acting Governor Fuller to Lord Stanley, July 9, 1842, CO 295/137.

49. Ibid.

50. "Terms under which the recently liberated Africans from Saint Helena have been Indented," enclosure in Lieutenant Governor MacLeod to Lord Stanley, June 27, 1842, CO 295/136. (The Colonial Office later rejected a new ordinance prepared by authorities in Trinidad to govern this immigration from Saint Helena. Among other things, the proposed ordinance attempted to set into law the system of having the employers of liberated Africans pay fees to help cover the costs of the immigration scheme—the system already used when the *Chieftan* brought its first group of Africans to Trinidad in 1842. After the rejection of the new ordinance the cost of transporting liberated African immigrants from Saint Helena to Trinidad reverted entirely to the government.)

51. Lieutenant Governor Henry MacLeod, Trinidad, to Lord Stanley, Principal Secretary of State, Colonial Department, February 15, 1842, and June 27, 1842, with replies, CO 295/136.

52. Lieutenant Governor MacLeod to Lord Stanley, February 15, 1842, with Stanley's response, CO 295/136.

53. Governor MacLeod to Lord Stanley, May 30, 1843, CO 295/139. Stipendiary magistrates were the officials responsible for monitoring the treatment of former slaves in the British West Indies after emancipation.

54. Ibid.

55. Governor MacLeod to Lord Stanley, September 11, 1843, CO 295/140.

56. "Present Condition of Trinidad as Exhibited by the Evidence Taken by the Agricultural and Immigration Society of the Colony . . . Revised by the Chairman,

The Honourable W. H. Burnley, [March–May 1841]," enclosure in Governor Mac-
Leod to Lord Russell, August 20, 1841, CO 295/134.

57. Enclosure in Governor MacLeod to Lord Stanley, May 18, 1844, CO
295/143.

58. Robert M. Guppy, "Report on the State of Emigration from Sierra Leone to
Trinidad, October 18, 1844," enclosure in Governor MacLeod to Lord Stanley, October 30, 1844, CO 295/144.

59. Governor MacLeod to Lord Stanley, October 30, 1844, CO 295/144.

60. Guppy, "Report on the State of Emigration," enclosure in MacLeod to Stanley, October 30, 1844, CO 295/144.

61. Ibid.

62. Christopher Fyfe, *A History of Sierra Leone* (New York: Oxford University
Press, 1962), 130, 133–134, 137–138, 267. See also Robert A. Clarke, *Sierra Leone: A
Description of the Manners and Customs of the Liberated Africans; with Observations
on the Natural History of the Colony, and a Notice of the Native Tribes* (London: James
Ridgway, 1843). This site was first known as the King's Yard but became the Queen's
Yard when Victoria succeeded William IV in 1837.

63. Fyfe, *A History of Sierra Leone*, 230.

64. Governor MacLeod to Lord Stanley, May 14, 1845, CO 295/146.

65. Governor MacLeod to Lord Stanley, September 2, 1845, CO 295/147.

66. Extract from the *Sierra Leone Watchman*, December 1845, MSS Brit Emp
s.22 G 76, Papers of the British and Foreign Anti-Slavery Society, British Empire
Manuscripts, Rhodes House Library, Oxford University.

67. Asiegbu, *Slavery and the Politics of Liberation*, 91.

68. Ibid., 91, 189.

69. Governor Harris, Trinidad, to Earl Grey, Principal Secretary of State, Colonial Department, June 6, 1848, CO 295/162.

70. Governor Harris to Earl Grey, July 6, 1849, CO 295/167.

71. Governor Harris to Earl Grey, August 27, 1850, and enclosures, and November 11, 1850, and enclosures, both in CO 295/171; Asiegbu, *Slavery and the Politics of
Liberation*, 140–143.

72. Charles William Day, *Five Years' Residence in the West Indies* (London: Colburn and Co., Publishers, 1852), 274–275. The short-lived H.M.S. *Growler* scheme
involved the attempt to recruit not only recently rescued Africans but also people
from the settled population of Sierra Leone and from other places in West Africa
such as the Kru coast and the Gambia. Day's first-hand account of the arrival of the
Growler clearly corresponds to the official reports of a voyage the *Growler* made to
Trinidad in December of 1847. On that trip, H.M.S. *Growler* collected 441 recently
liberated Africans and four immigrants from the settled population of Sierra Leone.
The ship afterward "touched at the Kroo Coast" but did not pick up any Kru immigrants before proceeding to Trinidad. See Thomas Anderson, M.D., Trinidad Inspector of Health of Shipping, to A. White, Trinidad Colonial Secretary, December
6, 1847, enclosure in Governor Harris to Earl Grey, December 8, 1847, CO 295/158.
Thus, the vast majority of the group Day observed were people taken directly from
the Liberated African Yard.

There seems to be little doubt that Day drew the figures he quoted in his text from government accounts of this voyage. The relevant passage from his book describes "a cargo of one hundred and fifty men, thirty-seven women, and two hundred and fifty-four children of both sexes"—a degree of specificity the author could hardly have gleaned from casual observation but that accords precisely with the numbers Dr. Anderson cited in his account of the group the *Growler* collected at Sierra Leone. But Day's account of the arrival of the *Growler* in Trinidad proves inaccurate because he neglected to subtract the forty-five people who died on the journey from Africa to the Caribbean.

73. Day, *Five Years' Residence,* 274–275.

74. Ibid.

75. Ibid.

76. Ibid.

77. Asiegbu, *Slavery and the Politics of Liberation,* 189.

78. Governor MacLeod to Lord Stanley, March 19, 1844, CO 295/142; Governor George Harris, Trinidad, to Earl Grey, December 4, 1846, CO 295/152; Governor Harris to Earl Grey, June 10, 1847, CO 295/157.

79. Governor Harris to Earl Grey, May 1, 1849, and May 19, 1849, and enclosures with both, CO 295/167.

80. Governor Harris to Earl Grey, July 21, 1849, and enclosures, CO 295/167.

81. Governor Harris to Earl Grey, October 13, 1849, CO 295/168.

82. Governor Harris to Earl Grey, September 7, 1850, and enclosures, CO 295/171.

83. Governor Harris to Earl Grey, December 4, 1846, CO 295/152.

84. Ibid.

85. "Rules and Regulations to be Observed by the Agent General of Immigrants at the Island of Trinidad (or the Person Acting in that Capacity) with the Consent of the Governor, with Regard to Liberated Africans Brought into that Colony," enclosure in Governor Harris to Earl Grey, March 18, 1847, CO 295/156.

86. Governor MacLeod to Lord Stanley, January 11, 1844, CO 295/142, reporting the arrival of the ship *Earl Grey* with 216 liberated Africans "who were all landed the following morning and found immediate employment upon the different sugar plantations"; Governor MacLeod to Lord Stanley, February 29, 1844, CO 295/142, reporting the arrival of the *Lancashire Witch* with 288 liberated Africans, who "were landed and distributed among the different Sugar Estates"; Governor Harris to Earl Grey, May 15, 1850, CO 295/170, reporting the arrival of the *Marion Leith* and the *Viscount Hardinge* with 110 and 213 liberated Africans, respectively; Governor Harris to Earl Grey, April 6, 1848, CO 295/160, referring to a group of liberated Africans who had been rescued from the slaver *Flor de Loando* and brought to Trinidad from Rio de Janeiro in February 1847. Harris did not provide specific details about how many immigrants had been rescued from the *Flor de Loando* in this 1848 communication or in any dispatch from early 1847.

87. See appendix 2. Johnson Asiegbu's figures for this decade (derived mostly from British parliamentary papers) amount to approximately 1,200 African immigrants, but arrivals described in governors' correspondence from this period total significantly less. See Asiegbu, *Slavery and the Politics of Liberation,* 189. It is possible that the discrepancy here relates to confusion in the records used by Asiegbu con-

cerning when particular vessels arrived in Trinidad, rather than to any major difference between the total number of African immigrants reported in Asiegbu's book (8,383) and my own total from the governors' correspondence (8,158) included in appendix 2.

88. See for example Walton Look Lai, *Indentured Labor, Caribbean Sugar: Chinese and Indian Migrants to the British West Indies, 1838–1918* (Baltimore, Md.: Johns Hopkins University Press, 1993); and K. O. Laurence, *A Question of Labour: Indentured Immigration into Trinidad and British Guiana 1875–1917* (Kingston, Jamaica: Ian Randle, 1994).

89. Governor Harris to Earl Grey, June 19, 1847, CO 295/157.

90. Governor Harris to the Duke of Newcastle, Principal Secretary of State, Colonial Department, February 23, 1853, CO 295/180. In addition to the 356 Indian immigrants aboard the *Harkaway,* Harris also reported the arrival of 296 "Coolie" immigrants on the *William Jardine.*

91. Asiegbu, *Slavery and the Politics of Liberation,* 189–190. For discussion of the uneven manner in which the illegal slave trade ended, see David Eltis, *Economic Growth and the Ending of the Transatlantic Slave Trade* (New York: Oxford University Press, 1987), 214–222. The developments addressed in Eltis's review, however, do not directly explain why the number of slave ships seized and prosecuted in the vice admiralty courts of Saint Helena and Sierra Leone reached a new peak in the early 1860s.

92. Governor Robert W. Keate, Trinidad, to the Duke of Newcastle, Principal Secretary of State, Colonial Department, March 9, 1860, and enclosures, CO 295/208.

93. Governor Keate to the Duke of Newcastle, March 20, 1860, and March 31, 1860, and enclosures with both, CO 295/208.

94. Henry Mitchell, Trinidad Agent General of Immigrants, to J. Scott Bushe, Trinidad Colonial Secretary, March 17, 1860, enclosure in Governor Keate to the Duke of Newcastle, March 20, 1860, CO 295/208

95. Henry Mitchell to J. Scott Bushe, March 24, 1860 and "Africans ex 'Brooklyne' distributed," enclosures in Governor Keate to the Duke of Newcastle, March 31, 1860. The list of the Africans rescued from the *Brooklyne* indicated the names and plantations of the various employers at a level of detail comparable to the records authorities prepared during the 1830s for the liberated Africans from Havana. This arguably indicates that the arrival of liberated Africans in Trinidad had once again acquired a novel and uncertain quality for local officials, who thus felt motivated to give more elaborate details of their actions for the information of their superiors. Henry Mitchell to J. Scott Bushe, June 30, 1860, enclosure in Lieutenant Governor James Walker, Trinidad, to the Duke of Newcastle, Principal Secretary of State, Colonial Department, July 6, 1860, CO 295/208.

96. Lieutenant Governor Walker to the Duke of Newcastle, July 6, 1860, CO 295/208.

97. Ibid.

98. Lieutenant Governor Walker to the Duke of Newcastle, July 21, 1860, and enclosures, CO 295/208. Both Mitchell and Walker pointed to the fact that the 1854 ordinance addressed only "immigrants introduced at the expense of the colony," a condition which, they explained, did not apply to the liberated Africans. No doubt

the Trinidad Council and attorney general framed the 1854 law to apply to the new system of labor immigration from East India. Nevertheless, given the arguments of Mitchell and Walker in this matter, it is not clear who covered the cost of conveying these later liberated African groups to the island.

99. Colonial Office to Lieutenant Governor James Walker, September 8, 1860, CO 295/208; Lieutenant Governor James Walker to the Duke of Newcastle, Principal Secretary of State, Colonial Department, March 22, 1861, with enclosure, CO 295/212.

100. It is important to understand that *awareness* of slaves' humanity was not incompatible with dehumanizing and brutal behavior on the part of slaveholders. That is, even the most violent and dehumanizing planter or slave trader knew that he was interacting with African, African-American, or African-Caribbean human beings. Slaves were legally chattel but still unavoidably human to the individuals who brutalized them daily. For detailed exploration of this complex social interaction, see Eugene Genovese's classic work *Roll, Jordan, Roll: The World the Slaves Made* (New York: Vintage Books, 1972); and the more recent work by Walter Johnson, *Soul by Soul: Life Inside the Antebellum Slave Market* (Cambridge, Mass.: Harvard University Press, 2001).

101. Massé, *Diaries of the Abbé Armand Massé,* 4:66–67; and William Drysdale, *In Sunny Lands: Out-Door Life in Nassau and Cuba* (New York: Harper & Brothers, 1885), 12–13, 43, 48–49.

3. "A fine family of what we call Creole Yarabas"

1. Philip Curtin's *The Atlantic Slave Trade: A Census* (Madison: University of Wisconsin Press, 1969) still provides the most comprehensive overview of the distribution of the slave trade throughout the Americas. It pays at least some attention to relationships between different sources for slaves in Africa and various New World destinations. Curtin's work in this regard is still valuable despite the controversies that continue over his low estimated figure for the total volume of the trade. On the contributions of Akan-Asante peoples to slave culture in the eighteenth-century Caribbean, see for example Orlando Patterson, *The Sociology of Slavery: An Analysis of the Origins, Development and Structure of Negro Slave Society in Jamaica* (Rutherford, N.J.: Fairleigh Dickinson University Press, 1969); Craton, *Testing the Chains*; and Mervyn Alleyne, *Roots of Jamaican Culture* (London: Pluto Press, 1989).

2. On the ethnic composition of the slave trade to French Saint Domingue, see for example Robert Louis Stein, *The French Slave Trade in the Eighteenth Century: An Old Regime Business* (Madison: University of Wisconsin Press, 1979); and Serge Daget and Jean Mettas, eds., *Répertoire des expéditions négrieres françaises au XVIIIe siècle* (Paris: Societe française d'histoire d'outre-mer, 1978).

On the contributions of Fon and Yoruba cultures to the formation of Haitian vodun, see for example Alfred Metraux, *Voodoo in Haiti,* translated by Hugo Charteris, with a new introduction by Sidney W. Mintz (1950; New York: Schocken Books, 1972); Maya Deren, *Divine Horsemen: Voodoo Gods of Haiti* (1953; London: Thames and Hudson, 1970); and Leslie Desmangles, *The Faces of the Gods: Vodou and Roman Catholicism in Haiti* (Chapel Hill: University of North Carolina Press, 1992).

3. See for example Joseph E. Holloway, "The Origins of African-American Culture," and Robert Farris Thompson, "Kongo Influences on African-American Artistic Culture," in Joseph E. Holloway, ed., *Africanisms in American Culture* (Bloomington: Indiana University Press, 1990), 1–18, 148–184.

4. Maya Deren's *Divine Horseman* and Leslie Desmangles' *Faces of the Gods* both offer discussions of Kongo influences on vodun, although Deren attempts to draw overly rigid distinctions between the different African ethnic inputs. Because of the heterogeneous and syncretic history and character of the religion, it seems likely that much blurring occurs among the several African influences.

5. Curtin's comprehensive work *The Atlantic Slave Trade* remains an important source in English on the slave trade to Cuba. See also Franklin W. Knight, *Slave Society in Cuba during the Nineteenth Century* (Madison: University of Wisconsin Press, 1970); and Bergad, García, and Barcia, *The Cuban Slave Market, 1790–1880.* Although *The Cuban Slave Market* focuses on the functioning of the Cuban slave trade as an economic enterprise, the essays provide some detail on the particularly fruitful supply routes from Yoruba regions of West Africa to the island. For discussions of Yoruba contributions to African-Cuban culture, see for example George Brandon, *Santeria from Africa to the New World: The Dead Sell Memories* (Bloomington: Indiana University Press, 1993); and Robert Farris Thompson, *Flash of the Spirit: African and Afro-American Art and Philosophy* (New York: Vintage Books, 1983). On the ethnic composition of the Brazilian slave trade, see Robert Edgar Conrad, *World of Sorrow: The African Slave Trade to Brazil* (Baton Rouge: Louisiana State University Press, 1986); and Pierre Verger, *Flux et reflux de la traite des nègres entre le Golfe de Benin et Bahia de Todos os Santos, du XVIIe au XIXe siècle* (Paris: La Haye, Mouton, 1968). On the Yoruba and Kongo presence in Brazilian slave culture, see for example Roger Bastide, *The African Religions of Brazil: Toward a Sociology of the Interpenetration of Civilizations,* translated by Helen Sebba (Baltimore, Md.: Johns Hopkins University Press, 1978); and Mary Karasch, *Slave Life in Rio de Janeiro, 1808–1850* (Princeton, N.J.: Princeton University Press, 1987).

6. For a succinct discussion of this period of Yoruba history, see Robert S. Smith, *Kingdoms of the Yoruba,* 3rd ed. (1969; Madison: University of Wisconsin Press, 1988), 99–140.

7. Records of the Anglo-Spanish Mixed Commission at Havana, FO 313/56-62. Unless otherwise indicated, translations of Spanish-language texts from these records are my own.

8. In other words, if a liberated African ended up recaptured, reenslaved, and once again rescued by the British, he could report his unique number to British authorities. This documentation would help secure continued funding for suppression of the slave trade by demonstrating the pervasive treachery of the trade. It is unfortunate that the numbering system could do little to prevent reenslavement from occurring in the first place.

9. My review of ethnic and geographic reference materials included atlases written in both English and Spanish, survey texts of African history and anthropol-

ogy, and various works on the Atlantic slave trade that examine in varying degrees the role of African ethnicity in the trading process. Of particular use were Curtin, *The Atlantic Slave Trade;* John Thornton, *Africa and Africans in the Making of the Atlantic World, 1400–1680* (New York: Cambridge University Press, 1992); Philip Curtin, Steven Feierman, Leonard Thompson, and Jan Vansina, *African History* (1978; Madison: University of Wisconsin Press, 1988); and Barry W. Higman, "African and Creole Slave Family Patterns in Trinidad," in Franklin Knight and Margaret Crahan, eds., *Africa and the Caribbean: The Legacies of a Link* (Baltimore, Md.: Johns Hopkins University Press, 1979). Atlases and anthropological reference texts most often consulted included J. D. Fage, *An Atlas of African History* (New York: Africana Publishing Company, 1978); M. Kwamena-Poh, J. Tosh, R. Waller, and M. Tidy, *African History in Maps* (1982; London: Longman Group Limited, 1987); Colin McEvedy, *Atlas of African History* (New York: Facts on File Inc., 1980); and George Peter Murdock, *Africa: Its Peoples and Their Culture History* (New York: McGraw-Hill Book Company, Inc., 1959). For an examination of early Spanish-language terms used to describe Africa and Africans, see Alonso de Sandoval, *Tomo primero de instauranda aethiopum salute: Historia de Aethiopia; naturaelça, policia sagrada y profana, costumbres, ritos y cathecismo evangelico de todos los aethiopes* . . . (Madrid: A. D. paredes, 1647).

10. For extensive examination of who the Carabalí were and the history of this terminology and identity in Cuba, see Enrique Sosa, *El Carabalí* (Ciudad de la Habana, Cuba: Editorial Letras Cubanas, 1984). Sosa explains the broadly encompassing nature of this term for "heterogeneous" African arrivals from southern Nigeria: "*De Nigeria del sur, durante el período de historia esclavista en Cuba y, con redoblada intensidad, desde finales del siglo XVIII hasta la década del cuarenta del XIX, llegaron constreñidos a costas cubanas miles de hombres y mujeres esclavizados. . . . En Cuba fueron denominados, por metátesis del término nigeriano Calabar e ignorando su heterogénea composición tribal con el nombre genérico de <<carabalíes.>>*" (From southern Nigeria, during the era of slavery in Cuba and, with redoubled intensity from the end of the 1700s through the 1840s, thousands of enslaved men and women arrived against their will on Cuban shores. . . . In Cuba they were collectively identified based on the Nigerian term Calabar, and having no regard for their heterogeneous tribal makeup, with the generic name "carablíes.") Sosa, *El Carabalí*, 7.

11. Register of Slaves, 1828, Archives of Havana Slave Trade Commission, FO 313/56. The captured vessel *Gerges* brought 385 Africans to Havana, 344 of whom the mixed commission identified as Carabalí followed by various suffixes. Authorities identified the remaining forty-one as Ybibi or Ibibi.

12. Register of Slaves, 1835, Archives of Havana Slave Trade Commission, FO 313/61. These 378 people came from a single vessel that had its own Calabar connections. The British captured the slave ship *Minfa*, which was sailing under the false name *Matanra* with 396 slaves aboard. Mixed commission officials marked eighteen of these as Carabalí Camaron and the remaining 378 simply as Camaron.

13. While numerous discussions of these particular ethnic identifications appear in both twentieth-century scholarship and the writings of nineteenth-century observers, I am particularly indebted for the summary of these ideas to Kwaku

Senah, Ph.D. candidate in history at the University of the West Indies at Saint Augustine, who presented a review of several of these African ethnic concepts in a History Department seminar in February 1994.

14. Murdock, *Africa: Its Peoples and Their Culture History,* 64 and 259.

15. This word introduces a particular confusion. Murdock cites "Bere" as an alternate term for the "Belle," whom he classifies as one of the Peripheral Mande groups. However, in her review of the African ethnic origins of the South Carolina Gullah community, Margaret Washington Creel cites the terms "beri" and "berimo" as alternate terms for the Poro secret society, a ritual subgroup of the Vai and other ethnic groups of the Sierra Leone area. See Murdock, *Africa,* 260 and Margaret Washington Creel, *"A Peculiar People": Slave Religion and Community-Culture among the Gullahs* (New York: New York University Press, 1988), 18–19.

16. I am indebted for this reminder to my colleague Dylan Penningroth of the Department of History at Northwestern University. See for example the work of John Thornton: "The African Experience of the '20 and Odd Negroes' Arriving in Virginia in 1619," *William and Mary Quarterly,* 3rd series, LV, no. 3 (July 1998) and "African Dimensions of the Stono Rebellion," *American Historical Review* 96, no. 4 (October 1991): 1101–1113. For one of the most recent overviews of the challenges of African ethnic and cultural terminology in the era of Atlantic slave trading, see "African Cultural Groups in the Atlantic World," in John Thornton, *Africa and Africans in the Making of the Atlantic World,* 2nd ed. (New York: Cambridge University Press, 1998).

17. See for example Schuler, *"Alas, Alas Kongo"*; and Maureen Warner-Lewis, *Guinea's Other Suns* and *Trinidad Yoruba: From Mother Tongue to Memory* (Tuscaloosa: University of Alabama Press, 1996).

18. See Warner-Lewis and Schuler on Yoruba groups in Trinidad (*Guinea's Other Suns*) and Kongo groups in Jamaica (*"Alas, Alas Kongo"*). For notes on an effort to repatriate Kongo people from the Bahamas, see Philip Cash, Shirley Gordon, and Gail Saunders, *Sources of Bahamian History* (London: Macmillan Caribbean, 1991).

19. Register of Slaves, 1835, Archives of Havana Slave Trade Commission, FO 313/61. For example, the captured vessel *Ricomar,* sailing under the false name *Zafira,* arrived with 186 slaves whom the mixed commission classified as follows: Lucumí 114, Mina Popo 22, Mina 14, Arara 34, and Arara Magi 2.

20. Register of Slaves, 1835, Archives of Havana Slave Trade Commission, FO 313/61. The words translated and paraphrased as "when they were very young" appear in Spanish in the register as "*desde muy miños,*" or literally "since very *miños.*" There is no obvious translation for the word "*miños*" in modern dictionaries. I interpret this as either a misspelling or a transcription of the word "*niños,*" meaning children.

21. Sterling Stuckey, *Slave Culture: Nationalist Theory and the Foundations of Black America* (New York: Oxford University Press, 1987), 194.

22. Ibid., 194–198.

23. "Crown Lands Office, 17th October, 1871," *The New Era* III, no. 107, November 13, 1871; "San Fernando Police Court, Monday, Feb. 17," *The Trinidad Chronicle,* no. 334, February 21, 1868; "Police Intelligence," *The New Era,* n.s., XV, no. 27, December 2, 1887.

24. *The Trinidad Chronicle*: "San Fernando Police Court, Friday," no. 303, November 5, 1867; "Supreme Criminal Court," no. 366, June 12, 1868.

25. "Supreme Criminal Court," *The Trinidad Chronicle*, no. 366, June 12, 1868.

26. "Supreme Criminal Court, Wednesday June 14," *The Trinidad Chronicle*, n.s., no. 188, June 16, 1871.

27. This assumption is consistent with the way that attachments to and cultural practices from home change over time for any immigrants. It is also supported by the fact that these kinds of names became less common with the passage of time and as the population contained fewer and fewer African-born people or their first-generation descendants. Legal slave trading to Trinidad ended in 1807, and no significant illegal trade existed. Therefore, in the second half of the nineteenth century, African-born people under the age of sixty (or people under the age of forty with African-born parents) likely belonged to the liberated African community.

28. "San Fernando Police Court, Saturday," *The Trinidad Chronicle*, no. 311, December 3, 1867.

29. "San Fernando Police Court, Monday, March 9," *The Trinidad Chronicle*, no. 340, March 13, 1868.

30. Samuel Grosvenor, letter to the editor, *The New Era*, n.s., XIII, no. 4, June 29, 1885.

31. "Country News—Mayaro," *The Trinidad Chronicle*, n.s., no. 245, January 2, 1872.

32. *The Trinidad Chronicle*: "Murder on Cupar Grange Estate," no. 289, September 17, 1867; "San Fernando Police Court, Friday," no. 293, October 1, 1867.

33. The newspaper reports I consulted for this study do not give any indication of how this case concluded. However, some earlier criminal records from the *Trinidad Chronicle* provide a clue about the identity of the accused murderer. In December 1864, a man at San Fernando identified as "Tony Congo" received a twelve-month prison sentence for severely beating another man with a stick. During the trial, different witnesses characterized the defendant as "crazy" and "in a foolish way." They testified that Tony claimed he beat his victim because he believed the man to be a "diablesse," or supernatural spirit. Because the Cupar Grange prisoner also had the name "Tony" and also belonged to the Kongo ethnic group, it seems possible that the same man committed both crimes. Such speculation gains further credence when one considers the issues of supernatural belief and mental instability in the 1864 matter and the rumors of suspicious poisoning in the 1867 murder. See "Criminal Court," *The Trinidad Chronicle*, no. 12, December 17, 1864 and no. 13, December 21, 1864.

34. "Arrest of the Pointe-a-Pierre Murderer," *The Trinidad Chronicle*, no. 312, December 6, 1867.

35. Land and Emigration Commission Letter Book, Colonial Office, West Indies, Africa, Saint Helena, from May 1851, vol. 14, enclosure in J. W. C. Murdoch and Frederic Rogers, Land Emigration Commissioners to Herman Merivale, Under Secretary of State, Colonial Department, May 26, 1851, CO 386/88.

36. Author's interview with Sylvia Ampson, February 24, 1994, Caratal, Trinidad.

37. See Warner-Lewis, *Guinea's Other Suns*; Warner-Lewis, *Yoruba Songs of Trinidad* (London: Kamak House, 1994); and Warner-Lewis, *Trinidad Yoruba*.

38. For a summary presentation of some of Warner-Lewis's interviews, see *Guinea's Other Suns*, 61–77.

39. Andrew Anthony Ali, "Lengua/Barrackpore: A Socio-Psychological Study" (B.A. thesis, University of the West Indies, Saint Augustine, Trinidad, 1975), 29–30.

40. *The Trinidad Chronicle*, n.s., no. 751, November 7, 1876. See also Bridget Brereton's discussion of this incident and other newspaper reports involving the Radas of Belmont in *Race Relations in Colonial Trinidad, 1870–1900* (New York: Cambridge University Press, 1979), 153–156.

41. For explorations of this issue with respect to slave societies, see for example Roger Bastide, *African Civilisations in the New World*, translated from the French by Peter Green with a foreword by Geoffrey Parrinder (New York: Harper & Row, 1971); Melville Herskovits, *The Myth of the Negro Past* (1941; Boston: Beacon Press, 1990); and Monica Schuler, "Ethnic Slave Rebellions in the Caribbean and the Guianas," *Journal of Social History* 3, no. 4 (1970): 374–385.

42. "Obeah," *The New Era* n.s., XIV, no. 15, September 13, 1886.

43. Brereton, *Race Relations in Colonial Trinidad*, 156. Brereton also notes that despite this definition, "as the word [obeah] was used in the late nineteenth century, it included any religious or magical practices which were considered to be 'African', including healing, and conjuring of all types—seeking success in family and love affairs, or favourable results in litigation, or injuring enemies."

44. Ibid., 155–165; "Scotched but Not Killed," *The New Era* XIV, no. 21, October 25, 1886. It is not surprising that the Supreme Court did not accept the validity of the arguments made on behalf of the appellant concerning the legitimacy of Rada religious practice. His Honor Sir John Gorrie explained in his decision that the court had quashed the conviction because of the entrapment-like methods the police had used to acquire evidence for the case.

45. Andrew Carr, *A Rada Community in Trinidad* (1953; Port-of-Spain: Paria Publishing Company, 1989), 2–4; and *African Notes*, Andrew Carr Papers, National Archives of Trinidad and Tobago, Port-of-Spain. (*African Notes* is literally a notebook, including loose enclosed pages, kept by Andrew Carr during his research on the Rada community during the 1950s.)

46. Registers of Slaves, 1828–1838, Archives of the Havana Slave Trade Commission, FO 313/57-62.

47. Andrew Carr, *A Rada Community in Trinidad*, 4.

48. Ibid.

49. A brief notice in the *Trinidad Chronicle* in June 1877 marked the death of a man identified as the Rev. Hou Tuervee, who was allegedly considered by some Radas to be the "assistant Curate of Belmont." A man thus described may have served as the leader of the other Rada compound rather than as an aide to Robert Antoine. See "Trinidadiana," *The Trinidad Chronicle*, n.s., no. 8, June 22, 1877. In March 1994, Sedley Antoine, the grandson of Robert and present leader of the family despite his residence in Canada during most of the year, reported that he had heard of the existence of a second Rada compound in Belmont but could not recall when it had ceased to exist. Author's interview with Sedley Antoine, March 15, 1994, Belmont, Port-of-Spain, Trinidad.

50. "African Tales (Rada) Religious—Collected by A. T. Carr," in *African Notes,* Andrew Carr Papers. This detailed version of Ahoorloo's story appears in notes apparently from an interview conducted by Andrew Carr with Andrew George and/or Henry Antoine on January 30, 1952. See also other references to Ahoorloo, on different pages using this same heading, in notes from an interview conducted with Andrew George on January 28, 1952.

51. "Map of Belmont Valley Road showing the Rada compound and the distribution of African families around 1890 from data obtained from Henry Antoine," in Carr, *A Rada Community,* n.p. (between pages 10 and 11).

52. Charles Ives, *The Isles of Summer; or Nassau and the Bahamas* (New Haven. Conn.: Published by the author, 1880), 53.

53. J. and E. E. Dickinson and S. E. Dowd, *A Winter Picnic: The Story of a Four Months' Outing in Nassau, told in the Letters, Journals, and Talk of Four Picnicers* (New York: Henry Holt and Company, 1888), 142. The terms Congo and Congar are possibly variations of one another, both referring to the large Kongo ethnic group. Similarly, the labels Nango and Nangobar possibly both refer to the Yoruba. The origins of the word Nango lie in the term Anago, which described an early variant of the Yoruba language. (For clarification of this terminology, I am indebted to the research of linguist Olabiyi Yai, in particular to the material explored in an unpublished paper entitled "Anago, Lucumi, Yoruba: On the Inventions of Yoruba Language/ Identity in Africa and the New World," presented to the African Studies Program at the University of Pennsylvania, December 2, 1994.) Finally, the term "Egba" refers to another ethnic group of southern Nigeria.

54. Ibid., 35, 148.

55. Ibid., 142.

56. Ibid., 143.

57. L. D. Powles, *The Land of the Pink Pearl; or, Recollections of Life in the Bahamas* (London: Sampson Low, Marston, Searle, & Rivington Limited, 1888), 147.

58. James Stark's 1891 *History and Guide to the Bahama Islands* also refers to these annual elections among ethnic groups. However, since the language Stark uses virtually duplicates that of Powles, it seems probable that he referred to the earlier work in preparing his own effort. Powles acknowledges using William Drysdale's 1885 work *In Sunny Lands* to develop two chapters on life and culture in Nassau, although he said he often "imbibed [Drysdale's] spirit and clothed it in his own matter." See James H. Stark, *Stark's History and Guide to the Bahama Islands, Containing a Description of Everything on or about the Bahama Islands of Which the Visitor or Resident May Desire Information* (Boston: James H. Stark, 1891), 188; and L. D. Powles, *Land of the Pink Pearl,* vi, 137.

59. "Crowning of the Eboe Queen," *The Nassau Guardian,* vol. XLI, no. 4058, February 18, 1885.

60. Williams, *Guide to African Villages in New Providence,* 5–8. Williams derives these descriptions from the correspondence of Governor William Colebrooke, who in 1835 reported to the Colonial Office on the history and nature of various Bahamian settlement patterns.

61. N.a., *Archives Exhibition of Settlements in New Providence* (Nassau: Bahamas Department of Archives, 1982), 22; Williams, *Guide to African Villages in New Providence,* 5–8. According these sources, surveyor Burnside selected the name Grant's Town in honor of former Bahamian Governor Major General Lewis Grant, under whom he had served.

62. *The Nassau Guardian*: "St. Agnes School Festival," LXII, no. 4634, May 5, 1886; XLIII, no. 4708, January 19, 1887; XLIV, no. 4670, August 4, 1888.

63. Patrice M. Williams, ed., *Colonial Secretary Papers: Report on the Bahamas 1861–1876* (Nassau: Bahamas Department of Archives, 2002), 7–10. I am indebted to Sean McWeeney and my father, Paul L. Adderley, for drawing to my attention the 2002 publication of this colonial secretary's report. At a relatively late stage in the development of this project, the report added further evidence to the arguments of this chapter. Archivist and public historian Patrice M. Williams's decades of research about the experience of liberated Africans for the Bahamian Department of Archives have been invaluable.

64. Ibid.

65. Ibid.

66. Ibid.

67. Ibid.

68. Author's interview with Cleveland W. Eneas, April 30, 1994, Bain Town, Nassau, Bahamas.

69. Gladys Manuel, *Historical Notes on the Fox Hill Community* (Nassau, Bahamas: n.p., 1988), 1–2, 8–9.

70. Ibid.

71. Baptisms June 1820 to June 1855, Nos. 1–781, Bahamas Methodist Church Papers, Department of Archives, Commonwealth of the Bahamas.

72. Transcript of interview with Virginia Brice, Fox Hill, August 4, 1970, by D. Gail Saunders, Bahamas Department of Archives, Nassau, Bahamas.

4. "Assisted by his wife, an African"

1. Marie Bertrand Cothonay, *Trinidad: Journal d'un Missionaire Dominicain des Antilles Anglaises* (Paris: Victor Retaux et Fils, Libraires-Editeurs, 1893), 290–291. Cothonay reported his encounter with the Angolan prince in a journal entry from Port-of-Spain in May 1885. However, it must be said here that parts of the prince's tale prove confusing. He describes the final African captors who sold him to the Portuguese as being "Yerabas," presumably a reference to the West African Yoruba group. Thousands of miles and complicated polities separated nineteenth-century Yorubaland from those parts of West-Central Africa that might have been referred to as Angola in this era. Thus, logistically his story seems problematic. But the exact geography of the prince's origins does not alter the way his biography offers insight into questions of marriage and family in the liberated African community.

2. The term "rehearse" here is borrowed from Willie Lee Rose's classic study *Rehearsal for Reconstruction: The Port Royal Experiment* (Indianapolis, Ind.: Bobbs-

Merrill, 1964). Rose's study dealt with Union soldiers in Port Royal, South Carolina, early in the Civil War, when full slave emancipation was a probability but not yet a certainty. Likewise, during the first quarter-century of suppression of the slave trade, although policies for liberated Africans were developed in the shadow of an ever-stronger British abolition movement, eventual emancipation was far from being assured.

3. Alexander Murray, Collector of Customs, Bahamas, to Earl Bathurst, Principal Secretary of State, Colonial Department, September 1816, CO 23/63. This is Murray's paraphrase of the relevant legal instructions. There is no small irony here for historians of comparative slavery concerning the relative hardships of cotton versus sugar cultivation. By many accounts, some of the harshest conditions of slavery existed in the cotton country of the Deep South of the United States of the mid-nineteenth century. However, on this occasion British authorities, seeking to somehow shield liberated African women from the rigors of sugar cultivation, deemed picking cotton sufficiently mild in character that "protected" women could participate safely. Given the onerous nature of cotton-picking, the criteria used in this gendered regimen reveals volumes about British attitudes toward the exploitation of liberated African labor, even in the case of specially protected women.

4. Alexander Murray, Collector of Customs, Bahamas, to Governor Charles Cameron, Bahamas, enclosure in Alexander Murray to Earl Bathurst, Principal Secretary of State, Colonial Department, September 1816, CO 23/63.

5. Alexander Murray, Collector of Customs, Bahamas, to the Earl of Liverpool, Principal Secretary of State, Colonial Department, April 1812, CO 23/59.

6. See David Eltis and Stanley L. Engerman, "Fluctuations in Sex and Age Ratios in the Transatlantic Slave Trade, 1663–1864," *Economic History Review*, n.s., 46, no. 2 (1993): 308–323.

7. See "Minute on the Condition and Disposal of the Captured Africans at the Havana, 24th October 1835," in Removal of Liberated Africans from Cuba, 1835, vol. 4, CO318/123.

8. Richard B. Jackson, Havana, to Governor George F. Hill, Trinidad, August 4, 1835, enclosure in Governor George F. Hill, Trinidad, to James Stephen, Under Secretary of State, Colonial Department, September 15, 1835, CO 295/107.

9. Ibid.

10. Sir Hans Sloane, *A Voyage to the Islands of Madera, Barbados, Nieves, St. Christopher and Jamaica* (1707), cited in Barbara Bush, *Slave Women in Caribbean Society 1650–1838* (Bloomington: Indiana University Press, 1990), 98.

11. Captain General Mariano Ricafort, Havana, to Governor George F. Hill, Trinidad, January 16, 1834, enclosed in Governor Hill to Lord Stanley, Principal Secretary of State, Colonial Department, February 12, 1834, CO 295/101.

12. Governor George F. Hill, Trinidad, to Lord Glenelg, October 6, 1835, CO 295/108.

13. Governor William Colebrooke, Bahamas, to the Earl of Aberdeen, Principal Secretary of State, Colonial Department, March 25, 1835, CO 23/9.

14. Rosalyn Terborg-Penn, "African Feminism: A Theoretical Approach to the History of Women in the African Diaspora" in Rosalyn Terborg-Penn and Andrea

Benton Rushing, eds., *Women in Africa and the African Diaspora: A Reader,* 2nd ed. (Washington D.C.: Howard University Press, 1996), 24.

15. Extract from the minutes of the Council of Government, June 7, 1836, enclosure in Governor George F. Hill, Trinidad, to Lord Glenelg, June 18, 1836, CO 295/111.

16. "Queries submitted through Mr. Munnings to His Majesty's Secretary of State in July 1812," enclosure in Governor Charles Cameron, Bahamas, to Earl Bathurst, Principal Secretary of State, Colonial Department, October 2, 1815, CO 23/62.

17. Governor Ralph Woodford, Trinidad, to Earl Bathurst, Principal Secretary of State, Colonial Department, November 10, 1816, CO 295/40. Responses of Colonial Office authorities to Governor Woodford are included with this archival copy of the governor's dispatch.

18. Robert Mitchell, Superintendent of American Refugees, to Governor Woodford, August 5, 1817, enclosure in Governor Woodford to Earl Bathurst, Principal Secretary of State, Colonial Department, August 10, 1817, CO 295/44.

19. Governor Woodford to Earl Bathurst, December 16, 1820, CO 295/51.

20. Governor Woodford to Earl Bathurst, April 11, 1821, CO 295/53.

21. Governor Woodford to Earl Bathurst, August 8, 1826, CO 295/72.

22. Governor Woodford to Earl Bathurst, April 27, 1826, CO 295/71; Governor Woodford to Earl Bathurst, Principal Secretary of State, Colonial Department, October 31, 1826, CO 295/72.

23. Governor Charles Cameron, Bahamas, to Earl Bathurst, January 24, 1816, CO 23/63.

24. Ibid., and enclosures.

25. Alexander Murray, Collector of Customs, Bahamas, to Governor Charles Cameron, Bahamas, January 3, 1816, enclosure in Governor Charles Cameron to Earl Bathurst, January 24, 1816, CO23/63.

26. House of Assembly Enquiry into Grievances of the 2nd West India Regt., January 1816, enclosure in Governor Cameron to Earl Bathurst, January 24, 1816, CO 23/63.

27. Amy Dru Stanley, *From Bondage to Contract: Wage Labor, Marriage and the Market in the Age of Slave Emancipation* (New York: Cambridge University Press, 1998), 140.

28. Clare Midgley, *Women Against Slavery: The British Campaigns 1780–1870* (New York: Routledge, 1992). See especially Chapter 5, "Perspectives, Principles and Policies."

29. Minutes of Evidence given by Robert Mitchell, Superintendent of Company Villages of Disbanded Colonial Marines [from the United States], before a Committee of His Majesty's Council for the purpose of attaining a more correct knowledge of the Negro Character, as exhibited in this Colony, in a state of Slavery and of Freedom, 1 February 1825, enclosure in Governor Woodford to Earl Bathurst, June 12, 1825, CO295/66.

30. Governor Charles J. Bayley, Bahamas, to the Duke of Newcastle, Principal Secretary of State, Colonial Department, September 15, 1863, in Bahamas 1863, vol. 2, August to December, CO 23/172.

31. "Legal Intelligence," *The New Era* XV, no. 39, February 24, 1888. My examination of Harriet Charles's life relies entirely on the details available in this newspa-

per account. A full genealogical investigation of Charles's family history in other Trinidad sources might amplify the details known of her life or at least reveal the ultimate fate of her property.

32. Oyèrónké Oyewùmí, *The Invention of Women: Making an African Sense of Western Gender Discourses* (Minneapolis: University of Minnesota Press, 1997), 30.

33. Niara Sudarkasa, "The 'Status of Women' in Indigenous African Societies," in Terborg-Penn and Rushing, eds., *Women in Africa and the African Diaspora*, 84.

34. "Legal Intelligence," *The New Era* XV, no. 39, February 24, 1888. Another son reported that his mother had lived on her land only fifteen years before her death, but that may be an error because it would make the date of her settlement one year after she received the grant.

35. Bridget Brereton, *A History of Modern Trinidad, 1783–1962* (London: Heinemann Educational Books 1981), 89.

36. Ibid., 89–90.

37. Ibid., 90.

38. Ibid., 91.

39. Sudarkasa, "The 'Status of Women' in Indigenous African Societies," 85.

40. "Legal Intelligence," *The New Era* XV, no. 39, February 24, 1888.

41. Ibid.

42. Carol P. MacCormack, "Control of Land, Labor and Capital in Rural Southern Sierra Leone," in Edna G. Bay, ed., *Women and Work in Africa* (Boulder, Colo.: Westview Press, 1992), 47.

43. Claire Robertson and Iris Berger, eds., *Women and Class in Africa* (New York: Africana Publishing, 1986), 5.

44. Ibid.

45. Brereton, *History of Modern Trinidad*, 90–91.

46. Oyeronke Olajubu, *Women in the Yoruba Religious Sphere* (Albany: State University of New York Press, 2003), 102.

47. Ibid.

48. Ibid., 135n.

49. Judith Byfield, "Women, Marriage, Divorce and the Emerging Colonial State in Abeokuta (Nigeria) 1892–1904," in Dorothy L. Hodgson and Sheryl A. McCurdy, eds. *"Wicked" Women and the Reconfiguration of Gender in Africa* (Westport, Conn.: Heinemann, 2001), 28–29.

50. "Legal Intelligence," *The New Era* XV, no. 39, February 24, 1888.

51. Ibid.

52. Technically, Victoria Charles had two surviving brothers, Thomas Charles and Daniel Charles, and one half-brother, Thomas Alexander George.

53. "Legal Intelligence," *The New Era* XV, no. 39, February 24, 1888.

54. Oyewùmí, *The Invention of Women*, 52.

55. Karin Barber, *I Could Speak Until Tomorrow: Oriki, Women, and the Past in a Yoruba Town* (Edinburgh: Edinburgh University Press for the International African Institute, 1991), 135.

56. "Legal Intelligence," *The New Era* XV, no. 39, February 24, 1888.

57. See Dylan C. Pennigroth, *The Claims of Kinfolk: African American Property and Community in the Nineteenth-Century South* (Chapel Hill: University of North

Carolina Press, 2003). One note of caution might be added here related to the age of Harriet Charles when she arrived from Africa. The youngest child whose age appears in the court proceedings was the son "Daniel Charles," who was born in 1862. A full examination of average child-bearing ages for victims of the nineteenth-century Atlantic slave trade lies beyond the scope of this study. The legal report used for evidence here does not indicate definitively who was the youngest surviving child. Of the five children surviving at the time of Harriet's death, one daughter, Mary Charles, did not testify, and Thomas and Victoria Charles did not report their ages to the court. But by almost any reasonable calculation, Harriet's date of birth would fall somewhere between 1825 and 1840. If she was born as late as 1840, she may have arrived in the Caribbean as a young child—a fact that could have had some influence on the degree of cultural knowledge and expectations she would have brought from an African society of origin. Most of the conclusions here assume that she arrived in the Caribbean with sufficient prior immersion in the traditions of the society of her birth to have those traditions influence her new Caribbean life.

58. "Legal Intelligence," *The New Era* XV, no. 39, February 24, 1888.

59. Yisa Kehinde Yusuf, "Sexism in English and Yoruba," *Linguistik Online* 11 (February 2002), 17.

60. Ibid., 18.

61. Exploration of the ways that such naming practices might have functioned among this community of African immigrants in Trinidad or elsewhere in the Americas would doubtless yield a fruitful analysis. Note, for example, that in Victoria Charles's testimony about her reputed uncle, Tom Yaraba, she identified his son by the name Simon Tom. A skeptical view might see the use of the father's first name as surname as a purely practical alternative to creating an endless proliferation of people not related by blood using the ethnic surname Yaraba or the even more general African. Alternately, one could see the use of the father's first name as a way of anglicizing the names of the first Caribbean-born generation. One response to this would point out that Harriet did not chose Charles Yaraba's other surname, Baptiste, for his children, even though this would have achieved the same practical goals mentioned above.

62. Oyewùmí, *The Invention of Women*, 27.

63. Byfield, "Women, Marriage, Divorce," 29.

64. Ibid., 40; see also Sylvia Ojukutu-Macauley, "British Colonial Policy toward Education and the Roots of Gender Inequality in Sierra Leone, 1896–1961," in Catherine Higgs, Barbara A. Moss, and Earline Rice Ferguson, eds., *Stepping Forward: Black Women in Africa and the Americas* (Athens, Ohio: Ohio University Press, 2002), 3–16.

5. Orisha Worship and "Jesus Time"

1. The name Shango refers to only one of many spirits, or orishas, involved in this religion and others similar to it, both in West Africa and in the New World. Some have argued that British observers mistakenly applied the name Shango to the religion as a whole. They prefer the term orisha worship as being both more accu-

rate and a rejection of colonial misunderstandings of African-derived culture. Since the official recognition (in the mid-1980s) of orisha worship as one of Trinidad's religions, most of the individuals who have served as representatives or spokespeople for orisha believers seem to prefer the labels orisha worship or even orisha movement. However, in everyday discourse, the term Shango remains current among both practitioners and nonpractitioners. According to folklorist J. D. Elder, the term orisha work has also had currency during the twentieth century. See J. D. Elder, "The Yoruba Ancestor Cult in Gasparillo (Its Structure, Organization and Social Function in Community Cohesion)," paper presented at the University of the West Indies, Saint Augustine, Trinidad, January 20, 1969. The term orisha worship will be used here, except where written sources or oral history informants use the term Shango.

2. Author's interview with Irene E. Joseph, February 26, 1994, Caratal, Trinidad.

3. The most extensive treatment of this subject appears in Warner-Lewis's *Guinea's Other Suns.* She explores the various particular influences of Yoruba culture in Trinidad, basing her work on interviews conducted in the late 1960s and early 1970s with the descendants of Yoruba people who arrived as liberated Africans in the nineteenth century. Other commentaries on this religious influence appear in Brereton's *Race Relations in Colonial Trinidad;* and Donald Wood's *Trinidad in Transition: The Years after Slavery* (New York: Oxford University Press, 1968). Both of these place the influence of the liberated Africans in the context of an increasingly plural society in post-emancipation Trinidad.

4. John Thornton includes a chapter entitled "African Religions and Christianity in the Atlantic World" in his book *Africa and Africans in the Making of the Atlantic World,* which argues for a much more holistic treatment of the question of religion for people of African descent on both sides of the Atlantic during the era of the Atlantic slave trade. Although most studies acknowledge the differences in religious developments across the African diaspora, few analyze those differences as a central concern. All the same, several propositions have emerged as key explanations for the religious variety. In *Slave Religion: The Invisible Institution in the Antebellum South* (New York: Oxford University Press, 1978), Albert Raboteau directly addresses the contrast between the obvious African influences in Haiti, Cuba, and Brazil and the apparent dominance of Christianity in the southern United States. Raboteau emphasizes two factors, one ecclesiastical (or even theological) and the other demographic. Like many other historians and anthropologists, Raboteau points out the congruence between the Roman Catholic concept of saints and various West African concepts of multiple spirit beings beneath a high god. (This particular phenomenon has received great attention as the epitome of syncretism within candomble, vodun, and santería, all of which venerate spirits that devotees simultaneously identify as saints with Christian names such as Michael or Mary and as orishas with African names such as Ogun or Yemanja.) Protestant Christianity, particularly the experiential—as opposed to the ritual—variety preached by dissenting missionaries, offered no such cognitive or practical niche for the continued veneration by slaves of African spirits. Raboteau explores these issues in his chapter

entitled "Death of the Gods." For the delineation of the specific factors that explain differences between the U.S. and other parts of the diaspora, see 87–92.

Raboteau also focuses on the unique demography of the U.S. slave population. Unlike other New World slave societies that relied on new shipments from Africa for their continued labor supply, the U.S. slave population became a self-reproducing one, replenishing itself by the birth of slave children more than by new African arrivals. By the late eighteenth century, African-born slaves constituted a minority, and after the abolition of the legal slave trade in 1808, such people became a rarity, despite illegal imports. Thus, scholars argue, U.S. slave society did not provide the context for the maintenance (or invigoration) of African religious knowledge by continually arriving immigrants.

5. See for example Monica Schuler, "Akan Slave Rebellions in the British Caribbean," *Savacou* 1 (1970): 8–31; Craton, *Testing the Chains*; and Michael Mullin, *Africa in America: Slave Acculturation and Resistance in the American South and the British Caribbean 1736–1831* (Chicago: University of Illinois Press, 1992).

6. The combined effects of formal recognition of orisha worship by the Trinidad government and Trinidad's Black Power movement of the 1970s has attracted a small but significant number of followers to the orisha movement who have adopted the religion as a preferred, or more authentic, spiritual practice for people of African descent. Many such latter-day converts downplay the mixing that has occurred between African origins and Roman Catholicism. Rather, they seek to cast orisha worship as the virtually pure epitome of cultural self-determination by Africans in diaspora.

7. John Brownell, Nassau, Bahamas, to Revd. Messr. Morley, Townley, and James, London, September 29, 1829, MMS 4C: West Indies (Various) 1833–1906, Box 128, File 1829, WMMS Papers.

8. The Spanish term *cedula* here denotes a population decree for the colony of Trinidad. For a detailed explanation of this decree, see Brereton, *History of Modern Trinidad,* 13.

9. Ibid., 22.

10. For the Yoruba presence in Trinidad, see Warner-Lewis, *Guinea's Other Suns.* For the Bahamas, see Eneas, *Bain Town.*

11. Warner-Lewis, *Guinea's Other Suns,* 37.

12. Elder, "The Yoruba Ancestor Cult in Gasparillo," 7.

13. For British colonies, legal slave-trading from Africa ended with the 1807 abolition law, and there was no large illegal trade. Therefore, the latest immigrants from Africa—those most likely responsible for family memories and cultural practices found in the twentieth century—were mostly liberated Africans.

14. Author's interview with Sylvia Ampson, February 24, 1994.

15. Ibid. Another Trinidadian, Norman Carr of Saint Mary's Village, Moruga, confirmed this characterization of Mayo in my 1994 interview with him.

16. "The Ward of Montserrat," *The Trinidad Chronicle,* no. 260, June 7, 1867.

17. Editorial, *The Trinidad Chronicle,* no. 337, March 3, 1868.

18. Williams, *Guide to African Villages in New Providence,* 9; and *Settlements in New Providence,* 53. The latter publication by the Bahamas Department of Archives

notes that between 1840 and 1850 a black businessman, Charles H. Bain, purchased the Bain Town land, which he then divided for resale "at moderate prices to African people."

19. Isaac Whitehouse, Nassau, Bahamas, to Rev. Elijah Hoole, WMMS, London, July 27, 1850, MMS 4C: West Indies (Various), 1833–1906, Box 218, File 1850, WMMS Papers.

20. Eneas, *Bain Town,* 28.

21. Ibid.

22. Ibid., 32–33.

23. "[An Appeal:] Mission at Montserrat, Trinidad, among Liberated Africans and Their Descendants," October 8, 1869, enclosed in W. Bovell Laurie, Rector of St. Philip's and St. Peter's Trinidad, to Society for the Propagation of the Gospel, London, June 17, 1870, Original Letters Received 1850–1938, D40 2A, West Indies 1861–1874, [Diocese of] Barbados 1868–1870, Archives of the United Society for the Propagation of the Gospel, Rhodes House Library, Oxford.

24. During the 1830s, at least two Anglican missionaries also worked in south Trinidad under the sponsorship of the multidenominational Church Missionary Society. At first glance, it seems possible that such Anglican missionaries could account for the nominal baptism of the Montserrat Africans, but several factors make this unlikely. First, most of Trinidad's liberated Africans arrived during the 1840s, after the heaviest years of activity documented for these missionaries in the CMS archives. Second, and perhaps more important, these CMS priests appear to have focused their efforts around Savanna Grande, located many miles to the south of the Montserrat hills. For documentation of the activities of these Anglican missionaries, see Correspondence, J. G. Mulhauser and A. W. Eckel, Papers of the Church Missionary Society, CWO Series, Special Collections, Main Library, University of Birmingham, Birmingham, UK.

25. Editorial, *The Trinidad Chronicle,* no. 337, March 3, 1868.

26. Richard Rawle, Bishop of Trinidad, Bishop's Address, Council of the Church of England in Trinidad Annual Meeting, July 13, 1876, Original Letters Received 1850–1938, D 44B, West Indies 1876, Archives of the United Society for the Propagation of the Gospel.

27. See George E. Simpson, *Religious Cults of the Caribbean: Trinidad, Jamaica, and Haiti* (San Juan: Institute of Caribbean Studies, 1970).

28. Elder, "The Yoruba Ancestor Cult in Gasparillo," 10–14.

29. Author's interview with Sylvia Ampson, February 24, 1994.

30. Correspondence, Charles Penney, Nassau, Bahamas, to General Secretaries, WMMS, January 10, 1832, MMS. 4C, West Indies (Various), 1833–1906, Box 131, File 1832, WMMS Papers.

31. Ibid.

32. Correspondence, John Corlett, Nassau, Bahamas, May 22, 1839, MMS. 4C, West Indies (Various), 1833–1906, File 1839, WMMS Papers.

33. "Letter to the Editor," *The Nassau Guardian,* February 20, 1993. Jacob Shaw wrote these words as part of an ongoing dispute in the Bahamian church over whether or not to separate from the regional Methodist District of the Caribbean

and Central America. That formal separation became a reality later in 1993, but legal and other disputes are still pending. Notably for this study, a few of the most prominent descendants of the liberated African founders have found themselves separated from Wesley Methodist as a result of their opposition to the recent decision.

34. 1844 Synod Report, Bahamas Circuit, cited in William Makepeace, "A History of Methodism in Grant's Town, Nassau, New Providence, Bahamas 1847–1947," in *Wesley Methodist Church: A Souvenir of the Centenary 1847–1947* (Nassau, 1947), 17.

35. N.a., "Leaders and Church Officers," in *Wesley Methodist Church,* 17. In interviews conducted during the 1993 and 1994, both Cleveland Eneas and Gaspare Weir—a former Wesley Methodist Church trustee—characterized this essay as deriving from the collective knowledge of various church members present in 1947.

36. *Wesley Methodist Church,* 42; author's interview with Gaspare Weir, September 24, 1994, Grant's Town, Nassau, Bahamas.

37. Grants for Adelaide Lots, Book L4 Registry, Department of Lands and Surveys, Commonwealth of the Bahamas, Nassau, Bahamas.

38. *Wesley Methodist Church,* 42. Author's note: Alliday Adderley is my paternal ancestor.

39. *The Nassau Guardian* XLI, no. 4572, September 30, 1885.

40. Ibid.

41. Drysdale, *In Sunny Lands,* 12.

42. Ibid.

43. For descriptions of the elements of "shouting," see Raboteau, *Slave Religion,* 66–73, 245, 339–340n69. Raboteau's research focuses on the United States, but he also cites the work of other scholars who have included descriptions of shouting or similar religious behavior in the Bahamas, Jamaica, and Haiti. See ibid., 70.

44. Drysdale, *In Sunny Lands,* 13.

45. Ibid.

46. "Letter," *The Nassau Guardian* XLI, no. 4520, April 1, 1885.

47. *The Nassau Guardian:* XLI, no. 4519, March 28, 1885; "(From a Correspondent), San Salvador, May 20, 1885," XLI, no. 4539, June 6, 1885; and "Hysteria," XLI, no. 4542, June 17, 1885. Two islands in the central Bahamas—San Salvador and Cat Island—have a complicated naming and re-naming history. From the eighteenth century until the 1920s, present-day Cat Island was regularly known as San Salvador, while present-day San Salvador was known as Watlings Island. The reports of religious "hysteria" in 1885 came from present-day Cat Island.

48. *The Nassau Guardian* XLI, no. 4519, March 28, 1885.

49. It also seems possible that the participants at Cat Island belonged to the Baptist faith, and therefore Wilshere might have a felt a duty to defend them in the face of criticism from the competing Anglican denomination. In his letter, Wilshere criticized the Anglican rector for referring to the Church of England as "the church," thus implying a lesser degree of importance or legitimacy for other Christian sects. Wilshere also boasts of having "paid a number of visits to the island and knowing every settlement." See "Letter to the Editor," *The Nassau Guardian* XLI, no. 4520, April 1, 1885.

50. Historian David V. Trotman draws a similar conclusion in a brief study of orisha worship and liberated African settlement in Trinidad and British Guiana. See "The Yoruba and Orisha Worship in Trinidad and British Guiana: 1838–1870," *African Studies Review* XIX, no. 2 (September 1976): 1–17. Trotman contrasts the development of widespread Yoruba-derived orisha worship in Trinidad with the absence of that development in British Guiana despite the fact that both colonies received a significant number of free Yoruba immigrants during the mid-nineteenth century. He emphasizes the relative isolation of liberated African settlements in parts of Trinidad and the presence of a large number of French planters and their former slaves who migrated there from the francophone Caribbean. Trotman notes the syncretic meeting of Roman Catholic and Yoruba beliefs and practices among the francophone population and the role the francophone group played in disrupting a coherent British cultural influence on the new immigrants. (He argues, for example, that the use of French patois among the population of African descent automatically disadvantaged any British Protestant missionary effort.) He contrasts this Trinidad experience with settlement patterns in British Guiana, where most liberated Africans were confined to a relatively small area near the coast where they not only mixed more freely with the population of former slaves but also faced more-intensive efforts from both the British colonial establishment and Protestant missionaries.

Trotman's work differs most significantly from this study in that his article does not challenge the implication that the development of orisha worship constituted a preferable path of acculturation or perhaps a path with greater African cultural integrity. (In an especially striking comment, he refers to the "de-Africanization" of the immigrants in British Guiana—an adjective that, while having some justification, would certainly seem an overstatement with respect to the liberated African Methodists of Grant's Town in the Bahamas.) Consistent with the focus on orisha worship in his work, Trotman offers little insight into the specific nature of the religious practices liberated Africans in British Guiana developed.

51. Celia R. Fullerton, "A Cross Cultural Comparison Between 'Shango' in Trinidad and 'Pocomania' in Jamaica" (B.A. thesis, University of the West Indies, Saint Augustine, Trinidad, 1970), 21.

52. John C. Richardson, Port-of-Spain, Trinidad, to General Secretaries, WMMS, December 8, 1859, MMS. 4C, West Indies (Various), 1833–1906, Box 228, File 1859, WMMS Papers.

53. Ibid.

54. Massé, *Diaries of the Abbé Armand Massé, 1878–1883*, 2:217.

55. Warner-Lewis, *Guinea's Other Suns*, 22, 71.

56. Author's interview with Ucarl DaSilva, February 18 and 25, 1994, Diego Martin, Trinidad; author's interview with Telpha Achille, February 25, 1994, Teixera Street, Diego Martin, Trinidad; and author's interview with McDonald Asseverro, March 11, 1994, Covigne Road, Diego Martin, Trinidad.

57. Stephen D. Glazier, *Marchin' the Pilgrims Home: A Study of the Spiritual Baptists of Trinidad* (1983; Salem, Wisconsin: Sheffield Publishing Company, 1991), 3.

58. Ibid.

59. For descriptions of the nature of Spiritual Baptist beliefs and practice, see Glazier, *Marchin' the Pilgrims Home,* 23–72; Eudora Thomas, *A History of the Shouter Baptists in Trinidad and Tobago* (Tacarigua, Trinidad: Calaloux Publications, 1987), 47–60; and Simpson, *Religious Cults of the Caribbean,* 142–153.

60. Jeannette H. Henney, "The Shakers of Saint Vincent: A Stable Religion," in Erika Bourguignon, ed., *Religion, Altered States of Consciousness, and Social Change* (Columbus: Ohio State University Press, 1973), 224, 230.

61. Glazier, *Marchin' the Pilgrims Home,* 33.

62. One intriguing comparison from beyond the Caribbean involves the Aladura movement of western Nigeria and Sierra Leone. In a University of the West Indies Caribbean Studies thesis, Ian Anthony Taylor introduces this comparison and explores a meditative and trance-involving rite in the Aladura churches of Sierra Leone that is very similar to Spiritual Baptist mourning in Trinidad. See Taylor, "The Rite of Mourning in the Spiritual Baptist Faith" (B.A. thesis, University of the West Indies, Saint Augustine, Trinidad, 1986), 22–27. This comparison clearly warrants further exploration. Like the numerous forms of Christianity in the African diaspora, the Aladura movement (which historian H. W. Turner dates to the early twentieth century) constitutes a product of cultural interaction between African religious systems and the Protestant Christianity introduced by European missionaries. See H. W. Turner, *History of an African Independent Church: The Church of the Lord (Aladura),* 2 vols. (New York: Oxford University Press, 1967).

63. Charles Gullick, "Shakers and Ecstasy," *New Fire* (Oxford: Society of St. John the Evangelist, 1971), 9: 7–11, cited in Glazier, *Marchin' the Pilgrims Home,* 37.

64. Dickinson, Dickinson, and Dowd, *A Winter Picnic,* 128. It is interesting to note that the Dickinsons and S. E. Dowd acknowledge that when planning their own holiday and their book, they took some inspiration from William Drysdale's travel account *In Sunny Lands* (1885), which included its own detailed description of his visit to Wesley Methodist Church in Grants Town.

65. Ibid., 129. For the biblical reference, see Revelations 1:9–10 (King James version), which reads: "I, John, who also am your brother, and companion in tribulation, and in Christ, was in the isle that is called Patmos, for the word of God, and for the testimony of Jesus Christ. I was in the Spirit on the Lord's day, and heard behind me a great voice, as of a trumpet." This passage begins John's description of his lengthy visions concerning the power of God and the fate of Christianity.

66. Cited in Dickinson, Dickinson, and Dowd, *A Winter Picnic,* 130.

67. John W. Work, *American Negro Songs and Spirituals* (New York: Bonanza Books, 1940), cited in Mechal Sobel, *Trabelin' On: the Slave Journey to an Afro-Baptist Faith* (1979; Princeton, N.J.: Princeton University Press, 1988), 108.

68. For example, in one of the more recent analyses of Baptist Christianity in the African diaspora (and one of the few truly comparative studies), William Pitts cites the use of the term "mourning" solely in reference to the Trinidad case. See William F. Pitts, *Old Ship of Zion: The Afro-Baptist Ritual in the African Diaspora* (New York: Oxford University Press, 1993), 173.

69. Aloysius Bernard Joseph, "The Spiritual Baptists of Trinidad and Tobago: A Study of the Origin and Present Operation of their Religion" (B.A. thesis, University of the West Indies, Saint Augustine, Trinidad, 1983), 25–29.

See Daniel 10:2–5 (King James version): "In those days I Daniel was mourning three full weeks. I ate no pleasant bread, neither came flesh nor wine in my mouth, neither did I anoint myself at all, till three whole weeks were fulfilled. And in the four and twentieth day of the first month, as I was by the side of the great river. . . . I lifted up mine eyes, and looked, and behold a certain man clothed in linen, whose loins were girded with fine gold of Uphaz."

70. Melville J. Herskovits and Frances S. Herskovits, *Trinidad Village* (New York: Alfred Knopf, 1947), 167, 342–345.

71. Glazier, *Marchin' the Pilgrims Home*, 38.

72. Ibid. For his descriptions of the history and nature of the 'Merikan Baptist communities, Glazier refers to John O. Stewart, "Mission and Leadership among the 'Merikan' Baptists of Trinidad," in Norman Whitten, ed., *Contributions to the Latin American Anthropology Group* (Washington D.C.: Latin American Anthropology Group, 1976), 17–25. Glazier also points to Bridget Brereton's *Race Relations in Colonial Trinidad*, in which she too doubts the linkage between the immigrant North American Baptists and the Spiritual Baptist movement. See Glazier, *Marchin' the Pilgrims Home*, 142.

73. W. H. Gamble, *Trinidad: Historical and Descriptive: A Narrative of Nine Years' Residence in the Island. With Special Reference to Christian Missions* (London: Yates and Alexander for the Author, 1866), 97–99.

74. Ibid., 116.

75. Demographer A. Meredith John's study of Trinidadian slave populations in the early nineteenth century finds that in 1813 most of the population of African-born slaves consisted of people aged 20 years and older. Thus, by 1863, the population of African-born former slaves would have been mostly people aged 60 and older. However, John also provides a population projection that hypothesizes that by 1863, the entire African-descended population would have consisted largely of people aged 50 years and younger. These calculations clearly imply that at the time of Gamble's writing, most African-born former slaves would have died. If this projection is correct, references to the African-born would most likely have referred to liberated African immigrants. See A. Meredith John, *The Plantation Slaves of Trinidad, 1783–1816: A Mathematical and Demographic Enquiry* (New York: Cambridge University Press, 1988), 48–49, 57, 169.

76. Gamble, *Trinidad: Historical and Descriptive*, 116.

77. Ibid. Gamble reports that the parents of William Carr migrated to Trinidad from the Bahamas during the final decades of slavery. As emancipation loomed during the early nineteenth century, several slaveholders obtained permission from the Colonial Office to transport slaves from marginally profitable colonies such as the Bahamas to colonies with more virgin land and greater economic promise, such as Trinidad and British Guiana. It remains unclear from Gamble's description whether the Carr family converted to the Baptist faith in the Bahamas or after their arrival in

Trinidad. The timing of their conversion, however, would not have altered the nature of the "chiefly African" congregation Carr "presided over" at the settlement of Matilda Boundary.

78. Glazier, *Marchin' the Pilgrims Home*, 39.

79. Rosita Forbes, *A Unicorn in the Bahamas* (New York: E. P. Dutton & Co., Inc., 1940), 193–194.

80. Ibid.

81. Max R. Deslèves, *Les îles de juin* (Paris: Éditions Berger-Levrault, 1963), 186–187.

82. Ibid.

83. Ibid.

6. "Powers superior to those of other witches"

1. See various works by both historians and anthropologists such as Edward Kamau Brathwaite, *The Folk Culture of the Slaves in Jamaica* (London: New Beacon Press, 1981); Mary Turner, *Slaves and Missionaries: The Disintegration of Jamaican Slave Society, 1787–1834* (Urbana: University of Illinois Press, 1982); Robert J. Stewart, *Religion and Society in Post-Emancipation Jamaica* (Knoxville: University of Tennessee Press, 1992); George Eaton Simpson, *Religious Cults of the Caribbean: Trinidad, Jamaica, and Haiti* (Rio Piedras: Institute of Caribbean Studies, University of Puerto Rico, 1980); Joseph M. Murphy, *Santería: An African Religion in America* (Boston: Beacon Press, 1988); and Jay D. Dobbin, *The Jombee Dance of Montserrat: A Study of Trance Ritual in the West Indies* (Columbus: Ohio State University Press, 1986).

2. Orlando Patterson, *The Sociology of Slavery*, cited in Basil C. Hedrick and Jeanette E. Stephens, *It's A Natural Fact: Obeah in the Bahamas*, Miscellaneous Series no. 39 (University of Northern Colorado, Museum of Anthropology, 1977), 5.

3. Timothy McCartney, *Ten, Ten the Bible Ten: Obeah in the Bahamas*, cited in Hedrick and Stephens, *It's A Natural Fact*, 6.

4. "Report of the Lords of the Committee of the Council appointed for the consideration of all matters relating to Trade and Foreign Plantations, London 1789," cited in Joseph Williams, *Voodoos and Obeahs*, 110–111.

5. De Verteuil, *Trinidad: Its Geography, Natural Resources, Administration, Present Condition and Prospects*, 161.

6. Ibid., 163.

7. Marie Bertrand Cothonay, *Trinidad: Journal d'un Missionaire Dominicain des Antilles Anglaises* (Paris: Victor Rétaux et Fils, Libraires-Éditeurs, 1893), 124 (author's translation).

8. Ibid.

9. "African Tales (Rada) Black Magic—Collected by A. T. Carr," in *African Notes*, Andrew Carr Papers, National Archives of Trinidad and Tobago, Port-of-Spain, Trinidad. Excerpt appears in notes from an interview Carr conducted with Henry Antoine on November 28, 1951,

10. "Port-of-Spain Police Court, Monday, May 11," *The Trinidad Chronicle,* no. 358, May 15, 1868.

11. Ibid.

12. Ibid.

13. "Couva Police Court, Saturday, October 3," *The Trinidad Chronicle,* no. 399, October 6, 1868.

14. Ibid.

15. Ibid.

16. "Editorial," *The Trinidad Chronicle,* no. 399, October 6, 1868.

17. "Couva Police Court, Saturday, October 3," *The Trinidad Chronicle,* no. 399, October 6, 1868.

18. For a condensed contemporary description of the multiple facets of obeah practice, see John A. Holm and Alison Watt Shilling, *Dictionary of Bahamian English* (Cold Spring, New York: Lexik House Publishers, 1982), 145. For a more lengthy descriptive study that explores these various manifestations during the eighteenth and nineteenth centuries, see Joseph J. Williams, *Voodoos and Obeahs: Phases of West Indian Witchcraft* (1932; New York: AMS Press, 1970).

19. "Couva Police Court, Saturday, October 3."

20. Ibid.

21. Ibid.

22. Ibid.

23. "The Witch of Couva," *The Trinidad Chronicle,* no. 409, November 10, 1868.

24. Charles Kingsley, *At Last: A Christmas in the West Indies* (1871; London: Macmillan and Co. Ltd., 1896), 238–239.

25. Ibid.

26. *The New Era,* ns., XVI: "The Laventille Tragedy," no. 34, January 18, 1889; "Signs of the Times," no. 34, January 18, 1889; and "The Laventille Tragedy," no. 35, January 25, 1889.

27. "Signs of the Times."

28. "The Laventille Tragedy," *The New Era,* n.s., XVI, no. 36, February 1, 1889.

29. "The Laventille Tragedy," January 18, 1889.

30. Wyatt MacGaffey, *Religion and Society in Central Africa: The BaKongo of Lower Zaire,* (Chicago: The University of Chicago Press, 1986), 130.

31. See for example James W. Fernandez, *Bwiti: An Ethnography of the Religious Imagination in Africa* (Princeton, N.J.: Princeton University Press, 1982), 399–408, 550–553, 645–647; and John S. Mbiti, *African Religions and Philosophy,* 2nd ed. (London: Heinemann International, 1990), 51, 190.

32. "The Laventille Tragedy," February 1, 1889.

33. "The Laventille Tragedy," January 18, 1889.

34. "The Laventille Tragedy," February 1, 1889.

35. Ibid.

36. "The Laventille Tragedy," *The New Era,* n.s., XVI, no. 36, March 1, 1889.

37. "Dreams and Dollars," *The Trinidad Chronicle,* no. 202, October 12, 1866.

38. See for example "Editorial," *The Trinidad Chronicle,* no. 399, October 6, 1868.

39. The Spiritual Baptist Church was banned from 1917 to 1951 by a colonial law known as the Shouter Prohibition Ordinance. Colonial authorities condemned this variant of Christianity for many reasons including its obvious African influences, and its loud worship services. The Shouter Prohibition Ordinance was repealed in 1951. In 1996 the Trinidadian government designated March 30 as an annual holiday known as Spiritual Baptist/Shouter Baptist Liberation Day to commemorate the struggles of the church against colonial persecution. See National Library and Information System Authority of Trinidad and Tobago, "Spiritual/Shouter Baptists of Trinidad and Tobago," available online at http://library2.nalis.gov.tt/Default.aspx?PageContentID=272&tabid=174. The Yoruba-derived practice of orisha worship was officially recognized as a religion by the government of Trinidad and Tobago in 1983.

40. The song narrates the protests of a man who is talking with a woman who seeks to use obeah to induce him to marry her. The man insists that all such schemes will fail and advises the woman that instead of using obeah, she should pay attention to matters such as personal grooming in her attempts to win a husband. As a kind of coup de grâce, the narrator further declares that in any case, she could never succeed in using obeah against him because the famous Papa Neezer—the obeah man of all obeah men—is his own grandfather.

41. Jack Warner, "Obeah: Fact or Fiction?" (B.A. thesis, University of the West Indies, Saint Augustine, Trinidad, 1969). For specific discussion of the distinction between the town of Moruga and the Moruga Road area, see author's interview with Otto Gonzalez, Sr., February 24, 1994, Gasparillo, Trinidad.

42. Author's interview with Joseph Hudlin, March 9, 1994, Lengua, Trinidad.

43. Ibid.

44. Author's interview with Priscilla Taylor, March 9, 1994, Lengua, Trinidad.

45. Compare the descriptions of Otto Gonzalez and Winifred Salazar Lendore. Author's interviews with Otto Gonzalez, Sr., February 24, 1994, Gasparillo, Trinidad; and Winifred Salazar Lendore, February 26, 1994, Tortuga, Trinidad. Gonzalez briefly recounts the story he heard in which Papa Neezer provided some nondescript curative assistance to a man doctors had been unable to cure. Meanwhile, Salazar Lendore and her niece, Naomi Toby (who was also interviewed), describe in some detail the preparation of an orisha celebration at the request of individual seeking healing from a difficult illness.

46. Warner, "Obeah: Fact or Fiction?"

47. Marion Bethel, "The Passion," in Bethel, *Guanahani, Mi Amor y Otros Poemas,* traducción de David Chericián (Havana: Casa de las Américas, 1994).

48. Jacqualine C. Rahming, "The History and Background of Fox Hill with Songs" (Teaching certificate thesis, College of the Bahamas, Nassau, 1974), 32–33. To the best of my knowledge, Zechariah Adderley bore no relation to Alliday Adderley, whose life history appears in Chapter 5.

49. Ibid., 36–37.

50. Author's interview with Rev. Dr. Phillip Rahming, May 1994, Bahamas Department of Archives, Nassau, Bahamas.

51. Ibid.

52. Another noteworthy statement of Pa Bay's identity as an obeah man appears in the transcript of an interview conducted by historian Gail Saunders with an elderly Fox Hill resident in August 1970:

Q: Do you believe in obeah, at all?

A: Obeah? Yeah.

Q: You know Pa Bay used to do . . . ?

A: Yeah, right, he supposed to be my uncle.

Q: Oh, he's dead now?

A: And I don't like to hear his name call believe me. [Laugh]

Q: Why is that?

A: Well, he is my uncle.

Q: Quite famous?

A: Yeah, but according to the name what he carrying, I don't like to hear that because you know God ain't got no dealing with that.

Unpublished transcript of interview with Virginia Brice, August 4, 1970, Department of Archives, Nassau, Bahamas.

53. Gladys Manuel, *Historical Notes on the Fox Hill Community* (Nassau, Bahamas: n.p., 1988), 1–2. It is important to note that in this discussion, Manuel addresses only the distribution of family names *within* the Fox Hill community. Her work in no way implies the extension of particular African ethnic connections to the same surnames elsewhere in the Bahamas. In her thesis, Jacqualine Rahming also discusses the existence of the different named areas within Fox Hill, but she does not discuss the distribution of surnames and does not explicitly link Pa Bay to any particular named area. See Rahming, "The History and Background of Fox Hill," 22–23.

7. "Deeply attached to his native country"

1. Daniel Wilshere, 1878–1892, Missionary Journals and Correspondence 1792–1914, West Indies, Archives of the Baptist Missionary Society, Angus Library, Regents Park College, Oxford University. The details of this intriguing case have been published in a textbook aimed at secondary schools and the junior college in the Bahamas: Philip Cash, Shirley Gordon, and Gail Saunders, *Sources of Bahamian History* (London: Macmillan Education, Limited, 1991).

2. For a discussion of the formation and function of friendly societies in the Bahamas, see Howard Johnson, "Friendly Societies in the Bahamas," *Slavery and Abolition* 12, no. 3 (December 1991): 183–199.

3. The details of the establishment of the various groups of Baptists in the Bahamas are presented in Antonina Canzoneri's "A History of the Baptist Denomination in the Bahamas" (1972), unpublished monograph, Bahamas Department of Archives. See also Michael Carrington Symonette and Antonia Canzoneri, *Baptists in the Bahamas: An Historical Review* (El Paso, Tex.: Baptist Spanish Publishing House, 1977).

4. The present headstones are new ones erected during the 1980s with an elaborate memorial to Wilshere. I am uncertain whether either or both of the bodies actually lie in the churchyard. But this fact is perhaps unimportant, given that although Wilshere worked with numerous congregations in the Bahamas and founded the Bahamas Baptist Union in 1892, to my knowledge, Mount Carey is the only church with such a prominent marker in his memory.

5. "Died," *The Nassau Guardian* LIV, no. 5928, August 27, 1898.

6. Author's interview with anonymous oral historian, April 1994, Nassau, Bahamas.

7. John H. Weeks, *Among the Primitive Bakongo* (1914; New York: Negro Universities Press, 1969), 298.

8. See Wyatt MacGaffey, *Religion and Society in Central Africa: The BaKongo of Lower Zaire* (Chicago: University of Chicago Press, 1986).

9. King Leopold II took individual control of an area of territory in the Kongo region in 1885 and, with the acquiescence of other European governments, ran the area as his own personal colony until 1908. After decades of financial impropriety and physical abuse of residents, King Leopold turned the territory which he had called the Congo Free State over to the control of the Belgian government, which renamed the area the Belgian Congo.

10. Franklin W. Knight and Margaret W. Crahan, "The African Migration and the Origins of an Afro-American Society and Culture," in Knight and Crahan, *Africa and the Caribbean*, 4.

11. Christopher Fyfe, *A History of Sierra Leone* (New York: Oxford University Press, 1962), 230–231. Fyfe explains that most liberated Africans never even left the Freetown shipyard before transfer to the Caribbean as immigrant workers.

12. John Corlett, Nassau, New Providence, to General Secretaries, WMMS, May 13, 1844, MMS. 4C, West Indies (Various) 1833–1906, Box 218, File 1844, Fiche Number 27 1315, WMMS Papers.

13. *The Trinidad Chronicle*, n.s., no. 503, June 23, 1874.

14. Ibid.

15. I am indebted in my thinking here to a conversation with Monica Schuler. Following her study of liberated Africans in Jamaica (*"Alas, Alas Kongo"*), Schuler moved on to research concerning ideas about returning to Africa among people of African descent in both Jamaica and Guyana during the nineteenth and twentieth centuries. Schuler suggests that the idea of return perhaps has had greatest resonance or popularity in Jamaica because this colony had the largest percentage of liberated Africans who received formal offers of repatriation from the British government.

16. Benitez-Rojo, *The Repeating Island*, 70. In seeking to use the plantation as metaphor, Benitez-Rojo perhaps overstates the singularity of this particular institution in the attempt by slave societies to "deculturate" African slaves. Certainly no other institution played as great a role in the New World effort to convert African people into chattel. However, the idea of a "deculturating regimen" would seem to apply equally well to many aspects of slave society beyond the plantation.

17. I am indebted in my thinking here to anthropologist colleague Yvonne Teh, who directed me to the work of contemporary West and West-Central African anthropologists such as Karin Barber and others who have considered ideas such as "the invention of Yoruba ethnicity" as relatively recent ethnic categorizations that have been popularized in many ways as a result of interaction with Europeans.

18. Minutes of Evidence before a Committee of His Majesty's Council for the Purpose of Attaining a More Correct Knowledge of the Negro Character, as Exhibited in this Colony, in a State of Slavery and of Freedom, February 1, 1825, enclosure in Governor Ralph Woodford, Trinidad, to Earl Bathurst, Principal Secretary of State, Colonial Department, June 12, 1825, CO 295/66.

19. Ibid.

20. John Dougan, Commissioner of Enquiry into the State of Captured Negroes in the West Indies, to Colonial Office, March 14, 1823, CO 318/84.

21. It is not clear how this specific word gained such widespread currency among African slaves throughout the New World. Most likely, this linguistic development reflects the usage of Europeans involved in slave trafficking.

22. For an efficient narrative history of the African colonization movement, see P. J. Staudenraus, *The African Colonization Movement 1816–1865* (New York: Columbia University Press, 1961).

23. Some of the African-American opponents of the Liberia emigration plan criticized the American Colonization Society for attempting to send free black people from the United States "into the savage wilds of Africa." See Staudenraus, *The African Colonization Movement*, 32.

24. For a description of the location of the "little village of New Guinea," see Johann David Schoepf, *Travels in the Confederation (1783–1784)*, edited by Alfred J. Morrison, 2 vols. (Philadelphia: William J. Campbell, 1911), cited in Thelma Peterson Peters, "The American Loyalists and the Plantation Period in the Bahama Islands" (Ph.D. diss., University of Florida, Gainesville, 1960), 49. The description of the location of New Guinea closely matches the location more commonly described in eighteenth- and nineteenth-century documents as Creek Village. The names possibly refer to the same settlement.

25. Notes of Chief Justice William Vesey Munnings concerning The King vs. William John Peters, Bahamas, In the General Court, Trinity Term 1833, enclosure in Lieutenant Governor Blaney T. Balfour, Bahamas, to Lord Stanley, Principal Secretary of State, Colonial Department, September 4, 1833, CO 23/89.

26. Charmaine Fletcher, "Emily Scope: c. 1875–1953. Daughter of Liberated Africans, Blackwoman, Wife and Mother" (B.A. thesis, University of the West Indies, Saint Augustine, Trinidad, 1989), 13.

27. Maureen Warner, "Africans in Nineteenth Century Trinidad," *African Studies Association of the West Indies Bulletin* 5 (1972): 48.

28. Fletcher, "Emily Scope," 29.

29. Author's interview with Winifred Salazar Lendore, February 26, 1994.

30. Warner, "Africans in Nineteenth Century Trinidad," 48.

31. Schuler, *"Alas, Alas, Kongo,"* 94.

32. Warner, "Africans in Nineteenth Century Trinidad," 48. Warner does not indicate any written source for this information. Over the centuries of the Atlantic trade, a small percentage of those who were enslaved committed suicide in this fashion. Perhaps Warner simply speculates that at least some liberated Africans did the same. It is also possible that oral history informants provided such information based on stories passed down from their nineteenth-century ancestors.

33. De Verteuil, *Trinidad: Its Geography, Natural Resources, Administration, Present Condition, and Prospects,* 2nd ed. (London: Cassell & Company, Limited, 1884), 342.

34. "Arouca," *The Trinidad Chronicle,* n.s., no. 223, October 17, 1871.

35. C. M. Vowell and John Young, "Report of the Liberated African Establishment at Saint Helena," enclosure in Governor Patrick Ross, Saint Helena, to Earl Grey, Principal Secretary of State, Colonial Department, June 12, 1849, CO 247/72.

36. Alexander Murray, Collector of Customs, Bahamas, to Governor Charles Cameron, Bahamas, 30 September 1815, enclosure in Governor Cameron to Earl Bathurst, Principal Secretary of State, Colonial Department, October 2, 1815, CO 23/62.

37. Quite often, for example, mourners report that their guide has provided them with a biblical verse or other phrase to use as a personal mantra in times of doubt or crisis.

38. Taylor, "The Rite of Mourning in the Spiritual Baptist Faith," 15. Another thesis addresses mourning travel to Africa and India but does not discuss the link between these visions and the immigrant origins of Trinidad's population. See Aloysius Bernard Joseph, "The Spiritual Baptists of Trinidad and Tobago: A Study of the Origin and Present Operation of Their Religion" (B.A. thesis, University of the West Indies, Saint Augustine, Trinidad, 1983).

39. Taylor, "The Rite of Mourning in the Spiritual Baptist Faith," 15.

40. Stephen Glazier reports that church leaders would sometimes encourage mourners to prefer one locale over another for their visions. He described churches where all mourners claimed that their spirit traveled only to China or only to India. He also describes one leader who privileged Africa so much that whenever a mourner claimed to have traveled to China or India, the leader would interrupt his tale, effectively coercing the individual to change the location of his or her vision to Africa. See Glazier, *Marchin' The Pilgrims Home,* 57.

41. Schuler, *"Alas, Alas, Kongo,"* 96.

42. Ibid., 95.

43. Ibid., 96. Schuler also considers the possibility that salt earned its negative symbolism as a result of the brine-preserved fish and pork that slaves and other working-class Jamaicans often received as food from their masters or employers.

44. Author's interview with Winifred Salazar Lendore, February 26, 1994.

45. Catherine Alves, "The Shango Religious Cult in Trinidad through the Eyes of Two Informants" (B.A. thesis, University of the West Indies, Saint Augustine, Trinidad, 1982), 10–13. According to Alves, her informant Francis Charles was a descendant of nineteenth-century Yoruba immigrants to Trinidad.

46. Ibid., 22–23.

47. For discussion of the nature of "saraka" or "sakara" feasts, see Herskovits and Herskovits, *Trinidad Village;* and Annette E. Collins, "The Rites of Passage in Trinidad and Tobago" (B.A. thesis, University of the West Indies, Saint Augustine, Trinidad, 1969). Although Collins refers to the work of Herskovits and Herskovits, she seems to have corroborated the information with interviews she conducted during the late 1960s. In an interview conducted in January 1994, Laura Toby of the town of Morne Diablo in south Trinidad described the exclusion of salt from saraka feasts she observed as a child in the mid-twentieth century.

48. Author's interview with Winifred Salazar Lendore, February 26, 1994.

49. Author's interview with Naomi Toby and Winifred Salazar Lendore, March 5, 1994, Tortuga, Trinidad.

50. Holm and Shilling, *Dictionary of Bahamian English,* 97. Holm and Shilling cite several references from studies of African-American people in the United States. For an extensive treatment of this subject, see David J. Hufford, *The Terror that Comes in the Night: An Experience-Centered Study of Supernatural Assault Traditions* (Philadelphia: University of Pennsylvania Press, 1982).

51. Claudia Harvey, "Seven Supernatural Characters of Trinidad Folklore" (B.A. thesis, University of the West Indies, Saint Augustine, Trinidad, 1969), 4, 9.

52. I am indebted for this information to literature professor Ian Gregory Strachan, author of *Paradise and Plantation: Tourism and Anglophone Caribbean Culture* (Charlottesville: University of Virginia Press, 2002).

53. Arnold Itwaru, "Exile and Commemoration," in Frank Birbalsingh, ed., *Indenture and Exile: The Indo-Caribbean Experience* (Toronto: TSAR Publications in association with the Ontario Association for Studies of Indo-Caribbean Culture, 1989), 204–205.

54. Bridget Brereton describes at some length the participation of the "black and coloured middle classes" in the creation of the liberal segment of Trinidad's print media during the late nineteenth century. She offers the following description with respect to the *New Era* specifically: "Black and coloured men were involved in the local press to a considerable extent. *New Era* was established by Samuel Carter and Joseph Lewis, both coloured, in 1869; Lewis conducted it alone from 1874 to 1891, when it closed down after his death. It was the self-acknowledged spokesman for the coloured middle class, whose interests it consistently upheld." Brereton, *Race Relations in Colonial Trinidad, 1870–1900,* 96.

55. "West Africa," *The New Era* IV, no. 18, whole no. 175, March 3, 1873.

56. "The West Africa University," *The New Era* IV, no. 25, whole no. 183, April 28, 1873.

57. Hollis R. Lynch, *Edward Wilmot Blyden: Pan-Negro Patriot 1832–1912* (New York: Oxford University Press), xv–xvi, 4–6.

58. "The Negro Newspaper," *The New Era* III, no. 147, August 19, 1872.

59. Brereton, *Race Relations in Colonial Trinidad,* 96.

60. Donald Wood, "Biographical Note," in J. J. Thomas, *Froudacity: West Indian Fables by James Anthony Froude* (1889; London: New Beacon Books, 1969), 10–15.

Thomas earned perhaps his greatest fame posthumously as a result of the 1889 publication of *Froudacity*, which critiqued the racist and culturally biased portrayals of Froude's 1888 work *The English in the West Indies.*

61. Ibid., 9.

62. *The Freeman* II, no. 3, March 20, 1888. The attribution at the conclusion of the paragraph reads "Am. paper"; the abbreviation "Am." presumably means "American." This is unusual; other reprinted material that appeared in *The Freeman* usually had more specific notations. The extract preceding this one, for example, identified a specific newspaper in Jacksonville, Florida.

63. Edward Wilmot Blyden, *Christianity, Islam and the Negro Race* (1887; New York: ECA Associates, 1990), 260–261.

64. "Dr. Blyden's New Book," *The Freeman* I, no. 40, December 6, 1887.

65. Hartley Cecil Saunders, *The Other Bahamas* (Nassau, Bahamas: BODAB Publishers, 1991), 49.

66. *The Freeman*: "Meeting of the Anglo-African League," I, no. 51, February 21, 1888; "Meeting of the Anglo-African League," II, no. 3, March 20, 1888.

67. Howard Johnson, "Friendly Societies in the Bahamas," 183. According to Johnson, newly emancipated slaves in Nassau founded the Bahama Friendly Society—sometimes also referred to as the Bahamas Friendly Society—on Emancipation Day in August 1834.

68. "The Humble Petition of the President, Vice-President and Members of Grant's Town Friendly Society to the King's Most Excellent Majesty," enclosure in Governor William Colebrooke, Bahamas, to Lord Glenelg, October 8, 1835, CO 23/94.

69. A *Freeman* report of an Anglo-African League meeting in February of 1888 listed delegates who attended from the following friendly societies, identified in the paper only by their initials: B.F.S, Y.M.C.S, E.B.S, U.B.S, C. No. 1, E.F.S, S.C.U. and G.T.F.S. The following list of explanations for these abbreviations derives from other references in *The Freeman* and information from the works of Howard Johnson and Hartley Saunders:

B.F.S.:   Bahama Friendly Society

Y.M.C.S.:   unclear; the initial "Y" possibly refers to a Yoruba group, although presumably not the "Yoruba Friendly Society" which did exist but no doubt would have had other initials.

E.B.S.:   possibly Egba or Eboe Burial Society. See also E.F.S.

U.B.S.:   United Burial Society

C. No. 1:   Congo No. 1 Society

E.F.S.:   most likely Egba Friendly Society. Both Johnson and Saunders refer to the existence of this group. Saunders, however, also refers to an "Ebo Friendly Society," which of course could have had this same abbreviation.

S.C.U.:   Ship Carpenters' Union

G.T.F.S.:   Grant's Town Friendly Society

See "The Anglo-African League: Enthusiastic Meeting at the U.B. Society's Hall," *The Freeman* I, no. 51, February 21, 1888. These eight organizations do not represent all the friendly societies involved in the Anglo-African League; these are the groups that sent delegates to the February 13, 1888 meeting. According to a February 21 editorial in *The Freeman,* the Anglo-African League included some twenty-two organizations—"all the various Friendly and Benevolent Societies in New Providence, with two exceptions, and all those located throughout the Out-islands . . . with an aggregate male membership of about four thousand."

70. Governor Henry Arthur Blake, Bahamas, to the Earl of Derby, Principal Secretary of State, Colonial Department, May 10, 1884, CO 23/224, cited in Howard Johnson, "Friendly Societies in the Bahamas," 190.

71. "Jubilee of the Landing of the Yoruba and Egba Tribes on the Free Shores of Nassau," *The Freeman* II, no. 10, May 8, 1888.

72. These two groups were the 1,000 Africans taken from the Portuguese vessels *Diligente* and *Camoens;* they were involved in the controversy over cancelled apprenticeships during the summer of 1838. See introduction and chapter 1.

73. Statement of John Laing, free African resident of New Providence, enclosure in Lieutenant Governor Blaney T. Balfour, Bahamas, to E. G. Stanley, Principal Secretary of State, Colonial Department, September 4, 1833, CO 23/89.

74. Craton and Saunders, *Islanders in the Stream,* 1:274–275.

75. Mullin, *Africa in America,* 284.

76. Statement of W. G. Winder, S.M.J., 2nd West India Regiment, New Providence; A. Hope Pattison, Lt. Colonel Commanding the 2nd West India Regiment, New Providence, "Return of a Man in Custody of the Civil Authorities, Head Quarters, New Providence, Bahamas 16th August 1833," both enclosures in Lieutenant Governor Blaney T. Balfour, Bahamas, to E. G. Stanley, September 4, 1833, CO 23/89.

77. Statement of Frederic Walker, Private, 2nd West India Regiment, sworn before Public Secretary Charles R. Nesbitt, August 19, 1833, enclosure in Lieutenant Governor Balfour to E. G. Stanley, September 4, 1833, CO 23/89.

78. Ibid.

79. See Phoebe Ottenberg, "The Afikpo Ibo of Eastern Nigeria," in James L. Gibbs, Jr., ed., *Peoples of Africa: Cultures of Africa South of the Sahara* (1965; Prospect Heights, Illinois: Waveland Press, Inc, 1988), 3–39.

80. Statement of W. G. Winder; Pattison, "Return of a Man in Custody."

81. For a concise economic and social history of the town and region, see A. J. H. Latham, *Old Calabar, 1600–1891: The Impact of the International Economy upon a Traditional Society* (New York: Oxford University Press, 1973).

82. Baptisms June 1820 to June 1855, nos. 1 to 781, Bahamas Methodist Church Papers, Department of Archives, Commonwealth of the Bahamas.

83. See references in Chapter 3 to Tony Congo and Peter Yaraba in reports of criminal trials from *The Trinidad Chronicle* during the latter half of the nineteenth century.

84. See M. Kwamenah-Poh, M. Tidy, J. Tosh, and R. Waller, *African History in Maps* (1982; London: Longman Group Limited, 1987). A claim of having originated from Baol would not necessarily imply Wolof ethnicity. In their survey text *African History,* Curtin, Feierman, Thompson, and Vansina identify this state but also dis-

cuss in some detail the ethnic, religious, and political confusion that characterized the Senegambia region through much of the eighteenth and nineteenth centuries, making the identification of definitive ethnic or political boundaries difficult if not impossible.

85. For patterns of both Bahamian and slave trade demography that support this supposition, see for example Craton and Saunders, *Islanders in the Stream,* vol. 1; Curtin, *The Atlantic Slave Trade: A Census*; Eltis, *Economic Growth and the Ending of the Transatlantic Slave Trade*; and B. W. Higman, *Slave Populations of the British Caribbean, 1807–1834* (Baltimore, Md.: Johns Hopkins University Press, 1984). According to Higman, in 1834 the Bahamian slave population included only sixty African males between the ages of 25 and 39 (470). Excluding liberated Africans, African-born people formed only a small minority of the free nonwhite population. Such facts strongly suggest that an African-born man in the Bahamas during the mid-1820s very likely arrived from a captured slave ship. See also Duplicate of Report on the State and Condition of Liberated Africans in the Bahamas, 1828, CO 23/79-80.

86. "Legal Intelligence," *The New Era,* n.s., XV, no. 39, February 24, 1888.

87. Itwaru, "Exile and Commemoration," 202.

88. Marie Bertrand Cothonay, *Trinidad: Journal d'un Missionaire Dominicain des Antilles Anglaises* (Paris: Victor Retaux et Fils, Libraires-Éditeurs, 1893), 290–291.

Conclusion

1. Missionary Journals and Correspondence 1792–1914, West Indies, Daniel Wilshere, 1878–1892, Archives of the Baptist Missionary Society.

2. "What Next?" *The Nassau Guardian* XLVI, no. 4879, September 5, 1888.

3. Mintz and Price, *The Birth of African-American Culture,* 45–46.

4. See ibid., chapters 2–5.

5. I am using the term "African-American" here in the way that Mintz and Price use it, in reference to the Americas broadly defined and not just to North America or the United States.

6. Mintz and Price mention the Rada community in Port-of-Spain. They highlight the fact that the founders of this community arrived in Trinidad as refugees from the slave trade in the latter half of the nineteenth century and therefore near the end of the slave trade migration as a whole. However, they do not discuss at any length the specific connections of this group to other liberated Africans or the overall characteristics of the liberated African experience. See ibid., 56–58.

7. *The Bahama Argus,* May 7, 1836, enclosure in Governor William Colebrook, Bahamas, to Lord Glenelg, Principal Secretary of State, Colonial Department, May 11, 1836, CO 23/96.

SELECT BIBLIOGRAPHY

Abbreviations

CO   Colonial Office
FO   Foreign Office
WO   War Office

Manuscripts

*National Archives of England, Wales and the United Kingdom,
Kew, Richmond, Surrey, United Kingdom*

CO 23   Bahamas Original Correspondence, 1807–1900
CO 27   Bahamas: Miscellanea, 1804–1900
CO 295   Trinidad Original Correspondence, 1807–1900
CO 300   Trinidad: Miscellanea, 1804–1900
CO 318   West Indies Original Correspondence
CO 386   Land and Emigration Commission Letter Book: West Indies, Africa, Saint
         Helena
FO 84   General Correspondence before 1906: Slave Trade, 1816–1892
FO 313   Records of the Anglo-Spanish Mixed Commission at Havana
WO 41   Secretary-at-War: Office of Army Accounts

*Department of Archives, Commonwealth of the Bahamas,
Nassau, Bahamas*

Minutes of the House of Assembly, 1818–1923 (with breaks)
Vice Admiralty Court Minutes, 1804–1911 (with breaks)
Methodist Baptism Registers, Nassau, 1842–1900
Methodist Marriage Registers, Nassau, 1820–1910
Oral History Transcripts Collection

*National Archives of Trinidad and Tobago, Port-of-Spain,
Trinidad and Tobago*

Blue Books, 1865–1900
Andrew Carr Papers

*West Indies Collection, Main Library, University of the
West Indies at Saint Augustine, Trinidad*

Andrew Pearse Papers
Report of the Royal Commission to Consider and Report as to the Proposed Fran-
chise and Division of the Colony into Electoral Districts, 1888

Library, School of Oriental and African Studies, University of London

Papers of the Wesleyan Methodist Missionary Society: West Indies Correspondence 1810–1900
Annual Reports of the Wesleyan Methodist Missionary Society, 1810–1900

Special Collections, Main Library, University of Birmingham, Birmingham, United Kingdom

Papers of the Church Missionary Society (CMS)

Angus Library Regents Park College, Oxford University

Archives of the Baptist Missionary Society (BMS)

Rhodes House Library, Oxford University

Papers of the United Society for the Propagation of the Gospel
Papers of the British and Foreign Anti-Slavery Society

Newspapers and Periodicals

Bahamas

The Bahama Argus
The Freeman
The Nassau Guardian

Trinidad

The New Era
The Port of Spain Gazette
The Trinidad Chronicle

Interviews

Bahamas

Adderley, Sheila. January 1, 1995. Nassau.
Anonymous. April 27, 1994. Nassau.
———. May 7, 1994. Fox Hill, Nassau.
Coakley, Lillian. April 30, 1994. Nassau.
Eneas, Cleveland. August 14, 1993. Bain Town, Nassau.
———. April 30, 1994. Bain Town, Nassau.
Henry, Euna. May 17, 1994. Nassau.
Johnson, Jack. May 1994. Grant's Town, Nassau.
Maillis, Pericles. May 4, 1994. Nassau.
Moss, Roland. October 3, 1994. Nassau.

Nicholls, Alma. December 1993. Nassau.
Nixon, James. October 3, 1994. Matthew Town, Inagua.
Rahming, Phillip. May 9, 1994. Fox Hill, Nassau.
Thompson, William. August 11, 1993. Nassau.
Weir, Emmett. August 10, 1993. Nassau.
Weir, Gaspare. September 24, 1994. Grant's Town, Nassau.

Trinidad

Achille, Telpha. February 25, 1994. Diego Martin.
Ampson, Sylvia. February 24, 1994. Caratal.
Antoine, Sedley. March 15, 1994. Belmont.
Anonymous. February 26, 1994. Diego Martin.
Asseverro, MacDonald. March 11, 1994. Diego Martin.
Bain, Emmanuel. March 9, 1994. Princes Town.
Benjamin, Judith and Ronald. December 5, 1993. Moruga Road.
Carr, Norman. February 27, 1994. Saint Mary's Village, Moruga.
———. March 9, 1994. Saint Mary's Village, Moruga.
De Silva, Ucarl. February 18, 1994. Diego Martin.
Elder, J. D. December 1, 1993. Port-of-Spain.
Gonzales, Nora. February 18, 1994. Diego Martin.
Gonzalez, Otto, Sr. February 24, 1994. Gasparillo.
Guerrero, Eulie. March 9, 1994. Lengua.
Hill, Mabel. March 9, 1994. Princes Town.
Hudlin, Joseph. March 9, 1994. Lengua.
Joseph, Irene. February 26, 1994. Caratal.
Lendore, Winifred Salazar. February 26, 1994. Tortuga.
——— (with her niece, Naomi Toby). March 5, 1994. Tortuga.
Pierre, Clifton. March 6, 1994. Poonah.
Rohlehr, Gordon. December 16, 1993. Saint Augustine.
Rostant, Joseph. February 24, 1994. Tortuga.
Rouse-Jones, Margaret. November 9, 1993. Saint Augustine.
Sampson, Eloid. March 6, 1994. Poonah.
Sylvester, Theresa. March 6, 1994. Gasparillo.
Taylor, Priscilla. March 9, 1994. Lengua.
Thomas, Orthelese. March 6, 1994, Gasparillo.
Toby, Naomi (with her aunt, Winifred Salazar Lendore). March 5, 1994. Tortuga.
Toby, Laura. January 26, 1994. Morne Diablo.

Primary Sources

Alexander, Joseph. *Recollections of a Trinidad Detective: A Biography.* Port-of-Spain, Trinidad: n.p., 1920.
Bethel, Marion. *Guanahani, Mi Amor y Otros Poemas.* Traducción de David Chericián. Havana: Casa de las Américas, 1994.

Burnley, William Hardin. *Observations on the Present Condition of the Island of Trinidad and the Actual State of the Experiment of Negro Emancipation by William Hardin Burnley, Chairman of the Agricultural and Immigration Society in that Colony.* London: Longman, Brown, Green, and Longman, 1842.

Collens, James Henry. *Guide to Trinidad. A Hand-Book for the Use of Tourists and Visitors.* Port-of-Spain, Trinidad: n.p., 1886.

Cothonay, Marie Bertrand. *Trinidad: Journal d'un Missionaire Dominicain des Antilles Anglaises.* Paris: Victor Retaux et Fils, Libraires-Éditeurs, 1893.

Daget, Serge, and Jean Mettas. *Répertoire des expéditions négrieres françaises au XVIIe siècle.* Paris: Société française d'histoire d'outre-mer, 1978.

Davy, John. *The West Indies, before and since slave emancipation, comprising the Windward and Leeward Islands' military command; founded on notes and observations collected during a three years' residence.* London: W. & F. G. Cash, 1854.

Day, Charles William. *Five Years' Residence in the West Indies.* London: Colburn and Co., Publishers, 1852.

Dickinson, J., E. E. Dickinson, and S. E. Dowd. *A Winter Picnic: The Story of a Four Months' Outing in Nassau, Told in the Letters, Journals, and Talk of Four Picnicers.* New York: Henry Holt and Company, 1888.

Drysdale, William. *In Sunny Lands: Out-Door Life in Nassau and Cuba.* New York: Harper & Brothers, 1885.

Gamble, W. H. *Trinidad: Historical and Descriptive: A Narrative of Nine Years' Residence in the Island. With Special Reference to Christian Missions.* London: Yates and Alexander for the Author, 1866.

Innes, John. *Letter to the Lord Glenelg, Secretary of State for the Colonies; Containing A Report, from Personal Observation on the Working of the New System in the British West India Colonies.* London: Longman, Rees, Orme, Brown, Green, and Longman, 1835.

Innis, L. O. *Reminiscences of an Octogenarian.* Port-of-Spain, Trinidad: J. D. Corrie, Acting Government Printer, for the Trinidad Historical Society, 1937.

Ives, Charles. *The Isles of Summer; or Nassau and the Bahamas.* New Haven, Conn.: Published by the Author, 1880.

Joseph, E. L. *History of Trinidad.* 1838; London: Frank Cass and Company Limited, 1970.

Kingsley, Charles. *At Last: A Christmas in the West Indies.* 1871; London: Macmillan and Co., 1896.

Massé, Armand. *The Diaries of the Abbé Armand Massé, 1878–1883.* Translated by M. L. de Verteuil. 4 vols. Port-of-Spain, Trinidad: Scrip-J Printers, 1980.

Meyer-Heiselberg, Richard. *Notes from the Liberated African Department: Extracts from Sources on the Trans-Atlantic Slave Trade 1808–1860 from the Archives at Fourah Bay College, the University College of Sierra Leone, Freetown, Sierra Leone.* Uppsala: Scandinavian Institute of African Studies, 1967.

Moore, Rachel Wilson. *Journal of Rachel Wilson Moore, kept during a tour to the West Indies and South America in 1863–1864 with Notes from the Diary of her Husband together with His Memoir by George Truman, M.D.* Philadelphia: T. Ellwood Zell, Publisher, 1867.

Northcroft, G. J. H. *Sketches of Summerland—Giving Some Account of Nassau and the Bahama Islands.* Nassau, Bahamas: The Nassau Guardian, 1900.

Powles, L. D. *The Land of the Pink Pearl; or, Recollections of Life in the Bahamas.* London: Sampson Low, Marston, Searle, & Rivington Limited, 1888.

Sandoval, Alonso de. *Tomo primero de instauranda aethiopum salute: Historia de Aethiopia; naturaleça, policia sagrada y profana, costumbres, ritos y cathecismo evangelico de todos los aethiopes.* Madrid: A. D. Paredes, 1647.

Stark, James H. *Stark's History and Guide to the Bahama Islands, Containing a Description of Everything on or about the Bahama Islands of Which the Visitor or Resident May Desire Information.* Boston: James H. Stark, Publisher, 1891.

———. *Stark's Guide-Book and History of Trinidad, including Tobago, Granada, and Saint Vincent; Also a Trip up the Orinoco and a Description of Everything Relating to These Places that Would be of Interest to Tourists and Residents.* Fully Illustrated, with Maps, Engravings and Photo-Prints. Boston: James H. Stark, Publisher, 1897.

Thomas, J. J. *Froudacity: West Indian Fables by James Anthony Froude.* 1889; London: New Beacon Books, 1969.

de Verteuil, Louis A. A. *Trinidad: Its Geography, Natural Resources, Present Condition, and Prospects.* 1858; London: Cassell & Company, Limited, 1884.

Wesley Methodist Church: A Souvenir of the Centenary, 1847–1947. Nassau, Bahamas, 1947.

Secondary Sources

Ali, Anthony Andrew. "Lengua/Barrackpore: A Socio-Psychological Study." B.A. thesis, University of the West Indies at Saint Augustine, Trinidad, 1975.

Alleyne, Mervyn. *Roots of Jamaican Culture.* London: Pluto Press, 1989.

Alleyne, Aletia, Gilbert James, Cheryl Julien, Gary Tagallie, and Dianne Thurab. "Chaguanas in the Early Twentieth Century: A Socio-Historical Study." B.A. thesis, University of the West Indies at Saint Augustine, Trinidad, 1985.

Alves, Catherine. "The Shango Religious Cult in Trinidad through the Eyes of Two Informants." B.A. thesis, University of the West Indies at Saint Augustine, Trinidad, 1982.

Amadiume, Ifi. *Male Daughters, Female Husbands: Gender and Sex in an African Society.* 1987; Atlantic Highlands, N.J.: Zed Books, 1995.

Asiegbu, Johnson U. J. *Slavery and the Politics of Liberation, 1787–1861: A Study of Liberated African Emigration and British Anti-Slavery Policy.* New York: Africana Publishing Corporation, 1969.

Barclay, Jeneaver. "The Black Woman in the Trinidad Family." B.A. thesis, University of the West Indies at Saint Augustine, Trinidad, 1987.

Barber, Karin. *I Could Speak until Tomorrow: Oriki, Women, and the Past in a Yoruba Town.* Edinburgh: Edinburgh University Press, 1991.

Bastide, Roger. *African Civilisations in the New World.* Translated from the French by Peter Green with a foreword by Geoffrey Parrinder. New York: Harper & Row, 1971.

————. *The African Religions of Brazil: Toward a Sociology of the Interpenetration of Civilizations.* Translated by Helene Sebba. Baltimore, Md.: Johns Hopkins University Press, 1978.

Bay, Edna G. *Women and Work in Africa.* Boulder, Colo.: Westview Press, 1983.

Benitez-Rojo, Antonio. *The Repeating Island: The Caribbean and the Postmodern Perspective.* Translated by James Maraniss. Durham, N.C.: Duke University Press, 1992.

Benn, D. M. "Historical and Contemporary Expressions of Black Consciousness in the Caribbean (An Analysis of the Structural Context, Idea-System, and Goal Orientation of Movements and Ideologies of Black Protest.)" M.S. thesis, University of the West Indies at Mona, Jamaica, 1972.

Bergad, Laird, Fe Iglesias Garcia, and María del Carmen Barca. *The Cuban Slave Market, 1790–1880.* New York: Cambridge University Press, 1995.

Bethel, Valerie G. "Morne Diable (A Study of Village Life)." B.A. thesis, University of the West Indies at Saint Augustine, Trinidad, 1977.

Bethell, Leslie. "The Mixed Commissions for the Suppression of the Transatlantic Slave Trade in the Nineteenth Century." *Journal of African History* 7, no. 1 (1966): 79–93.

————. *The Abolition of the Brazilian Slave Trade: Britain, Brazil, and the Slave Trade Question, 1807–1869.* New York: Cambridge University Press, 1970.

Birbalsingh, Frank, ed. *Indenture and Exile: The Indo-Caribbean Experience.* Toronto: TSAR in association with the Ontario Association for Studies of Indo-Caribbean Culture, 1989.

Birjah, Deborah D. "Changing Role of Women in Rural Families in Trinidad." B.A. thesis, University of the West Indies at Saint Augustine, Trinidad, 1990.

Blassingame, John. *The Slave Community: Plantation Life in the Antebellum South.* Rev. ed. 1972; New York: Oxford University Press, 1979.

Borde, Jennifer. "African Survival in Shango." B.A. thesis, University of the West Indies at Saint Augustine, Trinidad, 1969.

Bourguignon, Erika, ed. *Religion, Altered States of Consciousness, and Social Change.* Columbus: Ohio State University Press, 1973.

Brandon, George. *Santería from Africa to the New World: The Dead Sell Memories.* Bloomington: Indiana University Press, 1993.

Brathwaite, Edward Kamau. *The Folk Culture of the Slaves in Jamaica.* London: New Beacon Press, 1981.

Brereton, Bridget. *Race Relations in Colonial Trinidad, 1870–1900.* New York: Cambridge University Press, 1979.

————. *A History of Modern Trinidad, 1783–1962.* London: Heinemann Educational Books, 1981.

Blyden, Edward Wilmot. *Christianity, Islam and the Negro Race.* 1887; New York: ECA Associates, 1990.

Carr, Andrew. *A Rada Community in Trinidad.* 1953; Port-of-Spain: Paria Publishing Company, 1989.

Cash, Philip, Shirley Gordon, and Gail Saunders. *Sources of Bahamian History.* London: Macmillan Education, 1991.

Charles, Margaret Allison. "Dance in Trinidad: An Exposition of the African and East Indian Dance Forms of Our Land." B.A. thesis, University of the West Indies at Saint Augustine, Trinidad, 1990.

Charles, Rommel. "A Study of the Shango Cult in Trinidad." B.A. thesis, University of the West Indies at Saint Augustine, Trinidad, 1969.

Chatoor, Donna. "The Socio-Historical Development of the London Baptists in Trinidad." B.A. thesis, University of the West Indies at Saint Augustine, Trinidad, 1977.

Chaves, Ingrid. "A Study of the Historical Development of the Baptist Community of Trinidad." B.A. thesis, University of the West Indies at Saint Augustine, 1986.

Clarke, Margaret Gail. "Chaguanas: From Origins to 1960." B.A. thesis, University of the West Indies at Saint Augustine, Trinidad, 1988.

Collins, Annette E. "The Rites of Passage in Trinidad and Tobago." B.A. thesis, University of the West Indies at Saint Augustine, Trinidad, 1969.

Conniff, Michael L., and Thomas J. Davis. *Africans in the Americas: A History of the Black Diaspora.* New York: St. Martin's Press, 1994.

Conrad, Robert Edgar. *World of Sorrow: The African Slave Trade to Brazil.* Baton Rouge: Louisiana State University Press, 1986.

Costa, Emilia Viotti da. *Crowns of Glory, Tears of Blood: The Demerara Slave Rebellion of 1823.* New York: Oxford University Press, 1997.

Crahan, Margaret, and Franklin Knight, eds. *Africa and the Caribbean: The Legacies of a Link.* Baltimore, Md.: Johns Hopkins University Press, 1979.

Craton, Michael. *Testing the Chains: Resistance to Slavery in the British West Indies.* Ithaca, N.Y.: Cornell University Press, 1982.

Craton, Michael, and Gail Saunders. *Islanders in the Stream: A History of the Bahamian People.* Vol. 1, *From Aboriginal Times to the End of Slavery.* Athens: University of Georgia Press, 1992.

———. *Islanders in the Stream: A History of the Bahamian People.* Vol. 2, *From the Ending of Slavery to the Twenty-First Century.* Athens: University of Georgia Press, 1998.

Creel, Margaret Washington. *"A Peculiar People": Slave Religion and Community-Culture among the Gullahs.* New York: New York University Press, 1988.

Curtin, Philip. *The Atlantic Slave Trade: A Census.* Madison: University of Wisconsin Press, 1969.

Curtin, Philip, Steven Feierman, Leonard Thompson, and Jan Vansina. *African History.* 1978; Madison: University of Wisconsin Press, 1988.

Dalleo, Peter T. "Africans in the Caribbean: A Preliminary Assessment of Recaptives in the Bahamas, 1811–1860." *Journal of the Bahamas Historical Society* 6, no. 1 (October 1984): 15–24.

Deren, Maya. *Divine Horsemen: Voodoo Gods of Haiti.* 1953; London: Thames and Hudson, 1970.

Deslèves, Max R. *Les îles de juin.* Paris: Éditions Berger-Levreault, 1963.

Desmangles, Leslie. *The Faces of the Gods: Vodou and Roman Catholicism in Haiti.* Chapel Hill: University of North Carolina Press, 1992.

Dobbin, Jay D. *The Jombee Dance of Montserrat: A Study of Trance Ritual in the West Indies.* Columbus: Ohio State University Press, 1986.

Dowlath, Evangeline. "The Development of a Rural Community with Specific Reference to Penal Rock Road and Environs." B.A. thesis, University of the West Indies at Saint Augustine, Trinidad, 1986.

Du Bois, W. E. B. *The Suppression of the Atlantic Slave-Trade to the United States of America, 1638–1870.* New York: Longmans, Green and Co., 1904.

Edwards, Belinda. "A Social History of the Leprosarium on the Island of Chacachacare." B.A. thesis, University of the West Indies at Saint Augustine, Trinidad, 1989.

Eltis, David. *Economic Growth and the Ending of the Transatlantic Slave Trade.* New York: Oxford University Press, 1987.

Eneas, Cleveland W. *Bain Town.* Nassau, Bahamas: Cleveland and Muriel Eneas, 1976.

Fage, J. D. *An Atlas of African History.* New York: Africana Publishing Company, 1978.

Farrell, Jocelyn. "A Study of Cultural Persistence (Shango Cult in Trinidad)." B.A. thesis, University of the West Indies at Saint Augustine, Trinidad, 1972.

Felix, Lynette. "A Comparison between the Shango Cult and the Spiritual Baptist Community in Port of Spain." B.A. thesis, University of the West Indies at Saint Augustine, Trinidad, 1971.

Fernandez, James W. *Bwiti: An Ethnography of the Religious Imagination in Africa.* Princeton, N.J.: Princeton University Press, 1982.

Finlayson, Iris E. *A History of Saint Matthew's Anglican Church.* Nassau, Bahamas: The Nassau Guardian, 1987.

Fletcher, Charmaine. "Emily Scope: c. 1875–1953. Daughter of Liberated Africans, Blackwoman, Wife and Mother." B.A. thesis, University of the West Indies at Saint Augustine, Trinidad, 1989.

Forbes, Rosita. *A Unicorn in the Bahamas.* New York: E. P. Dutton & Co., 1940.

Friday, Edmie. "La Divina Pastora: Legends and Traditions." B.A. thesis, University of the West Indies at Saint Augustine, Trinidad, 1975.

Fuentes, Christopher A. "West African Religious Survivals in Trinidad with Specific Reference to the Yorubas." B.A. thesis, University of the West Indies at Saint Augustine, 1970.

Fullerton, Celia R. "A Cross Cultural Comparison between 'Shango' in Trinidad and 'Pocomania' in Jamaica." B.A. thesis, University of the West Indies at Saint Augustine, Trinidad, 1970.

Fyfe, Christopher. *A History of Sierra Leone.* New York: Oxford University Press, 1962.

Gibbs, James L., Jr., ed. *Peoples of Africa: Cultures of Africa South of the Sahara.* 1965; Prospect Heights, Ill.: Waveland Press, 1988.

Glazier, Stephen D. *Marchin' the Pilgrims Home: A Study of the Spiritual Baptists of Trinidad.* 1983; Salem, Wis.: Sheffield Publishing Company, 1991.

Gomez, Michael A. *Exchanging Our Country Marks: The Transformation of African Identities in the Colonial and Antebellum South.* Chapel Hill: University of North Carolina Press, 1998.

Goveia, Elsa. *Slave Society in the British Leeward Islands at the End of the Eighteenth Century.* New Haven, Conn.: Yale University Press, 1965.

Green, William. *British Slave Emancipation: The Sugar Colonies and the Great Experiment, 1830–1865*. Oxford: Clarendon Press, 1976.

Guanche, Jesús. *Componentes étnicos de la nacion Cubana*. Ciudad de la Habana, Cuba: Fundación Fernando Ortiz y Ediciones UNION, 1996.

Harvey, Claudia. "Seven Supernatural Characters of Trinidad Folklore." B.A. thesis, University of the West Indies at Saint Augustine, Trinidad, 1969.

Hedrick, Basil C., and Jeanette E. Stephens. *It's a Natural Fact: Obeah in the Bahamas*. Miscellaneous Series no. 39. University of Northern Colorado, Museum of Anthropology, 1977.

Herbert, Hermez C. K. "A History of Carenage: A Socio-Cultural Perspective from 1800 to the Present Day." B.A. thesis, University of the West Indies at Saint Augustine, Trinidad, 1990.

Herskovits, Melville J. *The Myth of the Negro Past*. 1941; Boston: Beacon Press, 1990.

Herskovits, Melville J., and Frances S. Herskovits. *Trinidad Village*. New York: Alfred Knopf, 1947.

Heywood, Linda M., ed. *Central Africans and Cultural Transformations in the American Diaspora*. New York: Cambridge University Press, 2001.

Higman, B. W. *Slave Populations of the British Caribbean, 1807–1834*. Baltimore, Md.: Johns Hopkins University Press, 1984.

Hodgson, Dorothy L., and Sheryl A. McCurdy. *"Wicked" Women and the Reconfiguration of Gender in Africa*. Portsmouth, N.H.: Heinemann, 2001.

Holloway, Joseph E., ed. *Africanisms in American Culture*. Bloomington: Indiana University Press, 1990.

Holm, John A., and Alison Watt Shilling. *Dictionary of Bahamian English*. Cold Spring, N.Y.: Lexik House Publishers, 1982.

Holt, Thomas C. *The Problem of Freedom: Race, Labor, and Politics in Jamaica and Britain, 1832–1938*. Baltimore, Md.: Johns Hopkins University Press, 1992.

Hufford, David J. *The Terror That Comes in the Night: An Experience-Centered Study of Supernatural Assault Traditions*. Philadelphia: University of Pennsylvania Press, 1982.

John, A. Meredith. *The Plantation Slaves of Trinidad, 1783–1816: A Mathematical and Demographic Enquiry*. New York: Cambridge University Press, 1988.

Johnson, Howard. *The Bahamas in Slavery and Freedom*. Kingston, Jamaica: Ian Randle, 1991.

———. "Friendly Societies in the Bahamas." *Slavery and Abolition* 12, no. 3 (December 1991): 183–199.

Johnston, Sir Harry Hamilton. *The Negro in the New World*. 1910; New York and London: Johnson Reprint Corporation, 1969.

Jones, Sandra P. "The Orisa Religion in Trinidad: A History of Its Origin and Growth." B.A. thesis, University of the West Indies at Saint Augustine, Trinidad, 1991.

Joseph, Aloysius Bernard. "The Spiritual Baptists of Trinidad and Tobago: A Study of the Origin and Present Operation of Their Religion." B.A. thesis, University of the West Indies at Saint Augustine, Trinidad, 1983.

Journey through New Providence. Nassau, Bahamas: Arawak Editors, 1971.

Karasch, Mary. *Slave Life in Rio de Janeiro, 1808–1850.* Princeton, N.J.: Princeton University Press, 1987.

Kielstra, Paul Michael. *The Politics of Slave Trade Suppression in Britain and France, 1814–48.* New York: St. Martin's Press, 2000.

Knight, Franklin W. *Slave Society in Cuba during the Nineteenth Century.* Madison: University of Wisconsin Press, 1970.

Kwamena-Poh, M., M. Tidy, J. Tosh, and R. Waller. *African History in Maps.* 1982; London: Longman Group, 1987.

Lalchan, Shelley. "The Sou Sou Land Project—A Final Solution to Housing Problems in Trinidad and Tobago." B.A. thesis, University of the West Indies at Saint Augustine, Trinidad, 1987.

Latham, A. J. H. *Old Calabar, 1600–1891: The Impact of the International Economy upon a Traditional Society.* New York: Oxford University Press, 1973.

LeBlanc, June. "Black Awareness in Trinidad Calypso." B.A. thesis, University of the West Indies at Saint Augustine, Trinidad, 1987.

Leveen, E. Phillip. *British Slave Trade Suppression Policies, 1821–1865.* New York: Arno Press, 1977.

Lloyd, Christopher. *The Navy and the Slave Trade: The Suppression of the African Slave Trade in the Nineteenth Century.* London: Frank Cass and Company Ltd., 1968.

Lynch, Hollis R. *Edward Wilmot Blyden: Pan-Negro Patriot, 1832–1912.* New York: Oxford University Press, 1967.

MacGaffey, Wyatt. *Religion and Society in Central Africa: The BaKongo of Lower Zaire.* Chicago: University of Chicago Press, 1986.

MacMaster, Richard Kerwin. "The United States, Great Britain and the Suppression of the Cuban Slave Trade 1835–1860." Ph.D. diss., Georgetown University, 1968.

Manuel, Gladys. *Historical Notes on the Fox Hill Community.* Nassau, Bahamas: n.p., 1988.

Mbiti, John S. *African Religions and Philosophy.* 2nd ed. London: Heinemann International 1990.

McEvedy, Colin. *Atlas of African History.* 1980; New York: Facts on File, 1982.

Métraux, Alfred. *Voodoo in Haiti.* Translated by Hugo Charteris, with a new introduction by Sidney W. Mintz. 1959; New York: Schocken Books, 1972.

Miers, Suzanne. *Britain and the Ending of the Slave Trade.* New York: Africana Publishing Company, 1975.

Mintz, Sidney W., and Richard Price. *The Birth of African-American Culture: An Anthropological Perspective.* Rev. ed. Boston: Beacon Press, 1992.

Mullin, Michael. *Africa in America: Slave Acculturation and Resistance in the American South and the British Caribbean 1736–1831.* Chicago: University of Illinois Press, 1992.

Mohammed, Irma. "The Shango Cult in Trinidad." B.A. thesis, University of the West Indies at Saint Augustine, Trinidad, 1969.

Morton, Lennard. "The Shango Movement in Trinidad." B.A. thesis, University of the West Indies at Saint Augustine, Trinidad, 1970.

Murdock, George Peter. *Africa: Its Peoples and Their Culture History.* New York: McGraw-Hill Book Company, 1959.

Murphy, Joseph M. *Santería: An African Religion in America.* Boston: Beacon Press, 1988.

Murray, David. "Communal Relations between Africans and Indians in Trinago." B.A. thesis, University of the West Indies at Saint Augustine, Trinidad, 1972.

Murray, David R. *Odious Commerce: Britain, Spain, and the Abolition of the Cuban Slave Trade.* New York: Cambridge University Press, 1980.

Nathasingh, Rowena. "A History of Syne Village." B.A. thesis, University of the West Indies at Saint Augustine, Trinidad, 1992.

Neely, Lofton. "A Look at Life in the Bluff, Andros." Teaching certificate thesis, College of the Bahamas, Nassau, 1978.

Olajubu, Oyeronke. *Women in the Yoruba Religious Sphere.* Albany: State University of New York Press, 1993.

Oyewùmí, Oyèrónké. *The Invention of Women: Making African Sense of Western Gender Discourses.* Minneapolis: University of Minnesota Press, 1997.

Patterson, Orlando. *The Sociology of Slavery: An Analysis of the Origins, Development, and Structure of Negro Slave Society in Jamaica.* Rutherford, N.J.: Fairleigh Dickinson University Press, 1969.

Peggs, A. Deans. *A Short History of the Bahamas.* Nassau, Bahamas: The Nassau Daily Tribune, 1951.

Peltier, Cheryl Ann. "The Development of the Spiritual Baptist Movement in Trinidad and Tobago with Special Reference to the St. Francis Triune Shouters (Don Miguel Road, San Juan)." B.A. thesis, University of the West Indies at Saint Augustine, Trinidad, 1990.

Peters, Thelma Peterson. "The American Loyalists and the Plantation Period in the Bahama Islands." Ph.D. diss., University of Florida, 1960.

Philip, Alana Avion. "A Comparison between the Abakua Secret Society of Cuba and the Shango Religion of Trinidad." B.A. thesis, University of the West Indies at Saint Augustine, Trinidad, 1991.

Phillips, Daphne. "Class Formation and Ethnicity in Trinidad: A Review of Development and Change in Social Classes in Trinidad, with Particular Emphasis on the Role of Leadership in the Creation of Working Class Consciousness in the Period 1970–1980." M.S. thesis, University of the West Indies at Saint Augustine, Trinidad, 1984.

Piper, Marina. "Afro-Brazilian Religious Traditions and Its Relation to Ecstatic Sects in Trinidad." B.A. thesis, University of the West Indies at Saint Augustine, Trinidad, 1989.

Pitts, H. C. *One Hundred Years Together: A Brief History of Trinidad from 1797 to 1897.* Port-of-Spain, Trinidad: The Trinidad Publishing Company, 1948.

Pitts, Walter F. *Old Ship of Zion: The Afro-Baptist Ritual in the African Diaspora.* New York: Oxford University Press, 1993.

Plowden, Stanley Kenneth. "A Social Psychological Study of Leadership in Community Based Voluntary Organizations: An Evaluation of the Community Development Process in Trinidad and Tobago." M.S. thesis, University of the West Indies at Saint Augustine, Trinidad, 1989.

Raboteau, Albert J. *Slave Religion: The "Invisible Institution" in the Antebellum South.* New York: Oxford University Press, 1978.

Rahming, Jacqualine C. "The History and Background of Fox Hill with Songs." Teaching certificate thesis, College of the Bahamas, Nassau, 1974.

Rasumair, Roland T. "Valencia: Origin, Growth and Present State." B.A. thesis, University of the West Indies at Saint Augustine, 1975.

Rocke, Elitha. "History of the Saint Joseph Roman Catholic Church: Its Role in the Society." B.A. thesis, University of the West Indies at Saint Augustine, Trinidad, 1990.

Rodgers, William Blackstock, III. "The Wages of Change: An Anthropological Study of the Effects of Economic Development on Some Negro Communities in the Out Island Bahamas (Abaco)." Ph.D. diss., Stanford University, 1965.

Rogers, Jasmine Glendine. "The Acculturation of the Negro Slave in the Caribbean." B.A. thesis, University of the West Indies at Saint Augustine, Trinidad, 1970.

Romany, Rodney. "A Village Called Paramin—A Case of Social Neglect." B.A. thesis, University of the West Indies at Saint Augustine, Trinidad, 1976.

Salina, Elspeth Ann. "The Cultural Contribution of Lopinot to the Trinidad Society." B.A. thesis, University of the West Indies at Saint Augustine, Trinidad, 1989.

Sarracino, Rodolfo. *Los que volvieron a Africa.* Havana: Editorial de Ciencias Sociales, 1988.

———. *Inglaterra: Sus dos caras en la lucha cubana por la abolicion.* Havana: Editorial Letras Cubana, 1989.

Saunders, Hartley Cecil. *The Other Bahamas.* Nassau, Bahamas: BODAB Publishers, 1991.

Saunders, Keith. "Bain Town Yesterday and Today." Teaching certificate thesis, College of the Bahamas, Nassau, 1978.

Schuler, Monica. "Akan Slave Rebellions in the British Caribbean." *Savacou* 1 (1970): 8–31.

———. "Ethnic Slave Rebellions in the Caribbean and the Guianas." *Journal of Social History* 3, no. 4 (1970): 374–385.

———. *"Alas, Alas, Kongo": A Social History of Indentured African Immigration into Jamaica, 1841–1865.* Baltimore, Md.: Johns Hopkins University Press, 1980.

———. *Liberated Africans in Nineteenth-Century Guyana.* Elsa Goveia Memorial Lecture Series. Kingston, Jamaica: Department of History, University of the West Indies, Mona, 1992.

Shilling, Alison Watt. *Black English as a Creole—Some Bahamian Evidence.* Society for Caribbean Linguistics Occasional Paper no. 18. St. Augustine, Trinidad: Society for Caribbean Linguistics, 1984.

Simpson, George Eaton. *Religious Cults of the Caribbean: Trinidad, Jamaica, and Haiti.* San Juan, Puerto Rico: Institute of Caribbean Studies, 1970.

Small, Barbara. "A Social History of Princes Town." B.A. thesis, University of the West Indies at Saint Augustine, Trinidad, 1990.

Smith, Robert S. *Kingdoms of the Yoruba.* 3rd ed. 1969; Madison: University of Wisconsin Press, 1988.

Sobel, Mechal. *Trabelin' On: The Slave Journey to an Afro-Baptist Faith.* 1979; Princeton, N.J.: Princeton University Press, 1988.

Sosa, Enrique. *El Carabali.* Ciudad de la Habana, Cuba: Editorial Letras Cubanas, 1984.

Staudenraus, P. J. *The African Colonization Movement, 1816–1865.* New York: Columbia University Press, 1961.

Stein, Robert Louis. *The French Slave Trade in the Eighteenth Century: An Old Regime Business.* Madison: University of Wisconsin Press, 1979.

Stewart, Robert J. *Religion and Society in Post-Emancipation Jamaica.* Knoxville: University of Tennessee Press, 1992.

Storr, Margaret A. "A Detailed Study of the Oakes Field Area, New Providence." Teaching certificate thesis, College of the Bahamas, Nassau, 1976.

Stoute, Marlene. "The Origin and Development of the Lopinot Complex." B.A. thesis, University of the West Indies at Saint Augustine, Trinidad, 1991.

Stuckey, Sterling. *Slave Culture: Nationalist Theory and the Foundations of Black America.* New York: Oxford University Press, 1987.

Taylor, Ian Anthony. "The Rite of Mourning in the Spiritual Baptist Faith with Emphasis on the Activity of the 'Spirit.'" B.A. thesis, University of the West Indies at Saint Augustine, Trinidad, 1986.

Terborg-Penn, Rosalyn, and Andrea Benton Rushing. *Women in Africa and the African Diaspora: A Reader.* 2nd ed. Washington, D.C.: Howard University Press, 1996.

Thomas, Eudora. *A History of the Shouter Baptists in Trinidad and Tobago.* Tacarigua, Trinidad: Calaloux Publications, 1987.

Thompson, Robert Farris. *Flash of the Spirit: African and Afro-American Art and Philosophy.* New York: Vintage Books, 1983.

Thornton, John. *Africa and Africans in the Making of the Atlantic World, 1400–1600.* 1992; New York: Cambridge University Press, 1998.

Trotman, David V. *Crime in Trinidad: Conflict and Control in a Plantation Society, 1838–1900.* Knoxville: University of Tennessee Press, 1987.

———. "The Yoruba and Orisha Worship in Trinidad and British Guiana: 1838–1870." *African Studies Review* 19, no. 2 (September 1976): 1–17.

Turner, H. W. *History of an African Independent Church: The Church of the Lord (Aladura).* 2 vols. New York: Oxford University Press, 1967.

Turner, Mary. *Slaves and Missionaries: The Disintegration of Jamaican Slave Society, 1787–1834.* Urbana: University of Illinois Press, 1982.

Verger, Pierre. *Flux et reflux de la traite des nègres entre le Golfe de Benin et Bahia de Todos os Santos, du XVIIᵉ au XIXᵉ siècle.* Paris: La Haye, Mouton, 1968.

Vincent, Dolores. "The Origin and Development of the Company Villages in South Trinidad." B.A. thesis, University of the West Indies at Saint Augustine, Trinidad, 1975.

Warner, Jack. "Obeah: Fact or Fiction?" B.A. thesis, University of the West Indies at Saint Augustine, Trinidad, 1969.

Ward, W. E. F. *The Royal Navy and the Slavers: The Suppression of the Atlantic Slave Trade.* London: George Allen & Unwin, 1969.

Warner, Maureen. "Africans in Nineteenth Century Trinidad." *African Studies Association of the West Indies Bulletin* 5 (1972): 40–52.

Warner-Lewis, Maureen. *Guinea's Other Suns: The African Dynamic in Trinidad Culture*. Dover, Mass.: The Majority Press, 1991.

———. *Trinidad Yoruba: From Mother Tongue to Memory*. Tuscaloosa: University of Alabama Press, 1996.

———, ed. *Yoruba Songs of Trinidad*. With translations. London: Kamak House, 1994.

Weeks, John H. *Among the Primitive Bakongo*. 1914; New York: Negro Universities Press, 1969.

Whitten, Norman, ed. *Latin American Anthropology Group Contributions*. Washington, D.C.: Latin American Anthropology Group, 1976.

Williams, Joseph J. *Voodoos and Obeahs: Phases of West India Witchcraft*. 1932; New York: AMS Press, 1970.

Williams, Patrice. *A Guide to African Villages in New Providence*. Nassau, Bahamas: Bahamas Department of Archives, 1979.

———. *Archives Exhibition of Settlements in New Providence*. Nassau, Bahamas: Bahamas Department of Archives, 1982.

Wood, Donald. *Trinidad in Transition: The Years after Slavery*. New York: Oxford University Press, 1968.

Wood, Peter H. *Black Majority: Negroes in Colonial South Carolina from 1670 through the Stono Rebellion*. New York: W.W. Norton & Company, 1975.

Work, John W., ed. *American Negro Songs and Spirituals: A Comprehensive Collection of 230 Folk Songs, Religious and Secular*. New York: Bonanza Books, 1940.

INDEX

Page numbers in italics refer to illustrations.

1st West India Regiment, 60
2nd West India Regiment: *Hebe* Africans, 57; makeup of, 215; near mutiny in, 137–140; Peters and, 230; Walker (Frederic) and, 230
3rd West India Regiment, 131
1807 Abolition Act. *See* Abolition Act (1807)

Abaco Island, 60, 254n1
Aberdeen, George Hamilton Gordon, 4th Earl of, 59
Abolition Act (1807): apprenticeships for liberated Africans, 25, 65, 127; definition of slave ships, 27; effect on plantation colonies, 9; emancipation, 3; enlistment of liberated Africans in armed forces, 25; liberated Africans, 1–2, 3; provisions, 1–2, 3, 25–26, 27, 28, 29, 34, 127; role of chief customs officers, 25–26; seventh clause, 25; ships seized in accordance with, 25; status of liberated Africans, 25; sugar plantations, 65; women's exclusion from agricultural labor, 127, 280n3; wording, 25
Adderley, Alliday, 170
Adderley, Zechariah, 200–202
Adelaide settlement, Bahamas: Carmichael-Smyth and, 18, 56; *Despique* Africans, 57; *Rosa* Africans, 56, 57; scholarly attention paid to, 253n33
Africa: African culture, 214; Central Africa, 8, 193; gender and family labor divisions in precolonial Africa, 145; as a homeland, 208, 209–210, 222, 233, 235; intercourse between groups in Africa before enslavement, 103; marriage in precolonial West Africa, 146–147; oath-taking, 238; religious and supernatural life (*see* obeah; orisha worship [Shango]); return to (*see* repatriation to Africa); truthfulness, 238; West Africa, 193; West-Central Africa map, *93*
Africa: Its Peoples and Their Culture History (Murdock), 100

Africa in America (Mullin), 229
African, Albert, 106, 107
African, George: family relationships, *149;* marriages, 150–151; resources at marriage, 147; surname of children of, 151; wife, 141, 232
African, Manuel, 106
African, Robert, 106
African, Thomas, 106
African Americans: African-American Christianity, 175; African-Caribbean and African-American cultures, 4–5; back-to-Africa projects conducted by, 213–214; conversion to Christianity, 213; Kongo people, 94; norms of, 236; recruitment of African-American missionaries, 214; in Trinidad, 210
"African Atlantic world," 251n12
African Board (in Nassau), 18, 52, 53
African-Brazilian culture, 94
African-Caribbean culture: African-American culture and, 4–5; invention of, 238–239; liberated Africans, 2, 4–5, 12; social history, 237
African Civilisations in the New World (Bastide), 156–157
African-Creole culture, 90–91
African-Cuban culture, 94
African culture, 214
African-derived religions: Africanness, 157; Aladura movement, 289n62; Bahamas, 180–181; black Christianity, 156; candomble, 155, 157, 159; Christianity, 156; Fon people, 157; friendly societies, 204; Haitian vodun (*see* Haitian vodun); liberated Africans in Trinidad, 154; Roman Catholicism, 172–173, 284n4; santería, 155, 159; scholarly attention paid to, 182; slaves, 154; U.S. slave society, 284n4; Yoruba influences, 159; Yoruba people, 157
African diaspora: acculturation of African people, 204; African-Creole culture, crucible of, 90; community formation, 149; cultural development, 236; cul-

tural history of, 4–5, 6; de-Africanization, 208; instructiveness of liberated
African experience, 238; liberated
Africans as exiles (*see* liberated
Africans as exiles); models of cultural
development, 236; New World Africans
as immigrants, 207–208, 209; religious
development, 154–156; repatriation to
Africa (*see* repatriation to Africa);
slaves' cultural memory, 207; syncretism, 207

African ethnic identity, 95–125; acceptance of, 107–108; African ethnic
communities in Bahamas, 118–125;
African ethnic communities in Trinidad, 110–117; conflict within/among
ethnic groups, 110–111; creolization,
236; cultural distinction within ethnic
groups, 110–117; definitions of,
102–103; descriptive data in Cuban
registers of liberated Africans, 95–97,
98, 102–103; ethnic breakdown of liberated Africans registered in Cuba,
97–102; ethnic labeling according to
port of departure, 97; ethnic self-identification, 104–105, 117; ethnic slurs/
insults, 108–109; ethnic surnames,
106–107, 149, 231–232, 276n27; ethnically organized cultural resistance, 103;
formation of African-American cultures, 114; group size, 157; intercourse
between groups in Africa before enslavement, 103; interpretations of,
105–106; intraethnic bonds, 104; linguistic identities, 118; in lives of liberated Africans, 105–106; maroon communities, 235; persistence of, 6, 117;
persistence of African languages, 118,
164; persistence of Yoruba language,
112; Peters case, 229–231; place of
birth as a surname, 231–232; queens,
annual selection of, 120, 121–122; regionally imagined homelands, 235; religious development during African
diaspora, 157; resistance to Christian
conversion, 111; social subgroups, 109;
town names, 124; twentieth-century,
112; use of father's first name as children's surname, 151, 283n61; veneration of African spirits, 284n4

African-influenced Christianity: Africanness, 157, 158; centers of, 155; Spiri-
tual/Shouter Baptists (*see*

Spiritual/Shouter Baptists); Vincentian "Shaker" church, 175–176, 178
African Religions of Brazil (Bastide),
156

Africanness: African-derived religions,
157; African-influenced Christianity,
157, 158; claims of, 223; of liberated
Africans, 12, 90; obeah, 196; orisha
worship (Shango), 158; salt consumption, 221; of slaves, 5, 90

Agnes (transport ship), 83, 247t

agricultural labor: in Bahamas, 42, 121;
Colonial Office concern about using
liberated Africans as plantation labor,
49, 65; liberated African women,
127–128, 280n3; in Trinidad, 15, 19

Águila (slave ship), 97

Ahoorloo (Rada woman), 117

Akan-Asante people ("Coromantees"):
Gold Coast, 92, 99, 229; influence,
157; slave trade, 92, 99

Aladura movement, 289n62

"Alas, Alas Kongo" (Schuler), 7, 8, 23

Alerto (slave ship), 30

Ali, Andrew, 112–113

Allada people, 99. *See also* Arada people;
Arara people; Rada people; Rara
people

Amalia (slave ship), 102, 128t

American Colonization Society,
212–213

Ampson, Sylvia, 160–161, 166, 174

Anderson, Thomas, 85

Andros Island, 180, 181

Anglican faith: ecclesiastical rights, 204;
liberated Africans in Bahamas, 166,
172; Trinidad parishes, 163–164;
Wilshere (Daniel) and, 287n49

Anglo-African League, 227, 228, 299n69

Anglo-Spanish Treaty for the Abolition of
the Slave Trade, 46

Anta (slave ship), 129t

*An Anthropological Approach to the Afro-
American Past* (Mintz and Price), 4–5,
236

anthropological texts, 237

Antigua, liberated African women from,
136–137

Antoine, Henry, 115–116, 185

Antoine, Robert (or John, also Nannee),
115–116, 120, 277n49

Antoine, Sedley, 277n49

Antonio (slave ship), 242t, 261n97

apprenticeships: Abolition Act (1807), 25, 65, 127; in Bahamas, 10, 16, 34, 35, 41, 42–44, 52, 57, 58, 60–61, 263n108; Cockburn on, 17–18; Colonial Office on, 18; marriage as an alternative to apprenticeship, 135; tax on individuals sponsoring, 34; termination of British West Indies system, 72; in Trinidad, 64, 70, 86, 135

Aquila (slave ship), 128t

Arada people, 113. *See also* Allada people; Arara people; Rada people; Rara people

Arara people, 99, 101t, 114. *See also* Allada people; Arada people; Rada people; Rara people

Arundel (transport ship), 85, 86, 246t

Asiegbu, Johnson U. J.: Colonial Land and Emigration Office, 74; liberated Africans in Trinidad, 86–87; number of liberated Africans in British Caribbean territories, 250n8; *Slavery and the Politics of Liberation 1787–1861*, 7–8; statistics about emigrants from Freetown, 83, 270n87

Athol Island, 60

Atlantic slave trade, abolition of, 6

The Atlantic Slave Trade: A Census (Curtin), 272n1

Atlantic (transport ship), 83–84, 247t

El Atrevido (slave ship), 31, 241t

Bahama Friendly Society, 227

Bahamas: Abaco Island, 60, 254n1; Adelaide settlement (*see* Adelaide settlement, Bahamas); African/black soldiers, 137, 208–209; African-derived religions, 180–181; African ethnic communities, 118–125; Andros Island, 180, 181; Athol Island, 60; Attorney General of, 28; Bahamian-born blacks, 61, 122, 263n105; Bain Town, 162–163, 166; Carmichael settlement, 53, 121, 253n33; Cat Island, 171, 287n49; Cay Lobos, 264n109; chickcharnies, 180–181; collector of customs, 121; conflict among African-born, 123; Creek Village (The Creek), 215; "creole negroes," 61; ecclesiastical rights, 204; employers in, 14, 15–16; encouragement of monogamy, 137; farming pineapples and oranges, 61; Fort Charlotte, 60; Fox Hill (*see* Fox

Hill, Bahamas); free blacks, 32–33, 35; friendly societies, 120–121, 122, 203–204, 228, 299n69; gender ratio, 132; governor of, 12, 27, 52, 57, 58; Grant's Town (*see* Grant's Town, Bahamas); Heath and, 10; Highburn Cay, 57, 261n90; Hog Island, 30; House of Assembly, 34, 42, 138; labor experiments, 14–15; labor supply, 21–22, 32; labor usage, 14; Lanyard's Cay, 60; Legislative Council, 34; liberated Africans in (*see* liberated Africans in Bahamas); location, 10, 27; Long Island, 39, 52; map, *24;* missionaries in, 49, 58, 166; Nassau (*see* Nassau, Bahamas); New Guinea, 215; New Providence (*see* New Providence); obeah, 200–202; Out Islands, 42, 43–44, 60, 61; as a peripheral island economy, 9; plantations in, 42; Rum Cay, 52; salt-raking, 42, 58, 61; Sandilands, 124; set-apart class of workers, 21; as Sierra Leone of Northern Caribbean, 10; sisal industry, 227; slaves in, 14, 16, 39–41, 229; tax on individuals sponsoring apprenticeships, 34; Turks and Caicos Islands and, 243t; white inhabitants, 14, 32–35, 37

Bain Town, Bahamas, 162–163, 166

Bain Town (Eneas), 162

BaKongo people. *See* Kongo people

Balfour, Blaney T., 57–58

Bangalore (transport ship), 246t

Baptist faith: ecclesiastical rights, 204; liberated Africans in Bahamas, 166; liberated Africans in Trinidad, 154; 'Merikan Baptists, 178; missionary presence in Caribbean, 159, 171; Shango Baptists, 175; slaves, 156; Spiritual/Shouter Baptists (*see* Spiritual/Shouter Baptists)

Baptist Missionary Society (BMS), 178, 204

Baptiste, Charles. *See* Yaraba, Charles

Baptiste, Eller Jean, 107

Barbados, liberated African women from, 134–135

Barber, Karin, 150, 210, 296n17

Barrackpore, Trinidad, 112

Barrow, George, 193–194

Barrow, Luther, 192–196, 197

Barrow, Margaret, 192

Bastide, Roger, 156–157

Bathurst (transport ship), 85, 247t
Bayley, Charles J., 59–62, 89, 263n105
Bayong, Philip (also known as Philip Wallace), 231–232
Bayong/Wallace, Thomas Philip, 231
"Belle," 275n15
Benitez-Rojo, Antonio, 209, 295n16
"Bere," 275n15
Bere people, 101
Berger, Iris, 145
Bermuda, H.M.S., 36, 241t
Bethel, Marion, 200
Bethell, Leslie, 45
"Bethel's Seizure," 242t
"big drum," 182
Bight of Benin, 99
Bight of Biafra, 97–99
The Birth of African-American Culture (Mintz and Price), 5, 67
Blake, Henry, 228
Blassingame, John, 4, 156
Blyden, Edward, 223–224, 226
Boladora (slave ship), 128t
Bom Amigo (slave ship), 29–30
"Boyd's Seizure," 241t
Brazil: African-Brazilian culture, 94; Anglo-Portuguese treaty, 45; candomble, 155, 157, 159; *emancipados,* 46; Great Britain and, 46; Kongo people, 94, 95, 96; liberated Africans from, 46–47, 86; Rio de Janeiro, 246t, 247t (*see also* Mixed Commission, Rio de Janeiro); seizure of slaves bound for, 15; slaves in, 129–130; Yoruba people, 94, 95
Brereton, Bridget: French influence on Trinidad, 159; middle-class Trinidadians, 298n54; *New Era* editors, 224; squatters in Trinidad, 143–144; Trinidadian law banning obeah, 115
Brice, Virginia, 124
Britain. *See* Great Britain
Britain and the Ending of the Slave Trade (Miers), 254n3
British abolitionism/abolitionists: agenda items, 30; emancipated slaves, hopes for, 13; government-managed emigration of liberated Africans, 73, 126–127; liberated Africans, 3; Sierra Leone, 3; tracking numbers assigned to liberated Africans, 96, 273n8
British and Foreign Anti-Slavery Society, 51

British Caribbean territories: administrative posts, 259n65; African-born population, 2; African-Caribbean culture (*see* African-Caribbean culture); African-influenced Christianity, 155; black population, 6; free blacks, 35; friendly societies, 120–121, 122; liberated Africans (*see* liberated Africans in British Caribbean territories)
British Guiana: governor of, 47; labor supply, 47; liberated Africans (*see* liberated Africans in British Guiana); preparedness to receive liberated Africans, 70–71; recruitment agent in Freetown, 73; sugar economy, 50
British Honduras (Belize), 47–48, 51
British navy: number of ships detained by, 2; seizure of Brazil-bound vessels, 15; seizure of Cuba-bound vessels, 15, 26–27; seizure of Portuguese slave ships, 54
British Slave Emancipation (Green), 13, 252n24
British West Indies: African-Creole culture, 90; Akan-Asante slaves, 92; apprenticeship system, termination of, 72; demographic creolization of, 1–2; emancipated slaves, 13; emigration of liberated Africans to, 74; labor supply, 46–47, 48; number of liberated Africans, 63; obeah, 7; persistence of African ethnic identity, 6; white elites, 37
Brookline (transport ship; also called *Brooklyne*), 88, 247t, 271n95
Brownell, John, 158
Burnley, William, 80, 210
Burnside, J. J., 121
Bush, Barbara, 131
Buxton, Thomas, 72
Byfield, Judith, 145
Byng, Henry Wylkes, 29

Calabar, 97–98
Camaron designation, 101t
Cameron, Charles: Colonial Office and, 27; governorship, 27; on liberated Africans in Bahamas, 141; Munnings and, 32; Murray (Alexander) and, 258n41; near mutiny in 2nd West India Regiment, 138, 139; unpreparedness for influx of liberated Africans, 27
Camoens (slave ship), 17–19, 59, 242t

candomble, 155, 157, 159

Carabalí designation, 97–98, 101t, 274n11

Caratal, Trinidad: African-derived religions, 174; African ethnic identity, 112; Joseph and, 153; liberated Africans in Caratal, 160, 199; location, 112; *Trinidad Chronicle* on, 161

Caridad Cubana (slave ship), 129t

Carlota (slave ship), 128t

Carlota Teresa (slave ship), 30

Carmichael settlement, Bahamas, 53, 121, 253n33

Carmichael-Smyth, James: Adelaide settlement, 18, 56; Balfour and, 57; British Guiana's preparedness to receive liberated Africans, 71; Carmichael settlement, 53, 253n33; Colebrooke and, 14; Colonial Office and, 12–13; governorship, 12, 47, 52, 57; Hill and, 71; on liberated Africans, 12–13; *Rosa* case, 18, 54–57, 261n90; slavery, 14

Carr, Andrew, 115–117, 185

Carr, William, 179, 290n77

Carter, Samuel, 298n54

Cassidy, Sarah, 186–187, 197

Cat Island, Bahamas, 171, 287n49

Cay Lobos, Bahamas, 264n109

Central Africans, 8, 193

Ceres (transport ship), 87, 247t

Charles, Daniel, *149*

Charles, Harriet (or Henrietta): age of, 282n57; daughters, 148, 282n57; disposition of land holdings of, 141–152; family of, *149;* gender and family expectations, 141; heirs, 141; husbands, 232; sons, 144; use of father's first name as children's surname, 151

Charles, Mary, *149,* 282n57

Charles, Thomas: age, 282n57; family relationships, *149;* father, 145; mother, 144; parents' property, 145; residence, 144

Charles, Victoria: age, 282n57; family relationships, *149;* mother, 148; uncle, 148, 283n61

chickcharnies, 180–181

Chieftain (transport ship): immigrants delivered to Trinidad, 78, 85, 245t, 246t, 268n50; MacLeod and, 86

Christian missionaries: in Bahamas, 49, 58, 166; Baptist missionaries, 159, 171; Baptist Missionary Society (BMS), 178, 204; Church Missionary Society, 286n24; in Freetown, 81; interaction with Africans, 173; Methodist missionaries, 159, 169; Methodist Missionary Society, 209; recruitment of African-American missionaries, 214; Roman Catholic, 159; source materials about liberated Africans, 11; in Trinidad, 164

Christianity: African Americans, 213; African-derived religions, 156; African-influenced forms (*see* African-influenced Christianity); Anglican parishes in Trinidad, 163–164; Anglicans (*see* Anglican faith); baptism, 163, 164, 174; Baptists (*see* Baptist faith); black Christianity, 156; liberated Africans, 90; Methodists (*see* Methodist faith); missionaries (*see* Christian missionaries); Protestantism (*see* Protestantism); resistance to Christian conversion, 111; Roman Catholicism (*see* Roman Catholicism); slave communities, 154. *See also* Anglican faith; Baptist faith; Methodist faith; Roman Catholicism

Christianity, Islam and the Negro Race (Blyden), 226

Chubasco (slave ship), 128t

Church Missionary Society, 286n24

The Claims of Kinfolk (Penningroth), 150

Clarendon (transport ship), 247t

Cleopatra, H.M.S., 243t

Cleopatra (transport ship), 77, 78, 245t

Cochrane, Alexander, 63–65

Cockburn, Francis: apprenticeships for liberated Africans, 17–18; Carmichael settlement, 253n33; Colonial Office and, 18; concerns about liberated Africans, 18; independent villages for liberated Africans, 18, 253n33; liberated Africans for British Honduras, 47–48; *Nepal* case, 261n97; *Washington* case, 261n97

Cocombre (thief), 113

Cole, Thomas, 187–190

Colebrooke, William: Carmichael settlement, 253n33; Carmichael-Smyth and, 14; Colonial Office, 48, 58; gender ratio in Bahamas, 132; on liberated Africans, 14; liberated Africans in Bahamas, 58

Colibre, H.M.S. (also H.M.B. *Colibre*), 31, 241t
College of the Bahamas, 11
Colonial Land and Emigration Office (Great Britain), 11, 73, 74
Colonial Office (Great Britain): Africans rescued from Portuguese slave ships, 56–57, 58–59; apprenticeships for liberated Africans, 18; Bahamian law for settlement of liberated Africans, 62; Balfour (Blaney T.) and, 57; Cameron and, 27; Carmichael-Smyth and, 12–13; "Cochrane's African Apprentices," 65; Cockburn and, 18; Colebrooke and, 48, 58; Colonial Land and Emigration Office, 73; Congo No. 1 Society, 234; control of recruiting liberated Africans, 73; designated emigration transports, 82; distribution of liberated Africans from *Manuelita,* 266n18; emigration from Saint Helena to Trinidad, 268n50; emigration of liberated Africans from Sierra Leone to British West Indies, 71–72; enforcement of anti–slave trade legislation, 37; gender-management policies, 130–131; Great Britain as benefactor of liberated Africans, 48; Harris and, 83, 84, 85; Hill and, 70–71, 71, 132, 265n10, 267n24; Hyde, Hodge and Company, 75; indentured servitude, limits on, 20; interventions by, 16; Jamaican post-emancipation policy, 252n24; labor supply concerns, 46–47, 130; liberated African children, 86; liberated Africans in Trinidad, 63, 70–71, 79, 89; MacLeod and, 80, 85; management of emigration of liberated Africans, 74–75; "Minute on the Condition and Disposal of Captured Africans at the Havana" (1835), 47–51, 52, 58; mixed commissions, 66; Munnings and, 35; Murray (Alexander) and, 42, 43–44, 218; oversight of/concern about treatment of liberated Africans, 11–12, 15, 18, 35–36, 44–45, 47, 237; permission to transport slaves, 290n77; petitions received by, 37; recordkeeping by, 95; self-congratulation, 43; sexual immorality among female liberated Africans, 133–134; source materials about liberated Africans, 10–11; transport of slaves by sea, 39; use of liberated Africans as plantation labor, 49, 65; Walker (James) and, 88–89; Woodford and, 134

community formation: African diaspora, 149; African ethnic labels, 149; liberated Africans, 50, 104; liberated Africans in Bahamas, 32, 38, 53, 120; liberated Africans in Trinidad, 68–69, 70, 88; maroon communities, 235; slaves, 157

Comus, H.M.S., 242t, 261n97
Congar (designation), 278n53
Congo (designation), 97, 102, 278n53
Congo, Allen, 106
Congo, Jim (or James), 106, 110
Congo, John, 106
Congo, Simon, 109
Congo, Tony, 276n33
Congo Hill, Trinidad, 112–113
"Congo Luanda" (designation), 105
"Congo Luango" (designation), 105
Congo No. 1 Society: Colonial Office, 234; Fox Hill, 204–205; liberated Africans in, 228; *Nassau Guardian,* 234–235; repatriation to Africa, 203–207, 214–215, 228; Wilshere (Daniel) and, 204, 206, 207, 234, 235
Congo River, 206
Congos, 8. *See also* Kongo people
Conyers, Thomas, 227–228
Corbin, Sergeant, 192
Corlett, John, 168–169, 209
Cornwall (transport ship), 87, 246t
Costa, Emilia da, 156
Cothonay, Marie Bertrand: obeah in Trinidad, 187; obeah-related figurine, 184; tale of African of royal blood, 126, 232–233
Cowen, George, 178
Crahan, Margaret, 207
Craton, Michael, 229, 263n107
Creek Village (The Creek), Bahamas, 215
Creel, Margaret Washington, 275n15
Creole Negroes, 249n4
"creole negroes," 61
Creole (slave ship), 242t, 261n97
Crowns of Glory, Tears of Blood (daCosta), 156
Cuba: African-Cuban culture, 94; descriptive data in registers about liberated Africans, 95–97, 98, 102–103;

emancipados, 46; ethnic breakdown of liberated Africans registered in, 97–102; Havana (*see* Havana); Kongo people, 95; liberated Africans from, 46–47, 50–52, 60, 65, 66, 68, 71, 80, 85, 131; Mixed Commission in (*see* Mixed Commission, Havana); santería, 155, 159; seizure of slaves bound for, 15, 26–27; slave trade in, 96, 262n99; slaves in, 129–130; sugar economy, 26; Yoruba people, 94, 95

Cuba (transport ship), 66, 242t

Cupar Grange Estate, Trinidad, 109, 276n33

Curtin, Philip, 272n1

Dahomey, 93, 99, 113

Daiva, Antonio, 107

"Dangbwe," 116

Darkholm, Ellen, 119

Darling, Richard, 80

David, Andrew, 77, 79, 81

Day, Charles William, 84, 269n72

de Bisao designation, 101t

de Verteuil, Louis, 183–184, 187, 217

de Verteuil, Maureen, 249n1

Decouverte, H.M.B., 241t

Deren, Maya, 273n4

Deslèves, Max, 180–181

Desmangles, Leslie, 155–156, 273n4

Despique (slave ship), 57, 242t

Diana (transport vessel), 242t

Dickinson, E. E., 118–120, 176, 289n64

Dickinson, J., 118–120, 176, 289n64

Dictionary of Bahamian English (Holm and Shilling), 222

Diego Martin valley, Trinidad, 174

Diligencia (slave ship), 102, 128t

Diligente (slave ship), 17–19, 59, 242t

Divine Horseman (Deren), 273n4

Dougan, John, 211

Dowd, S. E., 118–120, 176, 289n64

Dowson, William, 231–232

Drysdale, William, 90–91, 170–171

Du Bois, W. E. B., 255n10

Dyer, Henry Moreton, 30

Earl Grey (transport ship), 246t, 270n86

Ebo people. *See* Ibo people

Edwards, Peter: *Bom Amigo* case, 29–30; deafness, 37; Dyer and, 30; *El Volador* case, 30; *La Rosa* case, 37; "Pakenham's seizure," 37; *San Carlos* case, 29; *Sancta Isabel* case, 31; Wylly and, 37

Egba people, 119, 228

El Atrevido. See *Atrevido, El*

Elder, J. D.: ethnic ancestry, 161; orisha worship, 160, 165–166, 283n1

Elizabeth and Jane (transport ship), 75–78, 245t

Elk, H.M.B., 241t

Elliot, T. F., 61, 263n104

Elmina, Gold Coast, 99

emancipated slaves: British antislavery activists, 13; *emancipados,* 46; labor complaints about, 13, 252n24; recaptives, 3, 250n6; Trinidad, 13, 20; white West Indians, 13

emancipation: Abolition Act and, 3; documents prepared for legally emancipated Africans, 54, *55;* Great Britain, 46; liberated Africans as a pre-emancipation experiment in free black experience, 140

Emancipation Act (1833), 48, 267n28

Emilio (slave ship; alias *César*), 128t

Emma (transport ship), 85, 246t

Empresa (slave ship): capture of, 242t; distribution of Africans from, 52–53, *54;* gender ratio of Africans on, 129t

Eneas, Cleveland W., 162

Esperanza (slave ship), 242t

ethnic identity. *See* African ethnic identity

Euphrates (transport ship), 85–86, 247t

Ewe-Fon, 99, 101t. *See also* Fon people

exile. *See* liberated Africans as exiles

Expeditious (transport vessel), 243t

Experiencia (slave ship), 36, 241t

The Faces of the Gods (Desmangles), 155–156, 273n4

Fairy Queen (transport ship), 246t

Fame (slave ship), 264n2

family formation, 141–152; British encouragement of nuclear families, 130, 131–132; encouragement of monogamy, 137; family and gender expectations, 141–152; gender imbalance, 130; liberated Africans, 7; marital separation, 140

Felicidad (slave ship), 242t

Ferrity, Captain, 31

Fila (slave ship), 102, 103, 104; gender ratio of liberated Africans aboard, 128t

Fingal (slave ship), 128t

Firefly, H.M.S., 57, 242t

Firma (slave ship), 128t

Five Years' Residence in the West Indies (Day), 84, 269n72

Fletcher, Charmaine, 216–217

Flor de Loando (slave ship), 246t, 270n86

Flor de Tejo (slave ship), 242t

Fon people: African-derived religions, 157; Dahomey, 93; "Dangbwe," 116; descriptive data in Cuban registers of liberated Africans, 103; Haitian vodun, 93, 94, 155–156; Port-of-Spain, 185; proxies for references to, 99; Roman Catholicism, 155–156; "Sakpata," 116; spiritual powers, 117

Forbes, Rosita, 180, 181

Foreign Office (Great Britain), 11–12, 66, 95

Fort Charlotte, Bahamas, 60

Fox Hill, Bahamas: Congo No. 1 Society, 204–205; early settlement, 124–125; family names in, 294n53; liberated Africans in, 124–125, 202; location, 124; obeah, 200–201

Francisco, Slinger ("Mighty Sparrow"), 198

free blacks: Bahamas, 32–33, 35; liberated Africans as a pre-emancipation experiment in free black experience, 140

freed blacks. *See* emancipated slaves

The Freeman (newspaper): Blyden and, 226; directors/writers, 226–227; founder/principal editor, 226; friendly societies, 299n69; readership, 228; repatriation, 225–226, 228

Freetown, Sierra Leone: Christian missionaries in, 81; credit extended to settlers, 78; Liberated African Yard (Queen's Yard), 73–74, 81–82, 83, 85, 86, 269n72; Mixed Commission in (*see* Mixed Commission, Freetown); recruitment agents in, 73; statistics about emigrants from, 83; vice admiralty court, 82

friendly societies: African-derived religions, 204; Anglo-African League, 227–228, 299n69; Bahama Friendly So-ciety, 227; in Bahamas, 120–121, 122, 203–204, 228, 299n69; ethnically specific societies, 228; *The Freeman,* 299n69; Grant's Town Friendly Society (G.T.F.S.), 120–121, 227–228; Great Britain, 204; *Nassau Guardian* on, 122

Fula (or Fulani) people, 100, 122

Fyfe, Christopher, 82

Gallito (slave ship), 128t

Gamble, W. H., 178–179, 290nn75,77

Gammet, H.M.S., 242t

"Ganga," 100–103

Ganga designation, 101, 101t

Gasparillo, Trinidad: liberated Africans in, 160, 199; orisha, 160, 165–166, 197, 200; Roman Catholic Church, *165;* Yoruba people, 160, 165–166

gender ratio, 128–140; in Bahamas, 132; black soldiers, 136–137; of Brazilian slaves, 129; on captured slave ships, 128–129; Colonial Office's gender-management policies, 130–131; of Cuban slaves, 129; encouragement of nonwhite female immigration, 133, 134; family formation, 130; Hill and, 132; liberated African women, 130; of liberated Africans, 53, 62, 132; of liberated Africans in Bahamas, 53, 62, 132, 136; of liberated Africans in Trinidad, 50, 136; marriage as an alternative to apprenticeship, 135; near mutiny in 2nd West India Regiment, 137–140; in Trinidad, 134; written guarantees concerning, 131

George, Thomas: birth, 147; kinship relationships, 144, 147–150

George, Victoria, 148–150

Gerges (slave ship), 128t, 274n11

Gilbert, Thomas, 19–21

Glazier, Stephen: 'Merikan Baptists, 178; mourning, 297n40; spirit travel to Africa, 219; Spiritual/Shouter Baptists, 175–178, 179

Gordon, A. H., 143

Goree, H.M.S., 29

Gorrie, John, 277n44

Goveia, Elsa, 156

Grant's Town, Bahamas: founding, 161–162; liberated Africans in, 121, 141; location, 121, 160; major churches, 166; Montserrat compared to, 172–173; "mourning" in, 176–177; Protestant evangelism, 166–170; silk-cotton tree, 197, *198;* Wesley Methodist Church, *167,* 171, 176, 177; Yoruba people in, 162–163

Grant's Town Friendly Society (G.T.F.S.), 120–121, 227–228

Great Britain: acquisition of Trinidad, 9; Anglo-Portuguese treaties, 45; Anglo-Spanish treaties, 45, 46; Brazil and, 46; Colonial Land and Emigration Office, 11, 73, 74; Colonial Office (*see* Colonial Office); emancipation, 46; encouragement of monogamy, 137; encouragement of nuclear families, 130, 131–132; enforcement of anti–slave trade legislation, 3, 6, 59–60, 237; Foreign Office, 11–12, 66, 95; friendly societies, 204; liberated Africans, relationship with, 7, 19, 42, 46, 48, 140, 236–237; near mutiny in 2nd West India Regiment, 137–140; oath-taking, 238; Parliamentary investigation of conditions of liberated Africans in Bahamas, 16–19; Royal Navy (*see* British navy); self-interest in policies for settlement of liberated Africans, 46, 48; slave trade, 3; travel writing, 237; Treasury Department, 11; War Office, 11, 95

Green, William, 13, 252n24

Grenada, 51

Grey, William, 110

Growler, H.M.S.: distribution of Africans from, 84; recruitment of free Africans, 74, 269n72; repatriation to Africa, 208; as transport ship, 246t

Guinea's Other Suns (Warner-Lewis), 284n3

Gullick, Charles, 176

Gulston, Fredericka, 192, 195

Guppy, Robert, 80–81

hags, 222

Haitian Revolution, 154

Haitian vodun: African diaspora Christianity, 155; cultural resistance, 157; Fon people, 93, 94, 155–156; Kongo people, 94, 273n4; Roman Catholicism, 156; scholarly attention paid to, 182; Yoruba people, 93, 94, 155–156, 159

Hamilton, W., 74, 76–77

Harkaway (transport ship), 87, 247t

Harley, Constable, 188–190

Harris, George Francis Robert, Lord: Colonial Office, 83, 84, 85; East Indian indentured laborers, 87; Gilbert and, 19, 21; governorship, 19, 83; liberated African children, 86; on liberated Africans, 21; MacLeod and, 83, 85

Harvey, Claudia, 222

Hausa people, 122, 160

Havana: legal proceedings at, 242t, 243t, 245t; Mixed Commission in (*see* Mixed Commission, Havana)

Haynes, Sergeant, 186

Heath, Robert, 10

Hebe (slave ship), 56–57, 242t, 261n90

Hedrick, Basil, 183

Heroina (slave ship), 60–61, 243t

Herskovits, Frances, 177

Herskovits, Melville, 113, 177, 207

Higgs, William, 203, 206–207

Highburn Cay, Bahamas, 57, 261n90

Hill, George: Carmichael-Smyth and, 71; Colonial Office, 70–71, 132, 265n10, 267n24; distribution of liberated Africans from *Manuelita,* 66–69; distribution of liberated Africans from *Siete Hermanas,* 67, 69–70, 266n17; Earl of Aberdeen and, 59; gender ratio of liberated Africans, 132; transfer of liberated Africans from Havana, 47

Historical Notes on the Fox Hill Community (Manuel), 294n53

Hog Island, 30

Holm, John A., 222

Holt, Thomas, 13, 252n24

Housa soldiers, 209

Hudlin, Joseph, 199

Hyde, Hodge and Company, 75, 83

L'Hyppolite (slave ship), 242t

Ibibio people, 98, 101t

Ibo people: among liberated Africans in Bahamas, 122, 123; as a category, 98, 102, 230–231; Eboe Queen story, 120, 121–122; as percentage of liberated Africans registered in Cuba, 101t; Peters and, 230; suicide, 212; Walker (Frederic) and, 230

In Sunny Lands (Drysdale), 170–171, 289n64

Indagadora (slave ship), 128t
indentured servitude: in Bahamas, 10, 14–15, 16, 17, 23, 32, 34, 38; British policy, 7; Colonial Office policy, 20; East Indians, 21; Gilbert on, 20–21; limits on, 20; in Trinidad, 15, 71, 79, 84, 86, 88–89, 147
Indian, H.M.S., 29
Intrepido (slave ship), 128t
The Invention of Women (Oyewùmí), 142
Invincible (slave ship), 242t
Irish, Mary, 186–187
Irish, Peter, 108
Isabel (slave ship), 128t
Isabella (slave ship), 232. *See also* Sancta Isabel
The Isles of Summer (Ives), 118
Itwaru, Arnold, 222–223, 232
Ives, Charles, 118

Jamaica: Central Africans, 8; Colonial Office policy, 252n24; labor supply, 252n24; liberated Africans (*see* liberated Africans in Jamaica); nineteenth-century immigration, 8; obeah, 183; recruitment agent in Freetown, 73; salt taboo, 219–220, 297n43; Yoruba people, 8
Jane, Henry, 29
Janet (transport ship), 85, 247t
Jesus María (slave ship), 51; capture of, 242t; Dalleo on, 261n97; gender ratio of Africans on, 129t
Joanna (slave ship), 32, 241t
Joaquina (slave ship), 128t
John, A. Meredith, 290n75
Johnson, Howard, 227–228
Johnston, Thomas, 75
"jombee," 182
Josefa (slave ship; alias *Fortuna*), 128t
Joseph, Irene, 153, *155*, 174
Journal of Rachel Wilson Moore, 262n99
La Joven Reyna (slave ship), 102, 104, 128t
Julia (or Judy, a servant), 40
Julita (slave ship), 128t
Jumbo, John, 209

Kanga Wood, Trinidad, 160
Keate, Robert William, 87, 89
Kerr, Lewis, 229
Kerr, William, 34, 35
Kingsley, Charles, 191–192
Kissi people, 101

Kiyaga-Malindwa, D., 229
Knight, Franklin, 207
Kongo people: African-American culture, 94; Africanness of, 103; among liberated Africans, 97, 114; among liberated Africans in Bahamas, 62, 122, 123–124, 162, 203, 235; among liberated Africans in Trinidad, 109–110, 111, 160, 161; BaKongo people, 210, 220; Brazil, 94, 95, 96; Congo Borough neighborhood, 123; Conta Butta neighborhood, 123; Cuba, 95; descriptive data in Cuban registers of liberated Africans, 102; ethnic presence, 108–109; ethnic self-identification, 104–105; Haitian vodun, 94, 273n4; intraethnic bonds, 104; Kongo kingdom, 210; North American slave trade, 94; as percentage of liberated Africans processed at Havana Mixed Commission, 101t; Roman Catholicism, 210; slaves from, 96; wars, 94–95, 110
Kono people, 101
Kru people ("Kroomen"), 74, 78, 83
kumina, 182

La Joven Reyna. See Joven Reyna, La
Laing, John, 229
Lancashire Witch (transport ship), 246t, 270n86
Land of the Pink Pearl (Powles), 120, 121
Lanyard's Cay, Bahamas, 60, 62
Laurie, W. Bovell, 163–164
Leeward Islands, 63
Lemacy, Emmanuel, 194, 195
Lendore, Winifred, 217, 221–222
Lengua, Trinidad, 112, 199
Leopold II, King of Belgium, 203, 295n9
Leveen, E. Phillip, 249n3
Lewis, Joseph, 298n54
Lewis, Llewellyn, 192
Liberated African Emigration and British Anti-Slavery Policy (Asiegbu), 72
liberated African women: African-American men, 135; agricultural labor, 127–128, 280n3; from Antigua, 136–137; appropriate work roles, 140; in Bahamas, 139; from Barbados, 134–135; British policies, 137; certification husbands and wives not separated, 131; control over their lives, 134, 136, 137, 140–141; economic status, 130; encouragement of nonwhite female im-

migration, 133, 134; extramarital affairs, 141; gender and family expectations, 141–152; gender imbalance, 130; liberated African men, 135; marital separation, 140; marriage as an alternative to apprenticeship, 135; mores related to, 137; near mutiny in 2nd West India Regiment, 137–140; reliance on husband's income, 140; sexual immorality among female liberated Africans, 133–134; slave women compared to, 129; special treatment, 129; in Trinidad, 132, 134–137, 146; use of father's first name as children's surname, 151, 283n61
Liberated African Yard. *See under* Freetown, Sierra Leone
liberated Africans: Abolition Act, 1–2, 3; African acculturation under slavery, 237; African-Caribbean culture, 2, 4–5, 12; African-Caribbean social history, 237; African-Creole culture, 90–91; African ethnic identity in lives of, 105–106; Africanness of, 12, 90; after 1860, 75; agricultural labor (*see* agricultural labor); apprenticeships (*see* apprenticeships); Bahamas (*see* liberated Africans in Bahamas); from Bight of Biafra region, 97–99; Britain, relationship with, 7, 19, 42, 46, 48, 140, 236–237; British abolitionism, 3; British Caribbean territories (*see* liberated Africans in British Caribbean territories); British Guiana (*see* liberated Africans in British Guiana); British West Indies, 87; Carmichael-Smyth on, 12–13; Colonial Office concern, 11–12, 237; combining Africans taken from different ships, 66; community formation, 50, 104; in Congo No. 1 Society, 228; control of cultural practices, 196–197; from Dahomey, 99; de-Africanization, 208; designated emigration transports, 82; distinctiveness among black populations, 6, 20, 38, 80, 91, 210–211, 223; documents prepared for legally emancipated Africans, 54, 55; emigration procedures, 72–75; enlistment in armed forces, 25; ethnic composition, 94; ethnicity of (*see* African ethnic identity); as exiles (*see* liberated Africans as exiles); family formation, 7; Foreign Office concern,

11–12; gender ratios, 7, 50, 66; geographic/ethnic origins, 5–6; government-managed emigration of, 73, 74–75; as immigrants, 207–208, 209; indentured servitude (*see* indentured servitude); Kongo presence among, 97, 99, 114; long-term settlement of, 6; men among, 135; models of cultural development, 236; number of, 249n3; number of captured vessels, 249n3; obeah, 196–197, 202; other black populations and, 8, 38–40, 50, 56, 61, 70, 90, 210–211; persistence of African ethnic identity, 6, 251n16; as potential plantation laborers, 65; as a pre-emancipation experiment in free black experience, 140; recaptives, 3, 250n6; recruitment of, 73; repatriation (*see* repatriation to Africa); in Saint Helena, 74, 217; scholarly attention paid to, 2; from Senegambia, 100; shipmate relationships, 67, 88; Sierra Leone (*see* liberated Africans in Sierra Leone); source materials about, 10–11; studies of, 7–8, 252n17; suicide attempts, 217–218, 295n15; tracking numbers assigned to, 96, 273n8; Trinidad (*see* liberated Africans in Trinidad); women among (*see* liberated African women); Yoruba presence among, 97, 99, 114
"liberated Africans" (the term), 89
liberated Africans as exiles, 211–233; Africa as a homeland, 208, 209–210, 222, 233, 235; belief in afterlife in Africa, 211–212; dissatisfaction with life in New World, 212–213; ethnicity or place of birth as a surname, 231–232; exile, notion of, 207, 209, 235; experience of other Africans in the Americas, 215; flying back to Africa, 211, 216–217, 220, 221–222; physical return, 212–213, 215; preoccupation with places of origin, 231; regionally imagined homelands, 235; "return to Guinea," 215–216; returning home by walking eastward from Trinidad, 217; salt's supernatural powers, 212, 219–221, 297n43; self-identification as expatriates, 228–229; spiritual return/travel to Africa, 215, 220; suicide attempts, 217–218, 295n15; trance journeys to Africa, 218–219. *See also* repatriation to Africa

liberated Africans in Bahamas, 23–62; 1840s, 59; 1860s, 59–60; abandonment of, 41; at Adelaide settlement, 56, 57, 253n33; Africa as a homeland, 222; African Board and, 18; African-Christian-Protestants, 158, 166; agricultural labor, 42, 121; aloofness, 38–40; Anglican faith, 166, 172; apprenticeships, 10, 16, 34, 35, 41, 42–44, 52, 57, 58, 60–61, 263n108; arrivals in the colony, 23, 241–243; at Athol Island, 60; Baptist faith, 154, 166; British Parliament investigation of conditions of, 16–19; Cameron on, 141; at Carmichael settlement, 53, 121, 253n33; children, 53, 263n108; community formation, 32, 38, 53, 120; creation of African-Caribbean culture, 238–239; Egba people among, 228; enlistment in armed forces, 32, 57, 60–61, 137–138, 215; farming pineapples and oranges, 61; female apprentices, 43, 44; financial help covering expenses related to, 35, 36; flying back to Africa, 216–217, 222; in Fox Hill, 124–125, 202; gender ratios, 53, 62, 132, 136; in Grant's Town, 121, 141; health problems, 31, 41, 60; at Highburn Cay, 57, 261n90; at Hog Island, 30; Ibo people among, 123; incorporation into local economy and society, 89; indentured servitude, 10, 14–15, 16, 17, 23, 32, 34, 38; independent villages for, 18, 52, 253n33; industriousness, 14; Kongo people among, 62, 122, 162, 203, 235; last recorded settlement of, 62; on Long Island, 52; medical care of, 261n90; Methodist faith, 166–170, 173; missionaries, 58; Murray (Alexander) on, ix, 39–41; in Nassau, 23, 38–39, 51, 52, 225; need for, 10; on New Providence, 57, 180; number of, 2, 8, 23, 28, 32, 45, 59; oath-taking, 238; occupations, 10, 16–17, 19; other black populations and, 38–40, 50, 56, 61; on Out Islands, 42, 43–44, 60, 61; peak year for immigration, 168; petitions concerning, 32–36, 37; poor relief, 31, 32, 34; from Portuguese slave ships, 54–59; prostitution, 43; removal to Trinidad, 57, 58; repatriation to Africa, 203, 225–226; at Rum Cay, 52; salt-raking, 61; scholarly attention paid to, 21; settlement policy, 31, 36, 41–44,

52, 56–57, 61, 62; slaves and, 16, 39–41; slaves compared to, 14; soucouyants, 222; special status of, 17, 21, 38, 39; suicide among, 218; unemployment, 32, 34; unpreparedness for influx of, 27; white inhabitants of Bahamas, 32–35, 37, 38–40, 41–42, 44, 53, 56; Yoruba people among, 119–120, 122–124, 159, 162–163, 173, 228

liberated Africans in British Caribbean territories: from Brazil, 46–47; from Cuba, 46–47; distinctiveness among black populations, 6; early period of settlement, 26; number of, 2, 3–4, 75, 87, 250n8; organized immigration projects, 23; plantation colonies *vs.* peripheral islands, 8–9, 26; recognition of differences between African- and Caribbean-born people, 106

liberated Africans in British Guiana: number of, 8; settlement patterns, 288n50; from Sierra Leone, 82; source of, 7; sugar production, 50; Yoruba people among, 288n50

liberated Africans in Jamaica: post-emancipation decade, 23; repatriation to Africa, 295n15; salt consumption, 219–220, 221; from Sierra Leone, 82; source of, 7

liberated Africans in Saint Helena, 74, 217

liberated Africans in Sierra Leone: emigration of, 7–8; English-speaking, 9; indebtedness, 78; number of, 3, 249n3; recruitment of, 9–10

liberated Africans in Trinidad, 63–91; Africa as a homeland, 208, 222; African Americans in Trinidad compared to, 210; African-derived religions, 154; agricultural labor, 15, 19; among squatters, 161; apprenticeships, 64, 68, 70, 86, 135; Arabic language, 160; arrivals of, 68, 78, 84, 245–248, 271n95; baptism, 163, 174; Baptist faith, 154; from Brazil, 86; in Caratal, 160, 199; children, 68, 70, 79, 86, 87–88, 147; church attendance, 19–20; clothing, 71; "Cochrane's African Apprentices," 65; Colonial Office, 63, 70–71, 79, 89; community formation, 68–69, 70, 88; cost of transporting to Trinidad, 268n50, 271n98; creation of African-Caribbean culture, 238–239; from Cuba, 50–51, 52, 66, 68, 71, 80, 85; cul-

tural uniqueness, 21–22; distinctiveness among black populations, 80, 91, 210–211; distribution of, 49–50, 66–70; division into small groups, 68–69; domestic service, 68, 70; domestic service *vs.* agricultural labor, 15; ending of immigration system, 87; English speakers from Sierra Leone, 9; ethnic naming, 106; flying back to Africa, 221–222; food for, 71, 75, 78, 84; from Gambia River, 136; in Gasparillo, 160, 169; gender ratios, 50, 136; Hausa among, 160; health problems, 32, 85; indentured servitude, 15, 71, 79, 84, 86, 88–89, 147; industriousness, 80; Kongo people among, 109–110, 111, 160, 161; Koran, 160; Kru people among, 83; largest influx, 163–164; literacy of, 78, 224; marriage as an alternative to apprenticeship, 135; medical care, 71, 75; Methodist faith, 154; in Montserrat, 160–161; "mourning" by, 218–219; number of, 2, 8, 9, 63, 65, 72, 75, 86–87; obeah, 183–200; orisha worship (Shango), 153, 158, 159, 160, 163, 164–166, 173, 174, 177, 180, 283n1, 285n6, 288n50; other black populations and, 50, 70, 210–211; from Portuguese slave ships, 59; as post-emancipation work force, 89; as potential plantation laborers, 65; prior to 1830, 63; refugees from War of 1812, 178; repatriation to Africa, 84, 225–226; rumors about treatment of, 78; from Saint Helena, 69, 72, 73, 74, 78–79, 85–86, 268n50; salt's supernatural powers, 220–221; scholarly attention paid to, 21; from Senegal River, 136; from Sierra Leone, 69, 71, 75–77, 78, 80, 83, 84, 85, 86, 88; slaves and, 19; soucouyants, 222; source of, 7, 9–10; special status of, 21; Spiritual/ Shouter Baptists among, 175–178, 197, 293n39; sugar production, 50; suicide attempts, 217–218; terms of employment, 75; from Tortola, 63–65; wages, 71, 77; women among, 132, 134–137, 146; Yoruba people among, 109, 111, 141, 159, 160, 174, 186–187, 188–189, 200, 216, 220–221, 284n3
Little Dick (slave ship), 28, 241t
Lively (transport vessel), 242t

Liverpool, Charles Cecil Cope Jenkinson, 3rd Earl of, 36
Long Island (Bahamas), 39, 52
Louis, Elizabeth, 107–108
Louisa (transport ship), 246t
Luango (designation), 97
Lucumí, 97, 102
"Lucumí Eyó" (designation), 104–105
Lynch, Hollis, 223

MacGaffey, Wyatt, 193, 206
Maclean, Lieutenant Colonel, 139, 140
Macleay, William, 54
MacLeod, Henry: *Chieftain* Africans, 79, 86; Colonial Office, 80, 85; *Elizabeth and Jane* Africans, 75–76, 77–78; Harris and, 83, 85; liberated Africans from Sierra Leone, 78–79; *Senator* Africans, 82
Madden, Richard Robert, 51, 96
Mágico (slave ship), 128t
Makepeace, William, 169
Mande (or Manding) people, 100–103, 275n15
"Mandinga," 100–103
Mandinga people, 101t, 122, 123
Manuel, Gladys, 294n53
Manuelita (transport ship): distribution of liberated Africans from, 66–69, 266n18; gender ratio of liberated Africans aboard, 128t; immigrants delivered to Trinidad, 246t
Margaret (transport ship), 85, 246t
Maria (slave ship), 128t
María Christina (transport ship), 245t. See also *Reyna Cristina*
Marion Leith (transport ship), 247t, 270n86
Marte (slave ship), 128t
Martin, Diego, 196
Martin, William, 138
Mary Ann (transport ship), 88, 247t
Massé, Armand, 1, 174
Matilde (slave ship), 129t
Matthews, T. M., 229, 230
Maxwell, Frederick, 80
Mayo, Trinidad, 160, 161
McCartney, Timothy, 183
Meg Lee (transport ship), 242t, 243t
Melville, George, 108
Methodist faith: ecclesiastical rights, 204; liberated Africans in Bahamas, 166–170, 173; liberated Africans in

Trinidad, 154; Methodist chapel in Nassau, 159; missionaries, 169; missionary presence in Caribbean, 159
Methodist Missionary Society, 209
Métraux, Alfred, 155–156
Midas (slave ship), 128t
Midgely, Claire, 140
Miers, Suzanne, 254n3
"Mighty Sparrow" (Slinger Francisco), 198
Mina people, 99, 101t, 114
Minfa (slave ship; alias *Matanra*), 128t, 274n12
Mintz, Sidney: African-American culture, 4–5; African-American norms, 236; Rada community in Port-of-Spain, 301n6; shipmate relationships, 67
Mitchell, Henry, 87–88
Mitchell, Robert: African-American men, 135; Burnley and, 210; citation of, 143; in Montserrat, 161; Woodford and, 135
Mitchell, Stephen, 111, 122
mixed commission(s): authority, 45; Colonial Office, 66; decline of, 72; documents prepared for legally emancipated Africans, 54, *55;* seizure of Portuguese slave ships, 54; slave ships, 45; staff, 45
Mixed Commission, Freetown: Anglo-Brazilian Commission, 45; Anglo-Dutch Commission, 45; Anglo-Portuguese Commission, 45, 54, 56, 95; Anglo-Spanish Commission, 45; tracking numbers assigned to liberated Africans, 96, 273n8; volume of activity, 45
Mixed Commission, Havana (Anglo-Spanish): commissioners, 51, 96; condemnations by, 52, 71; descriptive data in Cuban registers of liberated Africans, 95–97, 98, 102–103; establishment of, 4, 45, 250n9; ethnic breakdown of liberated Africans registered by, 97–102; gender disparity in nineteenth-century slave trade, 128–129, 130; importance of, 45; superintendents of liberated Africans, 51
Mixed Commission, Rio de Janeiro (Anglo-Portuguese), 4, 45
Mixed Commission, Suriname (Anglo-Dutch), 45
Montan (transport ship), 245t
Montejo, Esteban, 217

Montserrat, Trinidad: Charles's (Harriet) holdings in, 144; Christian proselytizers, 173; ethnic diversity, 143; Grant's Town compared to, 172–173; liberated Africans in Trinidad, 160–161; orisha worship, 163, 164–166; Roman Catholicism, 163
Moore, Rachel Wilson, 262n99
Moorley, Constable, 107–108
Morgan, Philip, 5
Moruga, Trinidad, 198–199
Moselle (British brig), 30
Mount Pleasant, Trinidad, 110
"mourning" in religious and supernatural life: among liberated Africans in Trinidad, 218–219; in Grant's Town, 176–177; Spiritual/Shouter Baptists, 175, 176–177; spiritual travel, 218–219, 297n40; trances, length of, 175
Mullin, Michael, 229
Munnings, William Vesey, 27, 32–35
Murdock, George, 100
Murphy, Joseph, 156
Murray, Alexander: Cameron and, 258n41; Colonial Office, 42, 43–44, 218; employees of, 40; female apprentices, 43, 44; *La Rosa* case, 41, 258n41; on liberated Africans in Bahamas, ix, 39–41; near mutiny in 2nd West India Regiment, 138–139; "Pakenham's seizure," 41, 43–44; settlement of liberated Africans in Bahamas, 41–44, 52; transfer of his slaves between his plantations, 39
Murray, David (*Odious Commerce*): on debate over disposition of liberated Africans from Havana, 51–52, 71; on seizures of Cuba-bound ships, 27; on self-interest in British policies for settlement of liberated Africans, 46, 48
Musicongo (designation), 97
myalism, 182

Nango (designation), 278n53
Nangobar (designation), 278n53
Nassau, Bahamas: African Board, 18, 52, 53; Christian missionaries, 166; Collector of Customs, ix; Congo Borough neighborhood, 123; Conta Butta neighborhood, 123; Kongo people in, 123–124; legal proceedings at, 27–32, 36–38, 241t, 242t; liberated Africans in, 23, 38–39, 51, 52, 225; Methodist

chapel, 159; native African dialects, 118; vice admiralty court, 27; Yoruba people in, 123–124, 159

Nassau Guardian (newspaper): Adderley (Alliday) obituary, 170; Congo No. 1 Society, 234–235; Eboe Queen story, 120, 121–122; on friendly societies, 122; letter from Wilshere (Daniel), 171–172; Rahming (Guilliam) obituary, 204–205

Neezer, Papa, 198–200, *199,* 202, 293n40

Negrita (slave ship), 245t, 265n10

Negrito (slave ship), 128t

The Negro (newspaper), 224

Nepal (slave ship), 242t, 261n97

New Era (newspaper): on Antoine (Robert), 115; Barrow (Luther) case, 194; Barrow (Luther) murder, 193; Blyden and, 224; ethnic slurs/insults, report of, 108; founders, 298n54; identification with Africa, 223; legitimate heirs to Harriet Charles's land, 141; repatriation to Africa, 225; Thomas (John Jacob) and, 224–225

New Guinea, Bahamas, 215

"new negroes," 249n4. *See also* liberated Africans

New Providence (Bahamas): Christian missionaries, 166; desire to live near town, 121; Fox Hill (*see* Fox Hill, Bahamas); Hobby Horse Hall race track, 201; map, *33;* Methodists, 167–168; *Rosa* Africans, 57, 169; *A Winter Picnic,* 118

Nicols, Peter, 209

Niger Expedition, 72

Nimble, H.M.S.: 1834 seizure of Portuguese ship, 57; *Hebe* seizure, 56; *Negrita* seizure, 265n10; ships captured by, 242t, 245t

Nuevo Campeador (slave ship), 128t

"Nzadi," 206

oath-taking, 238

obeah, 183–200; African-born slaves, 183; Africanness, 196; Antoine (Robert) and, 115–117; Bahamas, 200–202; Barrow (Luther) murder case, 192–196, 197; Belmont neighborhood of Port-of-Spain, 113–117, 192–194; British West Indies, 7; Cassidy (Sarah) and, 197; Cole and, 187–190; Congo obeah, 185; definition, 115, 181, 183, 277n43;

Hobby Horse Hall race track, 201; Jamaica, 183; liberated Africans, 196–197, 202; liberated Africans as exiles, 212; liberated Africans in Bahamas, 197; liberated Africans in Trinidad, 183–200; media coverage, 197; necromancy, 185; necromantic nature, 183; Neezer and, 198–200; obeah-related murder, 192–194; obeah-related prosecutions, 186–197; "Obeah Wedding" (song), 198, 293n40; orality, 183; Pa Bay and, 200–202; playing cards for divination, 201; present-day, 197–198; scholarly attention paid to, 182; sentences for obeah-related crimes, 197; Shower (Phillis) case, 187–192, 197; silk-cotton trees, 193–195, 197, *198;* Trinidadian law banning, 115; twentieth-century representatives, 198; Walter (Jean Baptiste, Waldron) and, 194, 195–196; Williams (Jessie) and Irish (Mary) case, 186–187, 197; Yoruba people, 188–189

O'Brien, John, 203, 204, 206–207

Olajubu, Oyeronke, 145

Orestes (slave ship), 128t

orisha worship (Shango), 153–160; African cultural integrity, 288n50; Africanness, 158; contemporary Trinidad, 200; Joseph and, 153, *155;* liberated Africans in Trinidad, 153, 158, 159, 160, 163, 164–166, 173, 174, 177, 180, 197, 200, 283n1, 285n6, 288n50; official recognition by Trinidad, 197, 283n1, 285n6; Roman Catholicism, 164; salt's supernatural powers, 220–221; scholarly attention paid to, 154, 182; "Shango person," 199; Spiritual/Shouter Baptists, 175; Yoruba people, 159, 200, 220–221, 288n50

The Other Bahamas (Saunders), 226

Oyewùmí, Oyèrónké, 142, 148, 152

Pa B, 200

Pa Bay, 198, 200–202, 294n52

Pakenham, John, 36–38

"Pakenham's Seizure," 36–38; Edwards and, 37; Murray (Alexander) and, 41, 43–44; origin of phrase, 241t; Wylly and, 36–37. *See also Rosa, La* (slave ship, wrecked 1816)

Papa designation, 99

Parry, Bishop Thomas, 20
"The Passion" (Bethel), 200
Patterson, Orlando, 4, 182–183
Paupau designation, 99
Pawpaw designation, 99
Pearl, H.M.S., 242t
Pearse, Andrew, 185
Penney, Charles, 167
Penningroth, Dylan, 150
Persian (transport ship), 83, 247t
Peters, William John, 215, 229–231, 230
Peterson, John Eric, 252n17
Pickle, H.M.S., 54, 242t
Planeta (slave ship), 128t
Poitier, Charles, 121
Poonah, Trinidad, 160
Popo designation, 99
Port-of-Spain, Trinidad: Belmont neighborhood, 113–117, 185, 192–194, 277n49; Dry River neighborhood, 178–179; Fon people, 185; Laventille neighborhood, 192, 193, 194; Rada community, 185, 301n6; Thomas (John Jacob) and, 225
Portugal, 45
Potbury, Lieutenant John, 56
Powles, L. D., 120
Preciosa (slave ship), 129t
Price, Richard: African-American culture, 4–5; African-American norms, 236; Rada community in Port-of-Spain, 301n6; shipmate relationships, 67
Princes Town, Trinidad, 199
The Problem of Freedom (Holt), 13, 252n24
Protestantism: conversion of slaves, 156, 157–158, 176, 284n4; liberated Africans in Bahamas, 158, 166; Protestant evangelism, 166–170

"Queen of the Yarabas," 191
Queen's Yard (Liberated African Yard). *See under* Freetown, Sierra Leone

Raboteau, Albert, 284n4
Racer, H.M.S. (also H.M.B. *Racer*), 242t
"A Rada Community in Trinidad" (Carr), 115–117
Rada people, 99, 113–117, 185, 301n6. *See also* Allada people; Arada people; Arara people; Fon people; Rara people
Rahming, Guilliam, 205

Rahming, Jacqualine, 200, 294n53
Rahming, Moses, 205
Rahming, Phillip, 201–202
Ranch, Samuel, 203, 206–207
Rara people, 99. *See also* Allada people; Arada people; Arara people; Fon people; Rada people
Rattler, H.M.S., 31, 241t
receptives, 3, 250n6
Relampago (slave ship), 128t
Reliance (transport ship), 85, 247t
religious and supernatural life, 153–181; African-derived religions (*see* African-derived religions); African-influenced Christianity (*see* African-influenced Christianity); Anglicans (*see* Anglican faith); Baptists (*see* Baptist faith); chickcharnies, 180–181; Christian missionaries (*see* Christian missionaries); Christianity (*see* Christianity); conversion to Protestant religions, 156, 157–158, 166, 176; discouragement of non-Christian practices, 158; distinctiveness of liberated Africans, 20; ethnicity, 157; hags, 222; Methodists (*see* Methodist faith); "mourning" (*see* "mourning" in religious and supernatural life); obeah (*see* obeah); orisha worship (Shango) (*see* orisha worship [Shango]); Protestantism (*see* Protestantism); religious development and African diaspora, 154–156; Roman Catholics (*see* Roman Catholicism); sakara feasts, 221; salt's supernatural powers, 212, 220–221, 297n43; scholarly attention paid to, 182; shouting/ecstatic worship style, 170–171; silk-cotton trees, 193–195, 197, *198;* sorcery (*see* obeah); soucouyants, 222; supernatural beings flying back and forth between Africa and the New World, 212
repatriation to Africa, 203–215; achievement of, 7, 234; Africa as a homeland, 209–210; American Colonization Society, 212–213; back-to-Africa projects conducted by African Americans, 213–214; Blyden and, 224, 226; Congo No. 1 Society request for, 203–207, 214–215, 228; conversion to Christianity, 213; *The Freeman*, 225–226, 228; *Growler*, H.M.S., 208; hag figure, 222; of Housa soldiers, 209; of liberated

Africans in Bahamas, 203, 225–226; of liberated Africans in Jamaica, 295n15; of liberated Africans in Trinidad, 84–85, 225–226; motivating factors, 212, 213; *New Era,* 225; option for liberated Africans, 208–209, 214, 295n15; paradox of, 235–236; recruitment of African-American missionaries, 214; to Sierra Leone, 208–209

The Repeating Island (Benitez-Rojo), 295n16

return to Africa. *see* repatriation to Africa

Reyna Cristina (slave ship; also *María Cristina*), 69, 245t

Richardson, John, 173–174

Ricomar (slave ship; alias *Zafiro*), 128t

Ringdove, H.M.S., 242t

Rio de Janeiro: legal proceedings at, 246t, 247t. *See also* Mixed Commission, Rio de Janeiro

Robertson, Claire, 145

Roker, Phebe, 231

Roman Catholicism: African-derived religions, 155, 172–173, 284n4; baptism, 164; Fon people, 155–156; Gasparillo church, *165;* Haitian vodun, 156; Kongo people, 210; missionary presence in Caribbean, 159; orisha worship (Shango), 164; saints, concept of, 284n4; Trinidad, 158, 163–164, 173–174; Yoruba people, 155–156

Rosa (slave ship, captured 1831): capture of, 54–57, 242t; Carmichael-Smyth and, 18, 54–57; settlement of liberated Africans from, 54–57, 169

Rosa (slave ship, captured 1834): capture of, 245t; gender ratio of liberated Africans aboard, 128t

La Rosa (slave ship, wrecked 1816): capture of, 241t; legal proceedings against, 36–37; settlement of liberated Africans from, 41. *See also* "Pakenham's Seizure"

Rothery, Stephen, 49–50, 263n108

Royal Navy. *See* British navy

Rum Cay, Bahamas, 52

Saint Helena: governor of, 19; labor recruitment from, 19, 50; legal proceedings at, 245t, 246t, 247t; liberated Africans from, 69, 72, 73, 74, 78–79, 85–86, 268n50; liberated Africans in, 74, 217; as transitional processing point, 250n7; vice admiralty court, 72

St. Philip, Constable, 186

Saint Vincent (island), 175–176, 179

sakara feasts. *See* saraka feasts

"Sakpata," 116

salt-raking in Bahamas, 42, 58, 61

salt's supernatural powers, 212, 219–221, 297n43

San Carlos (slave ship), 29

San Rafael (slave ship), 28, 241t

Sancta Isabel (slave ship; also called *Isabella*), 31, 241t

Sandilands, Bahamas, 124

santería, 155, 159, 182

Santería (Murphy), 156

Santiago (slave ship), 128t

Sappho, H.M.B., 242t

saraka feasts (also sakara feasts), 182, 221

Sargent, Daddy, 185

Saunders, Gail, 124, 229, 263n107

Saunders, Hartley, 226, 228

Schenley, Edward, 51, 267n24

Schuler, Monica: "Alas, Alas Kongo," 7, 8, 23; BaKongo cosmology, 220; factors shaping African immigrant experience, 8; flying back to Africa, 217, 220; liberated Africans in creating Caribbean communities, 103; liberated Africans in Jamaica, 221; repatriation in Jamaica, 295n15; salt taboo in Jamaica, 219–220, 297n43

Scope, Emily, 216–217

Scorpion (slave ship), 242t

Segunda Rosario (slave ship), 129t, 243t

Senator (transport ship), 79–81, 82, 246t

Senegambia, 100

La Sentinelle (slave ship), 28, 241t

Sevenside (transport ship), 85, 86, 247t

Shango, 283n1. *See also* orisha worship (Shango)

Shango Baptists, 175

Shilling, Alison Watt, 222

Ship Carpenters' Union, 227

shipmate relationships, 67, 88

Shower, Phillis, 187–192, 197, 198

Shower, Thomas Emmanuel, 187–190

Sierra del Pilar (slave ship), 129t

Sierra Leone: Aladura churches, 289n62; British abolitionism/abolitionists, 3; emigration transports from, 73; English-speaking blacks, 9, 73; founding, 3, 26; Freetown (*see* Freetown, Sierra

Leone); labor recruitment from, 19, 50; legal proceedings at, 242t, 245t, 246t, 247t; Liberated African Department, 95; liberated Africans from, 69, 71, 75–77, 78, 80, 82, 84, 85, 86, 88; liberated Africans in (*see* liberated Africans in Sierra Leone); Mixed Commission in (*see* Mixed Commission, Freetown); repatriation to, 208–209; vice admiralty court, 72

Sierra Leone Watchman (newspaper), 82–83

Siete Hermanas (transport ship): distribution of liberated Africans from, 67, 69–70, 266n17; immigrants delivered to Trinidad, 245t

silk-cotton trees, 193–195, 197, *198*

Simpson, George, 165

The Slave Community (Blassingame), 4, 156

Slave Counterpoint (Morgan), 5

Slave Religion (Raboteau), 284n4

slave ships: definition of, in Abolition Act, 27; demographic profile of captives, 31; disposition of ships seized under Abolition Act, 25, 66, 267n30; family units, 66; mixing of ethnic groups, 103–104; nationality of, 261n97; number of captured vessels, 2, 249n3; overcrowding, 30; processing of captured ships at Saint Helena, 250n7; refugees from shipwrecks, 59, 264n109; seizure of Brazil-bound vessels, 15; seizure of Cuba-bound vessels, 15, 26–27; seizure of Portuguese slave ships, 54–59; West African coast, 26

Slave Society in the British Leeward Islands (Goveia), 156

slave trade: abolition by Great Britain, 263n107; abolition by U.S., 255n10; abolition of Atlantic slave trade, 6; Akan-Asante people, 92, 99; in Cuba, 96, 262n99; decline, 75, 87; early-eighteenth-century, 92; gender imbalance in nineteenth century, 130; Kongo people, 94; legal slave trading to Trinidad, 276n27; returnees to slave traders, 30–31; Windward Coast of West Africa, 100–101

slave trade, suppression of: enforcement of anti–slave trade legislation, 3, 6, 37, 59–60, 63, 72, 237; mutual policing of,

45; Spain's role, 26; vice admiralty courts, 72. *See also* British abolitionism/abolitionists; mixed commission(s)

slavery: African acculturation under, 237; Carmichael-Smyth and, 14; Cuba, 26; "deculturating regimen," 295n16; discouragement of non-Christian practices, 158. *See also* emancipation

Slavery and the Politics of Liberation 1787–1861 (Asiegbu), 7–8, 23

slaves: Africa as a homeland, 235; African-derived religions, 154; Africanness of, 5, 90; Akan-Asante slaves, 92; in Bahamas, 14, 16, 39–41, 229; Baptist faith, 156; in Brazil, 129–130; community formation, 157; conversion to Protestant religions, 156, 157–158, 176, 284n4; in Cuba, 129–130; death threat as a punishment, 211; demography of U.S. slave population, 284n4; emancipated slaves (*see* emancipated slaves); fertility of, 129; geographic/ethnic origins, 5–6; hiring out of, 40; humanity of, 90, 272n100; intraethnic bonds, 104; Kongo people, 96; mortality of, 129; mutilation of, 211–212; notion of exile, 209; obeah, 183; slave women compared to liberated African women, 129; suicide of, 212; in Trinidad, 19, 145, 154, 290n75; veneration of African spirits, 284n4

Slaves and Missionaries (Turner), 156

Sloane, Hans, 131–132

Smith, James Carmichael (editor, *The Freeman*), 226

Sobel, Mechal, 156, 177

The Sociology of Slavery (Patterson), 4, 182–183

soldiers: in Bahamas, 137, 208–209; gender ratio, 136–137; Housa troops, 209; liberated Africans' enlistment in armed forces, 25, 32, 57, 60–61, 137–138, 215; in Trinidad, 136–137, 208–209

Solomon, David, 189

sorcery. *see* obeah

soucouyants, 222

South Carolina (slave ship), 31, 241t

Spain, 26, 45, 46

Spiritual/Shouter Baptists: Aladura movement compared to, 289n62; banning of, 293n39; Glazier on, 175–178, 179; "mourning" (*see* "mourning" in religious and supernatural life); official sanction, 197; origins, 175, 178; orisha worship (Shango), 175; Shango Baptists, 175; Spiritual Baptist/Shouter Baptist Liberation Day (Trinidad), 293n39; in Trinidad, 175–178, 197, 293n39; Vincentian "Shaker" church, 175–176

Stanley, Amy Dru, 140

Stephen, James, 249n4

Stephens, Jeannette, 183

Stuckey, Sterling, 105, 106

Sudarkasa, Niara, 143, 144

Suriname, Mixed Commission in, 45

Syp (transport ship), 243t

Taplin, Lieutenant John, 54

Taylor, Ian Anthony, 219, 289n62

Taylor, Priscilla, 199

Terborg-Penn, Rosalyn, 133

The Theory and Practice of Creole Grammar (Thomas), 224–225

Thomas, Eudora, 177

Thomas, John Jacob, 224–225

Thunder, John, 215

Toby, Naomi, 221–222

Tom, Simon, 148, *149,* 283n61

Tortola, British Virgin Islands, 63–65, 245t

Tortuga, Trinidad, 160, 174

Trabelin' On (Sobel), 156

travel writing, 237

Travers, James, 60–61

Treasury Department (Great Britain), 11

Trinidad: acquisition by Great Britain, 9; African Americans in, 210; African/black soldiers, 136–137, 208–209; African ethnic communities, 110–117; Agricultural and Immigration Society, 76, 80; Anglican parishes, 163–164; Barrackpore, 112; Board of Council, 49; Caratal (*see* Caratal, Trinidad); Chinese in, 219; Christian missionaries, 164; cocoa industry, 144, 145, 146; Congo Hill, 112–113; Consolidated Immigration Ordinance (1854), 89; Cupar Grange Estate, 276n33; Diego Martin valley, 174; East Indians in, 21, 87, 219, 222; emancipated slaves, 13, 20; employers in, 15–16; encouragement of nonwhite female immigration, 133, 134; French influences, 158–159, 174, 288n50; Gasparillo (*see* Gasparillo, Trinidad); gender ratio, 134; immigrant laborers from Saint Vincent, 175–176, 179; Kanga Wood, 160; labor recruitment, 79, 80–81; labor supply, 9–10, 14, 15–16, 47, 65; as a large plantation colony, 9, 15; legal slave trading to, 276n27; Legislative Council, 133; Lengua, 112, 199; liberated Africans in (*see* liberated Africans in Trinidad); lieutenant governor of, 75, 88; map, *64;* Mayo, 160, 161; middle-class Trinidadians, 298n54; Montserrat (*see* Montserrat, Trinidad); Moruga, 198–199; Mount Pleasant, 110; "Ordinance for the Protection of, and the Promotion [of] the Industry and Good Conduct of Africans Transferred to [That] Island" (1835), 70–71; Poonah, 160; Port-of-Spain (*see* Port-of-Spain, Trinidad); preparedness to receive liberated Africans, 70–71; Princes Town, 199; recruitment agent in Freetown, 73; Roman Catholicism, 158, 163–164, 173–174; Shango Baptists, 175; Shouter Prohibition Ordinance, 293n39; slaves in, 19, 145, 154, 290n75; small landholders, 144; smallpox outbreak (1872), 109; Spanish influences, 158–159; Spiritual Baptist/Shouter Baptist Liberation Day, 293n39; squatting/squatters in, 21, 143–144, 161; sugar economy, 9, 50, 68; Tortuga, 160, 174

Trinidad Chronicle (newspaper): on Caratal, 161; Cupar Grange Estate murder, 276n33; missing children cases, 196; on Montserrat, 163; murder at Mount Pleasant, 110; persistence of African languages, 164; repatriation of Housa soldiers, 209; Shower case, 188, 189, 190, 191; theft of money from Rada community chest, 113–114; Williams and Irish case, 186; witchcraft cases, 186, 188, 189, 190, 191; on Yaraba (Joe), 107

Trinidad Constabulary Manual, 177

Trotman, David V., 288n50

Trovadore (slave ship), 243t
Try (transport ship), 243t
Tuervee, Hou, 277n49
Turks and Caicos Islands, 243t
Turnbull, David, 51, 96
Turner, Mary, 156
Tuskar (transport ship), 86, 247t
Tyburnia (transport ship), 87, 247t

United Burial Society, 227
University of the West Indies, 11

Variable, H.M.B., 241t
Vestal, H.M.S., 242t
Vigilante (slave ship), 238, 242t
Vincentian "Shaker" church, 175–176, 178
Viscount Hardinge (transport ship), 247t, 270n86
El Volador (slave ship), 30–31
Voodoo in Haiti (Métraux), 155–156

Walker, Frederic, 230
Walker, James, 88–89
Wallace, Philip (also known as Philip Bayong), 231–232
Walter, Jean Baptiste (also known as Waldron), 194, 195–196
Wanderer, H.M.B., 242t
War Office (Great Britain), 11, 95
Warner, Jack, 198
Warner, Magistrate, 108
Warner-Lewis, Maureen: Diego Martin valley in Trinidad, 174; flying back to Africa, 217; liberated Africans in creating Caribbean communities, 103; persistence of Yoruba language, 112; "suicide- or escape-wish" in Trinidad, 218, 297n32; Yoruba in Trinidad, 160, 216, 284n3
Warwick (transport ship), 245t
Washington (slave ship), 242t, 261n97
Weekly Tribune (newspaper), 234
Weeks, John, 206
Weir, Gaspare, 169–170
Weir, Mingo, 169
West-Central Africa map, *93*
Wilberforce, William, 64–65
William IV, King of Great Britain, 56
Williams, Jessie, 186–187
Williams, John, 215–216
Williams, Joseph J., 183

Wilshere, Charlotte, 205, *205*
Wilshere, Daniel: Anglicanism, 287n49; Baptist Missionary Society, 204; Congo No. 1 Society, 204, 206, 207, 234, 235; gravestone, 204, 295n4; monument to, *205,* 295n4; *Nassau Guardian,* letter to, 171–172
Wilson, John, 67
Windward Coast of West Africa, 99
Windward Islands, 41, 43
A Winter Picnic (Dickinson, Dickinson, and Dowd), 118–120, 121, 289n64
women. *See* liberated African women
Women against Slavery (Midgely), 140
Wood, Donald, 225
Woodford, Ralph, 134–137
Wyke, George, 136
Wylly, William: as abolitionist, 30; *Bom Amigo* case, 29–30; Edwards and, 37; *El Volador* case, 30; *La Rosa* case, 36–37; *Little Dick* case, 28; "Pakenham's Seizure," 36–37; settlement of liberated Africans in Bahamas, 30–31; as slaveholder, 30

Yaraba, Charles (or Charles Baptiste): family relationships, *149;* relationship to Harriet Charles, 150–151; resources at marriage, 147; son, 145; surname of children of, 151; wife, 141, 232
Yaraba, Jim, 106, 107
Yaraba, Joe, 107
Yaraba, Tom: family relationships, 148, *149,* 150; niece, 148, 283n61; sister, 232; son, 283n61
Yoruba people: African-Cuban culture, 94; African-derived religions, 157; Africanness of, 103; among liberated Africans, 97, 114; among liberated Africans in Bahamas, 119–120, 122–124, 159, 162–163, 173, 228; among liberated Africans in Bermuda, 122–123; among liberated Africans in British Guiana, 288n50; among liberated Africans in Trinidad, 109, 111, 141, 159, 160, 174, 186–187, 188–189, 200, 216, 220–221, 284n3; Brazil, 94, 95; bride-wealth, 148; candomble, 159; Cuba, 94, 95; ethnic presence, 108–109; ethnic self-identification, 104–105; in Gasparillo, 160, 165–166; Haitian vodun, 93, 94,

155–156, 159; industriousness, 80; influence on African-derived religions, 159; intraethnic bonds, 104; Jamaica, 8; kin among, 150; Lucumí, 97, 102; marital renaming, 151; marriage, 146–147; Nigeria, 93; obeah, 188–189; orisha worship (Shango), 159, 200, 220–221, 288n50; as percentage of liberated Africans processed at Havana Mixed Commission, 101t; persistence of Yoruba language, 112; "Queen of the Yarabas," 191; Roman Catholicism, 155–156; salt's supernatural powers, 220–221; santería, 159; scarification, 119; surnames, 151; wars, 94–95, 110; western ideas of gender, 142; widows among, 146

Yusuf, Yisa Kehinde, 151

ROSANNE MARION ADDERLEY is Associate Professor of History
at Tulane University in New Orleans, where she is also affiliated
with the Stone Center for Latin American Studies, the Center
for Cuban and Caribbean Studies, and the Program in
African and African Diaspora Studies.